THE
CIRCLE OF SOCRATES

*Readings in the
First-Generation Socratics*

THE
CIRCLE OF SOCRATES

*Readings in the
First-Generation Socratics*

Edited and Translated by
George Boys-Stones
and
Christopher Rowe

Hackett Publishing Co.
Indianapolis/Cambridge

Copyright © 2013 by Hackett Publishing Company, Inc.

All rights reserved
Printed in the United States of America

17 16 15 14 13   1 2 3 4 5 6 7

For further information, please address
Hackett Publishing Company, Inc.
P.O. Box 44937
Indianapolis, Indiana 46244-0937

www.hackettpublishing.com

Cover design by Abigail Coyle
Interior design by Elizabeth L. Wilson
Composition by William Hartman

Library of Congress Cataloging-in-Publication Data
Boys-Stones, G. R.
　The circle of Socrates : readings in the first-generation Socratics /
George Boys-Stones and Christopher Rowe.
　　p. cm.
　Includes bibliographical references (p.) and indexes.
　ISBN 978-1-60384-936-4 (pbk.) —
　ISBN 978-1-60384-937-1 (cloth)
　1. Philosophy, Ancient. 2. Socrates. I. Rowe, C. J. II. Title.
B171.B73 2013
183'.2—dc23   2012036535

The paper used in this publication meets the minimum requirements of American National Standard for Information Sciences—Permanence of Paper for Printed Library Materials, ANSI Z39.48–1984.

Contents

Abbreviations	*vi*
Introduction	*vii*

Chapter 1: Argument and Truth	1
Chapter 2: Happiness and the Good	28
Chapter 3: Virtue and Pleasure	63
Chapter 4: Body and Soul	124
Chapter 5: Education	147
Chapter 6: The Erotic Sciences	167
Chapter 7: Alcibiades and Politics	191
Chapter 8: Aspasia and the Role of Women	233
Chapter 9: God and the World	253
Chapter 10: Lesser Divinities and Socrates' "Sign"	278
Chapter 11: Debates and Rivalries	293

Bibliography	*299*
Index of Socratics	*302*
Index of Sources	*314*

Abbreviations

CAG   *Commentaria in Aristotelem Graeca* (various editors). 23 vols. (Berlin: G. Reimer, 1882–1909).

DK   H. Diels and W. Kranz, *Die Fragmente der Vorsokratiker*. 3 vols. 6th ed. (Berlin: Weidmann, 1954).

PCG   R. Kassel and C. Austin, *Poetae Comici Graeci* (Berlin: De Gruyter, 1983).

SSR   Giannantoni, G. (ed.). *Socratis et Socraticorum Reliquiae*. 4 vols. (Naples: Bibliopolis, 1990).

TrGF   B. Snell, R. Kannicht, and S. Radt, *Tragicorum Graecorum Fragmenta*. 5 vols. (Göttingen: Vandenhoeck & Ruprecht, 1986–2004).

FGrH   F. Jacoby et al., *Die Fragmente der griechischen Historiker*. 4 vols. (Leiden: Brill, 1926–1998).

Introduction

Scope and Purpose of the Volume

We know the titles of some two hundred works written by followers of Socrates; we possess fewer than forty-five of these works.[1] That statistic by itself says something about the difficulty that scholars have faced in assessing the legacy of Socrates. But consider next that those forty-five-or-so works are by just three people: Plato accounts for the vast majority of them (at least twenty-seven—precision is not possible because of unresolved debates over the authenticity of some items historically attributed to Plato), Xenophon for another fourteen (including the historical works), and we have two very short pieces by Antisthenes (translated here in full as an appendix to Ch. 1).

The fragments of Socrates' other followers were collected for the first time in 1983 by the Italian scholar Gabriele Giannantoni, in a volume called *Socraticorum Reliquiae* (The Remains of the Socratics), which he later expanded to include further texts relating to the life and work of Socrates himself (as well as the fragments of Aeschines, which the earlier volume omits). *Socratis et Socraticorum Reliquiae,* commonly known as *SSR,* is now the standard work of reference in the field. The fragments it collects testify to just how many individuals and philosophical traditions traced their inspiration to Socrates, how diverse they were in their thinking, and how much they could do to enrich our understanding of the context in which Plato and Xenophon (not to mention Antisthenes) were working.

The present volume is an attempt to highlight and make more readily available what we consider to be some of the more interesting and illuminating material by the first-generation followers of Socrates, and to make the case that it ought to be taken into account by mainstream scholarship on classical philosophy. By this, we have two main constituencies in mind. The first is scholars interested in Socrates. This book—and it is especially important to bear this in mind—is not itself about Socrates, at least not directly. But it *is* very much about the principal evidence for him. Since Socrates wrote nothing, his voice comes to us only as mediated through his followers, and a proper understanding of

---

1. Cf. Rossetti (2003); and see our Index of Socratics for the lists.

their conversations and the context in which they report and represent Socrates is a precondition for any attempt to approach the historical Socrates.[2]

The second existing constituency we have in mind consists of scholars working on Plato and Xenophon. What the most casual acquaintance with *SSR* shows is that, while Plato and Xenophon may have been preeminent among their contemporaries (a judgment made since antiquity, and by those who still had much fuller access to the evidence on which such a claim could be justified), we run the risk of serious distortion if we read their work as if it arose in a vacuum. Even to see where and how they were original requires that we know what their contemporaries were saying—and that, as we have found in preparing this volume, can lead to some surprising answers and fruitful new perspectives.

Less important to us—although it is a central organizing principle in *SSR*—is the notion of "Socratic schools": the movements and institutions that traced their origins back to first-generation Socratics. The most prominent of these (for the record) are the Cynics, of a tradition that traced itself via Diogenes of Sinope to Antisthenes; the Megarians (also known as the Eristics and the Dialectics), who belonged to a school founded by Euclides in his hometown of Megara; the Elians (later called the Eretrians), belonging to a school founded by Phaedo of Elis; the Cyrenaics, whose "founder" was Aristippus of Cyrene; and the Academics, members of Plato's school in Athens (known as the "Academy" from a shrine to the hero Academus on the land where it was founded). We have occasionally resorted to testimony about these schools to speculate about the views of their "founders," but cautiously, and as a last resort. In the course of our work for this volume, two things have become increasingly clear to us. First of all, that it is in general unhelpful to think of the work of any of the Socratics as if it were oriented toward the foundation of a distinctive "school" (rather than toward conversation with their peers). Secondly, our picture of the first-generation Socratics can be quickly distorted by anachronisms introduced by unchecked inferences from the work of the later schools to the views of their "founders." To take one striking example: we are told that Euclides was interested in various aspects of dialectic (the art, as it were, of philosophical conversation), but it turns out to be very

---

2. We say this without prejudice to the controversial question of whether the attempt can succeed. The point is that, if it can, it will be through the help of this material; if it cannot, the material itself will have to stand proxy for the figure who inspired it.

misleading to conceive of this interest as the sort of interest in *logic* that characterized the Megarian school later on (see texts and discussion in Ch. 1).

These, then, are the thoughts that have guided the selection of texts we have included here. We have tried to choose just those texts which bear witness to the thinking of first-generation followers of Socrates (or purport to do so), and which resonate with lines of thought to be found in Plato and Xenophon; and we have tried to provide just enough in the way of excerpts from Plato and Xenophon to show what the resonance is. We have brought together texts from as many first-generation Socratic thinkers as we could, but have been deliberately parsimonious with Plato and Xenophon, and the reader will quickly think of texts we might have added. That, of course, is part of the grounds for our parsimony: the reader is invited, indeed encouraged (and certainly able), to go back to the full texts that we possess to find resonances of their own. To include here even a significant fraction of what in Plato and Xenophon is relevant to any one of the themes would be to overwhelm the voices of the other Socratics and drown out the *conversations* that we are trying, in some measure, to recover.[3]

Membership of the "Circle" of Socrates

But what, exactly, do we have in mind when we talk of the "circle of Socrates"?

One thing which is evident about the historical figure of Socrates is that he was a conspicuous and charismatic figure: a public intellectual, in the literal sense of being highly visible (and notoriously ugly with it). To the ordinary eye, he would have counted as belonging to the type called "sophists," professional teachers of rhetoric and sometimes of other subjects, who claimed to be able to train people (mainly young, ambitious men) in the qualities and competences needed to succeed in life. How fair that is (or how fair it is to the sophists that followers of Socrates such as Plato tried so hard to deny the association) may be a matter for debate (there is some relevant discussion in Ch. 5). But what

---

3. One source we have not used (although some are included in *SSR*) are the so-called Socratic Epistles, thirty-five letters purporting to have been written by members of the circle to each other. In fact, they seem to be entirely fictional products, maybe of the third century CE; and, whatever their own sources, they also have remarkably little to say about the philosophical views of their purported authors. See Malherbe (1977), which includes an English translation.

does seem to have drawn people to Socrates was his commitment to dialogue or conversation with others (cf. Ch. 1), typically on ethical subjects (Ch. 2). This is, in turn, the simplest explanation of the fact that so many of them turned to dialogue writing—and that the dialogue form was especially associated with Socrates: the *Sôkratikos logos*, "Socratic conversation," was a recognized genre at least by the time of Aristotle.[4]

So the circle is constituted by people who regularly associated with Socrates for the purpose of conversation. Given that loose definition, there can be, of course, no agreed list of who exactly counts as a Socratic (a term we use in this volume interchangeably with "member of the circle"). Nevertheless, Plato and Xenophon both give us their perspective on who the most important of Socrates' followers were. There are, for example, those named by Plato's Socrates at *Apology* 33c–34a as having been drawn to Socrates by his mode of inquiry and having spent considerable time with him; those said by Plato's Phaedo to have been present at Socrates' execution—or notable by their absence from it (*Phaedo* 59bc); and the disciples (*homilêtai*), distinguished at Xenophon, *Memorabilia* 1.2.47–48 from those (like Critias and Alcibiades) who quickly tired of Socrates' questioning and turned away to politics (cf. **7.3**).

These lists are confessedly incomplete and obviously ideological (the deliberate exclusion of politically controversial figures of Critias and Alcibiades by Xenophon is striking testimony to that). In an attempt to widen our perspective a little, but still keeping it focused on people we can fairly assume to have been part of what the others would have recognized as their philosophical peer group, we are also including in our construction of the circle: (a) followers of Socrates who wrote Socratic dialogues (when we know this from their biographies), and (b) figures whom our ancient sources call Socratics (*Sôkratikoi*), in virtue of their having been acquainted with Socrates and taken a lead from him. That gives us twenty-nine figures—all of whom are listed, along with their works, in the Index of Socratics at the back of this volume. Not all of them are mentioned anywhere else: some are no more than names to us. But those who do feature in our texts are highlighted in bold when they are mentioned in the introductory sentences to our passages (see further, below).

Of those excluded from the list based on our criteria, there are three whom we think deserve an additional comment. One is Aspasia: she

---

4. See *Poetics* 1447b9–13, and, further, the prefatory remarks to the Index of Socratics.

was apparently an important figure for the circle (and is even called a Socratic once in our sources);[5] but she is always represented as a teacher, not as someone who took her lead from Socrates. The other two are Critias and Alcibiades. We are not simply led by Xenophon here, and recognize that both clearly were part of the Socratic milieu. However, there is no evidence that they took an active lead in conversations (or that they wrote dialogues), and it seems to be the enemies of Socrates who employ the label "Socratic" in their case (see, e.g., Xenophon, *Memorabilia* 1.2.12).

Using This Volume

Our texts are grouped thematically, according to the themes that they themselves suggested to us. Within each section, the order of presentation is guided by no more scientific principle than our own sense of the conversations to be had between the texts. To help the reader, we introduce each chapter with an overview of the topic and the main lines of thought as we see them. Each passage has an introductory sentence to explain its inclusion, and these sentences trace their own, complementary narrative. But we intend to be supportive rather than directive: to give an impression of what can be done with this material, rather than giving a definitive account of the conclusions to which it might lead.

One of the features of the material which the reader should bear in mind is the complexity and diversity of the evidence for the underlying conversations. Some of our texts are presented as rather straightforward reports of what particular Socratics said or thought. But of course these are not straightforward at all: many of them are late and may be secondhand reports at best; some are no doubt fabricated or confused. And that is before one reflects on how difficult and controversial the interpretation of Socratic dialogue can be in the first place. We are familiar enough with the fact that, when *we* say "Plato thinks *x*," we are not referring to something that Plato says in his own voice (unless we are talking about one of the Platonic letters, and we suppose it to be genuine), so that the claim is always open to some degree of question. But the same will very often be true of an ancient source that tells us that (for example) "Antisthenes thinks *x*." We need to be aware that that claim may derive from something that one of the characters in a dialogue by Antisthenes says—which may or may not be precisely what Antisthenes himself believed.

---

5. By the Cynic philosopher at Athenaeus, *The Learned Banqueters* 13, 569F.

The Socratic texts that survive are no more straightforward in what they tell us about their dialectical context. For example: to what extent can the conversations described by Plato and Xenophon *within* their dialogues be used as evidence for the historical figures depicted? (We have to bear in mind, of course, that many of these characters are themselves members of the circle and often authors of *Sôkratikoi logoi* in their own right.) Xenophon's representations of Antisthenes and Aristippus (characters in the *Memorabilia* and *Symposium*) are sometimes taken to be historically informative sources for Antisthenes and Aristippus, but it is rare that Plato's depictions of his contemporaries are used in a similar way. One reason for this difference, it could be suggested, is that there are times when it would be absurd to take Plato's portrayals literally. For example, we would find ourselves thinking that the whole of Plato's *Phaedo* was a direct historical source for the beliefs of Phaedo, who is, formally speaking, the narrator of the entire dialogue; or that the whole of the *Theaetetus,* for the same reason, was evidence for the thought of Euclides and not of Plato at all. But we should not assume that the choice before us is to take any given depiction, in Plato or Xenophon, *either* as historically accurate, *or* as pure fiction. The truth of the matter is likely to be something more interesting. When, for example, Xenophon writes a conversation between Antisthenes and Socrates, we should probably think that we are hearing *neither* Xenophon's voice through Socrates played off against a wholly fictionalized Antisthenes *nor* a historically accurate Antisthenes speaking with a similarly faithful representation of Socrates. What we are actually hearing are *three intersecting conversations* of different sorts. There is the conversation between Antisthenes and Socrates, but there is also a conversation between Xenophon and Antisthenes (played out in the way Xenophon portrays Antisthenes), and yet a third between Xenophon and Socrates (expressed in the way that Xenophon portrays Socrates). The same will be true for Plato— even (perhaps especially) in the *Phaedo* and *Theaetetus*. These rich layers of evidence are what we mean to keep in mind when we use expressions in this volume like "Xenophon's Antisthenes" or "Plato's Euclides."

And it gets still more interesting. Consider again Plato's *Theaetetus,* for example. If Plato makes Euclides its narrator, then its Socrates is really "Plato's Euclides' Socrates." Or the famously intricate *Symposium*: given the complex frame of this dialogue, its Socrates is, strictly speaking, "Plato's Apollodorus' Aristodemus' Socrates"—where Apollodorus and Aristodemus (like Euclides) are members of the circle, and people with whom we must assume Plato was in some level of engagement when he wrote the dialogue this way.

There are no easy answers, nor rules about how to unpick these nested and imbricated layers of evidence, but that is not an excuse to ignore them. Just as most scholars come to their ideas about what Plato himself thought by paying attention to the tendency of the conversations he portrayed as a whole, and by being sensitive to resonances between different works, so we can listen out for resonances between *different* thinkers and positions within the complexities offered by the dialogues of Plato and Xenophon, both on their own and alongside the other evidence we present in this volume. It is in order to encourage this that the names of members of the circle are highlighted in **bold** when they occur in the lines introducing each of the passages. We do not do this in full for every passage; it would be tedious and distracting if every quotation from Plato's *Phaedo*, for example, had to begin: "**Plato**'s **Phaedo**'s Socrates talks to **Plato**'s **Phaedo**'s **Simmias** about. . . . " But we do it enough, we hope, to pick out the main players and remind the reader what else they should be looking for.

Finally, a note about primary references. For each text we have given a reference to its original source (sometimes using more recent editions, or editions we prefer on other grounds to those used in *SSR*), and where applicable the *SSR* passage number with which it corresponds. (Note that our selections may be longer or shorter than the passages in *SSR*, so the "=" sign should be taken to mark *correspondence* and not strict *equivalence*.) The standard form of reference for *SSR* texts gives the section numbers rather than the name of the philosopher; for the sake of simplicity we give just the passage number in *SSR* attached to the relevant Socratic's name. Thus "*SSR* V A 10*" (the standard form of *SSR* reference) is abbreviated in this volume to "Antisthenes 10."

Translations

Translations of Plato are derived from the Hackett *Complete Works* (Cooper 1997), and most translations of Xenophon's *Memorabilia* from the forthcoming Hackett translation by Kirk Sanders. However, chiefly in order to achieve consistency of voice and translation across the volume, we have allowed ourselves to modify these translations—in some cases very considerably—so we take full responsibility for their appearance here. Three extracts from the *Memorabilia* (texts **2.22**, **4.13**, and **6.3**) are entirely our own, as are all other translations in the volume.

Thanks and Acknowledgments

We have had the privilege of discussion with and help from a growing community of scholars interested in Socrates and his followers, but four people in particular have provided assistance without which this volume could not have been produced. The first is Lloyd Gerson, who encouraged it at its inception, and brought us together with the second: Deborah Wilkes at Hackett, who has been supportive and patient in exactly the proportions we needed. Kirk Sanders is the third, for generously providing us with advance drafts of his translations of the *Memorabilia*. Finally, Don Morrison, who read early drafts of every chapter and gave invaluable, insightful, and learned help and advice on everything from which passages to include (and exclude), to issues of presentation. The volume would have been considerably different, and considerably worse, without his input.

GB-S
CJR

Chapter 1: Argument and Truth

Above all, the Socratics were interested in arguing—specifically, how a person could reach the truth through dialectical exchange; i.e., the give-and-take of philosophical conversation. The paradigm case envisages two people in conversation with each other (although by extension the same rules will govern *thought,* understood as a matter of "conversing with oneself"; **1.1–3**): they take as their topic an idea that seems promising to both of them; they carefully define their terms to ensure that they really are talking about the same thing (**1.4–6**; cf. **6.14**); and they proceed to discuss it by steps which maintain consistency and agreement—even if that means retracing the line of thought and revising earlier claims (**1.6–8**; cf. **3.18(b)**.[349c–d]; **3.53**).

> Extensive further contributions on the subject of definition by Plato include his methods of "collection and division" and "hypothesis." See, for the former in particular, *Phaedrus* 265c–266d and the whole of the *Sophist* and *Statesman* (especially *Sophist* 218d–221c, for an example meant to guide the exercise); for hypothesis, which emphasizes the provisional nature of interim conclusions, see especially *Republic* VI, 509d–513e. These developments are all part of Plato's construction of a more technical notion of "dialectic," used to distinguish philosophy with increasing clarity from anything we could confuse with "rhetoric." (In its later stages, it is linked with the theory of "forms," to see which is the highest achievement of Platonic philosophy. See especially, *Republic* VII, 531d–535a; 537c–538a.)

This process gives cardinal importance to the role of definition. Antisthenes in particular grappled with how to identify the essence of a thing (what it *always* is, rather than what it happens to be at a particular time; **1.4**), and it might be in this context that we should consider his adoption of what is often taken to be a mere "sophism" (i.e., a specious logical conundrum): his claim that "contradiction is not possible" (**1.9**; cf. Antisthenes, *Ajax* 7 in the appendix at the end of this chapter). The serious idea behind it, perhaps, is that people only get into a position where they (appear to) disagree because they have not established common ground for their discussions. For example, if two people have in mind different things when they talk about "virtue" and being "teachable," are they actually *contradicting* each other when one says and the other denies that "virtue is teachable" (as in the case of Socrates and Protagoras in Plato's *Protagoras*)?

It might, indeed, be inappropriate to talk about sophisms at all in this context, if we mean by that term the sort of puzzles that arise as a challenge to formal logic. In fact, logic itself, as distinct from dialectic, seems to be the invention of the next generation, notably Aristotle and thinkers in the Megarian school. Instead, we can more helpfully think of these puzzles as dialectical pitfalls, which can trip us up on their own, or be exploited by the unscrupulous—such as the sophists in Plato's *Euthydemus*, who exploit the paradoxical nature of Antisthenes' reflection on contradiction simply to manufacture artificial victory for themselves (**1.10**). Other such pitfalls include, for Euclides, the potentially beguiling use of analogy in argument (**1.14**) and, for Plato, reliance on mere probability (**1.15**), or ridicule and other forms of emotional manipulation (**1.16–17**).[1]

Responses to these pitfalls varied: Euclides seems to have had a particular interest in exploring their dangers (**1.11**), presumably with an eye to making them safe; but Antisthenes and Aristippus thought it best simply to circumvent them altogether (**1.12–13**). (Plato is on Euclides' side here; for his analysis of falsehood and contradiction in particular, see his *Theaetetus*, where the issues are raised, and the *Sophist*, where his final answer is to be found.)

Dialectic so conceived has a certain amount in common with rhetoric. It differs in that dialectic has as its aim a steady and consistent grasp of the truth (**1.18–20**); but dialectic also requires an orator's ability to adapt one's language to the needs of one's partners in discussion (**1.21–22**). Rhetoricians such as Gorgias (who lends his name to one of the longer Platonic dialogues) might come under fire for having too little concern for the truth, but the Socratics learned from them too. Gorgias himself is supposed to have taught Antisthenes (**1.23**) and influenced the writing style of Aeschines (**1.24–25**); Aeschines in his turn is supposed to have taught rhetoric (**1.26**). It is interesting to see how Plato develops this model (of rhetoric employed in the service of the goals set by dialectic) for his political thinking: he eventually comes to the conclusion that rhetoric is only legitimized when, and to the extent that, it is put at the service of the higher, more philosophical skill possessed by the statesman (**1.29–30**). Most Socratics seem to have had a more pragmatic view of government, and the role of rhetoric at its heart (**1.27–28**), even if they were critical of particular orators (see **7.7–13**).

---

1. This is not to say that emotional appeals never have dialectically constructive uses, something most evident in Socrates' encounters with Alcibiades; cf. **7.2**.

In an appendix at the end of this chapter, we print a connected pair of surviving works by Antisthenes: the *Ajax* and the *Odysseus*. They repay careful study for a number of reasons, but they are placed here on two grounds: first, because they are examples of rhetorical composition from the circle of Socrates (they are both speeches); and second, because their principal theme is precisely the use of language in the pursuit of truth.

Texts

1.1 Aristippus *on the dialectical nature of philosophy*

Asked what he had got out of philosophy, he said it was the ability to converse with everyone confidently. (Diogenes Laertius 2.68 = Aristippus 104)

1.2 Antisthenes *on the same*

Asked what he had got out of philosophy, he said it was the ability to converse with himself. (Diogenes Laertius 6.6 = Antisthenes 100)

1.3 *An unnamed visitor from Elea (southern Italy) in* **Plato** *applies the idea to thought*

"Aren't thought and speech the same, except that what we call thought is speech that occurs without the voice, inside the soul in conversation with itself?" (Plato, *Sophist* 263e)

1.4 Antisthenes *defines a statement*

He was the first person to define "statement" (*logos*), saying: "A statement is what reveals what something was or is." (Diogenes Laertius 6.3 = Antisthenes 151)

1.5 Antisthenes *and* **Xenophon** *on the importance of definition*

"The arguments of logic are pointless." We shall see about this; but even if one grants it, it is enough that these arguments can distinguish between the others and subject them to examination—to measure and weigh them, as one might say. [11] Who says all this? Just Chrysippus and Zeno and Cleanthes?[2] [12] Doesn't Antisthenes say it? (Or who wrote that "the beginning of education is the examination of terms"?) Doesn't Socrates say it? (Or of whom did Xenophon write that he began from the examination of terms to determine what each signifies?)[3] (Epictetus, *Discourses* 1.17.10–12 = Antisthenes 160)

1.6 *Plato's* Socrates (talking to Phaedrus) agrees

"If you wish to reach a good decision on any topic, my boy, there is [c] only one way to begin: You must know what the decision is about, or else you are bound to miss your target altogether. Ordinary people cannot see that they do not know the true nature of a particular subject, so they proceed as if they did; and because they do not work out an agreement at the start of the inquiry, they wind up as you would expect—in conflict with themselves and each other. Now you and I had better not let this happen to us since we criticize it in others." (Plato, *Phaedrus* 237b–c; followed by **6.14**)

1.7(a)   *Xenophon's* Socrates pursues clarity through dialectic

I shall also try to show how he made his companions more skilled at philosophical discussion. Socrates thought that people who understood the nature of any given thing would also be able to explain it to others; however, he claimed, it was no great surprise that people ignorant in this regard made mistakes themselves and caused others to make them. For this reason, he never stopped examining with his companions the nature of any given thing. It would be a major undertaking to go through all his definitions in detail; I shall recount only what I think will suffice to illustrate his method of inquiry. (Xenophon, *Memorabilia* 4.6.1)

1.7(b)   *An example of this procedure, with* **Xenophon's** *reflection on it*

SOCRATES: Do you claim that the person you're praising is a better citizen than the one I'm praising?

EUTHYDEMUS: I do claim that.

---

2. Stoics of the third century BCE. Chrysippus in particular was noted for his work on logic.

3. Cf. **1.7**, below.

SOCRATES: Then why don't we consider first what the function of a good citizen is?

EUTHYDEMUS: Let's do that.

SOCRATES: In the case of financial management, wouldn't the better man be the one who makes the state richer?

EUTHYDEMUS: Certainly.

SOCRATES: And in the case of war, the one who gives the state the upper hand over its rivals?

EUTHYDEMUS: Of course.

SOCRATES: And in the case of diplomacy, whoever makes friends instead of enemies?

EUTHYDEMUS: Presumably.

SOCRATES: And in political debate, the one who puts an end to discord and creates harmony?

EUTHYDEMUS: I think so.

When the arguments were unpacked in this way, the truth became obvious even to his [Socrates'] opponents. [15] Whenever he himself offered any detailed argument, he proceeded at every stage from generally accepted propositions, since he considered this to be the only safe method of reasoning. As a result, whenever he spoke, he secured the agreement of his audience far more than anyone I have known. He used to say that Homer also credited Odysseus with being a "safe speaker" because he was able to build his arguments from accepted opinions. (Xenophon, *Memorabilia* 4.6.14–15)

1.8 *An exchange in* **Plato** *which suggests the importance of allowing the discussion to change one's mind about a subject*

"But tell me," [said Socrates,] "if you think that a doctor, when he makes someone healthy, does something useful both for himself and for the person he [b] cures."

"Yes, I agree," [said Critias].

"And the man who does these things does what he ought?"

"Yes."

"And the man who does what he ought is moderate, isn't he?"

"Of course he is."

"And does a doctor have to know when he cures in a useful way and when he does not? And so with each of the craftsmen: does he have to know when he is going to benefit from the work he performs and when he is not?"

"Perhaps not."

"Then sometimes," I said, "the doctor doesn't know himself whether he [c] has acted beneficially or harmfully. Now if he has acted beneficially, then, according to your argument, he has acted moderately. Or isn't this what you said?"

"Yes, it is."

"Then it seems that on some occasions he acts beneficially and, in so doing, acts moderately and is moderate, but is ignorant of his own moderateness?"

"But this," he said, "Socrates, would never happen. And if you think it necessary to draw this conclusion from what I admitted before, then I [d] would rather withdraw some of my statements, and would not be ashamed to admit I had made a mistake, in preference to conceding that a man ignorant of himself could be moderate. As a matter of fact, this is pretty much what I say moderation is, to know oneself, and I agree with the inscription to this effect set up at Delphi. Because this inscription appears to me to have been dedicated for the following purpose, as though it were a greeting from the god to those coming in place of the usual 'Hail,' as though to say 'Hail' were an incorrect greeting, but we should rather urge [e] one another to 'be moderate.' It is in this fashion, then, that the god greets those who enter his temple, not after the manner of man—or so I suppose the man thought who dedicated the inscription. What he says to the person entering is nothing else than 'be moderate'; this is what he says. Now in saying this he speaks very darkly, as a seer would do. That 'know thyself' [165a] and 'be moderate' are the same (as the inscription claims, and so do I) might be doubted by some, and this I think to be the case with those who dedicated the later inscriptions 'nothing too much' and 'pledges lead to perdition.' Because these people thought that 'know thyself' was a piece of advice and not the god's greeting to those who enter, so, with the idea of dedicating some admonitions which were no less useful, they wrote these things and put them up. But here's the reason why I say all this, Socrates: I concede to you everything that was said before—perhaps you [b] said something more nearly right on the subject and perhaps I did, but nothing of what we said was really clear—but now I wish to give you an explanation of this definition, unless you already agree that to be moderate is to know oneself."

"But Critias," I replied, "you are talking to me as though I professed to know the answers to my own questions and as though I could agree with you if I really wished. This is not the case—rather, because of my own [c] ignorance, I am continually investigating in your company whatever is put forward. However, if I think it over, I am willing to say whether I agree or not. Just wait while I consider."

"Well, think it over," he said.

"Yes, I'm thinking," said I. (Plato, *Charmides* 164a–165c)

1.9 Antisthenes *claimed that contradiction was not possible*

Here,[4] he [Aristotle] criticizes Antisthenes for his simple-minded claim that a statement speaks about nothing other than that of which it is properly said, misled as he was by the thought that a false statement is, as such, a statement of nothing at all. (That is not to say that it does not exist at all; for it does not follow, if something is not unqualifiedly such-and-such, or in the primary sense, that it is not *tout court*.) Antisthenes thought that everything that exists is expressed by the statement proper to it, and that there is one statement for each thing, namely the one "proper" to it. A statement which signifies something, but does not belong to the thing of which it is said, is "alien" to it. From this, he tried to infer that contradiction is not possible, on the ground that people who contradict each other about something would have to be saying different things; but one cannot bring statements to bear on it that actually are different because there is one statement proper to each thing—one belongs to each thing, and to speak about the thing is to say that alone. The result is that if these people [who were supposed to be contradicting one another] were to be talking about the same matter, they would be saying the same as each other (because one statement corresponds to one thing)—and since they would be saying the same thing, they would not be contradicting each other. If they were to say different things, he claimed, they would not any longer be talking about the same thing (there being just one statement to be applied to the thing itself), whereas people who contradict each other must be talking about the same thing. That is how he inferred the impossibility of contradiction—and pretty much of falsehood too, since it is impossible to make any statement about a thing except its own, i.e., the one that properly belongs to it. That this is a simple-minded argument, he [Aristotle] shows from the fact that one does talk about a thing using statements which belong to something else as well as by using its own, "proper" statement, falsely, hastily, often, and readily, as for example if one applies the statement describing a circle to a triangle, or that of

---

4. I.e., at Aristotle, *Metaphysics* Δ.29, 1024b26–34.

a horse to a human being. . . . (Alexander, *On Aristotle's Metaphysics* 434.25–435.20 Hayduck = Antisthenes 152)

1.10(a) ***Plato's Socrates reports Euthydemus, in conversation with Ctesippus***, *exploiting the idea that it is not possible to say what is false*

"Why Ctesippus," said Euthydemus, "do you think it possible to tell lies?" "Good heavens, yes," he said, "I should be raving if I didn't." "When one speaks the thing one is talking about, or when one does not speak it?" "When one speaks it," he said. [284a] "So that if he speaks this thing, he speaks no other one of things that are except the very one he speaks?" "Of course," said Ctesippus. "And the thing he speaks is one of those that are, distinct from the rest?" "Certainly." "Then the person speaking that thing speaks what is," he said. "Yes." "But surely the person who speaks what is and things that are speaks the truth—so that Dionysodorus, if he speaks things that are, speaks the truth and tells no lies about you." "Yes," said Ctesippus, "but a person who speaks these things, Euthydemus, [b] does not speak things that are." And Euthydemus said, "But the things that are not surely do not exist, do they?" "No, they do not exist." "Then there is nowhere that the things that are not are?" "Nowhere." "Then there is no possibility that any person whatsoever could do anything to the things that are not so as to make them be when they are nowhere?" "It seems unlikely to me," said Ctesippus. "Well then, when the orators speak to the people, do they do nothing?" "No, they do something," he said. "Then if they do something, they also make something?" [c] "Yes." "Speaking, then, is doing and making?" He agreed. "Then nobody speaks things that are not, since he would then be making something, and you have admitted that no one is capable of making something that is not. So according to your own statement, nobody tells lies; but if Dionysodorus really does speak, he speaks the truth and things that are." (Plato, *Euthydemus* 283e–284c)

1.10(b) *More of the same: Dionysodorus takes over the conversation with* **Ctesippus**, *and extends the topic to contradiction*

And Dionysodorus answered, "Are you making your speech on the assumption that there exists such a thing as contradiction, Ctesippus?" "I certainly am," he said, "decidedly so. And do you think there is none, [e] Dionysodorus?" "Well you, at any rate, could not prove that you have ever heard one person contradicting another." "Do you really mean that?" he answered. "Well then, just listen to Ctesippus contradicting Dionysodorus, if you want to hear my proof." "And do you undertake to back that up?" "I certainly do," he said. "Well then," he went on, "are there words to describe each thing that exists?" "Certainly." "And do they describe it as it is or as it is not?" "As it is." "Now if you remember, Ctesippus," he said, "we showed a moment ago [286a] that no one speaks of things as they are not, since it appeared that no one speaks what does not exist. "Well, what about it?" said Ctesippus. "Are you and I contradicting each other any the less?" "Now would we be contradicting," he said, "if we were both to speak the description of the same thing? I suppose we would be saying the same things in that case." He agreed. "But when neither of us speaks the description of the thing, would we [b] be contradicting then? Or wouldn't it be the case that neither of us had the thing in mind at all?" He agreed to this too. "But when I speak the description of the thing whereas you speak another description of another thing, do we contradict then? Or is it the case that I speak it but that you speak nothing at all? And how would a person who does not speak contradict one who does?" (Plato, *Euthydemus* 285d–286b)

1.11 Euclides *was apparently keen to address the danger of "eristics,"*
i.e., wrangling merely for the sake of winning an argument

Seeing Euclides keen on eristic arguments, Socrates said: "Euclides, you will be able to handle sophists, but not human beings at all"—for he thought that splitting hairs in matters such as this was of no utility, as Plato also says in the *Euthydemus* (Diogenes Laertius 2.30 = Euclides 3)

1.12 Aristippus *thought it safer simply to*
avoid such arguments altogether

When someone brought him a riddle (*ainigma*) and said, "Unravel it!" he [Aristippus] said, "Why do you want me unravel it, you fool, when it causes trouble for us even while it is tied up?" (Diogenes Laertius 2.70 = Aristippus 116)

1.13 Antisthenes *likewise saw a limit to engagement*
with arguments he saw as "tricky"

And he [Zeno] once agreed with the same teacher [Parmenides] when he said that being is unmoved, and constructed five attempts to show that being is unmoved. Antisthenes the Cynic, unable to refute them, got up and walked around, thinking that active proof was more powerful than any theoretical refutation. (Elias, *On Aristotle's Categories* 109.18–22, Busse = Antisthenes 159)[5]

1.14 Aspects of **Euclides'** own dialectical methodology

Euclides used to attacked proofs not for their premises, but for their conclusion. And he rejected argument by analogy [*parabolê*], saying that it was based on things that were either similar or dissimilar; but if they were similar, it would be better to concentrate on the things themselves than what was similar to them; but if they were dissimilar, the comparison was forced. For these reasons, Timon[6] says the following about him, and the rest of the Socratics:

> But I don't care about these babblers, or any other:
> Not Phaedo, whoever he was; and not that quarrelsome
> Euclides, who cast among the Megarians the rage for debating.

(Diogenes Laertius 2.107 = Euclides 34)

1.15 **Simmias** to Socrates (as narrated by **Plato**'s **Phaedo**) warns against arguments from mere probability

"I know that arguments of which the proof is based on probability are pretentious and, if one does not guard against them, they certainly deceive one, in geometry and everything else." (Plato, *Phaedo* 92d)

1.16 **Plato**'s visitor from Elea cautions against appeals to dignity rather than truth

"Such a method of argument as ours is not more concerned with what is more dignified than with what is not, and neither does it at all despise the smaller more than the greater, but always reaches the truest conclusion by itself." (Plato, *Statesman* 266d)

---

5. This text is 29 A15 DK: see discussion at McKirahan (2011), 182. For Parmenides, see 28 B8 DK (= fr. 11.8 McKirahan). His pupil Zeno is, of course, to be distinguished from the Stoic in **1.5**.

6. Timon of Phlius (320–230 BCE), philosopher and author of satirical verses called the *Silloi*.

1.17 *Plato's Socrates similarly warns that
mockery has no place in dialectic*

"What's this, Polus? You're laughing? Is this now some further style of refutation, to laugh when somebody makes a point, instead of refuting him?" (Plato, *Gorgias* 473e)

1.18 *Plato's Socrates on the philosopher's preference for
the truth rather than what sounds right in the moment*

"As for that son of Clinias,[7] what he says differs from one time to the next, but what philosophy says always stays the same, and she's saying things that now astound you, although you were present [b] when they were said." (Plato, *Gorgias* 482a–b)[8]

1.19 *So as long as one's own position keeps shifting,
Plato's Socrates sees further dialectical work to be done*

EUTHYPHRO: But Socrates, I have no way of telling you what I have in mind, for whatever proposition we put forward goes around and refuses to stay put where we establish it.

SOCRATES: Your statements, Euthyphro, seem to belong to my ancestor, Daedalus. If I were stating them and putting them forward, you would [c] perhaps be making fun of me and say that because of my kinship with him my conclusions in discussion run away and will not stay where one puts them. As these propositions are yours, however, we need some other jest, for they will not stay put for you, as you say yourself.

EUTHYPHRO: I think the same jest will do for our discussion, Socrates, for I am not the one who makes them go round and not remain in the same place; it is you who are the Daedalus; for as far as I am concerned [d] they would remain as they were.

SOCRATES: It looks as if I was cleverer than Daedalus in using my skill, my friend, insofar as he could only cause to move the things he made himself, but I can make other people's move as well as my own. And the smartest part of my skill is that I am clever without wanting to be, for I would rather have your statements to me remain unmoved

---

7. Alcibiades. For his mercurial nature, and Socrates' relationship with him, see Ch. 6 and Ch. 7 below.

8. The point is recapped at *Gorgias* 491b.

than possess the wealth of Tantalus as well as the cleverness of Daedalus. (Plato, *Euthyphro* 11b–d)

1.20 Xenophon's Socrates is ridiculed by a sophist for his constancy

Hippias had arrived in Athens after a long absence and came across Socrates talking with some people. Socrates was expressing his amazement at the fact that if one wanted to have somebody trained in the arts of shoemaking, carpentry, metalworking, or horseback riding, there was no mystery about where to send him to get this training—and some people say that there are plenty of teachers around for anybody who wants to train a horse or ox to behave properly—but if somebody wanted to learn justice for himself, or to have a son or a servant trained in it, he would not know where to go to get this training. [6] When Hippias heard this, he mockingly interjected, "What, Socrates? Still saying the same old things I heard from you so long ago, Socrates?" "It's even worse than that, Hippias," replied Socrates. "I'm constantly repeating myself on the same subjects. As learned as you are, you probably never repeat yourself on the same subject." [7] "I do try to say something fresh every time," he replied. (Xenophon, *Memorabilia* 4.4.5–7: cf. **3.35** for text preceding and following this passage)

1.21 But if what you think *ideally remains constant*, Antisthenes argues that how you express *it ought to change depending on the audience*

[on *Odyssey* 1.1: "*Sing for me, Muse, the man of many modes*"][9] Antisthenes says that Homer is not praising Odysseus when he says that he is a *man of many modes* but rather criticizing him. After all, he does not make Agamemnon or Ajax *men of many modes,* but straightforward and noble. Nor, by Zeus, does he make the wise Nestor crafty and irresolute in his character, but someone who is straightforward in his intercourse with Agamemnon and everyone else: advising them if he has something worth saying, and not concealing anything. And Achilles abstained from this mode of behavior to such an extent that he reckoned him an enemy like death "who lays one thing in his heart but speaks another."[10]

---

9. "Of many modes" translates *polytropos*—more usually translated as "of many ways" (i.e., versatile, cunning). "Mode" is admittedly clumsy; but the passage as a whole hangs on Antisthenes' observation that *polytropos* could be applied to the command of *verbal* "tropes" as well.

10. Homer, *Iliad* 10.313.

Antisthenes then proposes a solution: Well, so what? Is Odysseus base because he is called *a man of many modes,* or does Homer call him this because he is wise? Does "mode" not mean two things, character on the one hand, and a way of using language on the other? A "modal" man has a character that lends itself to ready adaptation; linguistic modes are similar. Odysseus in fact modulates both his voice and the disposition of his limbs—as it is said of the nightingale: "Quickly turning she has a far-echoing voice."[11] And if the wise are those who are clever at speaking, and know how to express the same thought in many modes, and know many modes of speech, they would be *men of many modes* in this sense. But the wise are also good.[12] This is why Homer says that Odysseus is, as a wise man, a *man of many modes,* because he knows many modes of intercourse with men. In a similar way, Pythagoras is also said to have crafted his words appropriately when speaking to children, addressing them with childlike speech, and for women, speech appropriate for women; words of leadership for leaders, and youthful speech for the young. It is the work of wisdom to discover the fitting mode in which to relay wisdom in each case; it is the work of folly to use the same linguistic mode to people who are different. Medicine does the same thing when the art is exercised correctly, using many modes of therapy because of the various types of patient.

Modes represent changeability in character, a tendency to alter and not be steady. But a command of many modes in *speech,* and the use of varied language to varied audiences, amounts to consistency—for only one mode is suitable for each. So to say what suits each person amounts to reducing variation to serial consistency. On the other hand, since a single mode of speech is unsuitable for different audiences, one speech delivered for many audiences plays to them like a speech of many modes. (Porphyry, *Questions on Homer's Odyssey* 1.1–3.2 Schrader = Antisthenes 187)

---

11. Homer, *Odyssey* 19.521.

12. We reject the supplement to the text proposed by Schrader here (accepted by SSR). The supplement would give the sense: "If the wise are good *at associating with men,* then this is why. . . ." Schrader argues that his supplement is required by what Antisthenes goes on to say in the next sentence. But since the ultimate purpose of the argument is to show that Odysseus is a good man, the premise that the wise are also good (without the qualification) seems perfectly acceptable.

1.22 *Plato's Socrates agrees*

SOCRATES: Consider, then, what both Hippocrates and true argument say about nature. Isn't this the way to think systematically about the nature [d] of anything? First, we must consider whether the object regarding which we intend to become experts and capable of transmitting our expertise is simple or complex. Then, if it is simple, we must investigate its power: What things does it have the natural power to act on, and what power is it? By what things does it have the natural disposition to be acted upon, and what disposition is it? If, on the other hand, it takes many forms, we must enumerate them all and, as we did in the simple case, investigate how each is naturally able to act upon what and how it has a natural disposition to be acted upon by what.

PHAEDRUS: It seems so, Socrates.

SOCRATES: Proceeding by any other method would be like walking with [e] the blind. Conversely, whoever studies anything on the basis of an art must never be compared to the blind or the deaf. On the contrary, it is clear that someone who teaches another to make speeches as an art will demonstrate precisely the essential nature of that to which speeches are to be applied. And that, surely, is the soul.

PHAEDRUS: Of course.

SOCRATES: This is therefore the object toward which the speaker's whole [271a] effort is directed, since it is in the soul that he attempts to produce conviction. Isn't that so?

PHAEDRUS: Yes.

SOCRATES: Clearly, therefore, Thrasymachus and anyone else who teaches the art of rhetoric seriously will, first, describe the soul with absolute precision and enable us to understand what it is: whether it is one and homogeneous by nature or takes many forms, like the shape of bodies, since, as we said, that's what it is to demonstrate the nature of something.

PHAEDRUS: Absolutely.

SOCRATES: Second, he will explain how, in virtue of its nature, it acts and is acted upon by certain things.

PHAEDRUS: Of course. [b]

SOCRATES: Third, he will classify the kinds of speech and of soul there are, as well as the various ways in which they are affected, and explain what causes each. He will then coordinate each kind of soul with the kind of speech appropriate to it. And he will give instructions concerning the reasons why one kind of soul is necessarily convinced by one kind of speech while another necessarily remains unconvinced.

PHAEDRUS: This, I think, would certainly be the best way.

SOCRATES: In fact, my friend, no speech will ever be a product of art, whether it is a model or one actually given, if it is delivered or written in [c] any other way—on this or on any other subject. But those who now write *Arts of Rhetoric*—we were just discussing them—are cunning people: they hide the fact that they know very well everything about the soul. Well, then, until they begin to speak and write in this way, we mustn't allow ourselves to be convinced that they write on the basis of the art.

PHAEDRUS: What way is that?

SOCRATES: It's very difficult to speak the actual words, but as to how one should write in order to be as artful as possible—that I am willing to tell you.

PHAEDRUS: Please do. [d]

SOCRATES: Since the nature of speech is in fact to direct the soul, whoever intends to be a rhetorician must know how many kinds of soul there are. Their number is so-and-so many; each is of such-and-such a sort; hence some people have such-and-such a character and others have such-and-such. Those distinctions established, there are, in turn, so-and-so many kinds of speech, each of such-and-such a sort. People of such-and-such a character are easy to persuade by speeches of such-and-such a sort in connection with such-and-such an issue for this particular reason, while people of such-and-such another sort are difficult to persuade for those particular reasons. The orator must learn all this well, then put his theory into practice and [e] develop the ability to discern each kind clearly as it occurs in the actions of real life. Otherwise he won't be any better off than he was when he was still listening to those discussions in school. He will now not only be able to say what kind of person is convinced by what kind of speech; on [272a] meeting someone he will be able to discern what he is like and make clear to himself that the person actually standing in front of him is of just this particular sort of character he had learned about in school—to that he must now apply speeches of such-and-such a kind in this particular way in order to secure conviction about such-and-such an issue. When he has learned all this—when, in addition, he has grasped the right occasions for speaking and for holding back; and when he has also understood when the time is right for Speaking Concisely or Appealing to Pity or Exaggeration or for any other of the kinds of speech he has learned and when it is not—then, and only then, will he have finally mastered the art well and completely. But if his speaking, his teaching, or his writing lacks any one of these elements [b] and he still claims to be speaking with art, you'll be better off if you don't believe him. "Well, Socrates and Phaedrus," the author of this discourse might say, "do you agree? Could we accept an art of speaking presented in any other terms?"

PHAEDRUS: That would be impossible, Socrates. Still, it's evidently rather a major undertaking.

SOCRATES: You're right. And that's why we must turn all our arguments every which way and try to find some easier and shorter route to the art: [c] we don't want to follow a long rough path for no good reason when we can choose a short smooth one instead. Now, try to remember if you've heard anything helpful from Lysias or anybody else. Speak up.

PHAEDRUS: It's not for lack of trying, but nothing comes to mind right now. (Plato, *Phaedrus* 270c–272c)

1.23 *Antisthenes benefited from rhetorical training* . . .

He [Antisthenes] studied with the rhetorician Gorgias at first—that is where his dialogues, and especially the *Truth* and the *Protrepticus,* get their rhetorical shine from. (Diogenes Laertius 6.1 = Antisthenes 11 = Antisthenes 145)

1.24 . . . *and Aeschines was also inspired by Gorgias*

He was a man well versed in rhetoric, as is plain from the defense of his father, Phaeax, the general, and of Dion.[13] He imitated Gorgias of Leontini in particular. (Diogenes Laertius 2.63 = Aeschines 13; follows **7.41**)

1.25 *The same*

Aeschines, the follower of Socrates, whom you were interested in yesterday as someone who openly criticized the dialogues, did not shrink from Gorgianizing in the speech *On Thargelia.* He says something like

---

13. The brother-in-law, and son-in-law, of the tyrant of Syracuse (as **7.41** makes clear).

this: "Thargelia of Miletus going to Thessaly consorted with Antiochus of Thessaly, the king of all Thessalians." (Philostratus, *Letters* 73.28–34 = Aeschines 65; preceded by **8.6**)

1.26 ***Aeschines*** *as himself a teacher of rhetoric*

Socrates was clever in rhetorical matters, as Idomeneus[14] also says: and the Thirty forbade him from teaching technical rhetoric, as Xenophon says.[15] And Aristophanes satirizes him as someone who makes the weaker argument stronger. And indeed he was the first, along with his pupil Aeschines, to teach rhetoric, as Favorinus[16] says in the *Miscellaneous History*—and Idomeneus says this too, in his work *On the Socratics*. (Diogenes Laertius 2.20 = Aeschines 7)

1.27 *So, for **Antisthenes**, rhetoric is a useful adjunct to philosophy*

Asked by someone what to teach his son, Antisthenes said, "If he is going to live with gods, to be a philosopher; if with men, to be an orator." (Stobaeus, *Selections* 2.31.76 = Antisthenes 173)

1.28 *The Socrates of **Aeschines** thinks that even laws depended on rhetoric*

That is one reason why it is so unavoidable that rhetoric takes precedence and governs over laws. But secondly, what should we say that laws themselves are, by the gods, if they are not things said, set apart from others only in that they are written down? If I remember, Aeschines is our witness that Socrates is of the same view. [218] But apart from the evidence even of Socrates, one can see it by looking into the matter itself. (Aelius Aristides, *In Defense of Oratory* 217–18 = Aeschines 93)

---

14. An Epicurean philosopher writing around the turn of the third century BCE.
15. At *Memorabilia* 1.2.33–34, Critias merely forbids Socrates from conversing with the young; but **9.2(a)** (at 19b–c) shows that people really did think that Socrates practiced and taught rhetoric, and Plato feels the need to put a denial in Socrates' mouth at **1.31** below.
16. Second-century CE philosopher and orator.

1.29 *Plato's visitor from Elea and the younger Socrates agree, conversely, that rhetoric needs to be subordinated to statesmanship*

VISITOR: Well then: to which sort of expert knowledge shall we assign what is capable of persuading mass and crowd, through the telling of [d] stories, and not through teaching?

YOUNG SOCRATES: This too is clear, I think: it must be given to rhetoric.

VISITOR: And the matter of whether to do through persuasion whatever it may be in relation to some people or other, or else by the use of some sort of force, or indeed to do nothing at all: to what sort of expert knowledge shall we attach this?

YOUNG SOCRATES: To the one that controls the art of persuasion and speaking.

VISITOR: This would be none other, I think, than the capacity of the statesman.

YOUNG SOCRATES: Very well said.

VISITOR: This matter of rhetoric too seems to have been separated quickly [e] from statesmanship, as a distinct class, but subordinate to it.

YOUNG SOCRATES: Yes. (Plato, *Statesman* 304c–e)

1.30 *Plato's Socrates (with Gorgias and his young pupil Polus): rhetoric is not a science or art (as statesmanship is), merely a knack*

POLUS: Tell me, Socrates, since you think Gorgias is confused about rhetoric, what do you say it is?

SOCRATES: Are you asking me what art [*technê*] I say it is?

POLUS: Yes, I am.

SOCRATES: To tell you the truth, Polus, I don't think it's an art at all.

POLUS: Well then, what do you think rhetoric is?

SOCRATES: In the treatise that I read recently, it's the thing that you say has produced art. [c]

POLUS: What do you mean?

SOCRATES: I mean a knack [*empeiria*].

POLUS: So you think rhetoric's a knack?

SOCRATES: Yes, I do, unless you say it's something else.

POLUS: A knack for what?

SOCRATES: For producing a certain gratification and pleasure.

POLUS: Don't you think that rhetoric's an admirable thing, then, to be able to give gratification to people?

SOCRATES: Really, Polus! Have you already discovered from me what I say it is, so that you go on to ask me next whether I don't think it's admirable?

POLUS: Haven't I discovered that you say it's a knack? [d]

SOCRATES: Since you value gratification, would you like to gratify me on a small matter?

POLUS: Certainly.

SOCRATES: Ask me now what art I think pastry baking is.

POLUS: All right, I will. What art is pastry baking?

SOCRATES: It isn't one at all, Polus. Now say, "What is it then?"

POLUS: All right.

SOCRATES: It's a knack. Say, "A knack for what?"

POLUS: All right.

SOCRATES: For producing gratification and pleasure, Polus.

POLUS: So rhetoric is the same thing as pastry baking? [e]

SOCRATES: Oh no, not at all, although it *is* a part of the same practice.

POLUS: What practice do you mean?

SOCRATES: I'm afraid it may be rather crude to speak the truth. I hesitate to do so for Gorgias' sake, for fear that he may think I'm satirizing what he practices. I don't know whether this is the kind of rhetoric that Gorgias practices—in fact in our discussion a while ago we didn't get at all clear [463a] on just what he thinks it is. But what *I* call rhetoric is a part of some business that isn't admirable at all.

GORGIAS: Which one's that, Socrates? Say it, and don't spare my feelings.

SOCRATES: Well then, Gorgias, I think there's a practice that's not like an art, but one that a mind given to making hunches takes to, a mind that's bold and naturally clever at dealing with people. I call it flattery, basically. [b] I think that this practice has many other parts as well, and pastry baking, too, is one of them. This part *seems* to be an art, but in my account of it it isn't an art but a knack and a routine. I call rhetoric a part of this, too, along with cosmetics and sophistry. These are four parts, and they're directed to four objects. So if Polus wants to discover them, let him do so. [c] He hasn't discovered yet what sort of part of flattery I say rhetoric is. Instead, it's escaped him that I haven't answered that question yet, and so he goes on to ask whether I don't consider it to be admirable. And I won't answer him whether I think it's admirable or shameful until I first tell what it is. That wouldn't be right, Polus. If, however, you do want to discover this, ask me what sort of part of flattery I say rhetoric is.

POLUS: I shall. Tell me what sort of part it is.

SOCRATES: Would you understand my answer? By my reasoning, rhetoric is an image of a part of politics. [d]

POLUS: Well? Are you saying that it's something admirable or shameful?

SOCRATES: I'm saying that it's a shameful thing—I call bad things shameful—since I must answer you as though you already know what I mean.

GORGIAS: By Zeus, Socrates, I myself don't understand what you mean, either!

SOCRATES: Reasonably enough, Gorgias. I'm not saying anything clear yet. [e] This colt here is youthful and impulsive.

GORGIAS: Nevermind him. Please tell me what you mean by saying that rhetoric is an image of a part of politics.

SOCRATES: All right, I'll try to describe my view of rhetoric. [464a] If this isn't what it actually is, Polus here will refute me. There is, I take it, something you call "body" and something you call "soul"?

GORGIAS: Yes, of course.

SOCRATES: And do you also think that there's a state of fitness for each of these?

GORGIAS: Yes, I do.

SOCRATES: All right. Is there also an apparent state of fitness, one that isn't real? The sort of thing I mean is this. There are many people who *appear* to be physically fit, and unless one is a doctor or one of the fitness experts, one wouldn't readily notice that they're not fit.

GORGIAS: That's true.

SOCRATES: I'm saying that this sort of thing exists in the case of both the body and the soul, a thing that makes the body and the soul seem fit when in fact they aren't any more so. [b]

GORGIAS: That's so.

SOCRATES: Come then, and I'll show you more clearly what I'm saying, if I can. I'm saying that of this pair of subjects there are two arts. The one for the soul I call politics; the one for the body, though it is one, I can't give you a name for offhand, but while the care of the body is a single art, I'm saying it has two parts: gymnastics and medicine. And in politics, the counterpart of gymnastics is legislation, and the part that [c] corresponds to medicine is justice. Each member of these pairs has features in common with the other, medicine with gymnastics and justice with legislation, because they're concerned with the same thing. They do, however, differ in some way from each other. These, then, are the four parts, and they always provide care, in the one case for the body, in the other for the soul, with a view to what's best. Now flattery takes notice of them, and—I won't say by *knowing,* but only by *guessing*—divides itself into four, [d] masks itself with each of the parts, and then pretends to be the characters of the masks. It takes no thought at all of whatever is best; with the lure of what's most pleasant at the moment, it sniffs out folly and hoodwinks it, so that it gives the impression of being most deserving. Pastry baking has put on the mask of medicine, and pretends to know the foods that are best for the body, so that if a pastry baker and a doctor had to compete in front of children, or in front of men just as foolish as children, to determine which of the two, the doctor or the pastry baker, had expert knowledge of good food and bad, the doctor would die of starvation. [465a] I call this flattery, and I say that such a thing is shameful, Polus—it's you I'm saying this to—because it guesses at what's pleasant with no consideration for what's best. And I say that it isn't an art, but a knack, because it has no account of the nature of whatever things it applies by which it applies them, so that it's unable to state the cause of each thing. And I refuse to call anything that lacks such an account an art. If you have any quarrel with these claims, I'm willing to submit them for discussion. So pastry baking, as I say, is the flattery that wears the mask of medicine. [b] Cosmetics is the one that wears that of gymnastics in the same way; a mischievous, deceptive, disgraceful, and ill-bred thing, one that perpetrates deception by means of shaping and coloring, smoothing out and dressing up, so as to make people assume an alien beauty and neglect their own, which comes through gymnastics. So that I won't make a long-style speech, I'm willing to put it to you the way the geometers do—for perhaps you [c] follow me now—that what cosmetics is to gymnastics, pastry baking is to medicine; or rather, like this: what cosmetics is to gymnastics, sophistry is to legislation, and what pastry baking is to medicine, rhetoric is to justice. However, as I was saying, although these activities are naturally distinct in this way, yet because they are so close, sophists and orators tend to be mixed together as people who work in the same area and concern themselves with the same things. They don't know what to do with themselves, and other people don't know what to do with them. In fact, if the soul didn't govern the body but the body governed itself, and if pastry baking [d] and medicine weren't kept under observation and distinguished by the soul, but the body itself made judgments about them, making its estimates by reference to the gratification it receives, then the world according to Anaxagoras would prevail. Polus my friend—you're familiar with these views—all things would be mixed together in the same place, and there would be no distinction between matters of medicine and health, and matters of pastry baking. You've now heard what I say rhetoric is. It's the counterpart in the soul to pastry baking, its counterpart in the body. Perhaps I've done an absurd [e] thing: I wouldn't let you make long speeches, and here I've just composed a lengthy one myself. I deserve to be forgiven, though, for when I made my statements short you didn't understand and didn't know how to deal with the answers I gave you, but you needed a narration. So if I don't know how to deal with your answers either, you must spin out a speech, [466a] too. But if I do, just let me deal with them. That's only fair. And if you now know how to deal with my answer, please deal with it. (Plato, *Gorgias* 462b–466a)

1.31 **Plato's** *Socrates, at his trial, denies being an orator at all*

"Of the many lies they told, one in particular surprised me, namely that you should be [b] careful not to be deceived by an accomplished speaker like me. That they were not ashamed to be immediately proved wrong by the facts, when I show myself not to be an accomplished speaker at all, that I thought was most shameless on their part—unless indeed they call an accomplished speaker the man who speaks the truth. If they mean that, I would agree that I am an orator, but not after their manner, for indeed, as I say, [c] practically nothing they said was true." (Plato, *Apology* 17a–c)

Appendix: *The* Ajax *and* Odysseus *of Antisthenes*

Antisthenes' *Ajax* and *Odysseus* come down to us in manuscripts that also contain speeches of the orators of classical Athens, which may indicate that they owe their survival to their inclusion in ancient anthologies of such speeches. In any case, they are the only complete works from the Socratic circle except those of Plato and Xenophon to have survived intact. Although apparently to be thought of as separate works (they are listed separately in the catalogue of Antisthenes' output), they only make sense as a pair: Ajax is arguing that he rather than the (unnamed) Odysseus should be awarded the armor of Achilles; Odysseus responds to the very speech that Ajax gives (albeit, again, without naming him); together the speeches explore the question of whether and how arguments can be used to discover the truth. Their length (even when considered together) serves as a useful reminder that many of the named works attributed to the Socratics would have been very much shorter than the typical length of a Platonic dialogue—sometimes just a few pages, limited to a single argument or exchange (compare some of the dialogues incorporated in Xenophon's *Memorabilia,* or a number of the dialogues spuriously attributed to Plato).

Ajax, or *The Speech of Ajax*

[1] I could wish that we were being judged by the very men who were present at the events: for I know that I would have needed to keep silent, and *his* [sc. Odysseus'] speaking at greater length would count for nothing. As it is, those who were there when we acted are not here now; and you, who know nothing of it, are the judges. But what sort of justice can there be when the judges do not know, and the events are related through speeches? Fact lies in action.

[2] I rescued the body of Achilles and carried it away: this man carried his armor, knowing that the Trojans were keener to get possession of the body than the armor. If they could have gained possession of the body, they could have maltreated it and gained satisfaction for Hector. They would not have dedicated the armor to the gods, but would have hidden it [3] for fear of this good man, who had already, by night, plundered their temple for the statue of the goddess, and displayed it to the Greeks as if he had done a wonderful thing. I think I should take the armor myself so that I can give it back to his friends; but this man wants it to sell. He certainly would not dare to use it: no coward wants

to use conspicuous armor, knowing that that armor draws attention to his cowardice.

[4] The rest of what I have to say is in a similar vein. Those who arranged the contest, although they claimed to be kings, passed the business of judging virtue on to others—who for their part undertook to pass judgment on things of which they knew nothing. But this I know: no king capable of making a judgment about virtue hands the job over to others—any more than a doctor who is good at diagnosing illnesses passes the job on to someone else. [5] Even so, if I had been pitted against a man like myself, I would not have minded being beaten. As it is, there could be no greater difference between us. *He* is the sort of person to do nothing openly: I would not dare to do anything in secret. I cannot bear to be ill spoken of, because I cannot bear being ill used: but he would be hanged if he could make money out of it. [6] In fact, he allowed himself to be whipped by slaves, hit on the back with clubs, and punched in the face—then, clothed in rags, he went off to mix with the enemy at night by the walls and steal from their temple. He admits this. Perhaps his speech will persuade you that he acted well. But is it right that this rogue and temple robber take possession of the armor of Achilles?

[7] I say to you, judges and jury who do not know: do not examine words when you are judging virtue, but rather actions. For a battle too is decided not by word but by action. You cannot contradict your enemy: you fight, and either you win or you get enslaved—in silence. This is what you should consider and examine: even if you do not make the right judgment, know that words have no strength in the face of action, [8] nor is there anything a man can say to help you; and understand clearly that people give lots of long speeches because they are incapable of action. So either say that you do not have insight into what is being talked about, and go your way; or make your judgment honestly. And do not do this in secret, but out in the open, to help you understand that judges themselves are punished if they do not judge honestly. And then, perhaps, you might realize that you sit not as judges of what is said, but speculators about it. [9] I turn over to you the business of investigating me and my affairs, but I forbid you from thinking that you will know it all.

This is what I have to present concerning a man who went to Troy not willingly but unwillingly, and about me, who always fought at the front, and was the only one not to hide behind the wall. (= Antisthenes 53)

Odysseus, or On Odysseus

[1] The speech I have risen to give is addressed not just to you [Ajax],[17] but to everyone else as well—for I have done more for the army than any of you. I would have said this if Achilles were still alive, and I say it to you now he is dead: you have not fought any battle that I did not fight alongside you—but none of you know anything of the dangers I underwent on my own. [2] And yet, in the battles we shared, nothing more came of it even if you fought well. As to the perils I risked on my own, on the other hand: if I succeeded, you would have had everything accomplished for which we came here, but if I failed, you would have lost just me, one man. For we did not come here to fight with the Trojans, but to remove Helen and take Troy. [3] All of this was at stake in what I risked. When Troy was declared unassailable unless we first take the statue of the goddess which had been stolen from us, who brought the statue here but me? And now you [Ajax] judge me to be a temple robber. *You* know nothing if you brand the man who secured the statue a "temple robber"—rather than Alexander, who stole it from us![18] [4] All of you pray that Troy is taken; but you [Ajax] brand me, who has found a way to do this, a temple robber? Yet if it is a fine thing to take Troy, then it is a fine thing to discover the way to do it. Everyone else is grateful: you even blame me. Your ignorance means that you don't know what benefits you have received. [5] For my part, I am not blaming you for your ignorance—it is not something you or anyone else suffers from on purpose; but I do blame you for the fact that you have been saved by my "crimes" but will not believe it. You even threaten to harm these people if they vote me the armor. Well, you have often made all sorts of threats, before doing some petty thing;

---

17. Greek distinguishes singular and plural forms of "you," as modern English does not, so the addition of [Ajax] here and below is needed to show when Odysseus is not addressing the army at large (or indeed, his judges, as Ajax does).

18. The statue in question is the Palladion, an image of Athena. It is nowhere else suggested that it had been stolen from the Greeks, by Alexander (i.e., Paris) or anyone else (although Wörner, 1897–1902: 1304, makes a tentative connection between this passage and a fragment from a Hellenistic historian who said that it was made from the bones of Pelops, the father of Agamemnon and Menelaus: see *FGrH* 15 F3). The more usual belief was that the Palladion had fallen from the sky (and was made of wood). In a context where the reliability of words is one of the issues at stake, it is a possibility that Odysseus is simply introducing a falsehood here to convince the Greeks that he has not incurred the potentially deadly pollution that would follow if the theft was anything other than an act of restoration.

but if one should go by what is likely, I think that you will do yourself some harm thanks to your terrible anger.

[6] So, you blame me for being a coward when I have wrought harm on the enemy. You, then, have been an idiot, for laboring conspicuously with nothing to show for it. Or do you think you are better because you have done this in the company of everyone else? And then you speak about virtue to me? First of all, you don't even know how to fight, but are borne on your anger like a wild boar—and will probably end up encountering some harm and killing yourself. Do you not know that a good man suffers no harm at all at his own hand, or those of his companions, or his enemies? [7] Like a child you are delighted that these people say you are brave—but I say that you are the greatest coward of them all, and terrified of death. First of all, you have invulnerable armor than cannot be pierced, which means that you cannot be pierced. And what would you do if one of our enemies should come up to you with similar armor? It would be a noble and wonderful sight, with neither of you able to do anything! And yet you think there is a difference between having armor like this and sitting within the walls? You are the only one not to hide behind the wall, you say? You are the only one to construct a wall for yourself by surrounding yourself with seven ox hides! [8] I do not wear armor, and I do not skulk near the walls of the enemy—I attack those walls; I kill the watchmen of the walls in their armor; I lead and protect you and everyone else; I know what goes on here and among the enemy, and not because I send someone else to spy on them, but because I go myself. Just as helmsmen study the night and the day to protect their sailors, so I protect you and everyone else. [9] There is no danger I avoid because I consider it demeaning, if it provides an opportunity to harm the enemy. If people were going to see me, I would not show daring just out of eagerness for my reputation: I would make the attempt, whether I was going to harm the enemy as a slave or a beggar or a rogue; and I would make it if no one were to see as well. For war is not about how one is seen, but what one does, by day and by night. I don't have an array of armor in which to call the enemy out to fight; but I am always ready to face one or many, however they want it. [10] Nor, when I am weary of fighting, do I hand my armor on to others, as you do. When the enemy lets up, then I array myself, with whatever "armor" might best harm them. Night has never stopped me, as it has often made you pleased to stop fighting. When you are snoring, then I am protecting you, always harming the enemy with the armor of a slave's appearance, my rags and lashes—all of which allow you to sleep safely.

[11] You think that you are brave because you rescued the corpse and carried it away? If you could not carry it, two men would have done, and then they perhaps might have argued about virtue with us. My speech to them would have been the same. But what would your argument against them have been? Or would you not have despised two men, though being ashamed to admit that you were more cowardly than one? [12] Do you not know that the Trojans were not concerned with getting the corpse, but the armor? Their intention was to give the corpse back, but dedicate the armor to the gods in their temples. In the case of corpses, disgrace does not attach to those who fail to collect them, but to those who fail to return them for burial. So you rescued what they were ready to let go, while I took from them what they blamed me for. [13] You are sick with envy and ignorance—the most contradictory of ailments. One of them makes you desire what is beautiful, the other turns you away. It is a human failing: because you are strong, you think you are brave and do not realize that being strong is not the same as wisdom in war and bravery. Ignorance is the greatest evil for those who have it.

[14] If ever there is a poet who understands virtue, I think that he will make me daring and cunning and resourceful, sacker of cities, the sole captor of Troy. He will, I think, liken your character to slothful donkeys, oxen, beasts of burden, who submit to others to govern and yoke them. (= Antisthenes 54)

Chapter 2: Happiness and the Good

To what end should dialectic be put? There is no question that members of the Socratic circle thought that the most important truths to be sought were those concerning ethics. Ethics constituted the dominant subject of their researches, and the revolutionary approaches they developed in this field no doubt constituted the most distinctive collective feature of their discussions. In this chapter, we consider the evidence for their thinking about higher-level questions in ethics: the basis for ethical value and the goal of human ethical life. In Chapter 3, we turn to the discussions of virtue that these inform.

It is striking, from the outset, how wide the disagreements are between individual members of the circle (forcibly reminding us that the circle was, of course, never a school). Nevertheless, there are distinctive commonalities as well. They all, for example, tend to take positions that either explicitly or implicitly overturn ordinary assumptions; and in particular they seem to have converged in rejecting the idea—which was as common in contemporary Greek and Athenian society as it is in ours—that external things like beauty, wealth, and power are good in themselves. Indeed, they questioned whether such things were, properly speaking, good for us at all. Socrates constituted an emblem for their countercultural ideal: ugly, poor, simple in his tastes and needs, uninterested in conventional political power. An emblem and even, to some, a role model. While Aristippus at one extreme thought it perfectly acceptable to live a life of luxury (**2.6–10**),[1] Aristodemus went around aping Socrates' habits and dress (**6.8**).

The first question in ethics, then, is just this: what is "good" for a human being? What constitutes a good human life? In what does our *eudaimonia* consist? This key Greek term, *eudaimonia,* is conventionally translated into English as "happiness," but it is a happiness that is measured not in terms of subjective feelings of contentment, but rather in terms of success in achieving the possession of the good things in a human life, or (as it is sometimes put) what it is "useful" for us to have (**2.18–19**).[2]

---

1. NB: these texts should be read alongside Ch. 3 (esp. **3.43–44**) and Ch. 5 (esp. **5.12–13**) for the full picture; Aristippus' hedonism is not simple or crude.

2. The saying attributed to the Athenian lawgiver Solon, "Call no one *eudaimôn* until he is dead" (Herodotus, *Histories* 1.32), is meant to have an air of paradox about it; but Solon did not mean anything nearly so odd as it would be to say "Call no one happy until he is dead" in English.

One of the major topics of discussion and disagreement under this heading was the role of pleasure in the good life. Aristippus stands out as according more value to the pleasures of the body than others. Sometimes he is treated as a pure, indeed gross, hedonist, although most texts are more circumspect, claiming only that he thought that bodily and other pleasures were somehow the "foundation stone" of happiness (e.g., **2.6**, **2.9**). In either case, there is a degree of contrast between Aristippus and the other Socratics, who tend to treat "external goods" (things such as wealth and pleasure) as neither good nor bad in themselves (**2.16–22**). But his position does not seem to have isolated him altogether from the general consensus that it is "virtue" that is of central importance for happiness (see texts *passim* in this and the next chapter). There are clear signs that Aristippus' approval of pleasures went along with the claim that happiness depended on our being in control of our pleasures (e.g., **3.43–44**).

"Happiness" is the subject only of the first section of this chapter, however, because the inquiry into the nature of "good" and "bad" goes beyond the merely human good. For one thing, the Socratics recognize that there are non-human goods: god, or whatever holds the universe together, is an example (**2.30**, **2.31**; cf. also **2.34–38**). For another, these non-human goods might actually help to explain *why* the things that are good for human beings are so (see especially **2.29**). The boundary between Section i ("Happiness") and Section ii ("Goods and the Good") is by no means a rigid one, but is intended to help structure and contextualize Socratic thinking about the human good within a broader set of questions. The chapter ends with a scattering of texts (**2.34–38**) on one of the most famous treatments of the good as such from the period: Plato's mysterious public lecture *On the Good*. Some tantalizingly brief texts about Euclides' thinking on the good (**2.31–33**) might provide evidence that the metaphysical tendency of Plato's thinking on this topic was not, as we might have assumed, wholly original to him and his school.

> Plato's rich and multifaceted examination of the topic of this chapter is further represented here by excerpts from the *Philebus,* a long dialogue devoted to a discussion about the status, respectively, of knowledge and pleasure in relation to the good (**2.20(a)** from the beginning, and **2.20(b)** from the end), and the *Lysis,* a work as technical as the *Philebus,* in its own way, but much shorter (**2.25**). Both works repay further study in full. A passage from the *Phaedo* (**2.30**) points toward the idea—worked out more fully in the *Timaeus*— that there is a principle of goodness operating from the cosmic level

all the way down. Above all, interested readers should supplement their reading of this chapter with the *Republic,* a work centrally concerned throughout both with the good for humans and the good more generally.

Texts

i. Happiness

2.1 ***Plato's** Socrates is questioned by Diotima, a probably fictional seer, on what we all desire*

"Tell me, Socrates, a lover of good things has a desire; what does he desire?"

"That they become his own," I said.

"And what will he have, when the good things he wants have become his own?"

[205a] "This time it's easier to come up with the answer," I said. "He'll have happiness."

"That's what makes happy people happy, isn't it—possessing good things. There's no need to ask further, 'What's the point of wanting happiness?' The answer you gave seems to be final."

"True," I said. (Plato, *Symposium* 204e–205a)

2.2 ***Plato's** Socrates on the impossibility of desiring bad things*

MENO: I think, Socrates, that virtue is, as the poet says, "to find joy in beautiful things and have power." So I say that virtue is to desire beautiful things and have the power to acquire them.

SOCRATES: Do you mean that the man who desires beautiful things desires good things?

MENO: Most certainly.

SOCRATES: Do you assume that there are people who desire bad things, [c] and others who desire good things? Do you not think, my good man, that all men desire good things?

MENO: I do not.

SOCRATES: But some desire bad things?

MENO: Yes.

SOCRATES: Do you mean that they believe the bad things to be good, or that they know they are bad and nevertheless desire them?

MENO: I think there are both kinds.

SOCRATES: Do you think, Meno, that anyone, knowing that bad things are bad, nevertheless desires them?

MENO: I certainly do.

SOCRATES: What do you mean by desiring? Is it to secure for oneself?

MENO: What else? [d]

SOCRATES: Does he think that the bad things benefit him who possesses them, or does he know they harm him?

MENO: There are some who believe that the bad things benefit them, others who know that the bad things harm them.

SOCRATES: And do you think that those who believe that bad things benefit them know that they are bad?

MENO: No, that I cannot altogether believe.

SOCRATES: It is clear then that they do not desire bad things, these people [e] who don't recognize them for what they are; they desire the things they thought good. But these are actually *bad;* so it follows that those who don't recognize them for what they are and believe them to be good clearly desire good things. Is that not so?

MENO: It is likely.

SOCRATES: Well then, those who you say desire bad things, believing that bad things harm their possessor, know that they will be harmed by them?

MENO: Necessarily. [78a]

SOCRATES: And do they not think that those who are harmed are miserable to the extent that they are harmed?

MENO: That too is inevitable.

SOCRATES: And that those who are miserable are unhappy?

MENO: I think so.

SOCRATES: Does anyone wish to be miserable and unhappy?

MENO: I do not think so, Socrates.

SOCRATES: No one then wants what is bad, Meno, unless he wants to be such. For what else is being miserable but to desire bad things and secure them? [b]

MENO: You are probably right, Socrates, and no one wants what is bad. (Plato, *Meno* 77b–78b)

2.3 Plato's Socrates on the importance of virtue for happiness

POLUS: Current events quite suffice [to refute you], and to prove that many people who behave unjustly are happy.

SOCRATES: What sorts of events are these?

POLUS: You can picture this man Archelaus, the son of Perdiccas, ruling Macedonia, I take it?

SOCRATES: Well, if I can't picture him, I do hear things about him.

POLUS: Do you think he's happy or miserable?

SOCRATES: I don't know, Polus. I haven't met the man yet. [e]

POLUS: Really? You'd know this if you had met him, but without that you don't know straight off that he's happy?

SOCRATES: No, I certainly don't, by Zeus!

POLUS: It's obvious, Socrates, that you won't even claim to know that the Great King is happy.

SOCRATES: Yes, and that would be true, for I don't know how he stands in regard to education and justice.

POLUS: Really? Is happiness determined entirely by that?

SOCRATES: Yes, Polus, so I say anyway. I say that the admirable and good person, man or woman, is happy, but that the one who's unjust and wicked is miserable. [471a]

POLUS: So on your reasoning this man Archelaus is miserable?

SOCRATES: Yes, my friend, if he is in fact unjust. (Plato, *Gorgias* 470d–471a)[3]

2.4 *Antisthenes* on the importance of virtue for happiness

[Antisthenes] used to declare . . . that virtue was sufficient for happiness, being in need of nothing except the strength of Socrates. (Diogenes Laertius 6.11 = Antisthenes 134)[4]

---

3. Cf. Plato, *Statesman* 272b–d, where a similar point is made.

4. Compare, perhaps, Aristotle, *Nicomachean Ethics* VII.13, 1153b19–20 = Antisthenes 118: "Those who claim that the man being broken on the wheel and

2.5 Plato's Socrates on the "science," or knowledge (epistêmê), needed in order to be happy

"But whether acting scientifically would make us fare well and be happy, this we have yet to learn, my dear Critias."

"But on the other hand," he said, "you will not readily gain the prize of faring well by any other means if you eliminate scientific action."

"Instruct me on just one more small point," I said. "When you say that [e] something is scientifically done, are you talking about the science of cutting out shoes?"

"Good heavens no!"

"Of bronze working, then?"

"Certainly not."

"Then of wool or wood or some similar thing?"

"Of course not."

"Then," I said, "we no longer keep to the statement that the man who lives scientifically is happy. Because those who live in the ways we mentioned are not admitted by you to be happy, but rather you seem to me to define the happy man as one who lives scientifically concerning certain specific things. And perhaps you mean the person I mentioned a moment ago, [174a] the man who knows what all future events will be, namely the seer."

"Are you referring to this man or some other?"

"Both to this one," he said, "and another."

"Which one?" I said. "Isn't it the sort of man who, in addition to the future, knows everything that has been and is now and is ignorant of nothing? Let us postulate the existence of such a man. Of this man I think you would say that there was no one living who was more scientific."

"Certainly not."

"There is one additional thing I want to know: which one of the sciences makes him happy? Do all of them do this equally?"

"No, very unequally," he said.

"Well, which one in particular makes him happy? [b] The one by which he knows which one of the things are and have been and are to come? Will it be the one by which he knows checker playing?"

"Oh for heaven's sake," he said.

"Well, the one by which he knows calculation?"

"Of course not."

---

engulfed by great misfortunes is happy, provided he is a good character, are talking nonsense whether they mean to or not."

"Well, will it be that by which he knows health?"

"That's better," he said.

"But the most likely case," I said, "is that by which he knows what?"

"By which he knows good," he said, "and evil."

"You wretch," said I, "all this time you've been leading me right round [c] in a circle and concealing from me that it was not living scientifically that was making us fare well and be happy, even if we possessed all the sciences put together, but that we have to have this one science of good and evil. Because, Critias, if you consent to take away this science from the other sciences, will medicine any the less produce health, or cobbling produce shoes, or the art of weaving produce clothes, or will the pilot's art any the less prevent us from dying at sea or the general's art in war?"

"They will do it just the same," he said.

"But my dear Critias, [d] our chance of getting any of these things well and beneficially done will have vanished if this is lacking."

"You are right."

"Then this science, at any rate, is not moderation, as it seems, but that one of which the function is to benefit us. For it is not a science of science and absence of science but of good and evil." (Plato, *Charmides* 173d–174d; continued in **3.47**)

2.6 *Aristippus* on pleasure as a component of happiness

Aristippus was a friend of Socrates—Aristippus who founded the so-called Cyrenaic sect, from which Epicurus derived the idea for the end he established.[5] Aristippus was very soft and hedonistic in his life; he would not discuss the end in public at all, but in practice he said that the foundation stone of happiness lay in pleasures. For he was always giving speeches on pleasure with the effect that those coming to him got the idea that he was saying that the end is to live pleasurably. (Eusebius, *Preparation for the Gospel* 14.18.31 = Aristippus 173)

2.7 *Pleasure is easier to come by than you might think*

[Aristippus] was good at adapting to any place or time or person, and molding himself to fit any situation; which was why he was in greater

---

[5]. In fact, the Epicureans differed from the Cyrenaics by recognizing the absence of pain as a superior form of pleasure; but for polemical purposes the two schools are often conflated.

favor with Dionysius,[6] as he always made the best of everything that happened to him. He used to take pleasure in whatever was currently available, and did not go in for laboriously hunting down the enjoyment of things that weren't; all of which explains Diogenes' labeling him the "king's cur." Timon[7] sneered at him for having no backbone, and said something like this about him: "An effeminate nature like Aristippus', telling false from true | By groping." (Diogenes Laertius 2.66 = Aristippus 51)

2.8 *Again, Aristippus emphasizes the value of what is to hand*

Aristippus seems to have spoken with very great vigor, passing on the message to people not to labor either with going over the past or with working for the future; behaving that way would be a sign of cheerfulness and the proof of a happy mind. He told us to keep our mind on the day, and again within the day on that part of it in which each of us acts or thinks. For only the present is ours, he claimed, not what has gone by or what is to come, for the one has passed away, and it is uncertain that the other will be. (Aelian, *Historical Miscellany* 14.6 = Aristippus 174)

2.9 *Aristippus' views as the foundation for the Cyrenaic school*

And whole schools of philosophers contended for the choice of a life of luxury; one of which was the so-called Cyrenaic school, which took its rise from Aristippus the Socratic, who accepted the experience of pleasure and went on to say that this was the end, and that happiness is built on it. He said it belonged to the moment, and like profligates he thought neither the memory of past enjoyments nor the expectation of future ones were anything to him, [B] making the present the one and only criterion of the good, and regarding past and future enjoyments nothing to him because the first no longer existed and the second did not yet exist and it was uncertain that they would; which is the sort of way luxurious livers behave, thinking that it's the present that does them good. (Athenaeus, *The Learned Banqueters* 12, 544A–B = Aristippus 174)

---

6. Tyrant of Syracuse: cf. p. 194.
7. Of Phlius (320–230 BCE): philosopher and author of satirical verses.

2.10 *Xenophon's Socrates encourages restraint in* **Aristippus** *by recounting Prodicus' "Choice of Heracles," in which Heracles encounters personifications of Virtue and Vice*

As they got closer to Heracles, the one mentioned earlier [Virtue] kept a steady pace, while the other [Vice], wanting to be first, ran up to Heracles and said: "I see that you are puzzling over which path to take in life, Heracles. If you befriend me, I will guide you along the pleasantest and easiest path: you will taste every delight and live your entire life without ever knowing hardship. [24] In the first place, you will give no thought to wars or troubles. Instead, you will spend your time considering what food or drink you could find to tickle your fancy; what you would enjoy seeing, hearing, smelling, or touching; which young lover's company would cheer you most; how you could sleep most comfortably; and how you could obtain all these things with the least possible effort. [25] If scarcity ever becomes a concern, have no fear that under my guidance you will have to struggle or endure any physical or mental hardship to acquire these things. On the contrary, you will reap the fruits of other people's labor and abstain from no potential source of gain, since I grant my companions license to benefit themselves by every available means."

[26] When he heard this, Heracles said, "What is your name, lady?"

"My friends call me 'Happiness,'" she replied, "but my critics use the epithet 'Vice.'"

[27] At this point, the other woman approached and said, "I too have come to you, Heracles, because I know your parents and have gauged your character from your upbringing. And so I am confident that, should you follow the path that leads to me, you will become a consummate performer of high and noble deeds, and that I will come to be even more esteemed and distinguished for my beneficence. I will not deceive you with preludes about pleasure; instead, I will accurately describe the divinely ordained order of things. [28] The gods grant nothing truly noble to mankind without hard work and care. If you want the gods to show you favor, you must tend to the gods; if you wish to be loved by your friends, you must treat your friends well; if you desire to be honored by some state, you must serve that state; if you expect to be admired by all of Greece for your excellence, you must strive to benefit Greece; if you want the earth to yield plentiful crops, you must tend the earth; if you are determined to make money from livestock, you must care for the livestock; if you intend to strengthen yourself through war and you want to be able to liberate your friends and to subdue your enemies, you must learn the arts of war

from experts and train in tactics; and if you want to be physically fit, you must condition your body to submit to reason and put effort and sweat into your training."

[29] As Prodicus tells it, Vice replied by saying, "Do you understand how long and hard a path to enjoyment this woman here is describing to you, Heracles? I will take you on a short and easy path to happiness."
[30] "You wretch!" said Virtue. "What do you have of value, or what pleasure do you know, considering your refusal to expend any effort on their behalf? You do not even wait for the desire for pleasures; instead, you stuff yourself with everything before you even desire it, eating before you are hungry and drinking before you are thirsty. To make eating enjoyable, you surround yourself with gourmet cooks. In order to make drinking enjoyable, you provide yourself expensive wines and run around looking for ice during the summer. To make sleeping enjoyable, you provide yourself not only soft blankets but also bed frames, since your desire for sleep results not from fatigue but from boredom. You force yourself to indulge in sex before you feel any need, using every contrivance and treating men as women. This is how you educate your friends: by behaving wantonly at night and sleeping through the better part of the day." (Xenophon, *Memorabilia* 2.1.23–30)

2.11 *Antisthenes' response to Aristippus?*

To someone who praised luxury, he [Antisthenes] said: "May the sons of your enemies live in luxury." (Diogenes Laertius 6.8 = Antisthenes 114)

2.12 *Antisthenes had the opposite view of pleasure . . .*

Some have embraced pleasure as good, while others think the opposite, that it is bad—indeed, one of the philosophers shouted out loud: "I'd rather go mad than experience pleasure!" (Sextus Empiricus, *Outlines of Pyrrhonism* 3.181 = Antisthenes 122)[8]

2.13 *. . . although not all reports agree on the scope of his disapproval*

Antisthenes, while saying pleasure was a good thing, added the qualification "the pleasure one doesn't repent of." (Athenaeus, *The Learned Banqueters* 12, 513A = Antisthenes 127)

---

8. For the identification of Antisthenes as the author of this sentiment, see **3.45**; cf. 3.2.[39].

2.14 **Plato's** Socrates considers whether good and pleasant are coextensive

"What, Protagoras?" [I (Socrates) said.] "Surely you don't, like most people, call some pleasant things bad and some painful things good? I mean, isn't a pleasant thing good just insofar as it is pleasant, that is, if it results in nothing other than pleasure; and, on the other hand, aren't painful things bad in the same way, just insofar as they are painful?"

"I don't know, Socrates," [d] he [Protagoras] said, "if I should answer as simply as you put the question—that everything pleasant is good and everything painful is bad. It seems to me to be safer to respond not merely with my present answer in mind but from the point of view of my life overall, that on the one hand, there are pleasurable things which are not good, and on the other hand, there are painful things which are not bad but some which are, and a third class which is neutral—neither bad nor good."

"You call pleasant things those which partake of pleasure or produce pleasure?" I asked. [e]

"Certainly," he replied.

"So my question is this: Just insofar as things are pleasurable are they good? I am asking whether pleasure itself is not a good."

"Just as you always say, Socrates," he said, "let us inquire into this matter, and if your claim seems reasonable and it is established that pleasure and the good are the same, then we will come to agreement; otherwise we will disagree." (Plato, *Protagoras* 351c–e)

2.15 **Xenophon's** Socrates finds pleasure in sensing his own progress in virtue

Socrates said: "Do you find it amazing that god thinks it better for me to die now? Don't you know that I wouldn't concede that any person has lived a better or more pleasant life than I have up to this point? In my opinion, the people with the best life are those who take the best care to become as good as possible, and the ones with the most pleasant life are those who are most aware that they're improving. [7] This has been my own experience up to this point, and as I've encountered other people and compared myself to them, I've always come to this same conclusion about myself. Nor am I alone: my friends share the same opinion of me, not out of their fondness for me—since, in that case, anybody who was fond of someone else would feel the same way about him—but because they think that they too stand to become best by associating with me." (Xenophon, *Memorabilia* 4.8.6–7)[9]

ii. Goods and the Good

2.16 *Xenophon's* Socrates questions conventional views of what is good and bad

"Should I take it," said Socrates, "that you're completely versed in what kinds of things are good and what kinds are bad?"

"Absolutely," he [Euthydemus] replied. "If I didn't know that much, I'd be even worse than a slave."

"Go on, then, and tell me about them," he [Socrates] said.

"Well, that's not hard," he replied. "In the first place, I regard health as good in itself and sickness as bad. Then, in terms of their respective causes, I regard as good the foods, drinks, and habits that promote health, and as bad the ones that promote sickness."

[32] "Then would both health and sickness be good whenever they result in something good but bad whenever they result in something bad?" he asked.

"When could health result in something bad, or sickness in something good?" he replied.

"Why, surely in the case of a disastrous military campaign, or a calamitous voyage, or many other, similar circumstances," he said, "where able-bodied men take part and die but the infirm ones stay behind and are spared."

"You're right," he said, "but, as you can see, able-bodied men also take part in successful expeditions, while the infirm ones stay behind."

"So, given that these physical states are sometimes beneficial and sometimes detrimental," he said, "are they more good than bad?"

[33] "It certainly doesn't seem like it, at least not according to this argument. But surely wisdom is unquestionably good, Socrates. In what possible circumstance would a person not be better off if he were wise rather than ignorant?"

"Why, haven't you heard about Daedalus," he replied, "how because of his wisdom he was captured by Minos and forced to serve him; how he was at once deprived of both his homeland and his freedom; and

---

9. Cf. Plato, *Republic* IX, 581b–587a, for the superior pleasures of the philosophical life.

how, when he tried to escape with his son, he not only lost the boy but also failed to get himself to safety, and was instead carried off to a foreign land where he was again reduced to servitude?"

"That's certainly what they say," he replied.

"And haven't you heard about Palamedes' experiences? All the poets sing about how Odysseus killed him out of envy for his wisdom."

"They say that too," he replied.

"How many others, do you suppose, have been snatched off to the king of Persia's court on account of their wisdom and made to serve there?"

[34] "Happiness is probably the most unquestionable good, Socrates," he said.

"Provided that one doesn't compose it out of questionable goods, Euthydemus," he replied.

"But what element of happiness could be questioned?" he asked.

"None," he answered, "provided that we don't include in it beauty, physical strength, wealth, status, or anything else of that sort."

"Of course we'll include them," he said. "How could someone be happy without those?"

[35] "Then you can bet that we'll be including the sources of many troubles for humanity: beauty causes the ruin of many people at the hands of those aroused by youthful good looks; physical strength induces many people to attempt outsized tasks, with disastrous results; wealth causes the destruction of many people through either decadent living or hostile conspiracies; and status and political power have caused many people to suffer great harm." (Xenophon, *Memorabilia* 4.2.31–35)

2.17 **Plato**'s Socrates suggests that the goodness of conventional "goods" depends on the possession of virtue

"I [Socrates] go around doing nothing but persuading both young and old among you not to care for your body or your wealth in preference to or [b] as strongly for the best possible state of your soul, as I say to you: Wealth does not bring about excellence, but excellence makes wealth and everything else good for men, both individually and collectively." (Plato, *Apology* 30a–b; part of **3.54(b)**)

2.18 *Similarly,* **Xenophon**'s *Socrates (here with* **Critobulus**)

"Then the same things [said Socrates] are wealth to the person who knows how to use them, and not wealth to the person who doesn't; just as pipes are wealth to the competent flute player, but are no more than useless lumps of stone to the incompetent."

"Unless he were to sell them," [said Critobulus].

[11] "So now we see that in the case of people who do know how to play them, flutes are wealth to the ones who sell them, not to the ones who've got them and don't sell them."

"And our argument runs consistently with what we said, since our claim was that wealth is a matter of what benefits us: flutes not sold are not wealth, because they're not useful; if sold, they are."

[12] To which Socrates replied: "If the seller knows how to sell. If he sold them for something he didn't know how to use, then by your argument they're not wealth even when sold."

"You seem to be saying, Socrates, that money isn't wealth either, if one doesn't know how to use it."

[13] "And you seem to me to be agreeing that it will depend on whether one is able to be benefited by it. At any rate if someone used the money in such a way as to make body, soul, and household worse off, say by buying the services of a prostitute, how could money still be said to be benefiting him?"

"It couldn't, unless we're going to say that the plant they call 'henbane' is wealth too—the one that makes those who eat it mad."

[14] "Then one must keep a good distance from money, Critobulus, if one doesn't know how to use it. What about friends, if one knows how to put them to use and be benefited from them—what shall we say about them?"

"Zeus! That they're wealth too," replied Critobulus; "much more than one's cattle, if they're actually more use than cattle."

[15] "And by your account the same will go for enemies, if one knows how to benefit from them."

"I think so."

"So it's the business of a good estate manager to know how to use enemies too, in order to derive benefit from one's enemies."

"Emphatically so!" (Xenophon, *On Household Management* 1.10–15)

2.19(a) *Plato's Socrates considers the virtues alongside external goods . . .*

"Do all men wish to do well? Or is this question one of the ridiculous ones I was afraid of just now? I suppose it is stupid even to raise such a question, since there could hardly be a man who would not wish to do well."

"No, there is no such person," said Clinias.

"Well then," I said, [279a] "the next question is, since we wish to do well, how are we to do so? Would it be through having many good things? Or is this question still more simpleminded than the other, since this must obviously be the case too?"

He agreed.

"Well then, what kinds of existing things are good for us? Or perhaps this isn't a difficult question and we don't need an important personage to supply the answer because everybody would tell us that to be rich is a good—isn't that so?"

"Very much so," he said.

"And so with being healthy, [b] and handsome, and having a sufficient supply of the other things the body needs?"

He agreed.

"And, again, it is clear that noble birth, and power, and honor in one's country are goods."

He agreed.

"Then which goods do we have left?" I said. "What about being moderate [*sôphrôn*] and just and brave? For heaven's sake tell me, Clinias, whether you think we will be putting these in the right place if we class them as 'goods' or if we refuse to do so? Perhaps someone might quarrel with us on this point—how does it seem to you?"

"They are goods," said Clinias.

"Very well," said I. [c] "And where in the company shall we station wisdom?"

"Among the goods, or what shall we do with it?"

"Among the goods." (Plato, *Euthydemus* 278e–279c; followed by **3.61**)

2.19(b) . . . *and again concludes that external goods depend on virtue*

"We decided," I [Socrates] said, "that if we had many good things, we should be happy and do well."

He agreed.

"And would the possession of good things make us happy if they were of no advantage to us, or if they were of some?" [c]

"If they were of some advantage," he said.

"And would they be advantageous to us if we simply had them and did not use them? For instance, if we had a great deal of food but didn't eat any, or plenty to drink but didn't drink any, would we derive any advantage from these things?"

. . .

"Then are these two things, the possession of good things and the use of them, enough to make a man happy, Clinias?" [e]

"They seem so to me, at any rate."

"If," I said, "he uses them rightly, or if he does not?"

"If he uses them rightly."

"Well spoken," I said. "Now I suppose there is more harm done if someone uses a thing wrongly than if he lets it alone—in the first instance there is [281a] bad, but in the second neither bad nor good. Or isn't this what we maintain?"

He agreed that it was.

"Then what comes next? In working and using wood there is surely nothing else that brings about right use except the knowledge of carpentry, is there?"

"Certainly not."

"And, again, I suppose that in making utensils, it is knowledge that produces the right method."

He agreed.

"And also," I said, "with regard to using the goods we mentioned first—[b] wealth and health and beauty—was it knowledge that ruled and directed our conduct in relation to the right use of all such things as these, or some other thing?"

"It was knowledge," he said.

"Then knowledge seems to provide men not only with good fortune but also with well-doing, in every case of possession or action."

He agreed.

"Then in heaven's name," I said, "is there any advantage in other possessions without good sense and wisdom? Would a man with no sense profit more if he possessed and did much or if he possessed and did little? Look at [c] it this way: if he did less, would he not make fewer mistakes; and if he made fewer mistakes, would he not do less badly, and if he did less badly, would he not be less miserable?"

"Yes, indeed," he said.

"And in which case would one do less, if one were poor or if one were rich?"

"Poor," he said.

"And if one were weak or strong?"

"Weak."

"If one were held in honor or in dishonor?"

"In dishonor."

"And if one were brave and moderate [*sôphrôn*] would one do less, or if one were a coward?"

"A coward."

"Then the same would be true if one were lazy rather than industrious?"

He agreed.

"And slow rather than quick, and dull of sight and hearing rather than keen?" [d]

We agreed with each other on all points of this sort.

"So, to sum up, Clinias," I said, "it seems likely that with respect to all the things we called good in the beginning, the correct account is not that in themselves they are good by nature, but rather as follows: if ignorance controls them, they are greater bads than their opposites, to the extent that they are more capable of complying with a bad master; but if good sense [e] and wisdom are in control, they are greater goods. In themselves, however, neither sort is of any value."

"It seems," he said, "to be just as you say."

"Then what is the result of our conversation? Isn't it that, of the other things, no one of them is either good or bad, but of these two, wisdom is good and ignorance bad?"

He agreed.

[282a] "Then let us consider what follows: since we all wish to be happy, and since we appear to become so by using things and using them rightly, and since knowledge was the source of rightness and good fortune, it seems to be necessary that every man should prepare himself by every means to become as wise as possible—or isn't this the case?" (Plato, *Euthydemus* 280b–282a; follows **3.61**)

2.20(a) *Plato's* Socrates elsewhere considers the competing claims of body and mind . . .

SOCRATES: Well, then, Protarchus, consider just what the thesis is that you are now taking over from Philebus [who evidently was speaking before the dialogue begins]—and what *our* thesis is that you [b] are going to argue against, if you find that you do not agree with it. Shall we summarize them both?

PROTARCHUS: Yes, let's do that.

SOCRATES: Philebus holds that what is good for all creatures is to enjoy themselves, to be pleased and delighted, and whatever else goes together with that kind of thing. We contend that not these, but knowing, understanding, and remembering, and what belongs with them, right opinion [c] and true calculations, are better than pleasure and more agreeable to all who can attain them; those who can get the maximum benefit possible from having them, both those now alive and future generations. Isn't that how we present our respective positions, Philebus? (Plato, *Philebus* 11a–c)

2.20(b) *. . . and concludes that both have their role to play*

SOCRATES: Our discussion would then continue as follows: "Will you have any need to associate with the strongest and most intensive pleasures in addition to the true pleasures?" we will ask them [i.e., Intelligence and Reason]. "Why on earth should we need them, Socrates?" they might reply. "They are a tremendous impediment to us, since they infect the souls in which they dwell with madness or even prevent our own development altogether. Furthermore, [e] they totally destroy most of our offspring, since neglect leads to forgetfulness. But as to the true and pure pleasures you mentioned, you should pretty much regard those as our kin. And besides, also add the pleasures of health and of moderation and all those that commit themselves to virtue as to their deity and follow it around everywhere. But to forge an association between reason and those pleasures that are forever involved with foolishness and other kinds of vice would be totally unreasonable for anyone who aims at the best and [64a] most stable mixture or blend. This is true particularly if he wants to discover in this mixture what the good is in man and in the universe and to get some vision of the nature of the good itself." When reason makes this defense for herself, as well as for memory and right opinion, shall we not admit that she has spoken reasonably and in accord with her own standards?

PROTARCHUS: Absolutely.

SOCRATES: But see whether the following is also necessary and without it not a single thing could come to be.

PROTARCHUS: What is it? [b]

SOCRATES: Wherever we do not mix in truth nothing could truly come to be nor remain in existence once it had come to be.

PROTARCHUS: How should it?

SOCRATES: In no way. But now, if there is anything else missing in our mixture, it is up to you and Philebus to say so. To me at least it seems that our discussion has arrived at the design of what might be called an incorporeal order that rules harmoniously over a body possessed by a soul.

PROTARCHUS: Count me as one who shares that opinion, Socrates.

SOCRATES: Would there be some justification to our claim that we are by now standing on the very threshold of the good and of the house of every member of its family? [c]

PROTARCHUS: It would seem so, to me at least.

SOCRATES: What ingredient in the mixture ought we to regard as most valuable and at the same time as the factor that makes it precious to all mankind? Once we have found it, we will inquire further whether it is more closely related and akin to pleasure or to reason, in nature as a whole.

PROTARCHUS: You are right. [d] This would certainly be very useful in bringing us closer to our final verdict.

SOCRATES: But it is certainly not difficult to see what factor in each mixture it is that makes it either most valuable or worth nothing at all.

PROTARCHUS: What do you have in mind?

SOCRATES: There is not a single human being who does not know it.

PROTARCHUS: Know what?

SOCRATES: That any kind of mixture that does not in some way or other possess measure or the nature of proportion will necessarily corrupt its [e] ingredients and most of all itself. For there would be no blending in such cases at all but really an unconnected medley, the ruin of whatever happens to be contained in it.

PROTARCHUS: Very true.

SOCRATES: But now we notice that the force of the good has taken refuge in an alliance with the nature of the beautiful. For measure and proportion manifest themselves in all areas as beauty and virtue.

PROTARCHUS: Undeniably.

SOCRATES: But we did say that truth is also included along with them in our mixture?

PROTARCHUS: Indeed.

SOCRATES: Well, then, if we cannot capture the good in *one* form, [65a] we will have to take hold of it in a conjunction of three: beauty, proportion, and truth. Let us affirm that these should by right be treated as a unity and be held responsible for what is in the mixture, for its goodness is what makes the mixture itself a good one.

PROTARCHUS: Very well stated.

SOCRATES: Anyone should by now be able to judge between pleasure [b] and intelligence, which of the two is more closely related to the supreme good and more valuable among gods and men. (Plato, *Philebus* 63d–65b)

2.21 *Compare* **Aeschines**

From Aeschines: there is no poverty for a person in being fine and good. (Stobaeus, *Selections* 2.8.26 = Aeschines 95)[10]

2.22 **Xenophon's Aristippus** *tries to trap Socrates in his own snare*

Aristippus asked him [Socrates] if he knew of anything that was good, so that if he cited anything like food, drink, money, health, physical strength, or daring, he could show him that in some cases it was bad. But Socrates, knowing that if ever we're in any sort of trouble we need something to put a stop to it, answered in terms of what it's best for us to do.

"Are you asking me if I know anything good for a fever?"
"No, I'm not asking that."
"Are you after something good for eye-disease?"
"Not that either."
"Good for hunger?"
"Not for hunger either."
"Well," said Socrates, "if you're really going to ask me if I know of anything good that isn't good *for* something, I don't, and I don't need to know." (Xenophon, *Memorabilia* 3.8.2–3)

2.23 *Virtue is what we should aim for according to* **Antisthenes**, *too*

The Cynics also thought that the end (*telos*) was to live according to virtue, as Antisthenes says in the *Heracles*. (Diogenes Laertius 6.104 = Antisthenes 98)

2.24 **Xenophon's** *Socrates looks to the gods*

He also used to pray to the gods simply to give him good things, on the grounds that the gods know best what sorts of things are good. He

---

10. The phrase "fine and good" (*kalos kagathos*) represents the conventional virtue of the Athenian "pillar of society." Aeschines may be suggesting that it is a state of character that confers value on other things, rather than a social status partly conferred by wealth.

regarded praying for gold, silver, supreme power, or anything else of this sort as no different from anything else with an obviously unclear outcome. (Xenophon, *Memorabilia* 1.3.2; follows **3.56**)

2.25(a)–(b) *Plato's* Socrates with Menexenus and Lysis, on "friendship" (love, desire) for the good

[**2.25(a)**] "So like is not friend to like, nor is opposite friend to opposite."

"Apparently not."

"But there's this too we still ought to consider. [c] We may have overlooked something else, the possibility that the friend is none of these things, but something that is neither bad nor good but becomes the friend of the good just for that reason."

"What are you saying?" he [Menexenus] asked.

"By Zeus," I said, "I hardly know myself. I'm getting downright dizzy with the perplexities of our argument. Maybe the old proverb is right, and the beautiful is a friend. It bears a resemblance, at any rate, to something [d] soft and smooth and sleek, and maybe that's why it slides and sinks into us so easily, because it's something like that. Now I maintain that the good is beautiful. What do you think?"

"I agree."

"All right, now, I'm going to wax prophetic and say that what is neither good nor bad is a friend of the beautiful and the good. Listen to the motive for my mantic utterance. It seems to me that there are three kinds of things: the good, the bad, and the neither good nor bad. What about you?"

"It seems so to me too," he said.

"And the good is not a friend to the good, nor the bad to the bad, nor the good to the bad. [e] Our previous argument disallows it. Only one possibility remains. If anything is a friend to anything, what is neither good nor bad is a friend either to the good or to something like itself. For I don't suppose anything could be a friend to the bad."

"True."

"But we just said that like is not friend to like."

"Yes."

"So what is neither good nor bad cannot be a friend to something like itself."

"Apparently not."

"So it turns out that only what is neither good nor bad is friend to the good, and only to the good." [217a]

"It seems it must be so."

"Well, then, boys, are we on the right track with our present statement? Suppose we consider a healthy body. It has no need of a doctor's help. It's fine just as it is. So no one in good health is friend to a doctor, on account of his good health. Right?"

"Right."

"But a sick man is, I imagine, on account of his disease."

"Naturally."

"Now, disease is a bad thing, and medicine is beneficial and good."

"Yes."

"And the body, as body, is neither good nor bad."

"True." [b]

"And because of disease, a body is forced to welcome and love medicine."

"I think so."

"So what is neither good nor bad becomes a friend of the good because of the presence of something bad."

"It looks like it."

"But clearly this is before it becomes bad itself by the bad it is in contact with. Because once it has become bad, it can no longer desire the good or [c] be its friend. Remember we said it was impossible for the bad to befriend the good."

"It *is* impossible."

"Now consider what I'm going to say. I say that some things are of the same sort as what is present with them, and some are not. For example, if you paint something a certain color, the paint is somehow present with the thing painted."

"Definitely."

"Then is the thing painted of the same sort, as far as color goes, as the applied paint?"

"I don't understand," he said.

"Look at it this way," I said. [d] "If someone smeared your blond hair with white lead, would your hair then *be* white or *appear* white?"

"Appear white," he said.

"And yet whiteness would surely be present with it."

"Yes."

"But all the same your hair would not yet be white. Though whiteness would be present, your hair would not be white any more than it is black."

"True."

"But when, my friend, [e] old age introduces this same color to your hair, then it will become of the same sort as what is present, white by the presence of white."

"Naturally."

"Here at last is my question, then. When a thing has something present with it, will it be of the same sort as what is present? Or only when that thing is present in a certain way?"

"Only then," he said.

"And what is neither good nor bad sometimes has not yet become bad by the presence with it of bad, but sometimes it has."

"Certainly."

"And when it is not yet bad although bad is present, that presence makes it desire the good. But the presence that makes it be bad deprives [218a] it of its desire as well as its love for the good. For it is no longer neither good nor bad, but bad. And the bad can't be friend to the good."

"No, it can't."

"From this we may infer that those who are already wise no longer love wisdom, whether they are gods or men. Nor do those love it who are so ignorant that they are bad, for no bad and stupid man loves wisdom. There remain only those who have this bad thing, ignorance, but have not yet been made ignorant and stupid by it. They are conscious of not knowing [b] what they don't know. The upshot is that those who are as yet neither good nor bad love wisdom, while all those who are bad do not, and neither do those who are good. For our earlier discussion made it clear that the opposite is not friend to the opposite, nor is like friend to like. Remember?"

"Of course," they both answered.

"So now, Lysis and Menexenus, we have discovered for sure what the friend is and what it is [c] not. For we maintain that in the soul and in the body and everywhere, that which is neither good nor bad itself is, by the presence of evil, a friend of the good."

The two of them heartily agreed that this was the case, and I was pretty happy myself. I had the satisfied feeling of a successful hunter and was basking in it, when a very strange suspicion, from where I don't know, came over me. Maybe what we had all agreed to wasn't true after all. What an awful thought. "Oh, no!" I screamed out. "Lysis and Menexenus, it seems our wealth has all been a dream!" (Plato, *Lysis* 216b–218c)

[**2.25(b)**] "Look, this is how it stands. There are three things of which we have just been speaking—good, bad, and what is neither good nor bad. Suppose there remained only two, and bad were eliminated and could affect no one in body or soul or anything else that we say is neither good nor bad in and of itself. Would the good then be of any use to us, or would it have become useless? [d] For if nothing could still harm us, we would have no need of any assistance, and it would be perfectly clear to us that it was on account of the bad that we prized and loved the good—as if the good is a drug against the bad, and the bad is a disease, so that without the disease there is no need for the drug. Isn't the good by nature loved on account of the bad by those of us who are midway between good and bad, but by itself and for its own sake it has no use at all?"

"It looks like that's how it is," he [Menexenus] said.

"Then that friend of ours, [e] the one which was the terminal point for all the other things that we called 'friends for the sake of another friend,' does not resemble them at all [see 219c–220b]. For they are called friends for the sake of a friend, but the real friend appears to have a nature completely the opposite of this. It has become clear to us that it was a friend for the sake of an enemy. Take away the enemy and it seems it is no longer a friend."

"It seems it isn't," he said, "not, at least, by what we are saying now."

"By Zeus," I said, [221a] "I wonder, if the bad is eliminated, whether it will be possible to be hungry or thirsty or anything like that. Or if there will be hunger as long as human beings and other animals exist, but it won't do harm. Thirst, too, and all the other desires, but they won't be bad, because the bad will have been abolished. Or is it ridiculous to ask what will be then and what will not? Who knows? But we do know this: that it is possible for hunger to do harm, and also possible for it to help. Right?"

"Certainly."

"And isn't it true that thirst or any other such desires can be felt sometimes to one's benefit, [b] sometimes to one's harm, and sometimes to neither?"

"Absolutely."

"And if bad things are abolished, does this have anything to do with things that aren't bad being abolished along with them?"

"No."

"So the desires that are neither good nor bad will continue to exist, even if bad things are abolished."

"It appears so."

"And is it possible to desire and love something passionately without feeling friendly toward it?"

"It doesn't seem so to me."

"So there will still be some friendly things even if the bad is abolished."

"Yes."

"It is impossible, [c] if bad were the cause of something's being a friend, that with the bad abolished one thing could be another's friend. When a cause is abolished, the thing that it was the cause of can no longer exist."

"That makes sense."

"Haven't we agreed that the friend loves something, and loves it on account of something, and didn't we think then that it was on account of bad that what was neither good nor bad loved the good?"

"True."

"But now it looks like some other cause of loving and being loved has appeared." [d]

"It does look like it."

"Then can it really be, as we were just saying, that desire is cause of friendship, and that what desires is a friend to that which it desires, and is so whenever it does so? And that what we were saying earlier about being a friend was all just chatter, like a poem that trails on too long?"

"There's a good chance," he said.

"But," I said, [e] "what desires, desires whatever it is lacking. Right?"

"Yes."

"And what is lacking, in that case, is friend of whatever it is lacking?"

"I think so."

"And what becomes lacking is whatever has something taken away from it."

"Of course."

"Then it is what belongs to oneself, it seems, that passionate love and friendship and desire are directed toward, Menexenus and Lysis." (Plato, *Lysis* 220c–221e)

2.26 *Plato's Glaucon challenges Socrates: what (kind of) good is justice?*

"Tell me," [I (Socrates) said,] "do you think there is a kind of good we welcome, not because we desire what comes from it, but because we welcome it for its own sake—joy, for example, and all the harmless pleasures that have no results beyond the joy of having them?"

"Certainly, I think there are such things."

"And is there a kind of good we like for its own sake and also for the [c] sake of what comes from it—knowing, for example, and seeing and being healthy? We welcome such things, I suppose, on both counts."

"Yes."

"And do you also see a third kind of good, such as physical training, medical treatment when sick, medicine itself, and the other ways of making money? We'd say that these are onerous but beneficial to us, and we wouldn't choose them for their own sakes, but for the sake of the rewards [d] and other things that come from them."

"There is also this third kind. But what of it?"

"Where do you put justice?"

"I myself put it among the finest goods, [358a] as something to be valued by anyone who is going to be blessed with happiness, both because of itself and because of what comes from it."

"That isn't most people's opinion. They'd say that justice belongs to the onerous kind, and is to be practiced for the sake of the rewards and popularity that come from a reputation for justice, but is to be avoided because of itself as something burdensome."

"I know that's the general opinion. Thrasymachus faulted justice on these grounds a moment ago and praised injustice, but it seems that I'm a slow learner." (Plato, *Republic* II, 357b–358a)

2.27 Plato's Socrates with **Crito**, *on the effect of justice*

SOCRATES: Do we say that one must never in any way do wrong willingly, or must one do wrong in one way and not in another? Is to do wrong never good or admirable, as we have agreed in the past, or have all these [b] former agreements been washed out during the last few days? Have we at our age failed to notice for some time that in our serious discussions we were no different from children? Above all, is the truth such as we used to say it was, whether the majority agree or not and whether we must still suffer worse things than we do now, or will be treated more gently, that nonetheless, wrongdoing or injustice is in every way harmful and shameful to the wrongdoer? Do we say so or not?

CRITO: We do.

SOCRATES: So one must never do wrong.

CRITO: Certainly not.

SOCRATES: Nor must one, when wronged, inflict wrong in return, as the majority believe, since one must never do wrong.

CRITO: That seems to be the case. [c]

SOCRATES: Come now, should one do harm to anyone or not, Crito?

CRITO: One must never do so.

SOCRATES: Well then, if one is done harm, is it right, as the majority say, to do harm in return, or is it not?

CRITO: It is never right.

SOCRATES: Doing harm to people is no different from wrongdoing.

CRITO: That is true.

SOCRATES: One should never do wrong in return, nor do any man harm, [d] no matter what he may have done to you. (Plato, *Crito* 49a–d)

2.28 *Plato's* Socrates against a common view that injustice can be beneficial and preferable

SOCRATES: For I do believe that you and I and everybody else consider doing what's unjust worse than suffering it, and not paying what is due worse than paying it.

POLUS: And I do believe that I don't, and that no other person does, either. So you'd take suffering what's unjust over doing it, would you?

SOCRATES: Yes, and so would you and everyone else.

POLUS: Far from it! I wouldn't, you wouldn't, and nobody else would, either. (Plato, *Gorgias* 474b)[11]

2.29(a) *Plato's* Socrates with Adimantus, introducing the *"form"* of the good

"Aren't these virtues, then, the most important things?" he [Adimantus] asked. "Is there anything even more important than justice and the other virtues we discussed?"

"There is something more important," [I (Socrates) said]. "However, even for the virtues themselves, it isn't enough to look at a mere sketch, as we did before, while neglecting the most complete account. It's ridiculous, isn't it, to strain every nerve to attain the utmost exactness and clarity about other things of little value and not to consider the most important things worthy of [e] the greatest exactness?"

---

11. Cf. **3.37–39**.

"It certainly is. But do you think that anyone is going to let you off without asking you what this most important subject is and what it concerns?"

"No, indeed, and you can ask me too. You've certainly heard the answer often enough, but now either you aren't thinking or you intend to make trouble for me again by interrupting. And I suspect the latter, for you've [505a] often heard it said that the form of the good is the most important thing to learn about and that it's by their relation to it that just things and the others become useful and beneficial. You know very well now that I am going to say this, and, besides, that we have no adequate knowledge of it. And you also know that, if we don't know it, even the fullest possible knowledge of other things is of no benefit to us, any more than if we acquire any possession without the good of it. Or do you think that it is any advantage to have every kind of possession without the good of it? [b] Or to know everything except the good, thereby knowing nothing fine or good?"

"No, by god, I don't."

"Furthermore, you certainly know that the majority believe that pleasure is the good, while the more sophisticated believe that it is knowledge."

"Indeed I do."

"And you know that those who believe this can't tell us what sort of knowledge it is, however, but in the end are forced to say that it is knowledge of the good."

"And that's ridiculous."

"Of course it is. [c] They blame us for not knowing the good and then turn around and talk to us as if we did know it. They say that it is knowledge of the good—as if we understood what they're speaking about when they utter the word 'good.'"

"That's completely true."

"What about those who define the good as pleasure? Are they any less full of confusion than the others? Aren't even they forced to admit that there are bad pleasures?"

"Most definitely."

"So, I think, they have to agree that the same things are both good and bad. Isn't that true?"

"Of course." [d]

"It's clear, then, isn't it, why there are many large controversies about this?"

"How could it be otherwise?"

"And isn't this also clear? In the case of just and beautiful things, many people are content with what are believed to be so, even if they aren't really so, and they act, acquire, and form their own beliefs on that basis. Nobody is satisfied to acquire things that are merely believed to be good, however, but everyone wants the things that really *are* good and disdains mere belief here."

"That's right."

"Every soul pursues the good and does its utmost for its sake. [e] It divines that the good is something but it is perplexed and cannot adequately grasp what it is or acquire the sort of stable beliefs it has about other things, and so it misses the benefit, if any, that even those other things may give. Will we allow the best people in the city, to whom we [506a] entrust everything, to be so in the dark about something of this kind and of this importance?"

"That's the last thing we'd do."

"I don't suppose, at least, that just and fine things will have acquired much of a guardian in someone who doesn't even know in what way they are good. And I divine that no one will have adequate knowledge of them until he knows this."

"You've divined well."

"But won't our constitution be perfectly ordered, if a guardian who knows [b] these things is in charge of it?"

"Necessarily. But, Socrates, you must also tell us whether you consider the good to be knowledge or pleasure or something else altogether."

"What a man! It's been clear for some time that other people's opinions about these matters wouldn't satisfy you."

"Well, Socrates, it doesn't seem right to me for you to be willing to state other people's convictions but not your own, especially when you've spent [c] so much time occupied with these matters."

"What? Do you think it's right to talk about things one doesn't know as if one does know them?"

"Not as if one knows them," he said, "but one ought to be willing to state one's opinions as such."

"What? Haven't you noticed that opinions without knowledge are shameful and ugly things? The best of them are blind—or do you think that those who express a true opinion without understanding are any different from blind people who happen to travel the right road?"

"They're no different."

"Do you want to look at shameful, blind, and crooked things, then, when [d] you might hear illuminating and fine ones from other people?"

"By god, Socrates," Glaucon said, "don't desert us with the end almost in sight. We'll be satisfied if you discuss the good as you discussed justice, moderation, and the rest."

"That, my friend," I said, "would satisfy me too, but I'm afraid that I won't be up to it and that I'll disgrace myself and look ridiculous by trying. So let's abandon the quest for what the good itself is for the time being, for [e] even to arrive at my own view about it is too big a topic for the discussion we are now started on. But I am willing to tell you about what is apparently an offspring of the good and most like it." (Plato, *Republic* VI, 504d–506e)

2.29(b) **Plato**'s *Socrates, pressed by* **Glaucon**, *describes the "form" of the good by analogy with the sun*

"We say," I [Socrates] said, "that there are many beautiful things and many good things, and so on for each kind, and in this way we distinguish them in words."

"We do."

"And beauty itself and good itself and all the things that we thereby set down as many, reversing ourselves, we set down according to a single form of each, believing that there is but one, and call it 'the being' of each."

"That's true."

"And we say that the many beautiful things and the rest are visible but not intelligible, while the forms are intelligible but not visible."

"That's completely true."

"With what part of ourselves do we see visible things?" [c]

"With our sight," he [Glaucon] said.

"And so," I asked, "audible things are heard by hearing, and with our other senses we perceive all the other perceptible things."

"That's right."

I asked, "Have you considered how lavish the maker of our senses was in making the power to see and be seen?"

"I can't say I have," he replied.

"Well, consider it this way. Do hearing and sound need another kind of thing in order for the former to hear and the latter to be heard, a third [d] thing in whose absence the one won't hear or the other be heard?"

"No, they need nothing else," he said.

"And if there are any others that need such a thing," I said, "there can't be many of them. Can you think of one?"

"I can't," he replied.

"You don't realize that sight and the visible have such a need?"

"How so?"

"Sight may be present in the eyes, and the one who has it may try to use it, and colors may be present in things, but unless a third kind of thing is present, which is naturally adapted for this very purpose, you know that [e] sight will see nothing, and the colors will remain unseen."

"What kind of thing do you have in mind?" he asked.

"It's what you call light," I replied.

"You're right," he said.

"Then it isn't an insignificant kind of link that connects the sense of sight [508a] and the power to be seen—it is a more valuable link than any other linked things have got, if indeed light is something valuable."

"And, of course," he said, "it's very valuable."

"Which of the gods in heaven would you name as the cause and controller of this, the one whose light causes our sight to see in the best way and the visible things to be seen?"

"The same one you and others would name," he said. "Obviously, the answer to your question is the sun."

"And isn't sight by nature related to that god in this way?"

"Which way?"

"Sight isn't the sun, neither sight itself nor that in which it comes to be, namely, the eye." [b]

"No, it certainly isn't."

"But I think that it is the most sunlike of the senses."

"Very much so."

"And it receives from the sun the power it has, just like an influx from an overflowing treasury."

"Certainly."

"The sun is not sight, but isn't it the cause of sight itself and seen by it?"

"That's right," he said.

"Let's say, then," I went on, "that this is what I called the offspring of the good, which the good begot as its analog. What the good itself is in the intelligible realm, in relation to understanding and intelligible things, the sun is in [c] the visible realm, in relation to sight and visible things."

"How?" he asked. "Explain a bit more."

"You know," I explained, "that when we turn our eyes to things whose colors are no longer illuminated by the light of day but by night lights, the eyes are dimmed and seem nearly blind, as if clear vision were no longer in them."

"Of course," he replied.

"Yet whenever one turns them on things illuminated by the sun, they [d] see clearly, and vision appears in those very same eyes?"

"Indeed."

'Well, understand the soul in the same way: When it focuses on something illuminated by truth and what is, it understands, knows, and apparently possesses understanding, but when it focuses on what is mixed with obscurity, on what comes to be and passes away, it opines and is dimmed, changes its opinions this way and that, and seems bereft of understanding."

"It does seem that way."

"So that what gives truth to the things known and the power to know [e] to the knower is the form of the good. And though it is the cause of knowledge and truth, it is also an object of knowledge. Both knowledge and truth are beautiful things, but the good is other and more beautiful than they. In the visible realm, light and sight are rightly considered sunlike, but it is wrong to think that they are the sun, so here it is right [509a] to think of knowledge and truth as goodlike but wrong to think that either of them is the good—for the good is yet more prized."

"This is an inconceivably beautiful thing you're talking about," he said, "if it provides both knowledge and truth and is superior to them in beauty. You surely don't think that a thing like that could be pleasure."

"Hush!" I exclaimed. "Let's examine its image in more detail as follows."

"How?" [b]

"You'll be willing to say, I think, that the sun not only provides visible things with the power to be seen but also with coming to be, growth, and nourishment, although it is not itself coming to be."

"How could it be?"

"Therefore, you should also say that not only do the objects of knowledge owe their being known to the good, but their being is also due to it, although the good is not being, but superior to it in rank and power."

And Glaucon comically said: "By Apollo, what a daemonic superiority!"

"It's your own fault," I responded; [c] "you forced me to tell you my opinion about it." (Plato, *Republic* VI, 507b–509c)

2.30 Plato's Phaedo reports his Socrates (with **Simmias** and **Cebes**) on the role of goodness in the universe

"Again," [Socrates continued], "he [Anaxagoras] would mention other such causes for my talking to you: sounds and air and hearing, and a thousand other such things, but he would neglect to mention the true causes, that, after the Athenians decided [e] it was better to condemn me, for this reason it seemed best to me to sit here and more right to remain and to endure whatever penalty they ordered. For by the dog, I think these sinews and bones could long ago have been in [99a] Megara or among the Boeotians, taken there by my belief as to the best course, if I had not thought it more right and honorable to endure whatever penalty the city ordered rather than escape and run away. To call those things causes is too absurd. If someone said that without bones and sinews and all such things, I should not be able to do what I decided, he would be right, but surely to say that they are the cause of what I do, and not that I have chosen the best course, even though I act with my mind, is to [b] speak very lazily and carelessly. Imagine not being able to distinguish the real cause from that without which the cause would not be able to act as a cause. It is what the majority appear to do, like people groping in the dark; they call it a cause, thus giving it a name that does not belong to it. That is why one man surrounds the earth with a vortex to make the heavens [c] keep it in place, another makes the air support it like a wide lid. As for their capacity of being in the best place they could possibly be put, this they do not look for, nor do they believe it to have any divine force, but they believe that they will some time discover a stronger and more immortal Atlas to hold everything together more, and they do not believe that the truly good and 'binding' binds and holds them together. I would gladly become the disciple of any man who taught the workings of that kind of cause." (Plato, *Phaedo* 98d–99c)

2.31 Euclides *also had a unified view of the good*

A famous school was that of the Megarians, whose founder, as I see it recorded, was Xenophanes whom I mentioned just now;[12] next he was followed by Parmenides and Zeno (and so the school of thought derived

---

12. Of Colophon; a philosopher around the turn of the fifth century BCE, contemporary with Parmenides who, like his pupil Zeno, was based in Elea. The claim that Xenophanes, then Parmenides and Zeno, "founded" the Megarian school amounts to no more than the claim that the school lay in a tradition of thought initiated by them.

from them the name of Eleatic) and afterward by Euclides, the pupil of Socrates, a Megarian, from whom the same school obtained the title of Megarian; their doctrine was that the sole good is that which is always one and alike and the same. These thinkers also took much from Plato. (Cicero, *On Academic Scepticism* 2.129 = Euclides 31)

2.32 The same

So Euclides, founder of the Megarian school, is deservedly not obscure among philosophers. He disagreed with the others, and said that the highest good is that which is alike and the same forever. That is, he understood what the nature of the highest good was, even though he failed to explain it. (Lactantius, *Divine Institutes* 3.12.9 = Euclides 31)

2.33 The same

Euclides used to apply Parmenidean ideas. . . . He claimed that the good was one thing called by many names: sometimes wisdom, sometimes god, at other times intellect, etc. What was opposite to the good he eliminated, saying that it [what was opposite to the good] didn't exist. (Diogenes Laertius 2.106 = Euclides 30)

2.34–38 Plato's lecture on the good

[2.34] Perhaps it is better to go through the type of matter we are concerned with here, so that we recognize ahead of time the route we need to follow, as it were, and can travel easily because we know where we are on the road and don't come upon the matter without realizing it. It is as Aristotle always used to relate about what happened to most of the people in the audience for Plato's lecture on the Good: everyone went expecting to be regaled with one of the conventional human goods like wealth, health, strength—in short, some amazing form of happiness. But when the arguments turned out to be about mathematics and numbers and geometry and astronomy, and to cap it all, that the Good is one—I suppose it seemed completely contrary to what they were expecting, and some of them dismissed the whole matter, while others were critical. (Aristoxenus, *Harmonics* 39.4–40.4 da Rios)

[2.35] Alexander says that according to Plato the principles of everything, and of the forms themselves, are the One together with the Indivisible Dyad, which he called "the Great and the Small," as Aristotle records in his *On the Good*. One can also get this from Speusippus and

Xenocrates and others who were present at Plato's lecture on the Good: they all wrote down and preserved his view, and say that these are the principles he appealed to. (Simplicius, *On Aristotle's Physics* 151.6–11 Diels)

[2.36] "I eat anything anywhere," [says a parasite, or hungry guest], "even if they don't serve it up hot. The Good, as Plato says, is good everywhere—if you get me; and what's pleasant is always pleasant, anywhere." (Alexis *PCG* 98)

[2.37] "What good it could be you'll get from this girl here, master, I'm less certain than I am about Plato's Good." (Amphis *PCG* 6)

[2.38] "I told you not to get married, and to live a pleasant life. That's Plato's Good, Pheidylus, not to take a wife [i.e., to stay single/one], and not risk your luck in more things." (Philippides *PCG* 6)

Chapter 3: Virtue and Pleasure

In Chapter 2, we have already seen the importance that members of the Socratic circle accorded to virtue (or excellence: *aretê*) in their view of a good human life. Given their tendency to downplay the value of external goods at the same time, it is perhaps no surprise that their understanding of virtue in turn revolves around the concept of self-control (*enkrateia*). (The corresponding vice, lack of control, is *akrateia* or *akrasia,* sometimes unhelpfully translated as "weakness of will.") The clear majority view among the members of the circle seems to be that being virtuous requires keeping the passions and appetites—and especially desires for ordinary, irrational pleasures—under control. This view can also be found in Plato—at least in some contexts (e.g., **3.11**, **3.30**, **3.36–37**, **3.42**, **3.46**; but see further, below); it is probably to be found in Phaedo (cf. **4.11**); but it is most clearly expressed by Xenophon (**3.8–9**). For Xenophon, indeed, loss of control is an ever-present threat to us, and to our leading good and virtuous lives, however wise or foolish we may be. (Compare also Antisthenes, for whom virtue is said to be "sufficient for happiness, being in need of nothing except the strength of a Socrates" and thus, by implication, hard work for the rest of us to attain: **3.3**.) Self-control—in this context, controlling ourselves and our appetites and desires—thus becomes, as Xenophon puts it, the very "foundation stone" of virtue (**3.8**). Only if we are self-controlled can we possess moderation, courage, justice, or wisdom. Xenophon can at times say that "virtue is knowledge" (or "wisdom": see **3.14** with **3.22**, and cf. Antisthenes in **3.15**) because if one is, and stays, truly wise, one will never go wrong, and ignorance may be the cause if we do.[1] But ignorance, for Xenophon, is evidently not just a matter of an intellectual shortfall. We need wisdom, but wisdom, in his view (as **3.22** seems to confirm), can only be acquired if our desires have been controlled, or "enslaved," first. Xenophon also thinks virtue can be lost, here openly disagreeing with what he calls "self-styled philosophers" (**3.6**); perhaps he has in mind Antisthenes (**3.4**), or Aristippus (**3.5**). Like the Socrates

---

1. See the vignette, in his *Cyropaedia* (3.1.38–40), of the Armenian sophist or wise man, killed by the king because he supposedly made the king's son respect him more than he respected the king himself: "Don't be at all angry with your father, Tigranes, for putting me to death; he isn't doing it out of malevolence toward you, but out of ignorance, and all the things that people get wrong out of ignorance I count as not willingly done."

of Plato's *Protagoras*,[2] Xenophon thinks that knowledge and intelligence cannot be overcome by pleasure in particular; for an Antisthenes or an Aristippus, it evidently can be, and when they claim that virtue cannot be lost, they are perhaps making a statement about what it takes to be *truly* virtuous.

There is, however, another take on virtue, which uses the claim that "virtue is knowledge" in an unqualified sense. This is theory that is worked out in a number of texts by Plato (illustrated here by **3.13**, **3.16**, **3.18[b]–[c]**, **3.38–39**, **3.47–48**; cf. **3.27–28**). According to this view, knowledge is not just important for virtue: knowledge (i.e., a certain kind of knowledge) is what virtue *is*. The exploration of this possibility is nowhere more striking than in Plato's *Charmides*, which considers the virtue of moderation (*sôphrosunê*) without once mentioning what in this case was the standard contemporary view: that it precisely involved restraint about ordinary pleasures. Instead, Plato has Socrates wonder (albeit not with seeing difficulties in the position) whether it was some kind of knowledge or "science" (**3.47**).[3]

> It is worth noting that this so-called intellectualist position, despite its fringe status within the Socratic circle, was closely identified with Socrates himself in later thought. Aristotle for example ascribes the view to Socrates, sometimes with Platonic texts in mind, but sometimes apparently not: see *Eudemian Ethics* I.5, 1216b2–10, and VIII.1, 1246b32–36; *Nicomachean Ethics* VI.13, 1144b14–30; [Aristotle], *Magna Moralia* I.1, 1182a15–23, 1183b8–11, and I, 34.1198a10–22; also (relating specifically to courage) *Eudemian Ethics* III.1, 1229a12–16, 1230a7–10; *Nicomachean Ethics* III.11, 1116b3–5; [Aristotle], *Magna Moralia* I.20.1190b27–29. It is the strict version of this view that, as suggested by Aristotle's reports, generates the famous paradox that

---

2. *Protagoras* 352c: "[K]nowledge is a fine thing capable of ruling a person, and if someone were to know what is good and bad, then he would not be forced by anything to act otherwise than knowledge dictates, and intelligence would be sufficient to save a person."

3. How it comes about that we find both accounts in Plato is a matter of controversy: in one interpretation, Plato starts with the intellectualist approach in earlier works and later substitutes the more conventional approach. Another possibility is that Plato treats what one might term the "Xenophontic" kind of virtue as a civic or demotic version of the true, philosophical virtue that derives from (or is identical with) wisdom (for the contrast, cf. variously **3.11**, **3.16**, **3.26**, **3.27**, **3.31**). This latter explanation has the advantage of accounting for the fact that both varieties of virtue—intellectualist and Xenophontic—can appear side by side in the same text (see in addition to the texts just cited **3.28**, **3.36–37**, **3.42**, all from the *Republic*).

there is no such thing as *akrateia*—that is, no such thing as failing to be in control of our desires, because our desires never lead us astray. Later on, the Stoics took up their own version of this position, and thanks to them it enjoyed a long and distinguished history in ethics.

Given the fundamental difference between these two approaches to virtue, there are corresponding differences both about how to understand the relationship between the particular virtues (an issue addressed in the texts in Section iii below), and about how the particular virtues are to be understood in themselves (see texts in Sections iv–viii, below). Thus moderation, *sôphrosunê*, may be either: (1) a kind of knowledge (**3.47–48**; cf. **3.22**), or (2) a disposition to be self-controlled (or the behavior relating to such a disposition), which is at least partly non-rational (**3.30, 3.40–42**).[4] (In the latter case, moderation may actually become indistinguishable from self-control: **3.41–42**; cf. also **3.11**.) Similarly for courage (*andreia*) (knowledge: **3.50**; disposition/behavior: **3.30**), and for justice (*dikaiosunê*) (knowledge: **3.39**; disposition/behavior: **3.12, 3.36–37**). (**3.35** identifies the just with the lawful, i.e., what is laid down in the laws; but it then gives this apparently conventional position a radical slant by making law include unwritten as well as written law.) Wisdom (*sophia*), for its part, just is the whole of virtue in the "intellectualist" account; in the kind of account Xenophon typically gives, it is conditional on the control of irrational passions and appetites (**3.22, 3.30**).

Piety (*eusebeia*), understood as the proper way of behaving toward the gods (as opposed to merely believing in them), is treated somewhat separately from the other virtues. Sometimes, as, for example, in **3.1** or **3.18**, it appears in the list along with the other standard virtues (perhaps see also **3.51**, insofar as Aeschines seems there to treat piety as a part of what it is to be "noble and good," i.e., virtuous), and it is in principle capable of being understood like them (i.e., either in the "intellectualist" analysis as a kind of knowledge, or in terms of a type of disposition and/or behavior). This is clearly the case when, as in **3.53**, piety is treated as a part of justice: the thought is that piety is right behavior toward the gods, as justice is right behavior toward humans. But the most interesting texts on piety show a different kind of split, between what may be

---

4. A further distinction can be made between texts in which the self-control is exerted *by* oneself as a whole *over* oneself or one's desires (e.g., **3.40–41**), and texts in which the relevant relationship is between different parts of the soul (e.g., in the case of moderation: **3.30, 3.42**). See further Ch. 4 for different views about the nature of the soul and its relationship with the body.

called the dominant Platonic interpretation and the interpretation of Xenophon. These are, in fact, by no means mutually exclusive (especially given the apparent convergence between the two authors' views on the gods: see Ch. 10); but they can be distinguished as follows. Xenophon's line is that piety consists in observation of and participation in conventional rites, sacrifices, and prayers (**3.56–58**). The Platonic position, on the other hand, is that piety (although it no doubt includes ritual observance) more importantly involves a special kind of service or enslavement to god, or gods (**3.53–55**).[5] Other members of the circle seem less interested in piety than Plato (whose *Euthyphro* is specifically devoted to the topic) and Xenophon. This might be connected with the fact that—as far as we are able to tell from the surviving evidence—they are less directly preoccupied with the details of Socrates' trial and execution. Impiety was at the heart of the charge against Socrates, and it is a distinctive feature of their relationship with the historical events that Plato and Xenophon both seem keen to offer posthumous defense on this score (as on others).

There is one last virtue which might deserve a heading of its own: *karteria*—endurance—which most of all represents resistance to physical pain and hardship (see, e.g., **3.40**). It is closely connected with *enkrateia*, self-control (and derives from the same root, *krat-*, connoting power and strength). Lack of self-control, *akrateia*, is understood to prevent *karteria*, which we need for getting the most out of ordinary pleasures (**3.9**). Alternatively, endurance is an essential part of what makes for a good soul (Aristippus: **3.10**). Along with self-control, endurance also plays an important part in Xenophontic (and Platonic) ideas about education (see Ch. 5).

Finally, what of Aristippus and the love of pleasure? Despite polemical characterizations of Aristippus as a hedonist pure and simple (discussed in Ch. 2), it turns out that self-control is no less at the center of his vision of happiness—albeit with a twist. For Aristippus, self-control is not a matter of overcoming one's desires but rather, precisely of staying in control of them even while indulging in them: **3.5**, **3.43–44** (similarly **6.13**).

---

5. Compare also Plato's description of Socrates' role as a *divinely appointed* midwife to others' ideas (**6.5**).

Texts

i. On Virtue in General

3.1 Xenophon *reports that Socrates thought people mad who investigate the heavens when there is so much left to understand about human life*
His own conversation always concerned human affairs. He inquired into the nature of piety and impiety, virtue and vice, justice and injustice, sound-mindedness (*sôphrosunê*) and madness, courage and cowardice, state and statesman, government and governors, and everything else that he thought someone truly noble should know, or that anyone ignorant of would deserve to be labeled servile. (Xenophon, *Memorabilia* 1.1.16)

3.2 Xenophon's *Antisthenes* tells Socrates and
others why he counts himself as rich
"Come on, Antisthenes," said Socrates, "now you tell us how you pride yourself on your wealth when you have so little."
"It's because in my view, my friends, people's wealth or lack of it lie not in their property but in their souls. [35] I see many of them, private individuals, who have great quantities of money but still think themselves so poor that they subject themselves to any hardship and any danger provided it will bring them still greater riches. I know of brothers inheriting equal shares and managing them so that one of them has plenty enough to meet his expenses while the other has not an obol to his name. [36] I observe certain tyrants, too, so hungry for money that they do things much more terrible than the poorest among us. Want, obviously, causes people to steal, or break into people's houses, or make others their slaves; but there are tyrants who destroy whole houses, commit mass murder, and often reduce complete cities to slavery just for the sake of money. [37] These are the ones I really pity, prey as they are to an intolerable disease. Their position seems to me no different from that of someone who had plenty and ate plenty, but could never be satisfied. As for me, I have so many possessions that I can barely lay my hands on them myself, yet all the same I have more than enough to let me eat until I get to the point of not being hungry, drink until I'm not thirsty, and clothe myself so that when I'm outside I feel the cold no more than super-rich Callias here; [38] and when I get in the house, the walls are my warm tunics, the roofs my thick overgarments, and

the blanket on my bed is so comfortable that it's a job to wake me up in the morning. If my body needs sex, whatever is to hand will do; the women I approach are more than happy to have me because no one else will go near them. [39] In fact I find all these things so pleasant that I wouldn't pray for more pleasure from doing any of them, but rather for less; that's how much more pleasant some of them seem to me to be than is good for me. [40] The most valuable of the possessions in my treasure-house I count as the very fact that if someone took even what I have now from me, I see no work that would be so humble that it wouldn't provide sufficient to feed me. [41] And if I do feel inclined to indulge my appetite, instead of buying fancy things from the marketplace, since they're expensive, I draw from the store-house of my soul. It's a much greater pleasure to feed myself after waiting till I need it, than to have something fancy—like this wine from Thasos that someone's given me, so that I'm drinking it when I'm not thirsty. [42] And what's more, it's a fair bet that someone who's on the lookout for bargains will be more just than someone who's looking out to make himself rich; those most inclined to be satisfied with what they have will have less of an itch than anyone for other people's stuff. [43] And just note the way this sort of wealth of mine makes for open-handedness. Take Socrates here, from whom I got it all: he didn't count it out or weigh it when he gave it to me, he just loaded me with whatever I could carry. And I grudge it to no one myself; I display my abundance to all my friends, and invite any one of them who wishes to share in the wealth in my soul. [44] And there's that greatest luxury that I possess: the leisure you see me enjoy all the time, to see whatever is worth seeing and hearing whatever is worth hearing—and doing what I value most of all, spending my days with Socrates, untroubled by business. He too is one who is unimpressed by the quantity of gold someone has in his store; he goes on spending his time with those congenial to him."
(Xenophon, *Symposium* 4.34–44 = Antisthenes 82)

3.3 *Antisthenes on virtue and the ethical ideal (the "wise man")*

These are more of his [Antisthenes'] views. He used to declare that virtue was teachable. [11] Also that the same people were nobly born and possessed of virtue, and that virtue was sufficient for happiness, being in need of nothing except the strength of a Socrates. Virtue was something that had to be worked at, and didn't need so much by way of arguments or learning. The wise man, he held, was self-sufficient; for everything that belonged to anyone else belonged to him. Obscurity was a good thing, equal in rank with labor. The wise man would live his public life in accordance not with the established laws but with the law of virtue. He would marry for the sake of having children, sleeping with those women most naturally suited to the purpose; and he would be in love with them, because only the wise man knows which one should love. [12] Diocles also attributes the following sayings to him. To the wise man nothing is foreign, nothing beyond his capacity. The good man is worthy of love. Good men are friends. One should make allies of the courageous and just. If someone has virtue, it is a weapon that can never be taken from him. It is better to fight with a few good people against all the bad than with many bad people against a few good. One should pay attention to one's enemies, for they are the first to detect one's mistakes. One should give priority to a just person over a relation. Virtue is the same in a man as in a woman. Good things are fine, bad things shameful. Think of everything that is bad as alien. [13] Wisdom is the safest wall; for it can neither fall to pieces nor be betrayed. One must prepare walls for oneself in one's own impregnable reasonings. (Diogenes Laertius 6.10–13 = Antisthenes 134; part = **6.20**)

3.4 *The same*

The Cynics too think that virtue is teachable, as Antisthenes says in the *Heracles,* and cannot be lost; the sage is lovable and a friend to one like himself. (Diogenes Laertius 6.105 = Antisthenes 99; continued by **3.62** below)

3.5 *Aristippus acts as if he too thinks that virtue is not easily lost . . .*

It is said that, when once during drinking Dionysius told every guest he must dance dressed in purple, Plato refused and said: "I could not wear a woman's robe."[6] But Aristippus accepted it, and as he was about to dance, wittily riposted: "Because in the Bacchic dance | A moderate woman [*sôphrôn*] will her virtue keep." (Diogenes Laertius 2.78 = Aristippus 31)

---

6. Plato quotes Euripides, *Bacchae* 836 (the next line runs: "A man I was born, and from a manly race"); Aristippus' response quotes *Bacchae* 317–18. For Dionysus, the tyrant of Syracuse, see p. 194.

3.6 ... *but **Xenophon** thinks it certainly can:*
Critias and Alcibiades are examples

I also know that Socrates set a truly noble example for his companions, in addition to excelling at discussions of virtue and every other human concern. And I know that even those two men [i.e., Critias and Alcibiades] showed good sense [were moderate, *sôphrones*] for as long as they remained Socrates' companions, not because they feared punishment or a beating from Socrates, but because at the time they actually believed it best to behave that way. [19] Many self-styled "philosophers" perhaps would say that a just person could never become unjust, nor a moderate and sensible person insolent, and neither could anyone who had learned any other subject ever become ignorant of it. But I do not share this view of the matter. I note that just as people who do not train their bodies cannot perform physical tasks, so those who fail to train their minds cannot perform mental ones: they can neither do what they should do nor avoid what they should avoid. [20] It is for this reason that fathers keep their sons, even the sensible ones, away from bad company. They believe that good men's company is a training in virtue, while bad men's company is virtue's undoing. (Xenophon, *Memorabilia* 1.2.18–20 = Antisthenes 103)

3.7 *Plato's* *Socrates with Thrasymachus, on virtue*
as a matter of good human functioning

"Tell me," [I (Socrates) said,] "do you think there is such a thing as the function of a horse?"

"I do," [said Thrasymachus]. [e]

"And would you define the function of a horse or of anything else as that which one can do only with it or best with it?"

"I don't understand," he said.

"Let me put it this way: Is it possible to see with anything other than eyes?"

"Certainly not."

"Or to hear with anything other than ears?"

"No."

"Then, we are right to say that seeing and hearing are the functions of eyes and ears?"

"Of course."

"What about this? Could you use a dagger or a carving knife or lots of [353a] other things in pruning a vine?"

"Of course."

"But wouldn't you do a finer job with a pruning knife designed for the purpose than with anything else?"
"You would."
"Then shall we take pruning to be its function?"
"Yes."
"Now, I think you'll understand what I was asking earlier when I asked whether the function of each thing is what it alone can do or what it does better than anything else."
"I do understand," he said, [b] "and I think that this is the function of each."
"All right," I said. "Does each thing to which a particular function is assigned also have a virtue? Let's go over the same ground again. We say that eyes have some function?"
"They do."
"So there is also a virtue of eyes?"
"There is."
"And ears have a function?"
"Yes."
"So there is also a virtue of ears?"
"There is."
"And all other things are the same, aren't they?"
"They are."
"So think about this," I said: [c] "could eyes perform their function well if they lacked their peculiar virtue and had the vice instead?"
"How could they," he replied; "aren't you saying, if they had blindness instead of sight?"
"Whatever their virtue is," I said, "for I'm not now asking about that but about whether anything that has a function performs it well by means of its own peculiar virtue and badly by means of its vice?"
"That's true," he said, "it does."
"So ears, too, deprived of their own virtue, perform their function badly?"
"That's right."
"And the same could be said about everything else?" [d]
"So it seems."
"Come, then, and let's consider this: Is there some function of a soul that you couldn't perform with anything else, for example, taking care of things, ruling, deliberating, and the like? Is there anything other than a soul to which you could rightly assign these, and say that they are its peculiar function?"
"No, none of them."

"What of living? Isn't that a function of a soul?"

"It certainly is."

"And don't we also say that there is a virtue of a soul?"

"We do."

"Then, will a soul ever perform its function well, Thrasymachus, if it is deprived of its own peculiar virtue, or is that impossible?" [e]

"It's impossible."

"Doesn't it follow, then, that a bad soul rules and takes care of things badly and that a good soul does all these things well?" (Plato, *Republic* I, 352d–353e)

ii. The Basis for Virtue

3.8 **Xenophon's** Socrates rates self-control the foundation of virtue

Shouldn't every man [Socrates used to say] regard self-control as the foundation stone of virtue and make this fundamental to his mental character? [5] Without this, who could learn anything good or pursue it to any extent worth mentioning? What person wouldn't be physically and mentally degraded by enslavement to pleasures? It's my firm belief that every free man should pray not to get a slave like this, and that anyone enslaved to these kinds of pleasures should beg the gods for good masters, since that's the only way someone like this could find salvation. (Xenophon, *Memorabilia* 1.5.4–5)

3.9 More from **Xenophon's** Socrates on self-control

He [Socrates] also tried to make his companions better in practical terms, as I shall now show. As part of his belief that self-control was a good thing to have for anybody who hoped to accomplish something worthwhile, he first made clear to his companions his own unrivaled dedication to its practice; then, in his conversations, he advocated self-control to his companions above all else. [2] He was always mindful himself, and constantly reminding all his companions of what things promoted virtue. I know in particular that he once had a conversation of the following sort with Euthydemus about self-control:

"Tell me, Euthydemus," he said, "do you consider freedom a noble and splendid possession for both a man and a state?"

"As absolutely noble and splendid as possible," he replied.

[3] "So if someone is ruled by bodily pleasures and as a result incapable of acting in the best way, do you consider him a free man?"

"Not at all," he said.

"That's presumably because acting in the best way impresses you as fitting for a free man, and so you consider having people who will prevent you from acting in this way as something fit for a slave."

"Absolutely," he said.

[4] "Then you think that people lacking self-control are absolutely slavish?"

"Of course I do, naturally."

"And do you think that people lacking self-control are merely prevented from acting in the finest way, or are they also forced to act in the most shameful way?"

"In my opinion," he said, "they're just as much forced to do the one as they are prevented from doing the other."

[5] "What kind of masters do you suppose prevent what's best and compel what's worst?"

"The worst possible kind, of course," he said.

"And what form of slavery do you consider the worst?"

"For my part, slavery under the worst masters," he said.

"Then people lacking self-control endure the worst form of slavery?"

[6] "That's my opinion anyway," he said.

"Don't you think that lack of self-control precludes wisdom, our highest good, and so drives people to the opposite extreme? Or don't you think that it prevents them from paying attention to and understanding what's in their interest by distracting them with pleasures, or that it frequently distorts their perception of good and bad so as to make them choose the worse over the better?"

"That does happen," he said.

[7] "Could we name anyone for whom good sense matters less than someone lacking in self-control, Euthydemus? Surely the effects of good sense and lack of self-control are exact opposites."

"I agree with that too," he said.

"Do you think that there's any greater obstacle to attending to one's duties than lack of self-control?"

"Not as far as I'm concerned," he said.

"And do you think that there's anything worse for a person than what makes him prefer harms to benefits, persuades him to cultivate the former but neglect the latter, and forces him to act contrary to good sense?"

"There's nothing worse," he said.

[8] "So isn't it likely that self-control has an effect on people that's the opposite of lack of self-control?"

"Certainly," he said.

"And isn't the cause of these opposite effects in this case likely to be supremely good?"

"Yes, that's likely," he said.

"Then," he replied, "doesn't it stand to reason that self-control is the highest good for a person, Euthydemus?"

"It does stand to reason, Socrates," he said.

[9] "Have you ever given this any thought before, Euthydemus?"

"What?" he asked.

"The fact that lack of self-control can't even guide people to the very pleasures that seem to be its only goal, whereas self-control produces more pleasure than anything else."

"How so?" he asked.

"Lack of self-control prevents people from deriving any notable pleasure from the most necessary and recurrent activities, since it doesn't permit them to endure hunger or thirst or sexual desire or sleeplessness. But these are the only things that make eating, drinking, and sex pleasurable, and the same for rest and sleep, since waiting and refraining maximizes the satisfaction involved. Only self-control allows people to endure the things I named, and so it alone produces any pleasure worth mentioning in these activities."

"What you say is absolutely true," he replied.

[10] "Besides, people with self-control get pleasure from activities in which those lacking it have no part, such as learning something genuinely good or attending to any one of the kinds of things that allow someone to take good care of his own body, to manage his own household well, to be of use to both his friends and the state, and to defeat his enemies, all things that produce not only the greatest benefits but also the greatest pleasures. Could we name anyone for whom these sorts of things matter less than someone who's least able to accomplish them, since all his energies are focused on the pleasures nearest at hand?"

[11] "You seem to be saying that a man who's a slave to bodily pleasures has absolutely no part in virtue, Socrates," said Euthydemus.

"Yes, Euthydemus, since how can someone lacking self-control be any better than the most ignorant beast? How can someone who fails to consider what matters most and looks for every way to maximize his pleasure be any better than the dumbest ox? No, only the self-controlled are able to consider what things matter most and, by correctly classifying the good and the bad according to kind in both theory and practice, to choose the one and to abstain from the other."

[12] This is the way, he said, that men become best and happiest and most competent at philosophical discussion. He claimed that the very name "dialectic" derived from the practice of meeting together to deliberate and sorting (*dialegein*) things according to kind. So one should try as much as possible to prime himself for this and devote the greatest attention to it, since it's through this that men become the best and most suited for leadership and most skilled at philosophical conversation. (Xenophon, *Memorabilia* 4.5.1–12)

3.10 Aristippus: *endurance promotes virtue*

He said: "As our bodies grow by being fed, but get solid by being exercised, so the soul grows by practicing, but gets better by enduring (*karterousa*)." (*Vatican Sayings* 34 = Aristippus 124 = **5.13**)

3.11 Plato's *unnamed Athenian on the importance of possessing an "everyday" kind of moderation*

ATHENIAN: Then this is what he'll say: "Give me a state under the absolute control of a dictator, and let the dictator be young, with a good memory, quick to learn, courageous, and with a character of natural elevation. And [710a] if his other abilities are going to be any use, his dictatorial soul should also possess that quality which was earlier agreed to be an essential adjunct to all the parts of virtue."

CLINIAS: I think the "essential adjunct" our companion means, Megillus, is moderation. Right?

ATHENIAN: Yes, Clinias—but the everyday kind, not the kind we speak of in a heightened sense, when we compel self-control to be good judgment (*phronêsis*) as well. (Plato, *Laws* IV, 709e–710a)

3.12 Plato's *Socrates (with* **Glaucon**) *makes justice the foundation for the other virtues (here in the city; by implication also in the individual human beings, for whom the city is an analog)*

"So it turns out, my friend," I said, "that this doing one's own work—provided that it comes to be in a certain way—is justice. And do you know what I take as evidence of this?"

"No, tell me," he replied.

"I think," I said, "that this is what was left over in the city when moderation, courage, and wisdom have been found. It is the power that makes it possible for them to grow in the city and that preserves them when they've grown for as long as it remains there itself. [c] And of course we said that justice would be what was left over when we had found the other three."

"Yes, that must be so," he replied.

"And surely," I said, "if we had to decide which of the four will make the city good by its presence, it would be a hard decision. Is it the agreement in belief between the rulers and the ruled? Or the preservation among the soldiers of the law-inspired belief about what is to be feared and what isn't? [d] Or the wisdom and guardianship of the rulers? Or is it, above all, the fact that every child, woman, slave, freeman, craftsman, ruler, and ruled each does his own work and doesn't meddle with what is other people's?"

"How could this fail to be a hard decision?" he asked.

"It seems, then, that the power that consists in everyone's doing his own work rivals wisdom, moderation, and courage in its contribution to the virtue of the city." (Plato, *Republic* IV, 433b–d)

3.13 *Plato's* Socrates wonders whether virtue could be identified with knowledge

SOCRATES: So let us speak about virtue also, since we do not know either what it is or what qualities it possesses, and let us investigate whether it is teachable or not by means of a hypothesis, and say this: Among the things existing in the soul, of what sort is virtue, that it [c] should be teachable or not? First, if it is another sort than knowledge, is it teachable or not, or, as we were just saying, recollectable? Let it make no difference to us which term we use: is it teachable? Or is it plain to anyone that men cannot be taught anything but knowledge?

MENO: I think so.

SOCRATES: But, if virtue is a kind of knowledge, it is clear that it could be taught.

MENO: Of course.

SOCRATES: We have dealt with that question quickly, that if it is of one kind it can be taught; if it is of a different kind, it cannot.

MENO: We have indeed.

SOCRATES: The next point to consider seems to be whether virtue is knowledge or something else. [d]

MENO: That does seem to be the next point to consider.

SOCRATES: Well now, do we say that virtue is itself something good, and will this hypothesis stand firm for us, that it is something good?

MENO: Of course.

SOCRATES: If then there is anything else good that is different and separate from knowledge, virtue might well not be a kind of knowledge; but if there is nothing good that knowledge does not encompass, we would be right to suspect that it is a kind of knowledge.

MENO: That is so.

SOCRATES: Surely virtue makes us good? [e]

MENO: Yes.

SOCRATES: And if we are good, we are beneficent, for all that is good is beneficial. Is that not so?

MENO: Yes.

SOCRATES: So virtue is something beneficial?

MENO: That necessarily follows from what has been agreed.

SOCRATES: Let us then examine what kinds of things benefit us, taking them up one by one: health, we say, and strength, and beauty, and also wealth. We say that these things, and others of the same kind, benefit us, do we not?

MENO: We do.

SOCRATES: Yet we say that these same things also sometimes harm one. [88a] Do you agree or not?

MENO: I do.

SOCRATES: Look then, what directing factor determines in each case whether these things benefit or harm us? Is it not the right use of them that benefits us, and the wrong use that harms us?

MENO: Certainly.

SOCRATES: Let us now look at the qualities of the soul. There is something you call moderation, and justice, courage, intelligence, memory, munificence, and all such things?

MENO: There is.

SOCRATES: Consider whichever of these you believe not to be knowledge but different from it; [b] do they not at times harm us, at other times benefit us? Courage, for example, when it is not wisdom but like a kind of recklessness: when a man is reckless without understanding, he is harmed; when with understanding, he is benefited.

MENO: Yes.

SOCRATES: The same is true of moderation and mental quickness; when they are learned and disciplined with understanding they are beneficial, but without understanding they are harmful?

MENO: Very much so.

SOCRATES: Therefore, in a word, [c] all that the soul undertakes and endures, if directed by wisdom, ends in happiness, but if directed by ignorance, it ends in the opposite?

MENO: That is likely.

SOCRATES: If then virtue is something in the soul and it must be beneficial, it must be knowledge, since all the qualities of the soul are in themselves [d] neither beneficial nor harmful, but accompanied by wisdom or folly they become harmful or beneficial. This argument shows that virtue, being beneficial, must be a kind of wisdom.

MENO: I agree.

SOCRATES: Furthermore, those other things we were mentioning just now, wealth and the like, are at times good and at times harmful. Just as for the rest of the soul the direction of wisdom makes things beneficial, but harmful [e] if directed by folly, so in these cases, if the soul uses and directs them right it makes them beneficial, but bad use makes them harmful?

MENO: Quite so.

SOCRATES: The wise soul directs them right, the foolish soul wrongly?

MENO: That is so.

SOCRATES: So one may say this about everything; all other human activities depend on the soul, and those of the soul itself depend on wisdom [89a] if they are to be good. According to this argument the beneficial would be wisdom, and we say that virtue is beneficial?

MENO: Certainly.

SOCRATES: Then we say that virtue is wisdom, either the whole or a part of it?

MENO: What you say, Socrates, seems to me quite right.

SOCRATES: Then, if that is so, the good are not so by nature?

MENO: I do not think they are.

SOCRATES: For if they were, this would follow: [b] if the good were so by nature, we would have people who knew which among the young were by nature good; we would take those whom they had pointed out and guard them in the Acropolis, sealing them up there much more carefully than gold so that no one could corrupt them, and when they reached maturity they would be useful to their cities.

MENO: Reasonable enough, Socrates.

SOCRATES: Since the good are not good by nature, [c] does learning make them so?

MENO: Necessarily, as I now think, Socrates, and clearly, on our hypothesis, if virtue is knowledge, it can be taught.

SOCRATES: Perhaps, by Zeus, but may it be that we were not right to agree to this?

MENO: Yet it seemed to be right at the time.

SOCRATES: We should not only think it right at the time, but also now and in the future if it is to be at all sound.

MENO: What is the difficulty? [d] What do you have in mind that you do not like about it and doubt that virtue is knowledge?

SOCRATES: I will tell you, Meno. I am not saying that it is wrong to say that virtue is teachable if it is knowledge, but look whether it is reasonable of me to doubt whether it is knowledge. Tell me this: if not only virtue but anything whatever can be taught, should there not be of necessity people who teach it and people who learn it?

MENO: I think so.

SOCRATES: Then again, if on the contrary there are no teachers or learners of something, we should be right to assume that the subject cannot be taught?

MENO: Quite so, [e] but do you think that there are no teachers of virtue?

SOCRATES: I have often tried to find out whether there were any teachers of it, but in spite of all my efforts I cannot find any. And yet I have searched for them with the help of many people, especially those whom I believed to be most experienced in this matter. (Plato, *Meno* 87b–89e)

3.14 Xenophon *claims that Socrates really did identify the virtues with wisdom in some sense*

He claimed also that justice and every other form of virtue is wisdom, since just actions and all virtuous activities are truly noble. People who understand these things would never choose anything else instead, while those without the proper knowledge would be unable to perform them, and would fail even if they tried. So, since actions that are just or truly noble in any other form are all virtuous activities, it is clear that justice and every other form of virtue is wisdom.

[6] As for madness, he said it was opposed to wisdom. But he did not equate a lack of knowledge with madness, though it was his considered view that to lack self-awareness, and yet to form opinions about and presume to understand what one does not know, comes very close to madness. Ordinary people, he said, don't say that those who err about things most people don't know are mad; it's those who err about matters of common knowledge that they call mad. [7] For example, if someone imagines himself to be so tall that he stoops down when entering the city gates, or so strong that he tries to lift houses or to perform any other feat everyone knows to be impossible, they say he's mad. But most people do not think that a minor error qualifies someone as mad; instead, in the same way that they call only intense desire "erotic," they call only serious derangement "madness." (Xenophon, *Memorabilia* 3.9.5–7; follows **3.22**)

3.15 **Antisthenes** *agrees that wisdom has a special place in virtue*

[on *Iliad* 15.123: *"had Athena not, out of fear for all the gods"*:] Reasonably, as fearing her father and already taught not to oppose him, the grey-eyed goddess is concerned about what will happen. From this Antisthenes says that, if the wise man does something, he acts with the entirety of virtue, just as Athena three times warns Ares. (From the scholia to Homer's *Iliad* = Antisthenes 192)

3.16 **Plato's** Socrates with **Glaucon**: *the love of wisdom itself tends to generate other virtues*

"Let's agree," I [Socrates] said, "that philosophic natures always love the sort of learning that makes clear to them some feature of the being that always is and does not [b] wander around between coming to be and decaying."

"Let's do that," [responded Glaucon].

"And further," I said, "let's agree that, like the honor-lovers and erotically inclined men we described before,[7] they love all such learning and are not willing to give up any part of it, whether large or small, more valuable or less so."

"That's right," he replied.

"Consider next," I said, "whether the people we're describing must also have this in their nature." [c]

"What?"

"They must be without falsehood—they must refuse to accept what is false, hate it, and have a love for the truth."

"That's a reasonable addition, at any rate," he said.

"It's not only reasonable, my friend, it's entirely necessary, for it's necessary for a man who is erotically inclined by nature to love everything akin to or belonging to the boy he loves."

"You're right," he said.

"And could you find anything that belongs more to wisdom than truth does?"

"Of course not," he replied.

"Then is it possible for the same nature to be a philosopher—a lover of [d] wisdom—and a lover of falsehood?"

"Not at all."

"Then someone who loves learning must above all strive for every kind of truth from childhood on."

"Absolutely."

"Now, we surely know that, when someone's desires incline strongly for one thing, they are thereby weakened for others, just like a stream that has been partly diverted into another channel."

"Of course."

"Then, when someone's desires flow toward learning and everything of that sort, they'd be concerned, I suppose, with the pleasures of the soul itself by itself, and they'd abandon those pleasures that come through the body—if indeed he is a true philosopher and not merely a counterfeit one."

"That's completely necessary." [e]

"Then surely such a person is moderate and not at all a money-lover. It's appropriate for others to take seriously the things for which money and large expenditures are needed, but not for him."

"That's right."

---

7. The reference is to *Republic* V, 474c–475c.

"And of course there's also this to consider when you are judging whether a nature is philosophic or not." [486a]

"What's that?"

"If it is at all slavish, you should not overlook that fact, for pettiness is altogether incompatible with a soul that is always reaching out to grasp everything both divine and human as a whole."

"That's completely true," he said.

"And will a thinker high-minded enough to study all time and all being consider human life to be something important?"

"He couldn't possibly."

"Then will he consider death to be a terrible thing?" [b]

"He least of all."

"Then it seems a cowardly and slavish nature will take no part in true philosophy."

"Not in my opinion."

"And is there any way that an orderly person, who isn't money-loving, slavish, a boaster, or a coward, could become unreliable or unjust?"

"There isn't." (Plato, *Republic* VI, 485a–486b)

iii. Virtue and the Virtues

3.17 *Euclides' followers (and maybe he himself) taught the unity of virtue*

[Aristo of Chios] did not propose that there were many virtues, as Zeno did,[8] nor that there was one called by many names, as the Megarians did. (Diogenes Laertius 7.161 = Euclides 32)

3.18(a)–(c) *Plato's Socrates considers whether (and how) this is right*

[3.18(a)] "Now, then, Protagoras," [I (Socrates) said,] "I need one little thing, and then I'll have it all, if you'll just answer me this. You say that virtue is teachable, and if there's [c] any human being who could persuade me of this, it's you. But there is one thing you said that troubles me, and maybe you can satisfy my soul. You said that Zeus sent justice and a sense of shame to the human race. You also said, at many points in your speech, that justice and moderation and piety and

---

8. Zeno (of Citium) was the third-century BCE founder of Stoicism; Aristo was one of his pupils.

all these things were somehow collectively one thing: virtue. [d] Could you go through this again and be more precise? Is virtue a single thing, with justice and moderation and piety its parts, or are the things I have just listed all names for a single entity? This is what still intrigues me."

"This is an easy question to answer, Socrates," he replied. "Virtue is a single entity, and the things you are asking about are its parts."

"Parts as in the parts of a face: mouth, nose, eyes, and ears?" I asked. "Or parts as in the parts of gold, where there is no difference, except for size, between parts or between the parts and the whole?"

"In the former sense, I would think, [e] Socrates: as the parts of the face are to the whole face."

"Then tell me this," I said. "Do some people have one part and some another, or do you necessarily have all the parts if you have any one of them?"

"By no means," he replied, "since many are courageous but unjust, and many again are just but not wise."

"Then these also are parts of virtue—wisdom and courage?" I asked.

"Absolutely," he said, [330a] "and wisdom is the greatest part."

"Is each of them different from the others?" I asked.

"Yes."

"And does each also have its own unique power or function? In the analogy to the parts of the face, the eye is not like the ear, nor is its power or function the same, and this applies to the other parts as well: They are not like each other in power or function or in any other way. Is this how [b] it is with the parts of virtue? Are they unlike each other, both in themselves and in their powers or functions? Is it not clear that this must be the case, if our analogy is valid?"

"Yes, it must be the case, Socrates," he replied.

And I said, "In that case none of the other parts of virtue is like knowledge, or like justice, or like courage, or like moderation, or like piety?" (Plato, *Protagoras* 329b–330b)

[3.18(b)] "So right now," I [Socrates] said, "I want you to remind me of some of the questions I first [b] asked, starting from the beginning. Then I want to proceed together to take a good hard look at some other questions. I believe the first question was this: wisdom, moderation, courage, justice, and piety—are these five names for the same thing, or is there underlying each of these names a unique thing, a thing with its own power or function, each one unlike any [c] of the others? You said that they are not names for the same thing, that each of these names refers to a unique thing, and that all these are parts of virtue, not like the parts of gold, which are similar to each other and to the whole of which they are parts, but like the parts of a face, dissimilar to the whole of which they are parts and to each other, and each one having its own unique power or function. If this is still your view, say so; if it's changed in any way, make your new position clear, for I am certainly [d] not going to hold you accountable for what you said before if you want to say something at all different now. In fact, I wouldn't be surprised if you were just trying out something on me before."

"What I am saying to you, Socrates," said Protagoras, "is that all these are parts of virtue, and that while four of them are reasonably close to each other, courage is completely different from all the rest. The proof that what I am saying is true is that you will find many people who are extremely unjust, impious, unrestrained, and ignorant, and yet exceptionally courageous."

"Hold it right there," I said. [e] "This is worth looking into. Would you say courageous men are confident, or something else?"

"Confident, yes," he said, "and ready for action where most men would be afraid."

"Well, then, do you agree that virtue is something fine, and that you offer yourself as a teacher of it because it is fine?"

"The finest thing of all," he said, "unless I am quite out of my mind."

"Then is part of it worthless and part of it fine," I asked, "or all of it fine?"

"Surely it is all as fine as can be."

"Do you know who dives confidently into wells?" [350a]

"Of course, divers."

"Is this because they know what they are doing, or for some other reason?"

"Because they know what they are doing."

"Who are confident in fighting from horseback? Riders or nonriders?"

"Riders."

"And in fighting with shields? Shieldmen or nonshieldmen?"

"Shieldmen, and so on down the line, if that's what you're getting at. Those with the right kind of knowledge are always more confident than those without it, and a given individual is more confident after he acquires it than he was before."

"But," I asked, [b] "haven't you ever seen people lacking knowledge of all of these things yet confident in each of them?"

"I have," he said, "all too confident."

"Is their confidence courage?"

"No," he replied, "because courage would then be contemptible. These men are out of their minds."
"Then how do you describe the courageous?" I asked. "Aren't they those who are confident?"
"I still hold by that," he replied. [c]
"Then," I said, "*these* people, the ones that are so confident, turn out to be not courageous but mad? And, on the other side, the wisest are the most confident, and if the most confident, the most courageous? And the logical conclusion would be that wisdom is courage?"
"You are doing a poor job of remembering what I said when I answered your questions, Socrates," Protagoras responded. "When I was asked if the courageous are confident, I agreed. I was not asked if the confident are courageous. If you had asked [e] me that, I would have said, 'Not all of them.' You have nowhere shown that my assent to the proposition that the courageous are confident was in error. What you did show next was that knowledge increases one's confidence and makes one more confident than those without knowledge. In consequence of this you conclude that courage and wisdom are the same thing. But by following this line of reasoning you could conclude that strength and wisdom are the same thing. First you would ask me if the strong are powerful, and I would say yes. Then, if those who know how to wrestle are more powerful than those who do not, and if individual wrestlers became more powerful after they learn than they were before. Again I would say yes. After I had agreed to these things, it would be open to you to use precisely these points of agreement to prove that wisdom is strength. But nowhere in this process do I agree that the powerful [351a] are strong, only that the strong are powerful. Strength and power are not the same thing. Power derives from knowledge and also from madness and passionate emotion. Strength comes from nature and proper nurture of the body. So also confidence and courage are not the same thing, with the consequence that the courageous are confident, but not all those who are confident are courageous. For confidence, like power, comes from skill (and from passionate emotion and madness as well); courage, from nature and the proper nurture of the soul." (Plato, *Protagoras* 349a–351a)

[3.18(c)] "It seems to me," [I (Socrates) said,] "that our discussion has turned on us, and if it had a voice of its own, it would say, mockingly, 'Socrates and Protagoras, how [b] ridiculous you are, both of you. Socrates, you said earlier that virtue cannot be taught, but now you are arguing the very opposite and have attempted to show that everything is knowledge—justice, moderation, courage—in which case, virtue would appear to be eminently teachable. On the other hand, if virtue is anything other than knowledge, as Protagoras has been trying to say, then it would clearly be unteachable. But, if it turns out to be wholly knowledge, as you now urge, Socrates, it would be very surprising indeed if virtue could not be taught. Now, Protagoras maintained at first [c] that it could be taught, but now he thinks the opposite, urging that hardly any of the virtues turn out to be knowledge. On that view, virtue could hardly be taught at all.'" (Plato, *Protagoras* 361a–c)

iv. Wisdom

3.19–21 *Antisthenes on wisdom*

[3.19] Antisthenes said that the good (*asteios*) person is difficult to bear (*dusbastaktos*): as ignorance is light and flighty, <so> wisdom (*phronêsis*) is something firmly fixed, undeviating, and unshakable because of its weight. (Philo, *How Every Good Man Is Free* 28 = Antisthenes 106)

[3.20] [Antisthenes] said that virtue needed few words, whereas vice would go on forever. (*Vatican Sayings* 12 = Antisthenes 104)

[3.21] And to show Chrysippus[9] in conflict with himself we do not need to unroll another set of books; here in these very ones he now quotes and praises Antisthenes' saying, "One needs to get intelligence or a noose." [1041A] In fact by praising Antisthenes for wanting to force a noose onto those that lack intelligence he was criticizing <himself> for saying that viciousness was no reason for our taking leave of life. (Plutarch, *On Stoic Self-contradictions* 1039E–1040A = Antisthenes 105)

3.22 *Xenophon's Socrates equates wisdom and moderation*

He did not distinguish between wisdom and moderation but judged both wise and moderate the man who recognizes and utilizes what is truly noble as well as the one who understands and steers clear of what is shameful. When asked whether he held that people who know what they ought to do but do the opposite are wise and self-controlled, he replied: "No more so than unwise and un-self-controlled. I think that everyone chooses what he takes to be the most expedient among

---

9. Third-century BCE Stoic philosopher.

his available options and acts accordingly. So I hold that people who don't behave properly are neither wise nor moderate." (Xenophon, *Memorabilia* 3.9.4; follows **3.49**; followed by **3.14**)

3.23–25 *Aristippus on wisdom*

[**3.23**] Asked by Dionysius[10] why philosophers frequent the doors of the rich, whereas the rich do not return the compliment, [Aristippus] said: "That's because philosophers know what they need, and the rich don't." (Diogenes Laertius 2.69 = Aristippus 106)

[**3.24**] When someone said he always noticed philosophers at rich men's doors, [Aristippus] replied: "And you'll see doctors at the doors of the sick; but that wouldn't make anyone choose to be sick rather than a doctor." (Diogenes Laertius 2.70 = Aristippus 106)

[**3.25**] Once when asked what made the wise person better than someone who was not wise, [Aristippus] answered: "Send the two of them naked among strangers, and you'll soon know." (Diogenes Laertius 2.73 = Aristippus 120)

3.26 *Plato's Socrates (here with **Glaucon**) suggests that wisdom, uniquely, has innate roots*

"Now," [I (Socrates) said,] "it looks as though the other so-called virtues of the soul are akin to those of the body, for they really aren't there beforehand but are added [e] later by habit and practice. However, the virtue of reason [i.e., wisdom] seems to belong above all to something more divine, which never loses its power but is either useful and beneficial or useless and harmful, depending on the way [519a] it is turned. Or have you never noticed this about people who are said to be vicious but clever, how keen the vision of their little souls is and how sharply it distinguishes the things it is turned toward? This shows that its sight isn't inferior but rather is forced to serve bad ends, so that the sharper it sees, the more bad it accomplishes."

"Absolutely," said Glaucon.

"However," I went on, "if a nature of this sort had been hammered at from childhood and freed from the bonds of kinship with becoming, which have been fastened to it by feasting, greed, and other such

---

10. Cf. above **3.5**, and further p. 194.

pleasures, and which, like [b] leaden weights, pull its vision downwards—if, being rid of these, it turned to look at true things, then I say that the same soul of the same person would see these most sharply, just as it now does the things it is presently turned toward."

"Probably so." (Plato, *Republic* VII, 518e–519b)

3.27 Socrates and **Simmias** as recounted by **Plato**'s *Phaedo*: the reliance of the other virtues on wisdom

"Many men," [said Socrates,] "at the death of their lovers, wives or sons, were willing to go to the underworld, driven by the hope of seeing there those for whose company they longed, and being with them. Will then a true lover of wisdom, who has a similar hope and knows that he will never find it to any extent except in Hades, be resentful of dying and not gladly undertake the journey thither? One must surely think so, my friend, if he is a true [b] philosopher, for he is firmly convinced that he will not find pure knowledge anywhere except there. And if this is so, then, as I said just now, would it not be highly unreasonable for such a man to fear death?"

"It certainly would, by Zeus," he [Simmias] said.

"Then you have sufficient indication," said Socrates, "that any man whom you [c] see resenting death was not a lover of wisdom but a lover of the body, and also a lover of wealth or of honors, either or both."

"It is certainly as you say," the other agreed.

"And, Simmias," Socrates asked, "does not what is called 'courage' belong especially to men of this disposition?"

"Most certainly."

"And the quality of moderation which even the majority call by that name, that is, not to get swept off one's feet by one's passions, but to treat [d] them with disdain and orderliness, is this not suited only to those who most of all despise the body and live the life of philosophy?"

"Necessarily so," he said.

"If you are willing to reflect on the courage and moderation of other people, you will find them strange."

"In what way, Socrates?"

"You know that they all consider death a great evil?"

"Definitely," he said.

"And the brave among them face death, when they do, for fear of greater evils?"

"That is so."

"Therefore, it is fear and terror that make all men brave, except the philosophers. Yet it is illogical to be brave through fear and cowardice."

"It certainly is." [e]

"What of the moderate among them? Is their experience not similar? Is it licentiousness of a kind that makes them moderate? We say this is impossible, yet their experience of this simple-minded moderation turns out to be similar: they fear to be deprived of other pleasures which they desire, so they keep away from some pleasures because they are overcome by others. Now to be mastered by pleasure is what they call licentiousness, but what happens [69a] to them is that they master certain pleasures because they are mastered by others. This is like what we mentioned just now, that in some way it is a kind of licentiousness that has made them moderate."

"That seems likely."

"My good Simmias, I fear this is not the right exchange to attain virtue, to exchange pleasures for pleasures, pains for pains, and fears for fears, [b] the greater for the less like coins, but that the only valid currency for which all these things should be exchanged is wisdom. With this we have real courage and moderation and justice and, in a word, true virtue, with wisdom, whether pleasures and fears and all such things be present or absent. When these are exchanged for one another in separation from wisdom, such virtue is only an illusory appearance of virtue; it is in fact fit for slaves, without soundness or truth, whereas, in truth, moderation and courage and justice are a purging away of all such things, and wisdom itself is a kind of cleansing or purification."

(Plato, *Phaedo* 68a–69b)

3.28 *Later in the same dialogue, Socrates (now with **Cebes**) denigrates those who are virtuous merely out of habit*

"The happiest . . . ," said [Socrates], "who will also have the best destination [sc. in the underworld, after death], are those [b], aren't they, who have practiced popular and social virtue, which they call moderation and justice and which was developed by habit and practice, without philosophy or understanding?"

"How are they the happiest?"

"Because it is likely that they will again join a social and gentle group, either of bees or wasps or ants, and then again the same kind of human group, and so be moderate men."

"That is likely."

"No one may join the company of the gods who has not practiced philosophy [c] and is not completely pure when he departs from life, no one but the lover of learning." (Plato, *Phaedo* 82a–c)

3.29 Plato's unnamed Athenian agrees about the preeminent importance of wisdom

No mortal can ever attain a truly religious outlook without risk of relapse unless he grasps the two doctrines we're now discussing: first, that the soul is far older than any created thing, and that it is immortal and controls the entire world of matter; and second (a doctrine we've expounded often enough before) that reason is the supreme power among [e] the heavenly bodies. He also has to master the essential preliminary studies, survey with the eye of a philosopher what they have in common, and use them to frame consistent rules of moral action; and finally, when a reasoned [968a] explanation is possible, he must be able to provide it. No one who is unable to acquire these insights and rise above the level of the ordinary virtues will ever be good enough to govern an entire state, but only to assist government carried on by others. (Plato, *Laws* XII, 967d–968a)

3.30 Plato's Socrates (with **Glaucon**) on the contributions to virtue of the reasoning and "spirited" parts of a soul

"And," I [Socrates] said, "these two [sc. parts, the rational and the 'spirited'], having been nurtured in this way, and having truly learned their own roles and been educated in them, will govern the appetitive part, which is the largest part in each person's soul and is by nature most insatiable for money. They'll watch over it to see that it isn't filled with the so-called pleasures of the body and that it doesn't become so big and strong that it no longer does its own work but attempts to enslave and rule over the classes [b] it isn't fitted to rule, thereby overturning everyone's whole life."

"That's right," said [Glaucon].

"Then," I said, "wouldn't these two parts also do the finest job of guarding the whole soul and body against external enemies—reason by planning, spirit by fighting, following its leader, and carrying out the leader's decisions through its courage?"

"Yes, that's true."

"And it is because of the spirited part, I suppose, that we call a single [c] individual courageous, namely, when it preserves through pains and pleasures the declarations of reason about what is to be feared and what isn't."

"That's right," he said.

"And we'll call him wise because of that small part of himself that rules in him and makes those declarations and has within it the knowledge of what is advantageous for each part and for the whole soul, which is the community of all three parts."

"Absolutely."

"And isn't he moderate because of the friendly and harmonious relations between these same parts, namely, when the ruler and the ruled believe in common that the rational part should rule and don't engage in civil [d] war against it?"

"Moderation is surely nothing other than that," he said, "both in the city and in the individual." (Plato, *Republic* IV, 442a–d)

3.31 Plato's Socrates represents the philosopher as a "craftsman of popular virtue"

"Then the philosopher," [I (Socrates) said], "by consorting with what is ordered and divine and despite all the slanders around that say otherwise, himself becomes [d] as divine and ordered as a human being can."

"That's absolutely true," [said Adimantus].

"And," I said, "if he should come to be compelled to put what he sees there into people's characters, whether into a single person or into a populace, instead of shaping only his own, do you think that he will be a poor craftsman of moderation, justice, and the whole of popular virtue?" (Plato, *Republic* VI, 500c–d)

3.32 Xenophon's Socrates on the limits of human wisdom

Socrates also dealt with his close friends in the following way: regarding day-to-day matters, he advised them to do just as he thought would be best; but regarding matters whose outcome was uncertain, he sent them to consult an oracle about what to do. [7] He claimed that people who hope to succeed in managing public as well as private affairs have extra need of help from divination. Becoming adept at carpentry, metalwork, farming, governing, or the theoretical aspects of such occupations, or at mathematics, estate management, or military strategy—everything of this sort Socrates considered capable of being learned and grasped by human understanding. [8] But he claimed that even in these areas the gods keep the most important details to themselves, none of which are apparent to humans. Somebody who has done a good job planting a field for himself cannot tell who will reap the fruits; nor can somebody who has done a good job building a house for himself tell who will occupy it; nor can a military commander tell whether it is to his advantage to be in command; nor can a politician tell whether it is to his advantage to govern; nor can someone who marries a beautiful woman for his own enjoyment tell whether she will make him miserable; nor can somebody who has cultivated powerful political alliances tell whether he will end up exiled because of them. [9] People who think that these kinds of things are wholly within the realm of human understanding and that none of them exceeds reason are, he claimed, irrational. Equally irrational, however, are those who turn to divination for things the gods have granted human beings to study and make their own decisions about (such as asking "Is it better to get somebody experienced or inexperienced to drive my carriage?" or "Is it better to get somebody experienced or inexperienced to pilot my ship?"), or for things one can ascertain by simple calculation, measurement, or weighing. He considered it impious for people to ask the gods about such things. He maintained that it was necessary to learn through study what the gods grant us to learn in this way; but in the case of things not apparent to human beings, we must try to learn them from the gods through divination, since the gods provide signs to whomever they favor. (Xenophon, *Memorabilia* 1.1.6–9)

v. Justice

3.33 Xenophon's *Antisthenes* claims that courage and wisdom can harm others, but justice never can

"Well," said Socrates, "none of us objects to saying what each thinks is the most valuable knowledge he possesses."

[4] "So," said Callias, "I'll say what *I* pride myself on most. I think I have the power to make people better."

Antisthenes responded, "Is that by teaching some manual skill, or by teaching nobility?"

"The latter, if justice is nobility."

"Zeus!" exclaimed Antisthenes; "nobility of the least disputable kind. After all, courage and wisdom sometimes seem to be harmful both to friends and to city, whereas justice is never in the slightest respect mixed with injustice." (Xenophon, *Symposium* 3.3–4 = Antisthenes 78)

3.34 Xenophon's *Antisthenes* refutes a rich man's view of justice (or does he?)

Socrates was next, and said, "So it remains for each of us to show the value of what we've promised to defend."

"Let me go first, please," said Callias. "While you are all worrying about what justice is, I'm actually making people more just."

To which Socrates replied, "Splendid; how are you doing that?"

"Zeus!—by giving them money!"

[2] Antisthenes got up at that point and launched into some cross-questioning. "Callias, do people seem to you to keep justice in their souls or in their purse?"

"In their souls," said Callias.

"So you're making their souls juster by putting money in their purse?"

"Exactly."

"How so?"

"Because they know they've the wherewithal to buy what they need, so they won't put themselves at risk by committing crimes."

[3] "And do *you* get back from them," asked Antisthenes, "what they get from you?"

"Zeus! No," replied Callias.

"What about thanks instead of the money?"

"Zeus be my witness, not even that!" he said. "Some of them are even worse disposed toward me than before."

"Amazing!" exclaimed Antisthenes, with a look of triumph for refuting him; "so you're able to make them just toward everybody else, but not toward yourself!"

[4] "What's so amazing about that?" retorted Callias. "Don't you see plenty of carpenters and house builders making houses for lots of other people, but unable to make them for themselves, and having to rent? You're the one who's refuted, you sophist, so put up with it!"

[5] "Zeus! He'll have to," said Socrates. "I think seers too are said to be able to foretell the future for others, but not foresee what's coming for them." (Xenophon, *Symposium* 4.1–5 = Antisthenes 83; followed by **5.25**)[11]

---

11. For the view attributed to Callias here of the relation between wealth and justice, cf. Cephalus at Plato, *Republic* I, 330d–331b.

3.35 Xenophon *describes a conversation on justice between Socrates and Hippias*

In addition, far from concealing his views about justice, he [Socrates] demonstrated them by his very actions: in his personal life, he was invariably law-abiding and helpful; in his public life, he was so compliant to authority in everything required by law, as both a citizen and a soldier, that he stood out as a model of discipline. [2] When he was the presiding officer in the Assembly, he did not permit an illegal motion to carry; instead, he sided with the laws against a popular groundswell that no other person, in my opinion, could have resisted. [3] And when the Thirty Tyrants gave him an illegal order, he refused it. So it was when they forbade him from engaging in conversations with young men; and when they ordered him and some other citizens to bring in a certain man to be executed, he alone refused, on the grounds that the order he had been given was illegal. [4] While other defendants regularly ingratiate themselves to the jury, engage in flattery, and make illegal appeals, and although many of them frequently win acquittal by these means, when Socrates defended himself against the indictment brought by Meletus, he wanted nothing to do with the usual courtroom chicanery. He could easily have been acquitted by the jury if he had made even modest use of these means, but he preferred to die, abiding by the law, rather than to live by breaking it. [5] He frequently said as much in his conversations with others. I know of one particular conversation along the following lines that he had with Hippias about justice. Hippias had arrived in Athens after a long absence and came across Socrates talking with some people. Socrates was expressing his amazement at the fact that if one wanted to have somebody trained in the arts of shoemaking, carpentry, metalworking, or horseback riding, there was no mystery about where to send him to get this training—and some people say that there are plenty of teachers around for anybody who wants to train a horse or ox to behave properly—but if somebody wanted to learn justice for himself, or to have a son or a servant trained in it, he would not know where to go to get this training.

. . .

[7] "I'm confident," [said Socrates,] "that what I now have to say about justice is something that neither you nor anyone else could contradict."

[8] "Good heavens!" he said. "This discovery you claim to have made will be of great value, if it will stop jurors from splitting their votes; stop citizens from arguing, litigating, and quarreling over claims of justice; and stop cities from being at odds and waging war over the

same kinds of claims. I for one don't know how I could tear myself away from you before hearing this valuable discovery of yours."

[9] "Oh, no," he said. "You won't hear anything from me until you yourself say what you take justice to be. You content yourself with making fun of other people by posing questions and cross-examining everyone, but you yourself refuse to take a stand or to express an opinion about anything."

[10] "Why, Hippias," he replied, "haven't you noticed that I never stop revealing what I take to be just?"

"And just what's the nature of this account of yours?" he said.

"One I reveal by my actions, if not my words. Don't you think that actions are better evidence than words anyway?"

"Much better, of course," he said. "A lot of people talk about justice but act unjustly, but no one who acts justly could really be unjust."

[11] "Then have you ever known me to perjure myself, to bring trumped-up charges, to create strife between friends or within the state, or to commit any other injustice?"

"No, I haven't," he said.

"Don't you consider it just to abstain from injustice?"

"Even now, Socrates," he replied, "you're clearly trying to avoid revealing an opinion on what you take justice to be. You haven't said what just people do, only what they don't do."

[12] "Well," said Socrates, "I thought that refusal to do injustice was proof enough of justice. But if you don't think so, consider whether this satisfies you more: I maintain that what is lawful is just."

"Do you mean that 'lawful' and 'just' are the same thing, Socrates?"

"I do," he said.

[13] "Because I'm not quite sure what you have in mind by either 'lawful' or 'just.'"

"Are you familiar with the laws of states?" he asked.

"I am," he said.

"And what do you take them to be?"

"They're agreements the citizens enact that either mandate or prohibit certain actions," he replied.

"So," he said, "wouldn't the person who complies with these as a member of the community be lawful, and the one who breaks them be unlawful?"

"Certainly," he said.

"And wouldn't the person who obeys them be acting justly, while the one who disobeys would be acting unjustly?"

"Certainly."

"And wouldn't the person who acts justly be just, while the one who acts unjustly would be unjust?"

"Of course."

"Then the lawful person is just, and the unlawful one unjust."

[14] Hippias replied, "How could anyone put much stock in laws or obedience to them when the very same people who establish them often repudiate and alter them?"

"Yes, and cities that have gone to war often make peace again," said Socrates.

"Very true," he said.

"So," he asked, "do you think that there's any difference between denigrating people who obey the laws, just because the laws might be annulled, and criticizing people who show discipline in war, just because peace could arise? Or do you actually find fault with those who are eager to come to their country's aid in times of war?"

"Of course I don't!" he said.

[15] "Do you appreciate that Lycurgus the Lacedaemonian wouldn't have made Sparta any better than every other city," added Socrates, "if he hadn't made obedience to the laws a priority in it? And don't you know that the best leaders in government are the ones most responsible for making the citizens law-abiding, or that the state whose citizens are most law-abiding fares best in peacetime and is unstoppable in wartime? [16] Besides, harmony is considered to be the highest good for cities, and governing councils and members of the aristocracy very often call upon the citizens to live in harmony. Everywhere in Greece also legally requires its citizens to take an oath to live in harmony, and they take this oath everywhere. I don't imagine that the point of this requirement is to have the citizens vote for the same winning choruses, praise the same musicians, choose the same poets, or take pleasure in the same things, but to have them obey the laws. Cities become strongest and prosper most when their citizens abide by the laws, but in the absence of harmony no state can be well governed and no household well managed.

[17] "And what would make any private citizen less likely to incur penalties or more likely to earn honors from the state than obeying its laws? What would make him less likely to lose a court case or more likely to win one? To whom would anyone be more likely to entrust his fortune or his sons or his daughters? Whom would the state as a whole consider more trustworthy than someone law-abiding? From whom would parents, relatives, servants, friends, fellow citizens, or foreigners be more likely to receive fair treatment? Whom would enemies

trust more when it comes to making truces, treaties, or peace terms? To whom would people rather be allied than to someone law-abiding? To whom would allies rather entrust leadership, or charge over a garrison or cities? Whom would anyone expect to show more gratitude for favors than someone law-abiding? Or whom would one rather do a favor for than somebody from whom he believes he will receive the proper gratitude? Whom would anyone want more for a friend, or less for an enemy, than somebody like that? With whom would he be less likely to quarrel than somebody he wants most for a friend and least for an enemy, and who has the most people wanting to be friends and allies and the fewest wanting to be enemies and opponents?

[18] "So, for my part, I affirm that lawful and just are the same thing, Hippias. If you hold a contrary view, please explain it to me."

"Well, Socrates," replied Hippias, "I really don't think that my own view is contrary to what you've said about justice."

[19] "Do you know what 'unwritten laws' are, Hippias?" he asked.

"Yes," he said, "those observed in every country regarding the same circumstances."

"Would you say that these are man-made?" he asked.

"How could they be," he replied, "considering that not everyone could meet together and that they don't all speak the same language?"

"Then who in your opinion established these laws?" he asked.

"I suppose that the gods established these laws for human beings," he said. "At least, the first recognized law among all people is to worship the gods."

[20] "Isn't it also a recognized law everywhere to honor parents?"

"That too," he said.

"And likewise for parents and children not to engage in incest with one another?"

"This particular law doesn't seem divinely sanctioned to me, Socrates," he said.

"Why not?" he asked.

"Because I see that some people break it," he said.

[21] "Yes, and they break many other laws as well," he said. "But surely people who break divinely sanctioned laws incur a penalty they can't possibly escape in the way that some people who break man-made laws are able to escape punishment, whether by stealth or force."

[22] "And what is the penalty that parents who commit incest with their children or children who commit incest with their parents can't escape, Socrates?" he asked.

"Why, the greatest one of all," he replied. "What greater misfortune could be associated with procreation than to procreate badly?"

[23] "How is it that such people procreate badly," he said, "since nothing prevents the fathers in such cases from being good themselves, or from having children by good mothers?"

"Because it isn't enough just for the two parents to be good themselves," he replied. "They should also be in their physical prime. Or do you think that the seed of people in their prime is just like the seed of those who either haven't yet reached it or have already passed it?"

"No, that's certainly not likely to be the case," he said.

"Which is better?" he asked.

"Clearly the seed of those in their prime," he answered.

"So the seed of people not in their prime isn't of high quality?"

"It certainly seems unlikely that it would be," he said.

"Then they shouldn't procreate under these circumstances?"

"No, they shouldn't," he said.

"And those who do so would be procreating in a way that they shouldn't?"

"So it seems to me," he said.

"Who else would procreate badly then, if not these people?" he asked.

"I agree with you on this point too," he said.

[24] "Well, then, isn't it also a matter of law everywhere to return favors to people who have treated one well?"

"It is," he said, "but this law's also broken."

"Don't the people who break it also pay the price in terms of being left without good friends and forced to seek the company of people who hate them? Or isn't it the case that someone who treats his associates well is a good friend, whereas someone who doesn't return their favors incurs their hatred by his ingratitude but eagerly pursues their company anyway, because of how much he stands to profit from such associations?"

"You know, Socrates," he said, "all this really does seem like the gods' handiwork. I think that laws with built-in penalties for violators come from a source better than any human lawmaker."

[25] "So, Hippias, do you suppose that what the gods legislate is just or not?"

"It must be just, of course," he said. "It would be hard to see how what anyone else legislates could be just if this weren't true of a god."

"Then, Hippias, even the gods are satisfied with the identification of 'just' and 'lawful.'"

By words and actions of this sort, he made the people around him more just. (Xenophon, *Memorabilia* 4.4.1–5 and 7–25; the passage omitted here = **1.20**)[12]

3.36 Plato's Socrates and **Glaucon** find justice in the harmony of the soul

"Then the dream we had," [I (Socrates) said,] "has been completely fulfilled—our suspicion that, with the help of some god, we had hit upon the origin and pattern [c] of justice right at the beginning in founding our city."

"Absolutely."

"Indeed, Glaucon, the principle that it is right for someone who is by nature a cobbler to practice cobblery and nothing else, for the carpenter to practice carpentry, and the same for the others is a sort of image of justice—that's why it's beneficial."

"Apparently."

"And in truth justice is, it seems, something of this sort. However, it isn't concerned with someone's doing his own externally, but with what is [d] inside him, with what is truly himself and his own. One who is just does not allow any part of himself to do the work of another part or allow the various classes within him to meddle with each other. He regulates well what is really his own and rules himself. He puts himself in order, is his own friend, and harmonizes the three parts of himself like three limiting notes in a musical scale—high, low, and middle. He binds together those parts and any others there may be in between, and from having been [e] many things he becomes entirely one, moderate and harmonious. Only then does he act. And when he does anything, whether acquiring wealth, taking care of his body, engaging in politics, or in private contracts—in all of these, he believes that the action is just and fine that preserves this inner harmony and helps achieve it, and calls it so, and regards as wisdom the knowledge that oversees such actions. And he believes that the action that destroys this harmony is unjust, and calls it so, and regards the belief [444a] that oversees it as ignorance." (Plato, *Republic* IV, 443b–444a)

---

12. Compare the arguments Plato's Socrates puts in the mouth of the personified laws of Athens at *Crito* 50a–54d. For another, and important, discussion of justice in Xenophon, this time between Socrates and Euthydemus, see *Memorabilia* 4.2.11–21.

3.37 *The same on the bestial character of those who prefer injustice over justice*

"So then," I [Socrates] said, "since we've reached this point in the argument, let's return to the first things we said, since they are what led us here. I think someone said at some point that injustice profits a completely unjust person who is believed to be just. Isn't that so?"

"It certainly is."

"Now let's discuss this with him," I said, "since we've agreed on the respective powers that injustice and justice have."

"How?" asked [Glaucon].

"By fashioning an image of the soul in words, so that the person who says this sort of thing will know what he is saying."

"What sort of image?" he asked. [c]

"One like those creatures that legends tell us used to come into being in ancient times, such as the Chimera, Scylla, Cerberus, or any of the multitude of others in which many different kinds of things are said to have grown together naturally into one."

"Yes, the legends do tell us of such things," he agreed.

"Well, then, fashion a single kind of multicolored beast with a ring of many heads that it can grow and change at will—some from gentle, some from savage animals."

"That's work for a clever artist," he replied. [d] "However, since words are more malleable than wax and the like, consider it done."

"Then fashion one other kind, that of a lion, and another of a human being. But make the first much the largest and the other second to it in size."

"That's easier," he said, "—the sculpting is done."

"Now join the three of them into one, so that they somehow grow together naturally."

"They're joined."

"Then, fashion around them the image of one of them, that of a human being so that anyone who sees only the outer covering and not what's [e] inside will think it is a single creature, a human being."

"It's done."

"Then, if someone maintains that injustice profits this human being and that doing just things brings no advantage, let's tell him that he is simply saying that it is beneficial for him, first, to feed the multiform beast well and make it strong, and also the lion and all that pertains to him; second, [589a] to starve and weaken the human being within, so that he is dragged along wherever either of the other two leads; and, third, to leave the parts to bite and kill one another rather than accustoming them to each other and making them friendly."

"Yes," he said, "that's absolutely what someone who praises injustice is saying."

"But, on the other hand, wouldn't someone who maintains that just things are profitable be saying, first, that all our words and deeds should insure that the human being within this human being has the most control; second, [b] that he should take care of the many-headed beast as a farmer does his animals, feeding and domesticating the gentle heads and preventing the savage ones from growing; and, third, that he should make the lion's nature his ally, care for the community of all his parts, and bring them up in such a way that they will be friends with each other and with himself?"

"Yes, that's exactly what someone who praises justice is saying." (Plato, *Republic* IX, 588b–589b)

3.38 Plato's Socrates argues that it is better to commit injustice voluntarily than involuntarily

HIPPIAS: But it would be terrible, Socrates, if those who commit injustice voluntarily are to be better than those who do it involuntarily!

SOCRATES: But nonetheless they appear to be, at least given what's been said.

HIPPIAS: Not to me.

SOCRATES: But I thought, Hippias, that they appeared to be so to you, too. But answer again: isn't justice either some sort of power or knowledge, or both? Or isn't justice necessarily one of these things?

HIPPIAS: Yes. [e]

SOCRATES: So if justice is a power of the soul, isn't the more powerful soul the more just? For, my excellent friend, it appeared to us, didn't it, that one of this sort was better?

HIPPIAS: Yes, it did.

SOCRATES: And if it's knowledge? Then isn't the wiser soul more just and the more ignorant more unjust?

HIPPIAS: Yes.

SOCRATES: And if it's both? Then isn't the soul which has both—knowledge and power—more just, and the more ignorant more unjust? Isn't that necessarily so?

HIPPIAS: It appears so.

SOCRATES: This more powerful and wiser soul was seen to be better [376a] and to have more power to do both fine and shameful in everything it accomplishes?

HIPPIAS: Yes.

SOCRATES: Whenever it accomplishes shameful results, then, it does so voluntarily, by power and craft, and these things appear to be attributes of justice, either both or one of them.

HIPPIAS: So it seems.

SOCRATES: And to do injustice is to do bad, whereas to refrain from injustice is to do something fine.

HIPPIAS: Yes.

SOCRATES: So the more powerful and better soul, when it does injustice, will do injustice voluntarily, and the worthless soul involuntarily?

HIPPIAS: Apparently.

SOCRATES: And isn't the good man the one who has a good soul, and the bad man the one who has a bad soul? [b]

HIPPIAS: Yes.

SOCRATES: Therefore, it's up to the good man to do injustice voluntarily, and the bad man to do it involuntarily; that is, if the good man has a good soul.

HIPPIAS: But surely he has.

SOCRATES: So the one who voluntarily misses the mark and does what is shameful and unjust, Hippias—that is, if there is such a person—would be no other than the good man.

HIPPIAS: I can't agree with you in that, Socrates.

SOCRATES: Nor I with myself, Hippias. [c] But given the argument, we can't help having it look that way to us, now, at any rate. (Plato, *Lesser Hippias* 375d–376c)

3.39 *Plato's Socrates with Thrasymachus, on why it is the just person, not the unjust one, who is good and clever (wise)*

"Do you think," [I (Socrates) asked Thrasymachus,] "that a just person wants to outdo someone else who's just?"

"Not at all," he said, "for he wouldn't then be as polite and innocent as he is."

"Or to outdo a just action?"

"No, not even a just one," he replied.

"And would he claim that he deserves to outdo an unjust person and believe that it is just for him to do so, or wouldn't he believe that?"

"He'd want to outdo him," he said, "and he'd claim to deserve to do so, but he wouldn't be able."

"That's not what I asked," I said, "but whether a just person wants to outdo an [c] unjust person but not a just one, thinking that this is what he deserves?"

"He does."

"What about an unjust person? Does he claim that he deserves to outdo a just person or someone who does a just action?"

"Of course he does," he replied; "doesn't he think he deserves to outdo everyone?"

"Then will an unjust person also outdo an *unjust* person or someone who does an *unjust* action, and will he strive to get the most he can for himself from everyone?"

"He will."

"Then, let's put it this way," I said: "A just person doesn't outdo someone like himself but someone unlike himself, whereas an unjust person outdoes [d] both like and unlike."

"Very well put," he responded.

"An unjust person is clever (*phronimos*) and good," I asked, "and a just one is neither?"

"That's well put, too."

"So," I asked, "is an unjust person also like clever and good people, while the just person isn't?"

"Of course that's so," he replied. "How could he fail to be like them, when he has their qualities—and how could the other not fail to be like them?"

"Fine. Then each of them has the qualities of the people he's like?"

"Of course," he replied.

"All right, Thrasymachus. Do you call one person musical and another nonmusical?" [e]

"I do."

"Which of them is clever in music, and which isn't?"

"The musical one is clever, of course, and the other isn't."

"And the things he's clever in, he's good in, and the things he isn't clever in, he's bad in?"

"Yes."

"Isn't the same true of a doctor?"

"It is."

"Well, my fine friend, do you think that a musician, in tuning his lyre and in tightening and loosening the strings, wants to outdo another musician, claiming that this is what he deserves?"

"I do not."

"But he does want to outdo a nonmusician?"

"Necessarily."

"What about a doctor? Does he, when prescribing food and drink, want [350a] to outdo another doctor or any action that medical expertise prescribes?"

"Certainly not."

"But he does want to outdo a nondoctor?"

"Yes."

"In any branch of knowledge or ignorance, see if you think that a knowledgeable person would intentionally try to outdo other knowledgeable people or say something better or different than they do, rather than doing or saying the very same thing as those like him?"

"Well, perhaps it must be as you say," he replied.

"And what about an ignorant person? Doesn't he want to outdo both a [b] knowledgeable person and an ignorant one?"

"Probably."

"A knowledgeable person is clever [sophos]?"

"I agree."

"And a clever one is good?"

"I agree."

"Therefore, a good and clever person doesn't want to outdo those like himself but those who are unlike him and his opposite."

"So it seems."

"But a bad and ignorant person wants to outdo both his like and his opposite."

"Apparently."

"Now, Thrasymachus," I asked, "we found that an unjust person tries to outdo those like him and those unlike him? Didn't you say that?"

"I did," he admitted.

"And a just person won't outdo his like but his unlike?" [c]

"Yes."

"Then, a just person," I said, "is like a clever and good one, and an unjust is like an ignorant and bad one."

"It looks that way."

"But we agreed that each has the qualities of the one he resembles."

"Yes, we did."

"In that case a just person has turned out to be good and clever, and an unjust one ignorant and bad." (Plato, *Republic* I, 349b–350c)

vi. Moderation

3.40 *Xenophon attributes moderation to Socrates*

It also amazes me that some people were persuaded that Socrates corrupted young men. First, beyond what has already been said, he of all people was the most self-controlled with regard to sexual desires and appetites generally. Next, he was the most tolerant (*karterikôtatos*) of cold and heat and every hardship. And he had also trained himself to moderate his needs to such an extent that he was very easily contented despite his modest means. [2] Given the kind of person he himself was, how could he have made others impious, criminal, greedy, licentious, or unfit for hard work? On the contrary, he curbed these vices in many people by instilling in them a desire for virtue, and by giving them hope that if they took proper care of themselves they would achieve true nobility. [3] And while he certainly never put himself forward as a teacher of this [i.e., virtue], his shining example did make people who spent time with him hope that they could develop a similar character by imitating him. [4] In addition, he neither neglected his own body nor commended those who neglected theirs. He disapproved of bingeing followed by over-exercise, but he did approve of doing enough to work off reasonable portions of food, since, he claimed, this was a perfectly healthy practice and did not get in the way of cultivating one's mind. [5] He was certainly not the least bit fussy or pretentious in his dress, shoes, or any other aspect of his lifestyle. Nor did he by any means make his companions greedy, since he curbed all their desires other than that for his companionship, for which he charged them nothing. (Xenophon, *Memorabilia* 1.2.1–5)

3.41 *Plato's Socrates on moderation as self-rule*

SOCRATES: But tell me, my good fellow, once and for all, whom you mean by the better and the superior, and what they're better and superior in.

CALLICLES: But I've already said that I mean those who are intelligent [d] in the affairs of the city, and brave, too. It's fitting that they should be the ones who rule their cities, and what's just is that they, as the rulers, should have a greater share than the others, the ruled.

SOCRATES: But what of themselves, my friend?

CALLICLES: What of *what*?

SOCRATES: Ruling or being ruled?

CALLICLES: What do you mean?

SOCRATES: I mean each individual ruling himself. Or is there no need at all for him to rule himself, but only to rule others?

CALLICLES: What do you mean, rule himself?

SOCRATES: Nothing very subtle. Just what the many mean: being moderate [e] and master of oneself (*enkratês*), ruling the pleasures and appetites within oneself. (Plato, *Gorgias* 491c–e)

3.42 *The same, with* **Glaucon**

"Moderation," I [Socrates] said, "is surely a kind of order, the mastery (*enkrateia*) of certain kinds of pleasures and desires. People indicate as much when they use the phrase 'being stronger than oneself' and other similar phrases. I don't know just what they mean by them, but they are, as it were, traces moderation leaves behind it in the way we speak. Isn't that so?"

"Absolutely," said [Glaucon].

"Yet isn't the expression 'stronger than oneself' ridiculous? The stronger self that does the controlling is the same as the weaker self that gets controlled, [431a] so that only one person is referred to in all such expressions."

"Of course."

"Nonetheless," I said, "the expression is apparently trying to indicate that, in the soul of that very person, there is a better part and a worse one and that, whenever the naturally better part is in control of the worse, this is expressed by saying that the person is 'stronger than himself.' At any rate, one praises someone by describing him like that. But when, on the other hand, the smaller and better part is overpowered by the larger, because of bad upbringing or bad [b] company, this is called being 'weaker than oneself,' or 'unrestrained,' by way of reproach." (Plato, *Republic* IV, 430e–431b)

3.43 Aristippus *on having one's pleasures— and not being had by them*

He also resorted to the prostitute Lais, as Sotion tells us in Book 2 of his *Successions*.[13] [75] His response to those who criticized him for it was: "I have her, she doesn't have me—the best thing is controlling pleasures and not being controlled by them; it's not not having them." (Diogenes Laertius 2.74–75 = Aristippus 96)

3.44 *The same*

When once he was entering a prostitute's house and one of the lads with him was embarrassed, he said: "The hard part isn't going in, it's not to be able to leave." (Diogenes Laertius 2.69 = Aristippus 87)

3.45 *But Antisthenes argues that it is best not to have the pleasures at all*

And then there is Antisthenes, companion of Socrates and teacher of Diogenes, who put the highest value on moderation and was disgusted by pleasure. He is said to have declared about Aphrodite: "I would shoot Aphrodite if I could catch her; many a fine and good woman of ours she has corrupted." He called love one of nature's evils; yet the miserable individuals who come under her power, he said, call their disease a goddess! That's why his choice was rather to be mad than enjoy pleasure. (Theodoret, *Cure for Greek Maladies* 3.53 = Antisthenes 123)[14]

3.46 **Plato's** *Socrates thinks that restraint is better for the soul than a lack of it*

SOCRATES: Now, isn't it also true that doctors generally allow a person to fill up his appetites, to eat when he's hungry, for example, or drink when he's thirsty as much as he wants to when he's in good health, but when he's sick they practically never allow him to fill himself with what he has an appetite for? Do you also go along with this point, at least?

CALLICLES: Yes, I do.

---

13. This history of philosophy was written, probably by a member of Aristotle's school, in the early second century BCE.

14. Cf. **2.12–13**; **3.2**.[39].

SOCRATES: And isn't it just the same way with the soul, my excellent friend? [b] As long as it's corrupt, in that it's foolish, unrestrained and undisciplined, unjust and impious, it should be kept away from its appetites and not be permitted to do anything other than what will make it better. Do you agree or not?

CALLICLES: I agree.

SOCRATES: For this is no doubt better for the soul itself?

CALLICLES: Yes, it is.

SOCRATES: Now isn't keeping it away from what it has an appetite for, disciplining it?

CALLICLES: Yes.

SOCRATES: So to be disciplined and restrained is better for the soul than lack of restraint, which is what you yourself were thinking just now.

CALLICLES: I don't know what in the world you mean, Socrates. [c] Ask somebody else. (Plato, *Gorgias* 505a–c)

3.47 *Plato's Socrates (with Critias) on the difficulties of understanding moderation as a kind of science*

"You wretch," said I [Socrates], "all this time you've been leading me right round [c] in a circle and concealing from me that it was not living scientifically that was making us fare well and be happy, even if we possessed all the sciences put together, but that we have to have this one science of good and bad. Because, Critias, if you consent to take away this science from the other sciences, will medicine any the less produce health, or cobbling produce shoes, or the art of weaving produce clothes, or will the pilot's art any the less prevent us from dying at sea or the general's art in war?"

"They will do it just the same," he said.

"But my dear Critias, our chance of getting any of these things well and beneficially done will have vanished if this is lacking." [d]

"You are right."

"Then this science, at any rate, is not moderation, as it seems, but that one of which the function is to benefit us. For it is not a science of science and absence of science, but of good and bad. So that, if this latter one [sc. the science of good and bad] is beneficial, moderation would be something else for us."

"But why should not moderation be beneficial?" he said. "Because if [e] moderation really is a science of sciences and rules over the other sciences, then I suppose it would rule over this science of the good and would benefit us."

"And would this science make us healthy," I said, "and not the art of medicine? And would it perform the tasks of the other arts rather than each of them performing its own task? Didn't we protest solemnly just a moment ago that it is a science of science and absence of science only and of nothing else? We did, didn't we?"

"It seems so, at any rate."

"Then it will not be the craftsman of health?"

"Certainly not."

"Because health belonged to some other art, didn't it?" [175a]

"Yes, to another."

"Then it will be of no benefit, my friend. Because we have just awarded this work to another art, isn't that so?"

"Yes indeed."

"Then how will moderation be beneficial when it is the craftsman of no beneficial thing?"

"Apparently it won't be any benefit at all, Socrates." (Plato, *Charmides* 174b–175a; picking up from **2.5**)

3.48 *Plato's Socrates reports a conversation on a similar subject with Hippias, Prodicus, and Protagoras*

"'Now, I ask you, Hippias and Prodicus, as well as Protagoras—this is your conversation also—to say whether you think what I say is true or false.' They all thought that what I said was marvelously true.

"'So you agree,' I said, 'that the pleasant is good, the painful bad. I beg indulgence of Prodicus who distinguishes among words; for whether you call it "pleasant" [b] or "delightful" or "enjoyable," or whatever way or manner you please to name this sort of thing, my excellent Prodicus, please respond to the intent of my question.'

"Prodicus, laughing, agreed, as did the others.

"'Well, then, friends,' I asked, 'what about this? Are not all actions leading toward living painlessly and pleasantly honorable and beneficial? And isn't honorable activity good and beneficial?'

"They agreed.

"'Then if the pleasant is the good,' I said, [c] 'no one who knows or believes there is something else better than what he is doing, something possible, will go on doing what he had been doing when he could be doing what is better. To give in to oneself is nothing other than ignorance, and to control oneself is nothing other than wisdom.'" (Plato, *Protagoras* 358a–c)

vii. Courage

3.49 ***Xenophon's** Socrates thinks courage is acquired both by nature and training*

Again, when he was asked whether courage was something teachable or natural, he replied: "Just as one body is naturally stronger than another when it comes to physical labor, I think that one mind is naturally endowed with greater fortitude than another regarding danger, since I see that people raised under the same laws and customs differ markedly in terms of daring. [2] I do, however, believe that every nature can grow in courage through study and practice. The Scythians and Thracians clearly wouldn't dare take up full shields and spears to battle it out with the Spartans, and the Spartans obviously wouldn't want to compete against the Thracians with light shields and javelins, or against the Scythians with bows. [3] In my observation, it's the same with everything else: people differ naturally from one another and improve greatly through diligence. It's clear from this that everyone, whatever their natural talents, should study and practice the things in which they want to earn recognition." (Xenophon, *Memorabilia* 3.9.1–3; followed by **3.22**)

3.50 ***Plato's** Socrates on the subject of courage with the generals Nicias and Laches*

SOCRATES: You, Nicias, tell me again from the beginning—you know that when we were investigating courage at the beginning of the argument, we were investigating it as a part of virtue?

NICIAS: Yes, we were.

SOCRATES: And didn't you give your answer supposing that it was a part, and, as such, one among a number of other parts, all of which taken together were called virtue?

NICIAS: Yes, why not?

SOCRATES: And do you also speak of the same parts that I do? In addition to courage, I call moderation and justice and everything else of this kind parts of virtue. Don't you?

NICIAS: Yes, indeed. [b]

SOCRATES: Stop there. We are in agreement on these points, but let us investigate the grounds of fear and confidence to make sure that you don't regard them in one way and we in another. We will tell you what we think about them, and if you do not agree, you shall instruct us. We regard as fearful things those that produce fear, and as hopeful things those that do not produce fear; and fear is produced not by evils which have happened or are happening but by those which are anticipated. Because fear is the expectation of a future evil—or isn't this your opinion too, Laches?

LACHES: Very much so, Socrates.

SOCRATES: You hear what we have to say, [c] Nicias: that fearful things are future evils, and the ones inspiring hope are either future non-evils or future goods. Do you agree with this or have you some other view on the subject?

NICIAS: I agree with this one.

SOCRATES: And you declare that knowledge of just these things is courage?

NICIAS: Exactly so.

SOCRATES: Let us find out if we all agree on still a third point.

NICIAS: What one is that?

SOCRATES: I will explain. [d] It seems to me and my friend here that of the various things with which knowledge is concerned, there is not one kind of knowledge by which we know how things have happened in the past, and another by which we know how they are happening at the present time, and still another by which we know how what has not yet happened might best come to be in the future, but that the knowledge is the same in each case. For instance, in the case of health, there is no other art related to the past, the present, and the future except that of medicine, which, although it is a single art, surveys what is, what was, and what is likely [e] to be in the future. Again, in the case of the fruits of the earth, the art of farming conforms to the same pattern. And I suppose that both of you could bear witness that, in the case of the affairs of war, the art of generalship is that which best foresees the future and the other times—nor does this art [199a] consider it necessary to be ruled by the art of the seer, but to rule *it,* as being better acquainted with both present and future in the affairs of war. In fact, the law decrees, not that the seer should command the general, but that the general should command the seer. Is this what we shall say, Laches?

LACHES: Yes, it is.

SOCRATES: Well then, do you agree with us, Nicias, that the same knowledge has understanding of the same things, whether future, present, or past?

NICIAS: Yes, that is how it seems to me, Socrates.

SOCRATES: Now, my good friend, [b] you say that courage is the knowledge of the fearful and the hopeful, isn't that so?

NICIAS: Yes, it is.

SOCRATES: And it was agreed that fearful and hopeful things were future goods and future evils.

NICIAS: Yes, it was.

SOCRATES: And that the same knowledge is of the same things— future ones and all other kinds.

NICIAS: Yes, that is the case.

SOCRATES: Then courage is not knowledge of the fearful and the hopeful [c] only, because it understands not simply future goods and evils, but those of the present and the past and all times, just as is the case with the other kinds of knowledge.

NICIAS: So it seems, at any rate.

SOCRATES: Then you have told us about what amounts to a third part of courage, Nicias, whereas we asked you what the whole of courage was. And now it appears, according to your view, that courage is the knowledge not just of the fearful and the hopeful, but in your own opinion, it would [d] be the knowledge of practically all goods and evils put together. Do you agree to this new change, Nicias, or what do you say?

NICIAS: That seems right to me, Socrates.

SOCRATES: Then does a man with this kind of knowledge seem to depart from virtue in any respect if he really knows, in the case of all goods whatsoever, what they are and will be and have been, and similarly in the case of evils? And do you regard that man as lacking in moderation or justice and piety to whom alone belongs the ability to deal circumspectly [e] with both gods and men with respect to both the fearful and its opposite, and to provide himself with good things through his knowledge of how to associate with them correctly?

NICIAS: I think you have a point, Socrates.

SOCRATES: Then the thing you are now talking about, Nicias, would not be a part of virtue but rather virtue entire.

NICIAS: So it seems.

SOCRATES: And we have certainly stated that courage is one of the parts of virtue.

NICIAS: Yes, we have.

SOCRATES: Then what we are saying now does not appear to hold good.

NICIAS: Apparently not.

SOCRATES: Then we have not discovered, Nicias, what courage is. (Plato, *Laches* 198a–199e)

viii. Piety

3.51 Aeschines' Socrates (perhaps quoted from his Alcibiades) addresses Alcibiades

"Don't condemn me," I said, "Alcibiades, as if I had eccentric and atheistic views of chance and of divine matters, if I attribute all Themistocles' actions to knowledge, and if I hold that no mere chance was responsible for these deeds of his. I could much more easily prove to you that those who hold views opposite to mine are atheists than they could me, given that *they* suppose that good fortune attends equally on the bad and the good, and not that the fine and good, just because they are more pious, are better provided for in terms of what comes from the gods." (Aelius Aristides, *In Defence of the Four* 348 = Aeschines 50 = part of **7.4**)

3.52 Plato's Socrates relates piety to justice

SOCRATES: This is the kind of thing I was asking before, whether where [d] there is piety there is also justice, but where there is justice there is not always piety, for the pious is a part of justice. Shall we say that, or do you think otherwise?

EUTHYPHRO: No, but like that, for what you say appears to be right. (Plato, *Euthyphro* 12c–d)

3.53 *Later in the same discussion, he talks of piety as a kind of service to the gods—but what kind?*

SOCRATES: Very well, but what kind of care (*therapeia*) of the gods would piety be?

EUTHYPHRO: The kind of care, Socrates, that slaves take of their masters.

SOCRATES: I understand. It is likely to be a kind of service (*hupêretikê tis* [*technê*]) of the gods.

EUTHYPHRO: Quite so.

SOCRATES: Could you tell me to the achievement of what goal service to doctors tends? Is it not, do you think, to achieving health?

EUTHYPHRO: I think so.

SOCRATES: What about service to shipbuilders? [e] To what achievement is it directed?

EUTHYPHRO: Clearly, Socrates, to the building of a ship.

SOCRATES: And service to house builders to the building of a house?

EUTHYPHRO: Yes.

SOCRATES: Tell me then, my good sir, to the achievement of what aim does service to the gods tend? You obviously know since you say that you, of all men, have the best knowledge of the divine.

EUTHYPHRO: And I am telling the truth, Socrates.

SOCRATES: Tell me then, by Zeus, what is that excellent aim that the gods achieve, using us as their servants?

EUTHYPHRO: Many fine things, Socrates.

SOCRATES: So do generals, my friend. [14a] Nevertheless you could easily tell me their main concern, which is to achieve victory in war, is it not?

EUTHYPHRO: Of course.

SOCRATES: The farmers too, I think, achieve many fine things, but the main point of their efforts is to produce food from the earth.

EUTHYPHRO: Quite so.

SOCRATES: Well then, how would you sum up the many fine things that the gods achieve?

EUTHYPHRO: I told you a short while ago, Socrates, that it is a considerable [b] task to acquire any precise knowledge of these things, but, to put it simply, I say that if a man knows how to say and do what is pleasing to the gods at prayer and sacrifice, those are pious actions such as preserve both private houses and public affairs of state. The opposite of these pleasing actions are impious and overturn and destroy everything.

SOCRATES: You could tell me in far fewer words, if you were willing, the [c] sum of what I asked, Euthyphro, but you are not keen to teach me, that is clear. You were on the point of doing so, but you turned away. If you had given that answer, I should now have acquired from you sufficient knowledge of the nature of piety. As it is, the lover of inquiry must follow his beloved wherever it may lead him. Once more then, what do you say that piety and the pious are? Are they a knowledge of how to sacrifice and pray?

EUTHYPHRO: They are.

SOCRATES: To sacrifice is to make a gift to the gods, whereas to pray is to beg from the gods?

EUTHYPHRO: Definitely, Socrates.

SOCRATES: It would follow from this statement that piety would be a knowledge of how to give to, and beg from, the gods. [d]

EUTHYPHRO: You understood what I said very well, Socrates.

SOCRATES: That is because I am so desirous of your wisdom, and I concentrate my mind on it, so that no word of yours may fall to the ground. But tell me, what is this service to the gods? You say it is to beg from them and to give to them?

EUTHYPHRO: I do.

SOCRATES: And to beg correctly would be to ask from them things that we need?

EUTHYPHRO: What else?

SOCRATES: And to give correctly is to give them what they need from us, for it would not be skillful to bring gifts to anyone that are in no way needed. [e]

EUTHYPHRO: True, Socrates.

SOCRATES: Piety would then be a sort of trading skill between gods and men?

EUTHYPHRO: Trading yes, if you prefer to call it that.

SOCRATES: I prefer nothing, unless it is true. But tell me, what benefit do the gods derive from the gifts they receive from us? What they give us is [15a] obvious to all. There is for us no good that we do not receive from them, but how are they benefited by what they receive from us? Or do we have such an advantage over them in the trade that we receive all our blessings from them and they receive nothing from us?

EUTHYPHRO: Do you suppose, Socrates, that the gods are benefited by what they receive from us?

SOCRATES: What could those gifts from us to the gods be, Euthyphro?

EUTHYPHRO: What else, do you think, than honor, reverence, and what I mentioned just now, to please them?

SOCRATES: The pious is then, [b] Euthyphro, pleasing to the gods, but not beneficial or dear to them?

EUTHYPHRO: I think it is of all things most dear to them.

SOCRATES: So the pious is once again what is dear to the gods.

EUTHYPHRO: Most certainly.

SOCRATES: When you say this, will you be surprised if your arguments seem to move about instead of staying put? And will you accuse me of being Daedalus who makes them move, though you are yourself much more skillful than Daedalus and make them go round in a circle? Or do [c] you not realize that our argument has moved around and come again to the same place? You surely remember that earlier the pious and the god-loved were shown not to be the same but different from each other. Or do you not remember?

EUTHYPHRO: I do.

SOCRATES: Do you then not realize now that you are saying that what is dear to the gods is the pious? Is this not the same as the god-loved? Or is it not?

EUTHYPHRO: It certainly is.

SOCRATES: Either we were wrong when we agreed before, or, if we were right then, we are wrong now.

EUTHYPHRO: That seems to be so.

SOCRATES: So we must investigate again from the beginning what piety is, as I shall not willingly give up before I learn this. (Plato, *Euthyphro* 13d–15c)

3.54(a)–(b) Plato's Socrates tells his jury that he was engaged on his own special kind of service to god[15]

[3.54(a)] "What has caused my reputation is none other than a certain kind of wisdom. What kind of wisdom? . . . I shall call upon the god at Delphi as witness to the existence and nature of my wisdom, if it be such."

. . .

[21a] "He [Chaerephon] went to Delphi at one time and ventured to ask the oracle—as I say, gentlemen, do not create a disturbance—he asked if any man was wiser than I, and the Pythian replied that no one was wiser. Chaerephon is dead, but his brother will testify to you about this. [b] When I heard of this reply I asked myself: 'Whatever does the god mean? What is his riddle? I am very conscious that I am not wise at all; what then does he mean by saying that I am the wisest? For surely he does not lie; it is not legitimate for him to do so.' For a long time I was at a loss as to his meaning; then I very reluctantly turned to some such investigation as this; I went to one of those reputed wise, thinking [c] that there, if anywhere, I could refute the oracle. . . ." [continued at **7.7**]

. . .

[22e] "As a result of this investigation, men of Athens, I acquired much [23a] unpopularity, of a kind that is hard to deal with and is a heavy burden; many slanders came from these people and a reputation for wisdom, for in each case the bystanders thought that I myself possessed the wisdom that I proved that my interlocutor did not have. What is probable, gentlemen, is that in fact the god is wise and that his oracular response was saying that [b] human wisdom is worth little or nothing, and that when he says this man, Socrates, he is using my name as an example, as if he said: 'This man among you, mortals, is wisest who, like Socrates, understands that his wisdom is worthless.' So even now I continue this investigation as the god bade me—and I go around seeking out anyone, citizen or stranger, whom I think wise. Then if I do not think he is, I come to the assistance of the god and show him that he is not wise. Because of this occupation, I do not have the leisure to engage in public affairs to any extent, nor indeed to look after my own, but I live in great poverty because of my service (*latreia*) to the god." (Plato, *Apology* 20d, 21a–c, and 22e–23b; 21c–d is at **7.7**)

---

15. Xenophon (*Apology* 14) refers to the oracle too, though he makes it less central, and reports its utterance differently. Cf. **3.59**.

[3.54(b)] "This is the truth of the matter, men of Athens: wherever a man has taken a position that he believes to be best, or has been placed by his commander, there he must I think remain and face danger, without a [e] thought for death or anything else, rather than disgrace. It would have been a dreadful way to behave, men of Athens, if, at Potidaea, Amphipolis, and Delium, I had, at the risk of death, like anyone else, remained at my post where those you had elected to command had ordered me, and then, when the god ordered me, as I thought and believed, to [29a] live the life of a philosopher, to examine myself and others, I had abandoned my post for fear of death or anything else. That would have been a dreadful thing, and then I might truly have justly been brought here for not believing that there are gods, disobeying the oracle, fearing death, and thinking I was wise when I was not. To fear death, gentlemen, is no other than to think oneself wise when one is not, to think one knows what one does not know. No one knows whether death may not be the greatest of all blessings for a man, yet men fear it as if they knew that it is the greatest [b] of evils. And surely it is the most blameworthy ignorance to believe that one knows what one does not know. It is perhaps on this point and in this respect, gentlemen, that I differ from the majority of men, and if I were to claim that I am wiser than anyone in anything, it would be in this, that, as I have no adequate knowledge of things in the underworld, so I do not think I have. I do know, however, that it is wicked and shameful to do wrong, to disobey one's superior, be he god or man. I shall never fear or avoid things of which I do not know, whether they may not be [c] good rather than things that I know to be bad. Even if you acquitted me now and did not believe Anytus, who said to you that either I should not have been brought here in the first place, or that now I am here, you cannot avoid executing me, for if I should be acquitted, your sons would practice the teachings of Socrates and all be thoroughly corrupted; if you said to me in this regard: 'Socrates, we do not believe Anytus now; we acquit you, but only on condition that you spend no more time on this [d] investigation and do not practice philosophy, and if you are caught doing so you will die'; if, as I say, you were to acquit me on those terms, I would say to you: 'Men of Athens, I am grateful and I am your friend, but I will obey the god rather than you, and as long as I draw breath and am able, I shall not cease to practice philosophy, to exhort you and in my usual way to point out to any one of you whom I happen to meet: "Good sir, you are an Athenian, a citizen of the greatest city with the greatest [e] reputation for both wisdom and power; are you not ashamed of your eagerness to possess as much wealth, reputation, and honors as possible, while you do not care for nor give thought to wisdom or truth, or the best possible state of your soul?'" Then, if one of you disputes this and says he does care, I shall not let him go at once or leave him, but I shall question him, examine him and test him, and if I do not think he has attained the goodness that he says he has, I shall reproach him because he attaches [30a] little importance to the most important things and greater importance to inferior things. I shall treat in this way anyone I happen to meet, young and old, citizen and stranger, and more so the citizens because you are more kindred to me. Be sure that this is what the god orders me to do, and I think there is no greater blessing for the city than my service (*hupêresia*) to the god. For I go around doing nothing but persuading both young and old among you not to care for your body or your wealth in preference to or [b] as strongly as for the best possible state of your soul, as I say to you: 'Wealth does not bring about excellence, but excellence makes wealth and everything else good for men, both individually and collectively.'" (Plato, *Apology* 28d–30b; part = **2.17**)

3.55 *As recounted by* **Plato's Phaedo***, Socrates even describes himself (to* **Simmias***) as a slave to god*

"Really, Simmias, it would be hard for me to persuade other people that I do not consider my present fate a misfortune if I cannot persuade even you, and you are afraid that it is more difficult to deal with me than before. You seem to think me inferior to the swans in prophecy. They sing before too, but when they realize that they must die they sing most and most beautifully, as [85a] they rejoice that they are about to depart to join the god whose servants they are. But men, because of their own fear of death, tell lies about the swans and say that they lament their death and sing in sorrow. They do not reflect that no bird sings when it is hungry or cold or suffers in any other way, neither the nightingale nor the swallow nor the hoopoe, though they do say that these sing laments when in pain. Nor do the swans, but [b] I believe that as they belong to Apollo, they are prophetic, have knowledge of the future and sing of the blessings of the underworld, sing and rejoice on that day beyond what they did before. As I believe myself to be a fellow servant with the swans and dedicated to the same god, and have received from my master a gift of prophecy not inferior to theirs, I am no more despondent than they on leaving life." (Plato, *Phaedo* 84e–85b)

3.56 *Xenophon emphasizes Socrates' personal piety*

In relation to the gods both his actions and his words were conspicuously in line with the Pythia's responses to questions about how we should act in relation to sacrifices, duties to our ancestors, or anything like that; for the Pythia's answer is that acting piously will be acting by the city's laws, and that is both how Socrates acted himself and how he advised others to act, treating those who acted in some other way as engaged in pointless superstition. (Xenophon, *Memorabilia* 1.3.1; followed by **2.24**)

3.57 *The same*

He believed that by offering meager sacrifices from meager means he did nothing less than those who offer ample sacrifices from ample means. He said that it would reflect poorly on the gods if they took more pleasure in large offerings than in small ones, since in that case the sacrifices of wicked people would often please them more than those of honest ones; nor would life be worth living for human beings if the sacrifices of the wicked proved more pleasing to the gods than those of honest people. On the contrary, he believed that the gods took the greatest pleasure in honors paid to them by those who are most pious. He was an admirer of the line "According to your means, sacrifice to the gods,"[16] and he said that to act "according to your means" was also good advice for dealing with friends, strangers, and the other aspects of one's life. (Xenophon, *Memorabilia* 1.3.3)

3.58 *The same again*

"I'm quite sure that I won't neglect the divine in the slightest, Socrates," said Euthydemus. "But I'm discouraged at the thought that no single person could ever give the gods the gratitude they deserve for their kindnesses."

[16] "Don't let that discourage you, Euthydemus," he said. "You see the reply the god at Delphi makes whenever anyone asks how he might go about gratifying the gods: 'By following the customs of the state.' And it's presumably the custom everywhere to please the gods through the best offerings one is capable of. So what more excellent and pious way could there be for someone to honor the gods than by doing their bidding? [17] But he should be sure to do everything he's capable of,

---

16. Hesiod, *Works and Days* 336.

since whoever does less is clearly not honoring the gods. One should therefore honor the gods to the absolute best of one's ability and then confidently expect the greatest blessings. It wouldn't make sense to expect greater things from anyone else, or by any means other than pleasing those who are capable of conferring the greatest benefits. And how better could someone please them than by his strict obedience?" (Xenophon, *Memorabilia* 4.3.15–17; follows **9.23**)

3.59 **Xenophon** *reports* **Hermogenes'** *account of Socrates' reply to the charge of impiety at his trial*

"The first thing that I wonder at about Meletus, gentlemen, is what can possibly be the basis of his claim that I do not recognize the gods the city recognizes; for everyone who was there at the time, and indeed, if he wanted, Meletus himself, will have seen me sacrificing on the public altars at the communal festivals. [12] As for introducing 'new divinities,' how could I be doing that by claiming that a divine voice appears to me signaling what to do?[17] I imagine those who base themselves on the cries of birds and on human utterances of men are similarly relying on 'voices.' Nor will anyone surely dispute that thunder has a 'voice,' or that it is a portent of the greatest kind? Does not the priestess herself on her tripod at Delphi pass on the god's messages through a 'voice'?" (Xenophon, *Apology* 11–12)

ix. Virtue and Good Fortune

3.60 **Xenophon's** *Socrates thinks good fortune is a matter of virtue, not luck*

When someone asked him what he considered a man's best pursuit, he said: "Doing well." Asked in turn whether he held good luck to be a pursuit, he replied: "Personally, I regard luck and action as complete opposites: I think that happening upon something you need without looking for it is good fortune, but I believe that accomplishing something after study and practice is doing well; and I consider people who pursue this course to do well." [15] He claimed that the most accomplished people—whether farmers, doctors, or politicians—are the best and most divinely favored, but he said that the person who accomplishes

---

17. Socrates' *daimonion*: see Ch. 10.

nothing is neither good for anything nor divinely favored. (Xenophon, *Memorabilia* 3.9.14–15)

3.61 So does **Plato**'s

"Now be sure," I [Socrates] said, "we do not leave out any goods worth mentioning."

"I don't think we are leaving out any," said Clinias.

But I remembered one and said, "Good heavens, Clinias, we are in danger of leaving out the greatest good of all!"

"Which one is that?" he asked.

"Good fortune, Clinias, which everybody, even quite worthless people, says is the greatest of the goods."

"You are right," he said.

And I reconsidered a second time and said, [d] "Son of Axiochus, you and I have nearly made ourselves ridiculous in front of our visitors."

"How so?" he asked.

"Because in putting good fortune in our previous list we are now saying the same thing all over again."

"What are you talking about?"

"Surely it is ridiculous when a thing has already been brought up, to bring it up again and say the same things twice."

"What are you saying now?"

"Wisdom is surely good fortune," I said, "—this is something even a child would know."

He was amazed—he is still so young and simple-minded.

I noticed his surprise and said, [e] "You know, don't you, Clinias, that flute players have the best luck when it comes to success in flute music?"

He agreed.

"And writing masters at reading and writing?"

"Certainly."

"What about the perils of the sea—surely you don't think that, as a general rule, any pilots have better luck than the wise ones?"

"Certainly not."

"And again, if you were on a campaign, [280a] with which general would you prefer to share both the danger and the luck, a wise one or an ignorant one?"

"With a wise one."

"And if you were sick, would you rather take a chance with a wise doctor or with an ignorant one?"

"With a wise one."

"Then it is your opinion," I said, "that it is luckier to do things in the company of wise men than ignorant ones?"

He agreed.

"So wisdom makes men fortunate in every case, since I don't suppose she would ever make any sort of mistake but must necessarily do right and be lucky—otherwise she would no longer be wisdom."

We finally agreed (I don't know quite how) [b] that, in sum, the situation was this: if a man had wisdom, he had no need of any good fortune in addition. (Plato, *Euthydemus* 279c–280b; follows **2.19(a)**, and is followed by **2.19(b)**)

3.62 *Antisthenes agrees*

The wise person . . . entrusts nothing to luck. (Diogenes Laertius 6.105 = Antisthenes 99; continues **3.4**)

Chapter 4: Body and Soul

The focus on self-control in ethics naturally leads to a question: what, exactly, is doing the controlling, and what, exactly, is being controlled? They can hardly be the very same thing. There must be some part, or aspect, of a human being that accounts for potentially wayward impulses, and a part, or aspect, that is capable of reining them in.

The starting point for the Socratics' thinking about this question is the distinction they draw between body and soul (*psuchê*), based on the idea that "soul" names whatever it is that explains (a) life and (b) thought. In virtue of this distinction, it turns out that the soul is the true locus of personhood (**4.3**): to love someone, for example, is properly to love their soul (**4.4-6**; cf. also Ch. 6).

> It is unclear quite how novel this analysis was. On the one hand, *some* form of body–soul distinction is commonplace in earlier Greek thought, both technical and non-technical; the word *psuchê* is as old as Greek itself; and there is no evidence of controversy either within the circle or outside it raised by the basic division just outlined. On the other hand, earlier literature, philosophy, and even medical writings, are much less clear about what the nature of the distinction is. In these earlier contexts, "soul" (or sometimes "spirit," *daimôn*: cf. Ch. 10) is used more or less precisely to refer to one's character, or consciousness. In Homer, for example, it is what leaves the body when one faints (e.g., *Iliad* 5.696) or, ultimately, dies (e.g., *Iliad* 23.100). See further, Claus (1981).

A recurrent image among Socratic writers figures the soul as a container, in which one's experiences and memories are stored (**4.8**; cf. **3.2.**[41]). Plato himself uses the image (e.g., *Laches* 187b, *Protagoras* 314ab)—although he sometimes shows himself to be uncomfortable with the danger of its implying that the soul is a passive partner in the process. In **4.1**, then, the body "entombs" the soul, but the soul "encompasses" the body at the same time; cf. **4.3**, where the soul governs and employs the body as its instrument. For all the Socratics, in fact, there is no doubt that the answer to what is doing the controlling when one is self-controlled lies somehow or other with the soul—specifically, with its reasoning capacity.

The other part of the question (what it is that gets controlled in cases of self-control) is more difficult. We have seen in Chapter 3 that control is, one way or another, the control of pleasure, and it would give us a tidy dichotomy if one could say that pleasure was all about the body. But although pleasures—at least, the morally dangerous sort—tend to be closely associated with the body, they also involve experience, thought, and memory too. In other words, they also have a psychological dimension. But can we go so far as to say that pleasure (and pain, correlatively) is an experience of the soul which is merely *occasioned* by physical stimuli (cf. **4.7**)? Or should we tie them more closely to the body, and say that they are physical events which are properly extrinsic to the soul, even if they distract and affect it (**4.15**)? The issue has come to be familiar to us as one about the parts of the soul. The two positions on pleasure and pain just outlined correspond, respectively, to the positions (a) that soul itself contains a nonrational part which responds to pleasure, and which the rational part needs to control; and (b) that, on the contrary, the soul is purely rational, so that self-control is a matter of its ability to minimize and ignore bodily distractions. Plato mainly seems to align himself with the former view (argued, for example, and precisely as a defense of self-control, at *Gorgias* 491d–508c, part of which = **4.8**); indeed, in some works he takes it that there are *two* nonrational parts to the soul in addition to the rational part (argued at *Republic* IV, 435c–441d; compare *Phaedrus* 246a–256e). But he also presented the alternative view, that the soul is reason alone, both in the *Phaedo* (more commonly known in antiquity as *On the Soul*), and also in the *Republic*, when Socrates wonders whether the soul "in its pure state" (i.e., when it is not "maimed by its association with the body and other evils": X, 611b) "has many parts or just one, and whether or in what manner it is put together" (612a). One of the complicating factors in the question of how responsibility for conscious experience divides between soul and body is the fact that body and soul can affect and change each other. (It is important that the soul is not just a passive repository of experience; but it obviously *is* affected to some degree by what happens to the body.) Some ancient thinkers held that their mutual influence actually leads to the possibility of physiognomy—that is, of discerning psychological character from bodily traits. The term itself is, in fact, first found in this sense in the evidence for the Socratics. Aristippus talks of a soul manifesting its ugliness (**4.10**); Antisthenes, whose book *On the Sophists* is described in the catalogue as a "physiognomical" treatise, suggests in **4.9** that the soul is shaped by the body. Phaedo seems to have held the moderate view that a person might be born with character dispositions which corresponded to facts about the body, but that self-control could overcome one's determination by them (**4.11**). (If this means that Phaedo identified the soul with the intellect, identifying nonrational desires with the body, we can see why Plato might have chosen him as the narrator of the *Phaedo*.)[1] Even Plato and Xenophon, who seem to have had no time for physiognomy at all, both recognized that the state of the body directly affected the well-being of the soul—and vice versa (**4.13–14**).

It is important, finally, to note that "body" and "soul" are used as contrastive terms without prejudice to the question of how the soul is constituted (out of the same elements as the body, or out of some nonmaterial substance?) and whether it survives death: Plato outlines some alternatives at **4.16**.[2] Xenophon's Socrates hints that human souls derive from the divine intelligence that governs the world (**9.16**; Plato's Socrates argues this outright in **4.2**). **4.17** might be evidence that Antisthenes, whose catalogue of books contains a number of items on the subject of death (see our Index of Socratics), believed in the soul's survival (which would make a difference in how we read the attachment to life expressed in **4.18–22**). If we are right in our speculation about Phaedo's strong identification of the soul with the intellect along the lines proposed in the dialogue Plato named after him, then he may have agreed that it is immortal. But other members of the Socratic circle certainly did not agree. Plato has Glaucon affect surprise that someone could believe it (*Republic* X, 608d); the evidence for Aristodemus in **9.16**, though by no means conclusive, suggests that he might not have done so; cf. also Aristippus at **4.12**.

Texts

4.1 *Plato's Socrates on the soul as the "sustainer" of the body and source of its life*

HERMOGENES: We speak of the body and soul of a human being.

SOCRATES: Certainly.

HERMOGENES: Then let's try to analyze their names as we did the previous ones.

---

1. See Boys-Stones (2004).

2. Fuller arguments for the possibility of the soul's immortality are to be found in Plato's *Phaedo*; see also *Laws* X, 893b–897b; *Phaedrus* 245b–246a; *Republic* X, 608d–611b.

SOCRATES: Are you saying that we should investigate whether soul and then body are reasonably named?

HERMOGENES: Yes.

SOCRATES: Speaking off the top of my head, I think that those who gave soul its name had something like this in mind. They thought that when the soul is present in the body, it causes it to live and gives it the power [e] to breathe the air and be revitalized (*anapsuchon*), and that when this revitalization fails, the body dies and is finished. It's for this reason, I think, that they called it "soul" (*psuchê*). But hold on a minute, if you don't mind, for I imagine that the followers of Euthyphro would despise this [400a] analysis and think it crude. But I think I glimpse one they will find more persuasive. Have a look and see whether it pleases you.

HERMOGENES: Tell it to me and I will.

SOCRATES: When you consider the nature of every body, what, besides the soul, do you think sustains and supports it, so that it lives and moves about?

HERMOGENES: There isn't anything.

SOCRATES: What about when you consider the nature of everything else? Don't you agree with Anaxagoras that it is ordered and sustained by mind or soul?

HERMOGENES: I do. [b]

SOCRATES: So a fine name to give this power, which supports and sustains (*ochei kai echei*) the whole of nature (*phusis*), would be "nature-sustainer" (*phusechê*). This may also be pronounced more elegantly, *psuchê*.

HERMOGENES: Absolutely, and I also think this is a more scientific explanation than the other.

SOCRATES: Yes, it is. Nevertheless, it sounds funny when it's named in the true way, with its actual name (i.e., *phusechê*).

HERMOGENES: What are we going to say about the next one?

SOCRATES: Are you referring to the name "body"?

HERMOGENES: Yes.

SOCRATES: There's a lot to say, it seems to me—and if one distorted the name a little, there would be even more. Thus some people say that the [c] body (*sôma*) is the tomb (*sêma*) of the soul, on the grounds that it is entombed in its present life, while others say that it is correctly called a "sign" (*sêma*) because the soul signifies whatever it wants to signify by means of the body. I think it is most likely the followers of Orpheus who gave the body its name, with the idea that the soul is being punished for something, and that the body is an enclosure or prison in which the soul is securely kept (*sôzetai*)—as the name *sôma* itself suggests—until the penalty is paid; for, on this view, not even a single letter of the word needs to be changed. (Plato, *Cratylus* 399d–400b)

4.2 *Plato's Socrates argues that reason is a characteristic of soul, and that human souls derive from a soul that animates the entire cosmos*

SOCRATES: I guess you will give the same answer about the [d] earth here in animals when it is compared to earth in the universe, and likewise about the other elements I mentioned a little earlier. Is that your answer?

PROTARCHUS: Who could answer differently without seeming insane?

SOCRATES: No one at all. But now see what follows. To the combination of all these elements taken as a unit we give the name "body," don't we?

PROTARCHUS: Certainly.

SOCRATES: Now, realize that the same holds in the case of what we call the "ordered universe." [e] It will turn out to be a body in the same sense, since it is composed of the same elements.

PROTARCHUS: What you say is undeniable.

SOCRATES: Does the body of the universe as a whole provide for the sustenance of what is body in our sphere, or is it the reverse, and the universe possesses and derives all the goods enumerated from ours?

PROTARCHUS: That too is a question not worth asking, Socrates. [30a]

SOCRATES: But what about the following, is this also a question not worth asking?

PROTARCHUS: Tell me what the question is.

SOCRATES: Of the body that belongs to us, will we not say that it has a soul?

PROTARCHUS: Quite obviously that is what we will say.

SOCRATES: But where does it come from, unless the body of the universe which has the same properties as ours, but more beautiful in all respects, happens to possess a soul?

PROTARCHUS: Clearly from nowhere else.

SOCRATES: We surely cannot maintain this assumption, with respect to [b] our four classes (limit, the unlimited, their mixture, and their cause—which is present in everything): that this cause is recognized as all-encompassing wisdom, since among us it imports the soul and provides training for the body and medicine for its ailments and in other cases order and restitution, but that it should fail to be responsible for the same things on a large scale in the whole universe (things that are, in addition, beautiful and pure), for the contrivance of what has so fair and wonderful a nature.

PROTARCHUS: That would make no sense at all. [c]

SOCRATES: But if that is inconceivable, we had better pursue the alternative account and affirm, as we have said often, that there is plenty of the unlimited in the universe as well as sufficient limit, and that there is, above them, a certain cause, of no small significance, that orders and coordinates the years, seasons, and months, and which has every right to the title of wisdom and reason.

PROTARCHUS: The greatest right.

SOCRATES: But there could be no wisdom and reason without a soul.

PROTARCHUS: Certainly not.

SOCRATES: You will therefore say that in the nature of Zeus there is the soul of a king, [d] as well as a king's reason, in virtue of this power displayed by the cause, and that there are other fine qualities in other divinities, in conformity with the names by which they like to be addressed.

PROTARCHUS: Very much so.

SOCRATES: Do not think that we have engaged in an idle discussion here, Protarchus, for it comes as a support for the thinkers of old who held the view that reason is forever the ruler over the universe.

PROTARCHUS: It certainly does.

SOCRATES: It also has provided an answer to my query, that reason [e] belongs to that kind which is the cause of everything. But that was one of our four kinds. So there you already have the solution to our problem in your hands.

PROTARCHUS: I have indeed, and quite to my satisfaction, although at first I did not realize that you were answering.

SOCRATES: Sometimes joking is a relief from seriousness.

PROTARCHUS: Well said.

SOCRATES: By now, dear friend, we have arrived at a satisfactory explanation [31a] of the class that reason belongs to and what power it has. (Plato, *Philebus* 29d–31a)

4.3 Plato's Socrates argues that the soul, not the body, is the true "self"

SOCRATES: But the thing being used and the person using it—they're different, aren't they?

ALCIBIADES: What do you mean?

SOCRATES: A shoemaker, for example, cuts with a knife and a scraper, I think, and with other tools.

ALCIBIADES: Yes, he does.

SOCRATES: So isn't the cutter who uses the tools different from the tools he's cutting with?

ALCIBIADES: Of course.

SOCRATES: And likewise isn't the lyre player different from what he's playing with?

ALCIBIADES: Yes.

SOCRATES: This is what I was just asking—doesn't the user of a thing always seem to be different from what he's using? [d]

ALCIBIADES: It seems so.

SOCRATES: Let's think about the shoemaker again. Does he cut with his tools only, or does he also cut with his hands?

ALCIBIADES: With his hands, too.

SOCRATES: So he uses his hands, too.

ALCIBIADES: Yes.

SOCRATES: And doesn't he use his eyes, too, in shoemaking?

ALCIBIADES: Yes.

SOCRATES: Didn't we agree that the person who uses something is different from the thing that he uses?

ALCIBIADES: Yes.

SOCRATES: So the shoemaker and the lyre player are different from the hands and eyes they use in their work. [e]

ALCIBIADES: So it seems.

SOCRATES: Doesn't a man use his whole body, too?

ALCIBIADES: Certainly.

SOCRATES: And we agreed that the user is different from the thing being used.

ALCIBIADES: Yes.

SOCRATES: So a man is different from his own body.

ALCIBIADES: So it seems.

SOCRATES: Then what is a man?

ALCIBIADES: I don't know what to say.

SOCRATES: Yes, you do—say that it's what uses the body.

ALCIBIADES: Yes. [130a]

SOCRATES: What else uses it but the soul?

ALCIBIADES: Nothing else.

SOCRATES: And doesn't the soul rule the body?

ALCIBIADES: Yes.

SOCRATES: Now here's something I don't think anybody would disagree with.

ALCIBIADES: What?

SOCRATES: Man is one of three things.

ALCIBIADES: What things?

SOCRATES: The body, the soul, or the two of them together, the whole thing.

ALCIBIADES: Of course.

SOCRATES: But we agreed that man is that which rules the body. [b]

ALCIBIADES: Yes, we did agree to that.

SOCRATES: Does the body rule itself?

ALCIBIADES: It couldn't.

SOCRATES: Because we said it was ruled.

ALCIBIADES: Yes.

SOCRATES: So this can't be what we're looking for.

ALCIBIADES: Not likely.

SOCRATES: Well then, can the two of them together rule the body? Is this what man is?

ALCIBIADES: Yes, maybe that's it.

SOCRATES: No, that's the least likely of all. If one of them doesn't take part in ruling, then surely no combination of the two of them could rule.

ALCIBIADES: You're right.

SOCRATES: Since a man is neither his body, nor his body and soul together, [c] what remains, I think, is either that he's nothing, or else, if he is something, he's nothing other than his soul.

ALCIBIADES: Quite so.

SOCRATES: Do you need any clearer proof that the soul is the man?

ALCIBIADES: No, by Zeus, I think you've given ample proof. (?Plato, *Alcibiades* 129c–130c)[3]

4.4 *Socrates in* **Xenophon** *concurs*

When the soul (which is alone the indwelling center of intelligence) is gone out of a man, be he our nearest and dearest friend, we carry the body forth and bury it out of sight. [54] Even in life, he used to say, each of us is ready to part with any portion of his best possession—to wit, his own body—if it be useless and unprofitable. He will remove it himself, or suffer another to do so in his stead. Thus men cut off their own nails, hair, or corns; they allow surgeons to cut and cauterize them, not without pains and aches, and are so grateful to the doctor for his services that they further give him a fee. Or again, a man ejects the spittle from his mouth as far as possible. Why? Because it is of no use while it stays within the system, but is detrimental rather. (Xenophon, *Memorabilia* 1.2.53–54)

4.5 *The same (here in conversation with* **Hermogenes***): one corollary is that one ought to direct love toward souls, not bodies*

"I want to testify . . . that desire [*erôs*] for a soul is much greater than that for a body. [13] Everyone knows that intercourse without love [*philia*] is worthless. Well, love by those who admire character is said to be a sweet

---

3. "?Plato," because the authenticity of this work has been a matter of debate in modern times.

and willing necessity. But many of those who desire the body criticize the behavior of the objects of their love, and hate it. [14] Even if they care for both, the bloom of youth quickly peaks, and their love inevitably fades away with it. The soul, on the other hand, becomes even more desirable the longer it progresses toward wisdom. [15] What is more, there is a limit to the enjoyment of a physical beauty: one inevitably starts to feel about one's sweetheart what one feels about food when one is full. But love for the soul is pure and also less easily sated. That does not make it less erotic, as one might think; rather it brings clear fulfillment to our prayer to the goddess to supply us with erotic words and deeds. [16] That a flourishing soul which gives someone the beauty of the unaffected along with modesty and nobility of manner, a soul which is the obvious leader among its peers, but at the same time is kind—that such a soul admires and loves the object of its desire needs no argument. What I shall teach you is the likelihood that a soul like this will be loved in its turn by its sweetheart. . . ." (Xenophon, *Symposium* 8.12–16)

4.6 *Diotima, reported by* **Plato***'s Socrates, agrees with this*

"A lover who goes about this matter correctly must begin in his youth to devote himself to beautiful bodies. First, if the leader [sc. Love] leads aright, he should love one body and beget beautiful ideas there; then he should [b] realize that the beauty of any one body is brother to the beauty of any other, and that if he is to pursue beauty of form he'd be very foolish not to think that the beauty of all bodies is one and the same. When he grasps this, he must become a lover of all beautiful bodies, and he must think that this wild gaping after just one body is a small thing and despise it. After this he must think that the beauty of people's souls is more valuable than the beauty of their bodies, so that if someone is decent in [c] his soul, even though he is scarcely blooming in his body, our lover must be content to love and care for him and to seek to give birth to such ideas as will make young men better. The result is that our lover will be forced to gaze at the beauty of activities and laws and to see that all this is akin to itself, with the result that he will think that the beauty of bodies is a thing of no importance. After customs he must move on to various kinds of knowledge. The result is that he will see the beauty of knowledge and [d] be looking mainly not at beauty in a single example—as a servant would who favored the beauty of a little boy or a man or a single custom (being a slave, of course, he's low and small-minded)—but the lover is turned to the great sea of beauty, and, gazing upon this, he gives birth to many gloriously beautiful ideas and theories, in unstinting love of wisdom, until, having grown and been strengthened there, he catches sight of such [e] knowledge, and it is the knowledge of such beauty." (Plato, *Symposium* 210a–e)

4.7 **Plato**'s *Socrates sets out an argument to show that nonrational desire is part of the soul's activity*

SOCRATES: It seems we have first to determine what kind of a thing memory is; in fact I am afraid that we will have to determine the nature of perception even before that of memory, if the whole subject matter is to become at all clear to us in the right way.

PROTARCHUS: How do you mean?

SOCRATES: You must realize that some of the various affections of the body are extinguished within the body before they reach the soul, [d] leaving it unaffected. Others penetrate through both body and soul and provoke a kind of upheaval that is peculiar to each but also common to both of them.

PROTARCHUS: I realize that.

SOCRATES: Are we fully justified if we claim that the soul remains oblivious of those affections that do not penetrate both, while it is not oblivious of those that penetrate both?

PROTARCHUS: Of course we are justified.

SOCRATES: But you must not so misunderstand me as to suppose I meant that this "obliviousness" [e] gave rise to any kind of forgetting. Forgetting is rather the loss of memory, but in the case in question here no memory has yet arisen. It would be absurd to say that there could be the process of losing something that neither is nor was in existence, wouldn't it?

PROTARCHUS: Quite definitely.

SOCRATES: You only have to make some change in names, then.

PROTARCHUS: How so?

SOCRATES: Instead of saying that the soul is oblivious when it remains unaffected by the disturbances of the body, now change the name of what [34a] you so far called "obliviousness" to that of nonperception.

PROTARCHUS: I understand.

SOCRATES: But when the soul and body are jointly affected and moved by one and the same affection, if you call this motion "perception," you would say nothing out of the way.

PROTARCHUS: You are right.

SOCRATES: And so we know by now what we mean by perception?

PROTARCHUS: Certainly.

SOCRATES: So if someone were to call memory the "preservation of perception," he would be speaking correctly, as far as I am concerned.

PROTARCHUS: Rightly so. [b]

SOCRATES: And do we not hold that recollection differs from memory?

PROTARCHUS: Perhaps.

SOCRATES: Does not their difference lie in this?

PROTARCHUS: In what?

SOCRATES: Do we not call it "recollection" when the soul recalls as much as possible by itself, without the aid of the body, what she had once experienced together with the body? Or how would you put it?

PROTARCHUS: I quite agree.

SOCRATES: But on the other hand, when, after the loss of memory of [c] either a perception or again a piece of knowledge, the soul calls up this memory for itself, we also call all these events "recollection."

PROTARCHUS: You are right.

SOCRATES: The point for the sake of which all this has been said is the following.

PROTARCHUS: What is it?

SOCRATES: That we grasp as fully and clearly as possible the pleasure that the soul experiences without the body, as well as the desire. And through a clarification of these states, the nature of both pleasure and desire will somehow be revealed.

PROTARCHUS: Let us now discuss this as our next issue, Socrates.

SOCRATES: It seems that in our investigation we have to discuss many points about the origin of pleasure and about all its different varieties. [d] For it looks as if we will first have to determine what desire is and on what occasion it arises.

PROTARCHUS: Let us determine that, then. We have nothing to lose.

SOCRATES: We will certainly lose something, Protarchus; by discovering what we are looking for now, we will lose our ignorance about it.

PROTARCHUS: You rightly remind us of that fact. But now let us try to return to the further pursuit of our subject.

SOCRATES: Are we agreed now that hunger and thirst and many other things of this sort are desires?

PROTARCHUS: Quite in agreement. [e]

SOCRATES: But what is the common feature whose recognition allows us to address all these phenomena, which differ so much, by the same name?

PROTARCHUS: Heavens, that is perhaps not an easy thing to determine, Socrates, but it must be done nevertheless.

SOCRATES: Shall we go back to the same point of departure?

PROTARCHUS: What point?

SOCRATES: When we say "he is thirsty," we always have something in mind?

PROTARCHUS: We do.

SOCRATES: Meaning that he is getting empty?

PROTARCHUS: Certainly.

SOCRATES: But thirst is a desire?

PROTARCHUS: Yes, the desire for drink.

SOCRATES: For drink or for the filling with drink?

PROTARCHUS: For the filling with drink, I think. [35a]

SOCRATES: Whoever among us is emptied, it seems, desires the opposite of what he suffers. Being emptied, he desires to be filled.

PROTARCHUS: That is perfectly obvious.

SOCRATES: But what about this problem? If someone is emptied for the first time, is there any way he could be in touch with filling, either through sensation or memory, since he has no experience of it, either in the present or ever in the past?

PROTARCHUS: How should he?

SOCRATES: But we do maintain that he who has a desire desires something?

PROTARCHUS: Naturally. [b]

SOCRATES: He does, then, not have a desire for what he in fact experiences. For he is thirsty, and this is a process of emptying. His desire is rather of filling.

PROTARCHUS: Yes.

SOCRATES: Something in the person who is thirsty must necessarily somehow be in contact with filling.

PROTARCHUS: Necessarily.

SOCRATES: But it is impossible that this should be the body, for the body is what is emptied out.

PROTARCHUS: Yes.

SOCRATES: The only option we are left with is that the soul makes contact with the filling, and it clearly must do so through memory. Or could it [c] make contact through anything else?

PROTARCHUS: Clearly through nothing else.

SOCRATES: Do we understand, then, what conclusions we have to draw from what has been said?

PROTARCHUS: What are they?

SOCRATES: Our argument forces us to conclude that desire is not a matter of the body.

PROTARCHUS: Why is that?

SOCRATES: Because it shows that every living creature always strives toward the opposite of its own experience.

PROTARCHUS: And very much so.

SOCRATES: This impulse, then, that drives it toward the opposite of its own state signifies that it has memory of that opposite state?

PROTARCHUS: Certainly.

SOCRATES: By pointing out that it is this memory that directs it toward the objects of its desires, [d] our argument has established that every impulse, and desire, and the rule over the whole animal is the domain of the soul.

PROTARCHUS: Very much so.

SOCRATES: Our argument will, then, never allow that it is our body that experiences thirst, hunger, or anything of that sort.

PROTARCHUS: Absolutely not. (Plato, *Philebus* 33c–35d)

4.8 Plato's Socrates compares the soul to a jar

SOCRATES: But then the life of those people you call happiest is a strange one, too. I shouldn't be surprised that Euripides' lines are true when he says: "But who knows whether being alive is being dead | And being dead is being alive?" [493a] Perhaps in reality we're dead. Once I even heard one of the wise men say that we are now dead and that our bodies are our tombs, and that the part of our souls in which our appetites reside is actually the sort of thing to be open to persuasion and to shift back and forth. And hence some clever man, a teller of stories, a Sicilian, perhaps, or an Italian, named this part a "jar" [*pithos*], on account of its being a persuadable [*pithanon*] and [b] suggestible thing, thus slightly changing the name. And fools [*anoêtoi*] he named "uninitiated" [*amuêtoi*], suggesting that that part of the souls of fools where their appetites are located is their undisciplined part, one not tightly closed, a leaking jar, as it were. He based the image on its insatiability. Now this man, Callicles, quite to the contrary of your view, shows that of the people in Hades—meaning the unseen [*a-ides*]—these, the uninitiated ones, would be the most miserable. They would carry water into the leaking jar using another leaky thing, a sieve. That's why by the "sieve" he means [c] the soul (as the man who talked with me claimed). And because they leak, he likened the souls of fools to sieves; for their untrustworthiness and forgetfulness makes them unable to retain anything. This account is on the whole a bit strange; but now that I've shown it to you, it does make clear what I want to persuade you to change your mind about if I can: to choose the orderly life, the life that is adequate to and satisfied with its circumstances at any given time instead of the insatiable, undisciplined [d] life. Do I persuade you at all, and are you changing your mind to believe that those who are orderly are happier than those who are undisciplined, or, even if I tell you many other such stories, will you change it none the more for that?

CALLICLES: The latter thing you said is the truer, Socrates.

SOCRATES: Come then, and let me give you another image, one from the same school as this one. Consider whether what you're saying about each life, the life of the self-controlled man and that of the undisciplined one, is like this: Suppose there are two men, each of whom has many jars. The jars belonging to one of them are sound and full, one with wine, another [e] with honey, a third with milk, and many others with lots of other things. And suppose that the sources of each of these things are scarce and difficult to come by, procurable only with much toil and trouble. Now the one man, having filled up his jars, doesn't pour anything more into them and gives them no further thought. He can relax over them. As for the other one, he too has resources that can be procured, though with difficulty, but his containers are leaky and rotten. He's forced to keep on filling them, [494a] day and night, or else he suffers extreme pain. Now since each life is the way I describe it, are you saying that the life of the undisciplined man is happier than that of the orderly man? When I say this, do I at all persuade you to concede that the orderly life is better than the undisciplined one, or do I not?

CALLICLES: You do not, Socrates. The man who has filled himself up has no pleasure any more, and when he's been filled up and experiences neither joy nor pain, that's living like a stone, as I was saying just now. Rather, [b] living pleasantly consists in this: having as much as possible flow in.

SOCRATES: Isn't it necessary, then, that if there's a lot flowing in, there should also be a lot going out and that there should be big holes for what's passed out?

CALLICLES: Certainly.

SOCRATES: Now you're talking about the life of a stone curlew instead of that of a corpse or a stone. Tell me, do you say that there is such a thing as hunger, and eating when one is hungry?

CALLICLES: Yes, there is.

SOCRATES: And thirst, and drinking when one is thirsty?

CALLICLES: Yes, and also having all other appetites and being able to fill them and enjoy it, and so live happily. [c]

SOCRATES: Very good, my good man! Do carry on the way you've begun, and take care not to be ashamed. And I evidently shouldn't shrink from being ashamed, either. Tell me now first whether a man who has an itch and scratches it and can scratch to his heart's content, scratch his whole life long, can also live happily.

CALLICLES: What nonsense, Socrates. You're a regular crowd-pleaser.

SOCRATES: That's just how I shocked Polus and Gorgias and made them be ashamed. [d] You certainly won't be shocked, however, or be ashamed, for you're a brave man. Just answer me, please.

CALLICLES: I say that even the man who scratches would have a pleasant life.

SOCRATES: And if a pleasant one, a happy one, too?

CALLICLES: Yes indeed.

SOCRATES: What if he scratches only his head—or what am I to ask you further? [e] See what you'll answer if somebody asked you one after the other every question that comes next. And isn't the climax of this sort of thing, the life of a catamite, a frightfully shameful and miserable one? Or will you have the nerve to say that they are happy as long as they have what they need to their hearts' content?

CALLICLES: Aren't you ashamed, Socrates, to bring our discussion to such matters? (Plato, *Gorgias* 492e–494e)

4.9 *Antisthenes interprets Homer, as evidence for the possibility of physiognomy?*

[On *Iliad* 23.66: *"It [the soul of Patroclus] had his stature and beautiful eyes"*:] On the basis of this line, Antisthenes says that souls have the appearance of the bodies that surround them. (From the scholia to Homer's *Iliad* = Antisthenes 193)

4.10 *Aristippus thinks cosmetics cannot prevent the true character of the soul showing*

A woman applies cosmetics to her face, but shows an unshapely soul. (Antonius Melissa, *Commonplaces* II, 34.43 = Aristippus 139)

4.11 *Phaedo thinks that self-control can hide natural predispositions*

At one gathering, Zopyrus, who claimed to be able to perceive someone's nature from their physical appearance, inferred that he [Socrates] had many vices. Everyone else, who could not see these vices in Socrates, laughed at him; but Socrates encouraged him by saying that those vices had been implanted in him, but that he had cast them out of himself by reason. (Cicero, *Tusculan Disputations* 4.80)[4]

4.12 *Aristippus implies that death is a threat to the soul as well as the body*

He [Aristippus] was once sailing to Corinth when he got caught in a storm and was upset. Someone said, "We laymen are not afraid, but you philosophers act like cowards." "That," he said, "is because of the different types of soul we are fighting for!" (Diogenes Laertius 2.71 = Aristippus 49)

---

4. Not in *SSR*, but the anecdote almost certainly comes from Phaedo's *Zopyrus*: see Rossetti (1980).

4.13 Xenophon's Socrates suggests that the soul is weakened by physical indulgence

If he ever decided to accept an invitation to dinner, what most people find extremely hard work—taking care not to consume to excess—he managed with total ease. To people who couldn't do this his advice was to watch out for anything that might persuade them to eat when they were not hungry or drink when they were not thirsty; that, he said, was the ruin of stomachs, heads, and souls. He joked that he thought this was how Circe made people into pigs—by giving them lots of things like this for dinner; Odysseus avoided turning into a pig by not overindulging in such things, thanks to a combination of advice from Hermes and his own self-control. That was the way he used to jest about these things, all the time being quite in earnest. (Xenophon, *Memorabilia* 1.3.6–8; followed by **6.16**)

4.14 Plato's Socrates on the influence of the soul on the body

"You have probably heard this about good doctors," I [Socrates] said, "that if you go to them with a pain in the eyes, they are likely to say that they cannot undertake to cure the eyes by themselves, but that it will be necessary to treat the head at the same time if things are also to go well with the eyes. And again it would be very [c] foolish to suppose that one could ever treat the head by itself without treating the whole body. In keeping with this principle, they plan a regime for the whole body with the idea of treating and curing the part along with the whole. Or haven't you noticed that this is what they say and what the situation is?"

"Yes, I have," he [Charmides] said.

"Then what I have said appears true, and you accept the principle?"

"Absolutely," he said.

And when I heard his approval, I took heart and, little by little, my [d] former confidence revived, and I began to wake up. So I said, "Well Charmides, it is just the same with this charm. I learned it while I was with the army, from one of the Thracian doctors of Zalmoxis, who are also said to make men immortal. And this Thracian said that the Greek doctors were right to say what I told you just now. 'But our king Zalmoxis,' he said, 'who is a god, says that just as one should not attempt to cure [e] the eyes apart from the head, nor the head apart from the body, so one should not attempt to cure the body apart from the soul. And this, he says, is the very reason why most diseases are beyond the Greek doctors, that they do not pay attention to the whole as they ought to do, since if the whole is not in good condition, it is impossible that the part should be. Because,' he said, 'the soul is the source both of bodily health and bodily disease for the whole man, and these flow from the soul in the same way that the eyes are affected by the head. So it is necessary first [157a] and foremost to cure the soul if the parts of the head and of the rest of the body are to be healthy. And the soul,' he said, 'my dear friend, is cured by means of certain charms, and these charms consist of beautiful words. It is a result of such words that temperance arises in the soul, and when the soul acquires and possesses temperance, it is easy to provide health both for the head and for the rest of the body.' So when he taught me the [b] remedy and the charms, he also said, 'Don't let anyone persuade you to treat his head with this remedy who does not first submit his soul to you for treatment with the charm. Because nowadays,' he said, 'this is the mistake some doctors make with their patients. They try to produce health of body apart from health of soul.' And he gave me very strict instructions [c] that I should be deaf to the entreaties of wealth, position, and personal beauty. So I (for I have given him my promise and must keep it) shall be obedient, and if you are willing, in accordance with the stranger's instructions, to submit your soul to be charmed with the Thracian's charms first, then I shall apply the remedy to your head. But if not, there is nothing we can do for you, my dear Charmides." (Plato, *Charmides* 156b–157c)

4.15 *Plato's **Phaedo*** has Socrates associate pleasure with the body rather than the soul

"Do we believe that there is such a thing as death?"

"Certainly," responded Simmias.

"Is it anything else than the separation of the soul from the body? Do we believe that death is this, namely, that the body comes to be separated by itself apart from the soul, and the soul comes to be separated by itself apart from the body? Is death anything else than that?"

"No, that is what it is," he said.

"Consider then, my good sir, whether you share my opinion, for this will [d] lead us to a better knowledge of what we are investigating. Do you think it is the part of a philosopher to be concerned with such so-called pleasures as those of food and drink?"

"By no means," said Simmias.

"What about the pleasures of sex?"

"Not at all."

"What of the other pleasures concerned with the service of the body? Do you think such a man prizes them greatly, the acquisition of distinguished clothes and shoes and the other bodily ornaments? Do you think he values these or despises them, except insofar as one cannot do without them?"

"I think the true philosopher despises them," said Simmias.

"Do you not think," asked Socrates, "that in general such a man's concern is not with the body but that, as far as he can, he turns away from the body toward the soul?"

"I do."

"So in the first place, such things show clearly that the [65a] philosopher more than other men frees the soul from association with the body as much as possible?"

"Apparently."

"And I imagine it does seem to the majority, Simmias, that a man who finds no pleasure in such things and has no part in them has nothing worth living for; and indeed that someone who doesn't care at all for the pleasures that owe their existence to the body comes pretty close to being dead already."

"What you say is certainly true."

"Then what about the actual acquiring of knowledge? Is the body an obstacle when one associates with it in the search for knowledge? I mean, [b] for example, do men find any truth in sight or hearing, or are not even the poets forever telling us that we do not see or hear anything accurately, and surely if those two physical senses are not clear or precise, our other senses can hardly be accurate, as they are all inferior to these? Do you not think so?"

"I certainly do," he said.

"When then," Socrates asked, "does the soul grasp the truth? For whenever it attempts to examine anything with the body, it is clearly deceived by it." [c]

"True."

"Is it not in reasoning if anywhere that any reality becomes clear to the soul?"

"Yes."

"And indeed the soul reasons best when none of these senses troubles it, neither hearing nor sight, nor pain nor pleasure, but when it is most by itself, taking leave of the body and as far as possible having no contact or association with it in its search for reality."

"That is so."

"And it is then that the soul of the philosopher most disdains the body, [d] flees from it and seeks to be by itself?"

"It appears so."

"What about the following, Simmias? Do we say that there is such a thing as the Just itself, or not?"

"We do say so, by Zeus."

"And the Beautiful, and the Good?"

"Of course."

"And have you ever seen any of these things with your eyes?"

"In no way," he said.

"Or have you ever grasped them with any of your bodily senses? I am speaking of all things such as Bigness, Health, Strength, and, in a word, the reality of all other things, that which each of them essentially is. Is what is most true in them contemplated through the body, or is this the [e] position: whoever of us prepares himself best and most accurately to grasp that thing itself which he is investigating will come closest to the knowledge of it?"

"Obviously."

"Then he will do this most perfectly who approaches the object with thought alone, without associating any sight with his thought, or dragging [66a] in any sense perception with his reasoning, but who, using pure thought alone, tries to track down each reality pure and by itself, freeing himself as far as possible from eyes and ears and, in a word, from the whole body, because the body confuses the soul and does not allow it to acquire truth and wisdom whenever it is associated with it. Will not that man reach reality, Simmias, if anyone does?"

"What you say," said Simmias, "is indeed true." (Plato, *Phaedo* 64c–66a)

4.16 Plato's Socrates considers what death might be like

"Let us reflect in this way, too, that there is good hope that death is a blessing, for it is one of two things: either the dead are nothing and have no perception of anything, or it is, as we are told, a change and a relocating for the soul from here to another place. If it is complete lack of perception, [d] like a dreamless sleep, then death would be a great advantage. For I think that if one had to pick out that night during which a man slept soundly and did not dream, put beside it the other nights and days of his life, and then see how many days and nights had been better and more pleasant than that night, not only a private person but the great king would find them easy to count compared with the other days and nights. If death is [e] like this I say it is an advantage, for all eternity would then seem to be no more than a single night. If, on the other hand, death is a change from here to another place, and what we are told is true and all who have died are there, what greater blessing could there be, gentlemen of the jury? If [41a] anyone arriving in Hades will have escaped from those who call themselves jurymen here, and will find those true jurymen who are said to sit in judgment there, Minos and Rhadamanthus and Aeacus and Triptolemus and the other demigods who have been upright in their own life, would that be a poor kind of change? Again, what would one of you give to keep company with Orpheus and Musaeus, Hesiod and Homer? I am willing to die many times if that is true. It would be a wonderful way for me to spend my time whenever I met Palamedes and Ajax, the son of Telamon, [b] and any other of the men of old who died through an unjust conviction, to compare my experience with theirs. I think it would be pleasant. Most important, I could spend my time testing and examining people there, as I do here, as to who among them is wise, and who thinks he is, but is not. What would one not give, gentlemen of the jury, for the opportunity to [c] examine the man who led the great expedition against Troy, or Odysseus, or Sisyphus, and innumerable other men and women one could mention? It would be an extraordinary happiness to talk with them, to keep company with them and examine them. In any case, they would certainly not put one to death for doing so. They are happier there than we are here in other respects, and for the rest of time they are deathless, if indeed what we are told is true." (Plato, *Apology* 40c–41c; **9.24** and **10.8** extend the passage)

4.17 *Socrates continues his work after death (in an anecdote probably taken from* **Antisthenes***)*

Someone called Cyrsas, from Chios, came with the intention of spending time with Socrates. As he slept by the grave, he [Socrates] appeared in a dream and talked with him. He [Cyrsas] at once sailed home, having had only this much profit from the philosopher. (*Suda*, "Socrates," σ. 829.60–63)[5]

4.18–22 **Antisthenes** *encourages us to appreciate life and the good things it has to offer*

[4.18] Dionysius[6] was complaining that he was mortal. Antisthenes said: "When the time comes, you'll complain that you are not dead." (*Vatican Sayings* 5 = Antisthenes 32)

---

5. For the argument that this comes from a work by Antisthenes, see Brancacci (2003).
6. The Syracusan tyrant: cf. ch. 7, p. 194.

[4.19] Diogenes once came to him [Antisthenes, who was ill] carrying a dagger. Antisthenes said: "Who can free me from my pains?" Showing him the dagger, Diogenes said, "This can." He answered: "I said my pains, not my life!" (Diogenes Laertius 6.18 = Antisthenes 37)

[4.20] He said that those who wished to be immortal ought to live piously and justly. (Diogenes Laertius 6.5 = Antisthenes 176)

[4.21] He was asked what the most blessed circumstance available to a human being was: "To die while doing well," he said. (Diogenes Laertius 6.5 = Antisthenes 177)

[4.22] He was once initiated into the Orphic mysteries, when the priest said that initiates partook in many good things in Hades. "So," he said, "why don't you die?" (Diogenes Laertius 6.4 = Antisthenes 178)

Chapter 5: Education

For the Greek world at large, virtue was understood to be a purely and essentially *social* condition: an excellent ("virtuous") human being just is a well-functioning member of society. This explains why it is that goods that civic life had to offer, such as wealth and influence, could be considered legitimate and genuine human goods—and it also explains traditional ideas about education. If virtue is a matter of good citizenship, then the way to instill it is simply by induction into the norms and conventions of society. The example set by other citizens, and the codes of behavior enshrined in the law were, then, understood to be among the most important elements of a child's moral education. For those who could afford it, these influences might be complemented by formal tuition oriented around the study and detailed assimilation of the canonical poets, especially Homer. Again, this had a purpose that was much more political and ethical than purely aesthetic. The poems of ancient Greece are rich in reflection on human life, and provide both role models and object lessons—in any case, ample occasion to reflect on how one ought to behave.

Given this background, the claim that virtue is not (in the first place at least) a matter of how one behaves, but of one's internal, psychological condition, could easily be taken to have radical implications. We have already seen that the Socratics tend to challenge conventional notions of what is really "good" (Ch. 2). Would they go further and seek to question the authority of the values on which civil society was based? Did their teaching amount to a subversive alternative to traditional education, fostering the kind of cynical egoism associated with the so-called sophists, rather than social conformity? Was there any difference between the Socratics and the sophists? Socrates himself was certainly thought of as one of the sophists. This is how he is presented in Aristophanes' *Clouds,* for example, and it probably underlies the accusation against him that he corrupted the youths who associated with him. It is striking that Plato represents *both* of his accusers, on different occasions, as insisting against him that the best educators are the laws of the state: Meletus at *Apology* 24d–26a; Anytus at *Meno* 93a.

All of this would seem to be relevant background to the desire we see in members of Socrates' circle to distance themselves from the sophists—not least in the surprisingly conservative views they express about how the young should be educated. Xenophon explicitly aligns the interests of (Socratic) philosophy with those of the Athenians at large, and contrasts its aims with those of the sophists. *Philosophy* cherishes the young, and hates the idea of their corruption by *sophists*—whom Xenophon represents as predators (**5.1**). A similar strategy can be traced in Plato: he too depicts the sophists as "hunters" (**5.2**), distances Socrates from them by having him deny that he teaches at all (**5.3**), and affirms deference to the laws as our first educators, in terms surprisingly similar to those used by Meletus in the *Apology* (see **5.4**).

In general, the Socratics were careful not to present themselves as teachers, or even to present their philosophy as a desirable part of a child's formal education. They do, of course, reflect on whether and how virtue, in their sense, can be taught (see e.g., **1.20**, **3.3–4**, **3.13**, **3.18**, **3.31**, **3.40**, **3.46**, **3.49–50**):[1] if it can, it will presumably be philosophy that teaches it. But they tend to avoid saying as much, preferring to represent philosophy as a mode of social intercourse that complements conventional education rather than challenging it. Philosophers are friends (see **5.1** again) or lovers (cf. **6.18–19**) rather than teachers; their influence on the young is achieved if and when their own wisdom makes them good role models (**5.5–6**; cf. Xenophon in **3.40**).[2] Aristippus once again is the exception: at least, he drew pupils to himself, and even, like the sophists, charged them a fee (**5.7**; Aristotle, like his pupil Phaenias here, pointedly calls him a sophist in **9.4**). But he had very traditional views on what a child needs from an education (**5.8–13**, **5.17–18**), which suggests that he might have separated his roles as philosopher and educator. We find endorsement of the traditional curriculum in other Socratics as well. Xenophon, for example, argues that children ought to be taught the practical skills they will need when, as grown-ups, they have households and cities to run: **5.16** (and cf. Aristippus, **5.18**); he develops his ideas on this score at length in two works that should be consulted in their entirety: *On Hunting* and the *Cyropaedia*.

In the *Laws,* the last work he wrote, Plato finally ventures the idea that philosophical texts might be appropriate substitutes for poetical ones (**5.21**); but for most of his output he thought that the study of literature should underpin the ideal educational curriculum (even if, in the *Republic,* he adds that one would ideally vet the literature available

---

1. A dialogue attributed to Crito is called *That Learning Does Not Make Men Good,* and another by Simon is called *On Virtue, That It Is Not Teachable* (see for both our Index of Socratics).

2. Compare and contrast Phaedo's image of the "bite" in **5.6** with various examples of Socrates "biting" and "stinging" in Plato: e.g., *Apology* 30e; *Symposium* 218a (part of **6.11**); *Meno* 80a–b.

to ensure that it pointed the reader in the right direction from the start). This curriculum is outlined at length in the *Republic,* especially 376c–412b, which should be read alongside the texts in this chapter. In that work, Plato goes on to suggest that the curriculum ought to be extended into theoretical topics as well, and ultimately even dialectic (521d–541b), i.e., philosophy. (The imperative for this extension is pithily captured by an observation in **5.20** that the ultimate level of reality in Plato's philosophy, and the source of moral value, cannot even in principle be captured by poetry.) This might already seem like a significant departure from his peers; but, quite apart from the utopian context in which he says it, the higher levels of the Platonic curriculum are directed at people who would be considered beyond the regular school age by anyone else, and might better be considered specialist training than education in any straightforward sense.

Finally, some texts in this chapter clearly show that members of the Socratic circle were themselves highly educated (in the conventional sense), and ready to use poetic allusion and criticism in their own discussions and in engagement with others. Plato's Socrates knows his Homer backward, and on one occasion more than holds his own in a discussion of a poem by Simonides (**5.26**); the scholia (ancient commentaries) on Homer preserve a number of examples of Homeric exegesis by Antisthenes (**5.28–31**; further examples at **1.21, 3.15, 4.9**; cf. Xenophon's Socrates at **1.7(b)**), and the titles of many of Antisthenes' books show that he took Homer as the starting point for much of his work (although not, in his case, because he thought that Homer was infallible: **5.23**). The incident dramatized in his *Ajax* and *Odysseus* (Ch. 1, Appendix) is one we know from Pindar (*Nemean Ode* 8) and Sophocles (*Ajax*), not Homer; but his choice of language shows that he has Homer in mind as the poet "who understands virtue" (Antisthenes, *Odysseus* 14). **5.24** is a rare example of Antisthenes' engagement with another poet, Euripides, and an early example of "correction"—recasting what a poet ought to have said in cases where one comes to the conclusion that what they actually said could not be defended. (Aristippus does something similar in **7.37**.)

Texts

i. Philosophy on the Side of Conventional Education

5.1 Xenophon *contrasts the philosopher with the predatory "sophist"*
What I wonder at about the so-called sophists[3] is the way most of them claim that they lead them to excellence, when actually they lead them in the opposite direction. At any rate, I have not seen a single individual whose excellence can be laid at the door of the sophists of our generation, nor do they offer writings from which anyone should acquire it; instead they've written many things about fruitless subjects, [2] books that give the young empty pleasures but contain nothing by way of excellence. Anyone who vainly hopes they'll learn something from them finds them a waste of time, holds them back from learning what would be of use to them, and teaches them what's actually bad. [3] So to their large failings I attach larger blame; as for what they write, I blame them for combining a *recherché* expression with a complete absence of sentiments of the correct kind that might serve to educate younger people toward excellence. [4] I may be an amateur in these matters, but I know full well that the best thing is to be taught what is good from within one's own nature, and second best to be taught it by those who truly know something good, rather than by people that possess the arts of deception. [5] Well, perhaps the words I use are not formed as a sophist would form them, but neither is that my intention; what I mean to put down is a correct understanding of what the well-educated require for achieving excellence, since words will not educate anyone, but sentiments will, if they are of the right kind. [6] And there are plenty of other people besides me who criticize the present generation of sophists, not the philosophers, for professing a wisdom that consists in words rather than in thoughts.

I am well aware that one of their sort will probably claim that what is set out in a fine and orderly fashion is not finely written or ordered; it will be easy for them to come up with quick and misconceived criticisms. [7] But this is my purpose in writing: to get things right, and not make people into sophists but wise and good instead. I don't wish what I write to seem useful, I want it to *be* useful, so that it may stand unrefuted for all time. [8] The sophists, by contrast, talk in order to

---

3. "So-called" sophists, because a "sophist" (*sophistēs*) is a teacher of *sophia*, wisdom, which Xenophon claims that the individuals in question quite lack.

deceive, write with a view to their own profit, and are no help to anyone in anything: none of them is wise, or ever was—they are content, all of them, to be called "sophists," which to anyone in their right mind is a term of abuse. [9] So my advice is to be on one's guard against the pronouncements of the sophists, and not to disrespect the reasonings of philosophers; sophists hunt the rich and young, but philosophers are open to all and friends to all alike, and give neither more nor less respect to a man for what chance has bestowed upon him. (Xenophon, *On Hunting* 13.1–9)

5.2 *Plato on the same*

THEAETETUS: It's obvious. I think we've found the sophist. I think that's the name that would be suitable for him.

VISITOR: So according to our account now, Theaetetus, it seems that this [b] sort of expertise belongs to appropriation, taking possession, hunting, animal hunting, hunting on land, human hunting, hunting by persuasion, hunting privately, and money earning. It's the hunting of rich, prominent young men. And according to the way our account has turned out, it's what should be called "the expertise of the sophist." (Plato, *Sophist* 223a–b)

5.3 *Plato's Socrates distinguishes himself from the sophists*

"And if you have heard from anyone that I undertake to teach people and charge a fee for it, that is not true either. [e] Yet I think it a fine thing to be able to teach people as Gorgias of Leontini does, and Prodicus of Ceos, and Hippias of Elis. Each of these men can go to any city and persuade the young, who can keep company with [20a] anyone of their own fellow citizens they want without paying, to leave the company of these, to join with themselves, pay them a fee, and be grateful to them besides. Indeed, I learned that there is another wise man from Paros who is visiting us, for I met a man who has spent more money on Sophists than everybody else put together, Callias, the son of Hipponicus. So I asked him—he has two sons—'Callias,' I said, 'if your sons were colts or calves, we could find and engage a supervisor for them [b] who would make them excel in their proper qualities, some horse breeder or farmer. Now since they are men, whom do you have in mind to supervise them? Who is an expert in this kind of excellence, the human and social kind? I think you must have given thought to this since you have sons. Is there such a person,' I asked, 'or is there not?' 'Certainly there is,' he said. 'Who is he?' I asked, 'what is his name, where is he from? And what is his fee?' 'His name, Socrates, is Evenus, he comes from Paros, [c] and his fee is five minas.' I thought Evenus a happy man, if he really possesses this art, and teaches for so moderate a fee. Certainly I would pride and preen myself if I had this knowledge, but I do not have it, gentlemen." (Plato, *Apology* 19d–20c; follows **9.2(a)**)

5.4 *Plato's Socrates recognizes the laws' claims on the individual*

"'Reflect now, Socrates,' the laws might say, 'that if what we say is true, you are not treating us rightly by planning to do what you are planning. We have given you birth, nurtured you, educated you; we have given you and all other citizens a share of all the good things we [d] could. Even so, by giving every Athenian the opportunity, once arrived at voting age and having observed the affairs of the city and us the laws, we proclaim that if we do not please him, he can take his possessions and go wherever he pleases. Not one of us laws raises any obstacle or forbids him, if he is not satisfied with us or the city, if one of you wants to go and live in a colony or wants to go anywhere else, and keep his property. [e] We say, however, that whoever of you remains, when he sees how we conduct our trials and manage the city in other ways, has in fact come to an agreement with us to obey our instructions. We say that the one who disobeys does wrong in three ways, first because in us he disobeys his parents, also those who brought him up, and because, in spite of his agreement, he neither obeys us nor, if we do something wrong, does he [52a] try to persuade us to do better. Yet we only propose things, we do not issue savage commands to do whatever we order; we give two alternatives, either to persuade us or to do what we say. He does neither. We do say that you too, Socrates, are open to those charges if you do what you have in mind; you would be among, not the least, but the most guilty of the Athenians.'" (Plato, *Crito* 51c–52a)

5.5 *Euclides on the importance of role models*

From Euclides: "They learn the finest things who imitate the finest things." (Stobaeus, *Selections* 2.31.52 = Euclides 18)

5.6 *Philosophers do not need to teach to have a beneficial effect, according to* **Phaedo**

As Phaedo says: "There are tiny creatures whose bite we do not feel—such a subtle power they have, dangerous but unnoticed. A swelling signifies the bite, and no wound is visible even in the swelling itself. The same thing will happen to you in conversation with wise men: you will not notice how or when it benefits you, but you will notice that you have been benefited." (Seneca, *Letters* 94.41 = Phaedo 12)

5.7 ***Aristippus****, on the other hand, did teach*

Aristippus was born in Cyrene, but went to Athens drawn, so Aeschines says, by the fame of Socrates. He played the sophist, as Phanias of Eresus,[4] the Peripatetic, says: he was the first of the Socratics to charge fees and send money to his teacher. He once sent him 20 minae, but found them quickly back with him, Socrates having said that his *daimonion*[5] would not let him keep the money; he was disgusted with Aristippus for sending it. (Diogenes Laertius 2.65 = Aristippus 1)

5.8–10 ***Aristippus*** *on the humanizing effects of education*

[5.8] Asked how the educated differ from the uneducated, he [Aristippus] said: "As tamed from untamed horses." (Diogenes Laertius 2.69 = Aristippus 129)

[5.9] He said it was better to be a beggar than uneducated: the one lacks possessions, the other humanity. (Diogenes Laertius 2.70 = Aristippus 125)

[5.10] Asked by someone how his son would be any better with an education, he said: "If nothing else, when he is in the theatre he won't be one stone sitting on another." (Diogenes Laertius 2.72 = Aristippus 128)

5.11 *Consistently with these views,* ***Aristippus***
advocates one's seeking advice

Aristippus the Socratic . . . said that it was worse to need advice than to ask for it. (Plutarch fr. 42 Sandbach = Aristippus 126)[6]

---

4. More properly "Phaenias," a first-generation pupil of Aristotle.
5. See Ch. 10.
6. Plutarch is here commenting on Hesiod, *Works and Days* 293 ("The very best of men is he who works everything out for himself"), and it may be that Aristippus was speaking with the same line in mind.

5.12–13 *Aristippus* thinks that education involves hard work

[5.12] Someone swore that their son would become good and just. Aristippus said to him: "Swear that he becomes grammatical and musical too, and see if he turns out not to learn any of these things." (*Vatican Sayings* 33 = Aristippus 127)

[5.13] He said: "As our bodies grow by being fed, but get solid by being exercised, so the soul grows by practising, but gets better by enduring (*karterousa*)." (*Vatican Sayings* 34 = Aristippus 124 = **3.10**)

5.14 To this extent, he agrees with *Antisthenes* . . .

From Antisthenes: men who are going to become good must exercise their body by gymnastics, and their soul by education. (Stobaeus, *Selections* 2.31.68 = Antisthenes 163)

5.15 . . . and Socrates (as described by *Plato's Euclides*)

SOCRATES: And isn't it also true that bodily condition deteriorates with rest and idleness? While by exertion and motion it can be preserved for a long time?

THEAETETUS: Yes.

SOCRATES: And what about the condition of the soul? Isn't it by learning and study, which are motions, that the soul gains knowledge and is preserved [c] and becomes a better thing? Whereas in a state of rest, that is, when it will not study or learn, it not only fails to acquire knowledge but forgets what it has already learned?

THEAETETUS: That certainly is so.

SOCRATES: And so we may say that the one thing, that is, motion, is beneficial to both body and soul, while the other has the opposite effect?

THEAETETUS: Yes, that's what it looks like. (Plato, *Theaetetus* 153b–c)

ii. What Should a Child Be Taught?

5.16 *The Socrates of* **Xenophon** *advocates the learning of practical skills*

It is clear from what I have already said, I think, that Socrates candidly revealed his own views to the people who spent time with him. I shall now show that he also strove to make them independent in the activities to which they were suited. Out of everyone I have known, he was the most concerned to know the relevant expertise of each of his companions. He was also the most enthusiastic about teaching whatever he knew of the things that someone truly noble should know; for subjects with which he was personally less familiar, he referred them to experts.

[2] He also taught to what extent a properly educated person should familiarize himself with any given subject. For example, he maintained that one should study geometry until he was able, should the need ever arise, to measure land properly for the purpose of receiving, conveying, or dividing it up, or to check the work. And he said that this level of knowledge was so easily attained that anyone who put his mind to the calculation would at once know the size of the land and would leave with an understanding of how the calculation was made. [3] He opposed studying geometry up through the more complicated figures, on the grounds that he did not see how they were useful. Not that he was unfamiliar with them, but he said that they were enough to consume a person's life to the exclusion of many other, beneficial subjects of study.

[4] He encouraged them to familiarize themselves with astronomy as well, but only to the point of being able to determine the times of the night, month, or year; and, by distinguishing their respective phases, to have signs to use for a trip by land or sea, or for guard duty, or for all the other things taking place over the course of a night, month, or year. He said that this knowledge is also easily acquired from nighttime hunters, ship pilots, and many others who make it their business to know these things. [5] But he strongly discouraged studying astronomy to the point of acquiring knowledge of the objects that move in different orbits, such as planets and comets, and becoming consumed with investigating their distance from the earth, their trajectories, and the respective causes of these. Not that he was unversed in these studies either, but he said that they were also enough to consume a person's life to the exclusion of many beneficial subjects of study. [6] In general, he discouraged thinking too deeply about how god contrives each of the celestial phenomena, since he did not believe that these facts were discoverable

by human beings, and he thought that anyone who investigated things the gods chose not to reveal would not ingratiate himself to them. He claimed that whoever occupied himself with these matters would risk going as crazy as Anaxagoras, who took great pride in his exposition of the gods' workings. [7] In identifying the sun with fire, that man ignored the fact that people can readily gaze at a fire but are not able to stare into the sun; and that people exposed to sunshine have darker skin, but not those exposed to firelight. He also ignored the fact that no vegetation can experience healthy growth without sunlight, but that all plants wilt when heated by fire. And in claiming that the sun is a red-hot stone, he also ignored the fact that a stone placed in a fire neither glows nor lasts very long, whereas the sun outshines everything forever.

[8] He also encouraged the study of arithmetic. Here too, as in the other cases, he recommended guarding against idle treatments, and he himself assisted his companions in all their contemplations and investigations only to the extent that they were useful.

[9] He strongly encouraged his companions to take care of their health. He urged them to learn all they could from experts, and for each of them to be mindful throughout his life of what kinds of foods, drinks, and exercise suited him best and of how to make the proper use of them in order to live in the healthiest way possible. Anyone who did so, he claimed, would have as good a sense of what was conducive to his own health as any doctor.

[10] If anyone wanted help beyond what human wisdom could provide, he advised him to pursue divination, since, he said, someone expert in the means by which the gods convey signs about events to human beings would never lack divine counsel. (Xenophon, *Memorabilia* 4.7.1–10)

5.17–18 *Aristippus sees no point to the purely theoretical subjects*

[5.17] Aristippus was asked what beautiful boys needed to learn, and said: "Whatever they will use when they are men." (Diogenes Laertius 2.80 = Aristippus 121)

[5.18] Someone was priding himself for his wide learning, and Aristippus said: "Just as people who eat the most are not healthier than those who eat what they should, so the wise are not those who have learned a lot, but what is useful." (Diogenes Laertius 2.71 = Aristippus 122)

5.19 Antisthenes *thinks that book-learning can be distracting rather than helpful*

Antisthenes used to say that those who had become wise [*sôphronas*] had better not learn books, so as not to be diverted by matters alien to them. (Diogenes Laertius 6.103 = Antisthenes 161)

5.20 Plato*'s Socrates on the educative journey of the soul, imagined as a charioteer driving one bad and one good horse toward a region uncelebrated by mere earthly poets*

"The heaviness of the bad horse drags its charioteer toward the earth and weighs him down if he has failed to train it well, and this causes the most extreme toil and struggle that a soul will face. But when the souls we call immortals reach the top, they move outward and take their stand on the high ridge of heaven, where its circular motion carries [c] them around as they stand while they gaze upon what is outside heaven. The place beyond heaven—none of our earthly poets has ever sung or ever will sing its praises enough!" (Plato, *Phaedrus* 247b–c)

5.21 Plato*'s Athenian advocates his own political philosophy as an alternative to the study of poetry*

ATHENIAN: Best foot forward, then. Now, what I say is this. We have a great many poets who compose in hexameters and trimeters and all the standard meters; some of these authors try to be serious, while others aim at a comic effect. Over and over again it's claimed that in order to educate young people properly we have to cram their heads full of this stuff; we [811a] have to organize recitations of it so that they never stop listening to it and acquire a vast repertoire, getting whole poets off by heart. Another school of thought excerpts the outstanding work of all the poets and compiles a treasury of complete passages, claiming that if the wide knowledge of a fully informed person is to produce a sound and sensible citizen, these extracts must be committed to memory and learned by rote. I suppose you're now pressing me to be quite frank and show these people where they are right and where they've gone wrong?

CLINIAS: Of course.

ATHENIAN: Well then, in a nutshell, [b] what sort of estimate will do them all justice? I imagine everybody would agree if I put it rather like this. Each of these authors has produced a lot of fine work, and a lot of rubbish too—but if that's so, I maintain that learning so much of it puts the young at risk.

CLINIAS: So what recommendation would you give the Guardian of the Laws?

ATHENIAN: What about?

CLINIAS: The model work that will enable him to decide what material [c] all the children may learn, and what not. Tell us, without any hesitation.

ATHENIAN: My dear Clinias, I suspect I've had a bit of luck.

CLINIAS: How's that?

ATHENIAN: Because I haven't got far to look for a model. You see, when I look back now over this discussion of ours, which has lasted from dawn up till this very moment—a discussion in which I think I sense the inspiration of heaven—well, it's come to look, to my eyes, just like a literary composition. Perhaps not surprisingly, I was overcome by a feeling of [d] immense satisfaction at the sight of my collected works, so to speak, because, of all the addresses I have ever learned or listened to, whether in verse or in this kind of free prose style I've been using, it's *these* that have impressed me as being the most eminently acceptable and the most entirely appropriate for the ears of the younger generation. So I could hardly commend a better model than this to the Guardian of the Laws in charge of education. Here's what he must tell the teachers to teach the children, and if he comes across similar and related material while working [e] through prose writings, or the verse of poets, or when listening to unwritten compositions in simple prose that show a family resemblance to our discussion today, he must on no account let them slip through his fingers, but have them committed to writing. His first job will be to compel the teachers to learn this material and speak well of it, and he must not employ as his assistants any teachers who disapprove of it; he should employ only those who endorse his own high opinion, and entrust them with the teaching [812a] and education of the children. That, then, is my doctrine on literature and its teachers, so let me finish there.

CLINIAS: Well, sir, as far as I can judge from our original program, we've not strayed off the subjects we set out to discuss. But is our general policy the right one, or not? I suspect it would be difficult to say for sure.

ATHENIAN: That, Clinias, as we have often remarked, is something which will probably become clearer of its own accord when we've completely finished expounding our laws. (Plato, *Laws* VII, 810e–812a)

iii. Examples of Poetical Exegesis

5.22 ***Xenophon's*** *Socrates (in conversation with Niceratus and* ***Antisthenes****): it is one thing to know a poem, another to know its meaning*

"Well, you next, Niceratus," he [Socrates] said: "tell us what skill you pride yourself on."

And he said, "My father was concerned about my how I might become a good man, and he made me learn all of Homer. Even now, I can recite the whole of the *Iliad* and *Odyssey* by heart."

[6] "Haven't you noticed that all rhapsodes know these epics?" said Antisthenes.

"How could I not have noticed," replied Niceratus, "when I hear them almost every day?"

"So do you know any more naïve kind of person than a rhapsode?" asked Antisthenes.

"No, by Zeus," said Niceratus, "I really don't think I do."

"That," said Socrates, "is clearly because they don't know the underlying meaning. But you have given a lot of money to Stesimbrotus and Anaximander and many others so that none of the valuable things they know escapes you." (Xenophon, *Symposium* 3.5–6 = Antisthenes 185)[7]

5.23 ***Antisthenes*** *on saving Homer from contradiction*

Zeno[8] found nothing to criticize in Homer but interpreted and taught him according to the principle that he had written some things according to his own opinion, some according to the truth, so that he could be seen to be free of self-contradiction even where he seemed to say contradictory things. This theory, that the poet sometimes articulated his opinion, sometimes the truth, was held before him by Antisthenes;

---

7. Cf. Euthyphro's literalistic view of the poets' depiction of the gods (**9.10**). "Underlying meaning" here translates *huponoiai*, for which cf. also Plato, *Republic* II, 378d.
8. Of Citium (not to be confused with Zeno of Elea, pupil of Parmenides: **1.13**): third-century BCE founder of Stoicism.

but Zeno showed how it worked in detail. (Dio, *Orations* 53(36).4–5 = Antisthenes 194)

5.24 Antisthenes *"improves"* Euripides

So the "improvements" of Cleanthes and Antisthenes are not bad. Antisthenes, when he saw the Athenians in the theatre stirring at the line "What is disgraceful, except it seem to those involved?"[9] at once offered the alternative: "Disgraceful is disgraceful if so it seem or not." (Plutarch, *How the Young Should Listen to Poetry* 33C = Antisthenes 195)

5.25 Xenophon's Antisthenes *mocks a naïve view of Homer*

Then Niceratus said, "Listen how you will be improved if you spend time with me. Well, you know that Homer in his enormous wisdom has written about pretty well all human affairs? So, anyone among you who wishes to learn how to manage a household or a city or an army— or to be like Achilles or Ajax, or Nestor, or Odysseus—should cultivate me: I know all of this."

"Even how to be a king?" said Antisthenes. "Because of course you know that Homer praises Agamemnon as 'a good king and a strong spearsman.'"

"Indeed, yes!" he said. (Xenophon, *Symposium* 4.6 = Antisthenes 186; follows **3.34**)

5.26 *An interpretation of Simonides by* **Plato's** *Socrates*

"All right, then," I [Socrates] said, "I will try to explain to you what I think this poem is about. Philosophy, first of all, has its most ancient roots and is most widespread among the Greeks in Crete and Lacedaemon, and those [b] regions have the highest concentration of sophists in the world. But the natives deny it and pretend to be ignorant in order to conceal the fact that it is by their wisdom that they are the leaders of the Greek world, something like those sophists Protagoras was talking about. Their public image is that they owe their superiority to their brave fighting men, and their reason for promoting this image is that if the real basis for their superiority were discovered, i.e., wisdom, everyone else would start cultivating it. This is top secret; not even the Spartanizing cults in the other cities know about [c] it, and so you have all these people getting their ears mangled aping the Spartans,

---

9. Euripides fr. 19 *TrGF*, from his lost play *Aeolus*.

lacing on leather gloves, exercising fanatically and wearing short capes, as if Sparta's political power depended on these things. And when the citizens in Sparta want some privacy to have free and open discussions with their sophists, they pass alien acts against any Spartanizers and other foreigners in town, and conceal their meetings from the rest of the world. [d] And so that their young men won't unlearn what they are taught, they do not permit any of them to travel to other cities (the Cretans don't either). Crete and Sparta are places where there are not only men but women also who take pride in their education. You know how to test the truth of my contention that the Spartans have the best education in philosophy and [e] debate? Pick any ordinary Spartan and talk with him for a while. At first you will find he can barely hold up his end of the conversation, but at some point he will pick his spot with deadly skill and shoot back a terse remark you'll never forget, something that will make the person he's talking with (in this case, you) look like a child. Acute observers have known this for a long time now: To be a Spartan is to be a philosopher [343a] much more than to be an athlete. They know that to be able to say something like that is the mark of a perfectly educated man. We're talking about men like Thales of Miletus, Pittacus of Mytilene, Bias of Priene, our own Solon, Cleobulus of Lindus, Myson of Chen, and, the seventh in the list, Chilon of Sparta. All of these emulated, loved, and studied Spartan culture. You [b] can see that distinctive kind of Spartan wisdom in their pithy, memorable sayings, which they jointly dedicated as the first fruits of their wisdom to Apollo in his temple at Delphi, inscribing there the maxims now on everyone's lips: 'Know thyself' and 'Nothing in excess.' What is my point? That the characteristic style of ancient philosophy was laconic brevity. [c] It was in this context that the saying of Pittacus—'It is hard to be good'—was privately circulated with approval among the sages. Then Simonides, ambitious for philosophical fame, saw that if he could score a takedown against this saying, as if it were a famous wrestler, and get the better of it, he would himself become famous in his own lifetime. So he composed this poem as a deliberate attack against this maxim. That's how it seems to me. Let's test my hypothesis together, to see whether what I say is true. If [d] all the poet wanted to say was that it is hard to become good, then the beginning of the poem would be crazy, for he inserted there an antithetical particle. It doesn't make any sense to insert this unless one supposes that Simonides is addressing the Pittacus maxim as an opponent. Pittacus says it is hard to be good; Simonides rebuts this by saying, 'No, but it is hard for a man to become good, Pittacus, truly.' Notice that he does not say [e] 'truly good'; he is not talking about truth in the context of some things being truly good and other things being good but not truly so. This would create an impression of naiveté very unlike Simonides. The position of 'truly' in the verse must be a case of hyperbaton. We have to approach this maxim of Pittacus by imagining him speaking and Simonides replying, something like this: Pittacus: 'Gentlemen, it is hard to be good.' Simonides: [344a] 'What you say is not true, Pittacus, for it is not being but becoming good, in hands and feet and mind foursquare, blamelessly built—that is hard truly.' This way the insertion of the antithetical particle makes sense, and the 'truly' feels correct in its position at the end. Everything that comes after is evidence for this interpretation. The poem is full of details that testify to its excellent composition; indeed, it is a lovely and exquisitely [b] crafted piece, but it would take a long time to go through it from that point of view. Let's review instead the overall structure and intention of the ode, which is from beginning to end a refutation of Pittacus' maxim. A few lines later he states (imagine he is making a speech): 'To become good truly is hard, and although it may be possible for a short period of [c] time, to persist in that state and to be a good man, as you put it, Pittacus, is not humanly possible. God alone can have this privilege. *But that man inevitably is bad whom incapacitating misfortune throws down.* Whom does incapacitating misfortune throw down when it comes to, say, the command of a ship? Clearly not the ordinary passenger, who is always susceptible. You can't knock down someone already supine; you can only knock down someone standing up and render him supine. In the [d] same way, incapacitating misfortune would overthrow only someone who is capable, not the chronically incapable. A hurricane striking a pilot would incapacitate him, a bad season will do it to a farmer, and the same thing applies to a doctor. For the good is susceptible to becoming bad, as another poet testifies: "The good man is at times bad, at times good." But the bad is not susceptible to becoming bad; it must always be bad. So that when incapacitating misfortune throws down a man who is capable, [e] wise, and good, he must "inevitably be bad." You say, Pittacus, that it is hard to be good; in fact, to become good is hard, though possible, but to be good is impossible. *Faring well, every man is good;*

'*Bad, faring ill.* What does it mean to fare well in letters; what makes a man good at [345a] them? Clearly, the learning of letters. What kind of faring well makes a good doctor? Clearly, learning how to cure the sick. "Bad, faring ill": who could become a bad doctor? Clearly, someone who is, first, a doctor and, second, a good doctor. He could in fact become a bad doctor, but we who are medical laymen could never by faring ill become doctors or carpenters [b] or any other kind of professional. And if one cannot become a doctor by faring ill, clearly one cannot become a bad one either. In the same way a good man may eventually become bad with the passage of time, or through hardship, disease, or some other circumstance that involves the only real kind of faring ill, which is the loss of knowledge. But the bad man can never become bad, for he is so all the time. If he is to become bad, he must [c] first become good. So the tenor of this part of the poem is that it is impossible to be a good man and continue to be good, but possible for one and the same person to become good and also bad, and those are best for the longest time whom the gods love.' All this is directed at Pittacus, as the next few lines of the poem make even clearer: *'Therefore never shall I seek for the impossible, cast away my life's lot on empty hope, a quixotic quest for a blameless man among those who reap the broad earth's fruit,* [d] *but if I find him you will have my report.'* This is strong language, and he keeps up his attack on Pittacus' maxim throughout the poem: *'All who do no wrong willingly I praise and love. Necessity not even the gods resist.'* This is spoken to the same end. For Simonides was not so uneducated as [e] to say that he praised all who did nothing bad willingly, as if there were anyone who willingly did bad things. I am pretty sure that none of the wise men thinks that any human being willingly makes a mistake or willingly does anything wrong or bad. They know very well that anyone who does anything wrong or bad does so involuntarily. So also Simonides, [346a] who does not say that he praises those who willingly do nothing bad; rather he applies the term 'willingly' to himself. He perceived that a good man, an honorable man, often forces himself to love and praise someone utterly different from himself, one's alienated father perhaps, or mother, or country. Scoundrels in a similar situation are almost happy to see their parents' or country's trouble and viciously point it out and denounce it [b] so that their own dereliction of duty toward them will not be called into question. They actually exaggerate their complaints and add gratuitous to unavoidable hostility, whereas good men conceal the trouble and force themselves to give praise, and if they are angry because their parents or country wronged them, they calm themselves down and reconcile themselves to it, and they force themselves to love and praise their own people. I think that Simonides reflected that on more than one occasion he himself had eulogized some tyrant or other such person, not willingly but because [c] he had to. So he is saying to Pittacus: 'Pittacus, it is not because I am an overcritical person that I am criticizing you, since, *enough for me a man who is not bad nor too intractable, who knows civic Right, a sound man. I shall not blame him, for I am not fond of blame. Infinite the tribe of fools,'* the implication being that a censorious person would have his hands full blaming them. *'All is fair in which foul is not mixed.'* The sense here is not that all is white in which black is not mixed, which [d] would be ludicrous in many ways, but rather that he himself accepts without any objection what is in between. 'I do not seek,' he says, *'for a blameless man among those who reap the broad earth's fruit, but if I find him you will have my report.'* The meaning is that 'on those terms I will never praise anyone, but I am happy with an average man who does no wrong, since I willingly *praise and love all'*—note the Lesbian dialect form of the verb 'praise,' since he is addressing [e] Pittacus—*'all who do no wrong'* (this is where the pause should be, before 'willingly') *'willingly I praise and love,* but there are some whom I praise and love unwillingly. So if you spoke something even moderately reasonable and true, Pittacus, I would never [347a] censure you. But the fact is that you have lied blatantly yet with verisimilitude about extremely important issues, and for that I do censure you.' And that, Prodicus and Protagoras," I concluded, "is what I think was going through Simonides' mind when he composed this ode." [b] Then Hippias said, "I am favorably impressed by your analysis." (Plato, *Protagoras* 342a–347b)

5.27 **Xenophon** *on an accusation brought against Socrates' interpretation of Hesiod*

His accuser claimed that Socrates singled out the most disgraceful lines from the most respected poets and used them as support in teaching his companions to be miscreants and tyrants. In reference to Hesiod's line "Work is no disgrace; idleness is the disgrace,"[10] Socrates is alleged to have said that the poet enjoins people not to shun any work, however unjust or shameful, but to do anything for gain. [57] While Socrates agreed that being a worker is both advantageous and good for a person, whereas being an idler is harmful and bad—or, in other words, that work is good and idleness bad—he maintained that only those people who were accomplishing some good were actually engaged in work and being good workers, whereas those playing dice or taking part in any other disgraceful and harmful activity he labeled idlers. Understood in this way, "Work is no disgrace; idleness is the disgrace" would be accurate.

---

10. Hesiod, *Works and Days* 311.

[58] His accuser claimed that Socrates often cited the passage from Homer that says of Odysseus:

> Whenever he encountered a chieftain or the like,
> He tried to restrain him with gentle words:
> "What's gotten into you? I don't mean to frighten you
> As if you were a coward, but sit down here yourself
> And make your men sit down."
> . . .
> But if he caught any of the ordinary soldiers yelling,
> He would belt him with the staff and bawl him out:
> "You there, who do you think you are? Sit still
> And listen to your betters. You're a weakling,
> Unfit for combat, a nothing in battle and in council."[11]

He allegedly interpreted these lines to mean that the poet approved of beating ordinary citizens of modest means. [59] But that is not what Socrates had in mind. On that view, he would have had to think that he needed to be beaten himself. Instead, he claimed that people who contributed nothing useful in word or deed, and who in time of need were incapable of offering assistance to the army, the state, or the citizenry itself, should be kept in check by every possible means, especially if they were also reckless, and even if they happened to be very rich. (Xenophon, *Memorabilia* 1.2.56–59)

5.28 *Antisthenes on the* Iliad

[on *Iliad* 11.636: "*The old man Nestor lifted it without trouble*":] Why does he [Homer] say that Nestor alone lifted the drink? Antisthenes: He is not speaking about its weight in the hand, but signifying that he was not drunk: he took the wine easily. (Porphyry, *Questions on Homer's Iliad* 168.15–16 Schrader = Antisthenes 191)

5.29–31 *Antisthenes on the* Odyssey

[5.29] [on *Odyssey* 7.257: "*She said she would make me immortal and ageless forever*":] Antisthenes says that lovers necessarily lie in their promises: for she could not do this without Zeus. (Porphyry, *Questions on Homer's Odyssey* 69, n. 2 Schrader = Antisthenes 188)

---

11. Homer, *Iliad* 2.188–203, omitting 192–98. The translation is from S. Lombardo, *Homer: Iliad* (Indianapolis: Hackett Publishing Co., 1997).

[5.30] [on *Odyssey* 9.106: *"To the land of the lawless, overbearing Cyclopes"*:] How can he call the Cyclopes overbearing and lawless and villainous if he says that they have all good things unstintingly from the gods? One should say that they are overbearing because of the excessive size of their body, and lawless in the sense of not having a written law, since each is in charge of his own affairs ("each lays down the law | for his wife and children"[12])—one mark of lawlessness. Antisthenes says that only Polyphemus is unjust, for he genuinely has no concern for Zeus. The rest, then, are just—this is why, he says, the earth gives them all things spontaneously; and not working the earth is the work of the just. (Porphyry, *Questions on Homer's Odyssey* 86.14–87.6 Schrader = Antisthenes 189)

[5.31] [on *Odyssey* 9.525: *"Not even Poseidon will cure your eye"*:] Why does Odysseus so stupidly belittle Poseidon, saying, "Not even Poseidon will cure your eye"? Antisthenes says that it is because he knows that it is not Poseidon who is the physician but Apollo. (Porphyry, *Questions on Homer's Odyssey* 94.26–95.3 Schrader = Antisthenes 190)

---

12. Homer, *Odyssey* 9.114–15.

Chapter 6: The Erotic Sciences

We have seen that pleasure and its control are at the center of the Socratics' thinking about virtue (especially Ch. 3), so it is perhaps no wonder that they had a lot to say in particular about the "greatest and maddest" of the pleasures (**6.17**): sex. It might not be too much of a stretch to say that the expertise in erotics ascribed to Socrates (**6.1–2**) is intended partly as a way of qualifying the disavowal of ethical knowledge typically associated with him. To know something about erotics is to know something about the control of pleasure; and that, as we have seen, will be to know something about virtue after all.

The metaphors of "ruling" and "enslavement," familiar from the discussion of virtue and pleasure, are in evidence once again to describe the power of erotic attraction (**6.12–16**).

> Relevant here is the biographical tradition concerning Phaedo of Elis: "It happened that he was first captured and made a prisoner of war by Indians, then sold to a pimp, and prostituted by him in Athens. Meeting Socrates holding forth, he fell in love with his arguments and begged him to free him. Socrates persuaded Alcibiades to buy him, and from that point on he was a philosopher" (from the *Suda* entry "Phaedo" [φ.154] = Phaedo 1). There is some question about the historicity of the story (see McQueen and Rowe 1989); but its symbolic potential is obvious.

Love is also, especially in Plato, a form of madness (**6.16–18**): submission to erotic desire is the exact antithesis to the restraint that accompanies sound understanding in the dominant theory of virtue illustrated in Chapter 3.

The way to deal with erotic attraction, then (allowing, as no Socratic seems to have denied, that sexual desire is ineliminable, like the desire for food and drink: **6.16**.[15], **6.25(a)**), is through some form of rational control. This might involve willfully redirecting the impulse toward a genuinely *loving* relationship, one which starts with a person's soul not their body: cf. Antisthenes on the ideal relationship in **6.20**; also **4.5–6** for Xenophon and Plato. At the other extreme, one can ensure that the sex one has is made as cheap and meaningless as possible: Antisthenes seems to have recommended this approach to the non-sage (**6.21–23**, cf. also **3.2**.[38]). As Aristippus taught, the great thing was to avoid its taking over your life (**6.13**, **6.24**; cf. discussion in Ch. 3). Plato was less optimistic that this was possible: explicit discussion of the control of sexual desire, which is to be found mainly in the course of his construction of the good society, treats unregulated sex as an unqualifiedly bad thing (**6.25**).

But in parallel with this line of thought, many of our texts also recast or reapply the conventional language of erotic attraction to describe the activity of philosophy and philosophers. Philosophers are drawn to young men on whom they wish to heap gifts . . . of improvement (**6.19(c)**, **6.27**); in a further inversion of Greek erotic conventions, young men might be enflamed by the philosopher and desire to enjoy the beauty . . . of their wisdom (**6.7–8**, **6.11**). In this metaphorical sense, Socrates' expertise in erotics involves encouraging love, not overcoming it: he becomes an expert in "potions, charms and magic wheels"—wheels that will bring one's lover back (**6.3**); he prides himself on his skill as a procurer (**6.4**; cf. **6.7**); he is matchmaker and midwife (**6.5**). He is also a lover on his own account, albeit of a special kind—one who is simultaneously lover and beloved (**6.6–11**).

There is evident scope here for post-Freudians to talk of sublimation, insofar as the idea is that the erotic impulse can be rechanneled; but it is worth remembering too that the subversion of the discourse around conventional goods is something of a Socratic speciality—comparable to Antisthenes' denying that (conventional) wealth is a human good and at the same time asserting that he derives (real) "wealth" from his healthy psychological state (**3.2**). One thing that does seem to distinguish the case of sex, however, is that we find positive redescriptions not only of the desire itself, but also of the madness associated with it (**6.18**). Erotic intercourse turns out to be a model for philosophical intercourse not only for the obvious structural reasons, but also because the word *sunousia* ("intercourse"; literally: "being together") can be used concerning both. It is also a model for philosophical intercourse because philosophy, especially as personified by Socrates, inspires a mental revolution: a madness (as the world at large might see it) which is really the way to wisdom.

> The relationship between Socrates and Alcibiades (especially **6.9–10**) might be considered in this light: a paradigm philosopher pursuing a paradigm beauty,[1] with the aim, as we shall see in the next chapter, of bringing him to his senses.

---

1. "If Achilles was not like him, then Achilles was not beautiful," said Antisthenes (Olympiodorus, *On Plato's* Alcibiades 28.21–22 Westerink = Antisthenes 199; cf. Athenaeus, *The Learned Banqueters* 12, 534C = Antisthenes 198).

Philosophy, then, becomes the new sex, the highest form or expression of *erôs*. This is a theme which is developed at length by Plato's Socrates both in the *Symposium*—reporting what the priestess Diotima says about the "higher mysteries" of love: 210a–212b (including **4.6**)—and in the *Phaedrus*, in his great speech at the center of the dialogue (244a–257b). These passages, and the dialogues in which they come, deserve to be read in full alongside this chapter; so does the *Lysis*, a dialogue which is officially concerned with the subject of friendship (*philia*), rather than erotic love (*erôs*), but which in fact starts and ends by being about the latter—and is generally little concerned with maintaining the boundary between them.

Texts

i. Socrates as an Expert in Erotics and Associated Arts

6.1(a) *Erôs is one—the only—thing* **Plato's** *Socrates understands . . .*

"The only thing I say I understand is the art of love," [said Socrates]. (Plato, *Symposium* 177e)[2]

6.1(b) *. . . having learned it (he says) from a wise woman, a seer*

"I shall try to go through for you the speech about Love I once heard from a woman of Mantinea, Diotima—a woman who was wise about many things besides this: once she even put off the plague for ten years by telling the Athenians what sacrifices to make. She is the one who taught me the art of love, and I shall go through her speech as best I can on my own." (Plato, *Symposium* 201d)[3]

6.2(a) **Plato's** *Socrates (in conversation with Hippothales at a wrestling school) can recognize a lover . . .*

"Who is the teacher here?" [I (Socrates) asked.]
"Your old friend and admirer, Mikkos," replied [Hippothales].

---

2. Cf. *Phaedrus* 257a; similarly in the pseudo-Platonic *Theages* 127e–128b.
3. Socrates' description of Diotima's account which follows makes Love, or *erôs*, the cause of all productive and creative—and philosophical—activity.

"Well, god knows," I said, "he's a serious person and a competent instructor."

"Well, then," he responded, "won't you please come in and see who's here?"

"First I'd like to hear what I'm coming in for—and the name of the best-looking person here." [b]

"Each of us has a different opinion on who that is, Socrates," he said.

"So tell me, Hippothales, who do you think it is?"

He blushed at the question, so I said, "Aha! You don't have to answer that, Hippothales, for me to tell whether you're in love with any of these boys or not—I can see that you are not only in love but pretty far gone too. I may not be much good at anything else, but I have this god-given ability to recognize [c] quickly a lover and an object of love." (Plato, *Lysis* 204a–c)

6.2(b) . . . *and advise him on how he should address his beloved*

"What different advice can you give me about what one should say or do so his prospective boyfriend will like him?" [asked Hippothales].

"That's not easy to say. But if you're willing to have him talk with me, I might be able to give you a demonstration of how to carry on a conversation with him instead of talking and singing the way your friends here say you've been doing." (Plato, *Lysis* 206c)[4]

6.3 *Xenophon's* Socrates has magical charms to attract people to him . . .

There was once a beautiful woman in the city called Theodote, the sort who would go with anyone who could persuade her. One of those present mentioned her, saying that her beauty was inexpressible in words, and adding that painters went to her to paint her. He said she would show just as much of herself as was proper. "So we'd better go and take a look at her," said Socrates; "what can't be expressed in words can't be grasped by hearsay."

[2] "So come with me now," said Socrates' informant, and they went off to Theodote's, where they found her posed for a painter. When the painter came to a pause, Socrates asked, "Which of us should be grateful—ourselves to Theodote, for displaying her beauty to us, or rather

---

4. Socrates goes on to say that one should begin by humbling one's beloved, and showing him he knows nothing: cf. the attempts at humbling Alcibiades to make him receptive to philosophy in **7.1–4**.

Theodote to us for looking at her? Should the gratitude be on her side if showing herself to us is more useful to her, and on ours if we get the greater use from looking at her?"

[3] Someone said that was right. "Well," said Socrates, "she is already showing a profit from our praise, and when we report back to others she'll gain more; whereas we want to touch what we've seen, we'll go off still a bit excited, and we'll miss her when we've gone. Naturally then we'll be paying her court, and she'll be the one courted."

"Zeus!" said Theodote. "In that case it's I who should be grateful to you for looking."

[4] Next Socrates noticed that she was expensively dressed, and that her mother was with her, dressed in choice clothes and jewelry; she also had many pretty maids waiting on her whose own appearance was far from neglected, and her house was otherwise well provided.

"Tell me, Theodote," said Socrates: "do you have any land?"

"No, I don't," she replied.

"A house, perhaps, that brings in money?"

"No, I've no house either," she said.

"Craftsmen, maybe?"

"No craftsmen," she said.

"So where do you get your resources?" asked Socrates.

"If someone becomes my friend," she said, "and wants to be good to me—that's how I make my living."

"By Hera, Theodote," said Socrates, [5] "that's a fine resource— much better than having a friendly flock of sheep, or goats, or oxen. So do you trust to luck, then, and wait to see if a friend settles on you like some fly, or do you have devices of your own to get one?"

[6] "And what would I devise that would do that?" she asked.

"Something—Zeus!—*much* more appropriate than the spider's web. . . . [Think of the different kinds of hounds used to catch a hare. Then for the hounds] [9] substitute someone who'll track down rich men for you with an eye for beauty, and when he's found then will contrive for them to fall into your nets."

[10] "And what sorts of nets do *I* have?" she asked.

"There's certainly one that's pretty close-folding," said Socrates, "— your body; and within that you have a soul that will teach you how to bring pleasure with your glances, delight with pretty phrases, welcome as needed the one who cares for you with open arms, shut out the one who mocks you, care attentively for a friend when he's in ill health, join in his delight when he has a stroke of luck, be at the service—with all your soul—of the one who pays *you* attention. When it comes to loving, I'm sure you know how to do that with both gentleness and good will; you persuade your friends to be nice to you not by pretending but by doing."

"Zeus, no!" said Theodote. "I don't use any devices like that!"

[11] "All the same," said Socrates, "to behave naturally and correctly to someone makes a big difference. You certainly can't catch or keep a friend by force. A beast like that is caught and kept if you treat him well and give him pleasure."

"True enough," she said.

[12] "So," said Socrates, "those who care for you need at first to be asked for the sorts of things they wouldn't think twice about, and then you should respond with favors of a similar kind. That way they're most likely to become your friends, they'll stay your friends for longest, and they'll do the best by you. [13] And your favors will be best deployed if you give only when they ask. It's as with food: you know for yourself that the most delightful foods seem lacking if they're produced before they're wanted, and they're positively nauseating to those already sated; if you stoke someone's hunger before you offer it, even mediocre food seems quite delightful."

[14] "So how can I stoke up a hunger in any of my men?" she asked.

"Zeus!" exclaimed Socrates. "First, by not offering to them if they're already sated, and not hinting anything until they've stopped being full and are needy again; then, when they are, by making any hint you do make with behavior toward them that's as restrained as it could be, shows no wish on your part to grant them favors, even the opposite—until that point when they need you most; the very same gifts are worth far more then than if they're given before they're wanted."

[15] To which Theodote responded, "So, Socrates, why don't you become my partner in the hunt for friends?"

"Zeus, yes!" he replied; "if you can persuade me."

"So how should I persuade you?" she asked.

"You'll look for yourself," he said, "and devise the answer, if there's anything you need from me."

"So come and visit me often," said Theodote.

[16] Making fun of his own lack of political engagement, Socrates said. "It's not easy for me, Theodote, not easy at all, to find the time—I've that much private business, and public, to occupy me; and there are also my women friends, who won't let me leave them day or night as they study their potions and charms from me."

[17] "So you know about those too, Socrates?" she said.

"Why do you think Apollodorus here and Antisthenes are never away from my side?" asked Socrates. "Why do you think Cebes and Simmias visit me from Thebes? You can be sure that these things don't happen without lots of potions and charms and magic wheels."

[18] "So lend me your wheel," she replied, "and I'll use it on you first, to draw you back to me."

"Zeus!" he exclaimed. "What I want is not for me to be drawn back to you; it's for you to come to me."

"I'll come," she said; "make sure you give me a welcome."

"I certainly shall," he said, "unless there's a girl I love more than you with me already." (Xenophon, *Memorabilia* 3.11)

6.4 *. . . and prides himself on his skill as a procurer*

"And what about you, Socrates?" asked Callias. "What is it about you that you pride yourself on?"

Socrates screwed up his face into a thoroughly solemn expression: "On my procuring (*mastropeia*)," he said. (Xenophon, *Symposium* 3.10)

6.5 *Plato's Socrates describes himself both as matchmaker and as midwife*

SOCRATES: But there is also an unlawful and unscientific practice of bringing men and women together, which we call procuring (*proagôgia*); and because of that the midwives—a most august body of women—are very reluctant to undertake even lawful matchmaking. They are afraid that if they practice this, they may be suspected of the other. And yet, I suppose, reliable matchmaking is a matter for no one but the true midwife.

THEAETETUS: Apparently.

SOCRATES: So the work of the midwives is a highly important one; but it is not so important as my own performance. And for this reason, that [b] there is not in midwifery the further complication, that the patients are sometimes delivered of phantoms and sometimes of realities, and that the two are hard to distinguish. If there were, then the midwife's greatest and noblest function would be to distinguish the true from the false offspring—don't you agree?

THEAETETUS: Yes, I do.

SOCRATES: Now my art of midwifery is just like theirs in most respects. The difference is that I attend men and not women, and that I watch over [c] the labor of their souls, not of their bodies. And the most important thing about my art is the ability to apply all possible tests to the offspring, to determine whether the young mind is being delivered of a phantom, that is, an error, or a fertile truth. For one thing which I have in common with the ordinary midwives is that I myself am barren of wisdom. The common reproach against me is that I am always asking questions of other people but never express my own views about anything, because there is no wisdom in me; and that is true enough. And the reason of it is this, that god compels me to attend the travail of others, but has forbidden me to [d] procreate. So that I am not in any sense a wise man; I cannot claim as the child of my own soul any discovery worth the name of wisdom. But with those who associate with me it is different. At first some of them may give the impression of being ignorant and stupid; but as time goes on and our association continues, all whom god permits are seen to make progress—a progress which is amazing both to other people and to themselves. And yet it is clear that this is not due to anything they have learned from me; it is that they discover within themselves a multitude of beautiful things, which they bring forth into the light. But it is I, with god's help, who [e] deliver them of this offspring. And a proof of this may be seen in the many cases where people who did not realize this fact took all the credit to themselves and thought that I was no good. They have then proceeded to leave me sooner than they should, either of their own accord or through the influence of others. And after they have gone away from me they have resorted to harmful company, with the result that what remained within them has miscarried; while they have neglected the children I helped them to bring forth, and lost them, because they set more value upon lies and phantoms than upon the truth; finally they have been set down for ignorant [151a] fools, both by themselves and by everybody else. One of these people was Aristides, the son of Lysimachus; and there have been very many others. Sometimes they come back, wanting my company again, and ready to move heaven and earth to get it. When that happens, in some cases the divine sign that visits me forbids me to associate with them; in others, it permits me, and then they begin again to make progress.

There is another point also in which those who associate with me are like women in child-birth. They suffer the pains of labor, and are filled day and night with distress; indeed they suffer far more than women. And this pain my art is able to bring on, and also to allay.

[b] Well, that's what happens to them; but at times, Theaetetus, I come across people who do not seem to me somehow to be pregnant.

Then I realize that they have no need of me, and with the best will in the world I undertake the business of match-making; and I think I am good enough—god willing—at guessing with whom they might profitably keep company. Many of them I have given away to Prodicus; and a great number also to other wise and inspired persons. (Plato, *Theaetetus* 150a–151b)

ii. Socrates as Lover—and Beloved

6.6(a) *Plato's Socrates struck by Charmides' physical beauty* . . .

"You mustn't judge by me, my friend," I [Socrates] said. "I'm a broken yardstick as far as handsome people are concerned, because practically everyone of that age strikes me as beautiful. But even so, at the moment Charmides came in [c] he seemed to me to be amazing in stature and appearance, and everyone there looked to me to be in love with him, they were so astonished and confused by his entrance, and many other lovers followed in his train. That men of my age should have been affected this way was natural enough, but I noticed that even the small boys fixed their eyes upon him and no one of them, not even the littlest, looked at anyone else, but all gazed at him as if he were a statue. And Chaerephon called to me and said, 'Well, Socrates, what do you think of the young man? Hasn't he a [d] splendid face?' 'Extraordinary,' I said. 'But if he were willing to strip,' he said, 'you would hardly notice his face, his body is so perfect.'" (Plato, *Charmides* 154b–d)

6.6(b) . . . *and claims to be (almost) overwhelmed by it*

"Boy," [said Critias], "call Charmides and tell him I want him to meet a doctor for the weakness he told me he was suffering from yesterday." Then Critias said to me, "You see, just lately he's complained of a headache when he gets up in the morning. Why not pretend to him that you know a remedy for it?"

"No reason why not," I said, "if he will only come."

"Oh, he will come," he said.

He did come, and his coming caused a lot of laughter, because every one of us who was already seated began pushing hard at his neighbor so as to make a place for him to sit down. The upshot of it was that we made the man sitting at one end get up, and the man at the other end was toppled off sideways. In the end he came and sat down between me and Critias. And then, my friend, I really was in difficulties, and although I had thought it would be perfectly easy to talk to him, I found my previous brash confidence quite gone. And when [d] Critias said that I was the person who knew the remedy and he turned his full gaze upon me in a manner beyond description and seemed on the point of asking a question, and when everyone in the palaestra surged all around us in a circle, my noble friend, I saw inside his cloak and caught on fire and was quite beside myself. And it occurred to me that Cydias was the wisest love poet when he gave someone advice on the subject of beautiful boys and said that "the fawn should beware lest, while taking a look at the lion, he should provide part of the lion's dinner," because I felt as if I had been snapped up by such a creature. All the same, when he asked me if I knew the headache remedy, I managed somehow to answer that I did. (Plato, *Charmides* 155b–d)

6.7 *Xenophon's* **Antisthenes** *in love with Socrates*

"Are you the only person, Antisthenes," [asked Socrates,] "who is not in love with anyone?"

[4] "By the gods, no!" he replied. "I'm very much in love with you."

Socrates replied with a teasing, coquettish air, "Don't bother me just now; you can see I'm otherwise engaged."

[5] At which Antisthenes said, "How transparent you are, procuring for yourself as you always do—now you use your *daimonion* as an excuse for not talking to me, now it's because you're after someone else."[5]

[6] "By the gods, Antisthenes," replied Socrates, "just don't beat me up, please! Any other unpleasantness from you I'll put up with you as I always do, in a friendly manner. But," he added, "let's conceal your love, because it's not for my soul, it's for my shapeliness." (Xenophon, *Symposium* 8.3–6 = Antisthenes 14)

6.8 *Aristodemus in love with Socrates,*
according to **Plato's Apollodorus**

"So it really was a long time ago," he [Glaucon] said. "Then who told you about it? Was it Socrates himself?" "Oh, for god's sake, of course not!" I [Apollodorus] replied. "It was the very same man [b] who told Phoenix, a fellow called Aristodemus, from Cydatheneum, a small man, who always went barefoot. He went to the party because, I think,

---

5. For the *daimonion*, see Ch. 10.

he was in love with Socrates—one of the worst cases at that time." (Plato, *Symposium* 173a–b)

6.9–10 *Plato's Socrates in pursuit of Alcibiades* . . .

[6.9] FRIEND: Where have you just come from, Socrates? No, don't tell me. [309a] It's pretty obvious that you've been hunting the ripe and ready Alcibiades. Well, I saw him just the other day, and he is certainly still a beautiful man—and just between the two of us, "man" is the proper word, Socrates: his beard is already filling out.

SOCRATES: Well, what of it? I thought you were an admirer of Homer, [b] who says that youth is most charming when the beard is first blooming—which is just the stage Alcibiades is at.

FRIEND: So what's up? Were you just with him? And how is the young man disposed toward you?

SOCRATES: Pretty well, I think, especially today, since he rallied to my side and said a great many things to support me. (Plato, *Protagoras* 309a–b)

[6.10] "Well, Callicles," [Socrates said,] "if human beings didn't share common experiences, some sharing one, others sharing another, but one of us had some [d] unique experience not shared by others, it wouldn't be easy for him to communicate what he experienced to the other. I say this because I realize that you and I are both now actually sharing a common experience: each of the two of us is a lover of two objects, I of Alcibiades, Clinias' son, and of philosophy, and you of the *dêmos* [people] of Athens and the Demos who's the son of Pyrilampes." (Plato, *Gorgias* 481c–d)

6.11 . . . *and pursued by him in turn*

"Believe me," [said Alcibiades,] "it couldn't matter less to him whether a boy is beautiful. You can't imagine how little he [e] cares whether a person is beautiful, or rich, or famous in any other way that most people admire. He considers all these possessions beneath contempt, and that's exactly how he considers all of us as well. In public, I tell you, his whole life is one big game—a game of irony. I don't know if any of you have seen him when he's really serious. But I once caught him when he was open like Silenus' statues, and I had a glimpse of the figures he keeps hidden within: they were so godlike—so bright and beautiful,

[217a] so utterly amazing—that I no longer had a choice—I just had to do whatever he told me. What I thought at the time was that what he really wanted was *me,* and that seemed to me the luckiest coincidence: all I had to do was to let him have his way with me, and he would teach me everything he knew—believe me, I had a lot of confidence in my looks. Naturally, up to that time we'd never been alone together; one of my attendants had always been present. But with this in mind, I sent the attendant away, and met [b] Socrates alone. (You see, in this company I must tell the whole truth: so pay attention. And, Socrates, if I say anything untrue, I want you to correct me.) So there I was, my friends, alone with him at last. My idea, naturally, was that he'd take advantage of the opportunity to tell me whatever it is that lovers say when they find themselves alone; I relished the moment. But no such luck! Nothing of the sort occurred. Socrates had his usual sort of conversation with me, and at the end of the day he went off. [c] My next idea was to invite him to the gymnasium with me. We took exercise together, and I was sure that this would lead to something. He took exercise and wrestled with me many times when no one else was present. What can I tell you? I got nowhere. When I realized that my ploy had failed, I decided on a frontal attack. I refused to retreat from a battle I myself had begun, and I needed to know just where matters stood. So what I did was to invite him to dinner, as if *I* were his lover and he my young prey! To tell the truth, it took him quite a while to accept my [d] invitation, but one day he finally arrived. That first time he left right after dinner: I was too shy to try to stop him. But on my next attempt, I started some discussion just as we were finishing our meal and kept him talking late into the night. When he said he should be going, I used the lateness of the hour as an excuse and managed to persuade him to spend the night at my house. He had had his meal on the couch next to mine, so he just made himself comfortable and lay down on it. No one else was there. [e] Now you must admit that my story so far has been perfectly decent; I could have told it in any company. But you'd never have heard me tell the rest of it, as you're about to do, if it weren't that, as the saying goes, 'there's truth in wine when the slaves have left'—and when they're present, too. Also, would it be fair to Socrates for me to praise him and yet to fail to reveal one of his proudest accomplishments? And, furthermore, you know what people say about snakebite—that you'll only talk about it with your fellow victims: only they will understand the pain and forgive you [218a] for all the things it made you do. Well, something much more painful than a snake has bitten me in my most sensitive part—I mean my heart, or my soul, or whatever you

want to call it, which has been struck and bitten by philosophy, whose grip on young and eager souls is much more vicious than a viper's and makes them do the most amazing things. Now, [b] all you people here, Phaedrus, Agathon, Eryximachus, Pausanias, Aristodemus, Aristophanes—I need not mention Socrates himself—and all the rest, have all shared in the madness, the Bacchic frenzy of philosophy. And that's why you will hear the rest of my story; you will understand and forgive both what I did then and what I say now. As for the house slaves and for anyone else who is not an initiate, my story's not for you: block your ears! [c] To get back to the story. The lights were out; the slaves had left; the time was right, I thought, to come to the point and tell him freely what I had in mind. So I shook him and whispered: 'Socrates, are you asleep?' 'No, no, not at all,' he replied. 'You know what I've been thinking?' 'Well, no, not really.' 'I think,' I said, 'you're the only worthy lover I have ever had—and yet, look how shy you are with me! Well, here's how I look at it. It would [d] be really stupid not to give you anything you want: you can have me, my belongings, anything my friends might have. Nothing is more important to me than becoming the best man I can be, and no one can help me more than you to reach that aim. With a man like you, in fact, I'd be much more ashamed of what wise people would say if I did *not* take you as my lover, than I would of what all the others, in their foolishness, would say if I did.' He heard me out, and then he said in that absolutely inimitable ironic manner of his: [e] 'Dear Alcibiades, if you are right in what you say about me, you are already more accomplished than you think. If I really have in me the power to make you a better man, then you can see in me a beauty that is really beyond description and makes your own remarkable good looks pale in comparison. But, then, is this a fair exchange that you propose? You seem to me to want more than your proper share: you offer me the merest appearance of beauty, and in return you want the thing itself, "gold [219a] in exchange for bronze." Still, my dear boy, you should think twice, because you could be wrong, and I may be of no use to you. The mind's sight becomes sharp only when the body's eyes go past their prime—and you are still a good long time away from that.' When I heard this I replied: 'I really have nothing more to say. I've told you exactly what I think. Now it's your turn to consider what you think best for you and me.' [b] 'You're right about that,' he answered. 'In the future, let's consider things together. We'll always do what seems the best to the two of us.' His words made me think that my own had finally hit their mark, that he was smitten by my arrows. I didn't give him a chance to say another word. I stood up immediately and placed my mantle over the light cloak which, though it was the middle of winter, was his only clothing. I slipped underneath the cloak and put my arms around this man—this utterly [c] unnatural, this truly extraordinary man—and spent the whole night next to him. Socrates, you can't deny a word of it. But in spite of all my efforts, this hopelessly arrogant, this unbelievably insolent man—he turned me down! He spurned my beauty, of which I was so proud, members of the jury—for this is really what you are: you're here to sit in judgment of Socrates' amazing arrogance and pride. Be sure of it, I swear to you by all the gods and goddesses together, my night with Socrates went no [d] further than if I had spent it with my own father or older brother! How do you think I felt after that? Of course, I was deeply humiliated, but also I couldn't help admiring his natural character, his moderation, his fortitude—here was a man whose strength and wisdom went beyond my wildest dreams! How could I bring myself to hate him? I couldn't bear to lose his friendship. But how could I possibly win him over? I knew [e] very well that money meant much less to him than enemy weapons ever meant to Ajax, and the only trap by means of which I had thought I might capture him had already proved a dismal failure. I had no idea what to do, no purpose in life; ah, no one else has ever known the real meaning of slavery!" (Plato, *Symposium* 216d–219e)

iii. Love as Tyrant and Slave Master

6.12 *Plato's Cephalus is relieved to be free of sexual desire*

"I [Cephalus] was once present when someone asked the poet Sophocles: 'How are you as far as [c] sex goes, Sophocles? Can you still make love with a woman?' 'Quiet, man,' the poet replied, 'I am very glad to have escaped from all that, like a slave who has escaped from a savage and tyrannical master.' I thought at the time that he was right, and I still do, for old age brings peace and freedom from all such things. When the appetites relax and cease to importune us, everything Sophocles said comes to pass, and we escape [d] from many mad masters. In these matters and in those concerning relatives, the real cause isn't old age, Socrates, but the way people live. If they are moderate and contented, old age, too, is only moderately onerous; if they aren't, both old age and youth are hard to bear." (Plato, *Republic* I, 329b–d)

6.13 *Aristippus* resists capture by love

[on Horace, *Epistles* 1.17.36: *"It is not for everyone to sail to Corinth":*] He [Horace] uses a Greek proverb that refers to Aristippus: "It is not for everyone to sail to Corinth." That is, it is not safe for everyone, as it is for Aristippus, to sail to Corinth. When many people who did sail to Corinth were captured by love for Lais, talk of it drew Aristippus there too, and even when he had enjoyed her, love for her did not vanquish him. When he boasted that he hadn't been taken, as others had, people mocked him for merely having had a prostitute; to which he replied: "I may have had her, but I'm not had by her." (pseudo-Acron, *Scholia on Horace* = Aristippus 95)

6.14 *Plato's* Socrates makes the case against yielding to someone "tyrannized" by their love

"Because you and I are about to discuss whether a boy should make friends with a man who loves him [d] rather than with one who does not, we should agree on defining what love is and what effects it has. Then we can look back and refer to that as we try to find out whether to expect benefit or harm from love. Now, as everyone plainly knows, love is some kind of desire; but we also know that even men who are not in love have a desire for what is beautiful. So how shall we distinguish between a man who is in love and one who is not? We must realize that each of us is ruled by two principles which we follow wherever they lead: one is our inborn desire for pleasures, the other is our acquired judgment that pursues what is best. Sometimes these two [e] are in agreement; but there are times when they quarrel inside us, and then sometimes one of them gains control, sometimes the other. Now when judgment is in control and leads us by reasoning toward what is best, that [238a] sort of self-control is called 'being in your right mind'; but when desire takes command in us and drags us without reasoning toward pleasure, then its command is known as 'outrageousness.' Now outrageousness has as many names as the forms it can take, and these are quite diverse. Whichever form stands out in a particular case gives its name to the person who has it—and that is not a pretty name to be called, not worth earning at all. If it is desire for food that overpowers a person's reasoning about what is best and suppresses his other desires, it is called gluttony and it [b] gives him the name of a glutton, while if it is desire for drink that plays the tyrant and leads the man in that direction, we all know what name we'll call him then! And now it should be clear how to describe someone appropriately in the other cases: call the man by that name—sister to these others—that derives from the sister of these desires that controls him at the time. As for the desire that has led us to say all this, it should be obvious already, but I suppose things said are always better understood than things unsaid: The unreasoning desire that overpowers a person's [c] considered impulse to do right and is driven to take pleasure in beauty, its force reinforced by its kindred desires for beauty in human bodies—this desire, all-conquering in its forceful drive, takes its name from the word for force (*rhômê*) and is called *erôs*." (Plato, *Phaedrus* 237c–238c; follows **1.6**)

6.15 *Erotic desire is both like a tyrant and a cause of tyrannical behavior according to* **Plato**'*s Socrates*

"And when," I [Socrates] said, "the other desires—filled with incense, myrrh, wreaths, wine, and the other pleasures found in their company—buzz around the drone, nurturing it and making it grow as large as possible, they plant the sting of longing in it. Then this leader of the soul adopts madness as its bodyguard and becomes frenzied. If it finds any beliefs or desires in the man [b] that are thought to be good or that still have some shame, it destroys them and throws them out, until it's purged him of moderation and filled him with imported madness."

"You've perfectly described the evolution of a tyrannical man," said Adimantus.

"Is this the reason," I asked, "that erotic love has long been called a tyrant?"

"It looks that way," he said.

"And a drunken man too, my friend," I said "—doesn't he have something of a tyrannical mind?"

"Yes, he has."

"And a man who is mad and deranged attempts to rule not just human beings, but gods as well, and expects that he will be able to succeed."

"He certainly does," said Adimantus.

"The upshot, my fine friend," I said, "is that a man becomes tyrannical precisely when either his nature or his way of life or both of them together make him drunk, filled with erotic desire, and mad."

"Absolutely."

"This, then, it seems, is how a tyrannical man comes to be, and what he's like."...

[573d] "And don't many terrible desires grow up day and night beside the tyrannical one, needing many things to satisfy them?"

"Indeed they do."
"Hence any income someone like that has is soon spent."
"Of course."
"Then borrowing follows, and expenditure of capital." [e]
"What else?"
"And when everything is gone, won't the violent crowd of desires that has nested within him inevitably shout in protest? And driven by the stings of the other desires and especially by erotic love itself (which leads all of them as its bodyguard), won't he become frenzied and look to see [574a] who possesses anything that he could take, by either deceit or force?" (Plato, *Republic* IX, 573a–c and 573d–574a)

iv. Further on Love as Madness

6.16 ***Xenophon's*** *Socrates on the dangers to one's sanity of a kiss*

He advised steadfastly refraining from sex with beautiful people, since, he claimed, it was not possible for someone in this kind of relationship to remain sensible (*sôphronein*). . . . And so, when he once learned that Crito's son, Critobulus, had kissed Alcibiades' beautiful son, he put the following question to Xenophon in Critobulus' presence:

[9] "Tell me, Xenophon," he said, "didn't you once consider Critobulus more of a sensible person than a rash one, and more cautious than thoughtless and reckless?"

"Certainly," said Xenophon.

"Well, from now on consider him a complete hothead capable of anything. This one here would even somersault into a ring of knives or jump into a fire."

[10] "What did you see him do to accuse him of this?" asked Xenophon.

"Didn't he dare to kiss Alcibiades' extremely attractive and youthful son?" he replied.

"Well, if this is the kind of recklessness you mean," said Xenophon, "that's one risk even I'd be willing to take, I think."

[11] "What audacity!" said Socrates. "And what do you think would happen to you after you kissed someone beautiful? Wouldn't you instantly become a slave instead of a free man, start spending a lot of money on harmful pleasures, have little spare time for attending to anything truly noble, and be forced to take seriously things that even a madman wouldn't?"

[12] "Good heavens!" said Xenophon. "What terrible power you ascribe to a kiss."

"Does this surprise you?" said Socrates. "Don't you know that with just a touch of the mouth, spiders no bigger than a small coin inflict crushing pain on people and drive them out of their minds?"

"Yes, of course," said Xenophon. "That's because spiders inject something when they bite."

[13] "You're being dense," said Socrates. "Do you think that beautiful people don't inject anything when they kiss, just because you don't see it? Don't you know that this creature they call 'youthful beauty' is more terrible than any spider? Spiders need to make contact, but if anybody so much as looks on youthful beauty, even from a distance and without any contact, it injects a poison that's enough to drive him crazy. Maybe that's why Cupids are called 'archers,' considering how beautiful people inflict wounds from a distance. But my advice to you, Xenophon, is to flee as fast as you can whenever you spy someone beautiful. As for you, Critobulus, I recommend going abroad for a year. That might be just enough time for you to heal from your bite."

[14] In the same way, he thought that people whose resistance to sexual desires was shaky should limit themselves to sex with the kind of partners that the mind would reject out of hand if the physical need were not great, and who would cause no trouble whenever the need did exist. He himself was so clearly well equipped in this regard that he resisted youthful beauty more easily than others resist the ugly and those well past their prime.

[15] Such was his attitude toward eating, drinking, and sex; and he believed that he would experience no less abundant pleasures, and far fewer pains, than people who expended a lot of effort in pursuit of these things. (Xenophon, *Memorabilia* 1.3.8–15; follows **4.13**)

6.17 *Plato's Socrates (here with* **Glaucon***) on the madness of erotic desire . . .*

"Can you think of a greater or keener pleasure than sexual pleasure?" [I (Socrates) asked.]

"I can't—or a madder one either," he said.

"But the right kind of love is by nature the love of order and beauty that has been moderated by education in music and poetry?"

"That's right."

"Therefore, the right kind of love has nothing mad or licentious about it?"

"No, it hasn't."

"Then sexual pleasure mustn't come into it, and the lover and the boy [b] he loves must have no share in it, if they are to love and be loved in the right way?"

"By god, no, Socrates," he said, "it mustn't come into it."

"It seems, then, that you'll lay it down as a law in the city we're establishing that if a lover can persuade a boy to let him, then he may kiss him, be with him, and touch him, as a father would a son, for the sake of what is fine and beautiful, but—turning to the other things—his association [c] with the one he cares about must never seem to go any further than this, otherwise he will be reproached as untrained in music and poetry and lacking in appreciation for what is fine and beautiful."

"That's right," he said. (Plato, *Republic* III, 403a–c)

6.18 . . . *but the right kind of "lover" is mad in the right kind of way*

SOCRATES: "There's no truth to that story,"[6]—that when a lover is available you should give your favors to a man who doesn't love you instead, because he is in control of himself, while the lover has lost his head. That would have been fine to say if madness were bad, pure, and simple; but in fact the best things we have come from madness, when it is given as a gift of the god. [b] The prophetess of Delphi and the priestesses at Dodona are out of their minds when they perform that fine work of theirs for all of Greece, either for an individual person or for a whole city, but they accomplish little or nothing when they are in control of themselves. We will not mention the Sybil or the others who foretell many things by means of god-inspired prophetic trances and give sound guidance to many people—that would take too much time for a point that's obvious to everyone. But here's some evidence worth adding to our case: The people who designed our language in the old days never thought of madness as something to be ashamed of or worthy of blame; otherwise they would not have used the word "manic" for the finest experts of all—the ones who tell the future—thereby weaving [c] insanity into prophecy. They thought it was wonderful when it came as a gift of the god, and that's why they gave its name to prophecy; but nowadays people don't know the fine points, so they stick in a *t* and call it "mantic." Similarly, the clear-headed study of the future, which uses birds and other signs, was originally called *oionoïstic*, since it uses reasoning to bring intelligence (*nous*) and learning (*historia*)

---

6. Socrates here quotes the poet Stesichorus, retracting a claim he subsequently realized was blasphemous.

into human thought; but now modern speakers call it *oiônistic,* putting on airs with their long *ô.* [d] To the extent, then, that prophecy, *mantic,* is more perfect and more admirable than sign-based prediction, *oiônistic,* in both name and achievement, madness (*mania*) from a god is finer than self-control of human origin, according to the testimony of the ancient language givers.

Next, madness can provide relief from the greatest plagues of trouble that beset certain families because of their guilt for ancient crimes: it turns up among those who need a way out; it gives prophecies and takes refuge [e] in prayers to the gods and in worship, discovering mystic rites and purifications that bring the man it touches through to safety for this and all time to come. So it is that the right sort of madness finds relief from present hardships for a man it has possessed.

Third comes the kind of madness that is possession by the Muses, [245a] which takes a tender virgin soul and awakens it to a Bacchic frenzy of songs and poetry that glorifies the achievements of the past and teaches them to future generations. If anyone comes to the gates of poetry and expects to become an adequate poet by acquiring expert knowledge of the subject without the Muses' madness, he will fail, and his self-controlled verses will be eclipsed by the poetry of men who have been driven out of their minds.

There you have some of the fine achievements—and I could tell you [b] even more—that are due to god-sent madness. We must not have any fear on this particular point, then, and we must not let anyone disturb us or frighten us with the claim that you should prefer a friend who is in control of himself to one who is disturbed. Besides proving that point, if he is to win his case, our opponent must show that love is not sent by the gods as a benefit to a lover and his boy. And we, for our part, must prove the opposite, that this sort of madness is given us by the gods to ensure our greatest good fortune. It will be a proof that convinces the wise if not [c] the clever.

Now we must first understand the truth about the nature of the soul, divine or human, by examining what it does and what is done to it. (Plato, *Phaedrus* 244a–245c)

6.19(a)–(c) ***Aeschines'*** *Socrates (perhaps in his dialogue* Alcibiades*) suggests that the benefit he, too, conferred as a lover was due to "inspiration" rather than technical skill*

[6.19(a)] "If I [Socrates] thought that I could be of any help through some art (*technê*), I would convict myself of very great stupidity. As it is,

I thought this had been granted me, in respect to Alcibiades, by divine gift. There is nothing to be amazed at in this." (Aelius Aristides, *In Defense of Oratory* 61 = Aeschines 53)

[6.19(b)] "Among the sick, too, some become well through human expertise, some by divine gift. Well, those who become well through human expertise are cured by doctors; as for those cured 'by divine gift,' desire guides them to what will benefit them—they wanted to vomit when it was going to be good for them." (Aelius Aristides, *In Defense of Oratory* 62 = Aeschines 53)

[6.19(c)] "The genuine love that I had for Alcibiades made me no different from the Bacchants. For whenever the Bacchants become inspired, sources from which others cannot even draw water allow *them* to draw honey and milk. Just so I have no knowledge of any subject that I can benefit a person by teaching him, and yet I thought that by being with him I would make him better, through my loving him." (Aelius Aristides, *In Defense of Oratory* 74 = Aeschines 53)

v. Dealing with *Erôs*

6.20 *Marriage—**Antisthenes'** ideal for the sage?*

[Antisthenes' view was that the wise man] would marry for the sake of having children, sleeping with those women most naturally suited to the purpose; and he would be in love with them, because only the wise man knows which one should love. (Diogenes Laertius 6.11 = Antisthenes 58; part of **3.3**)

6.21 *But **Antisthenes'** non-sage might not be so fortunate*

To someone who asked what sort of wife one should marry, he said: "If she's beautiful you'll share her; but if she's ugly, you'll have your punishment already." (Diogenes Laertius 6.3 = Antisthenes 57)[7]

---

7. But this same anecdote is ascribed to Aristippus at Antonius Melissa, *Commonplaces* II, 34.42.

6.22 Antisthenes *advises sex without commitment* . . .

On one occasion he saw an adulterer in flight, and said: "Sad man! How much danger you could have avoided for an obol!" (Diogenes Laertius 6.4 = Antisthenes 60)

6.23 . . . *and preferably without cost*

Best sleep with women who will be grateful to you for it. (Diogenes Laertius 6.3 = Antisthenes 56)

6.24 Aristippus *agrees*

In these cases of desire for women, if things turn out as well as they can, there remains pleasure to be got in the enjoyment of a young body. Aristippus was witness to this, when in response to the accusation that Lais did not love him, he said [E] he thought the wine and the fish didn't love him either, but he enjoyed having both of them. (Plutarch, *Dialogue on Love* 750D–E = Aristippus 93)

6.25(a) **Plato's** *Socrates (with* **Glaucon***) thinks that potentially reproductive sex would be regulated in the ideal society* . . .

"Then you, as their lawgiver," I [Socrates] said, "will select women just as you did men, with natures as similar to theirs as possible, and hand them over to the men. And since they have common dwellings and meals, rather than [d] private ones, and live together and mix together both in physical training and in the rest of their upbringing, they will, I suppose, be driven by innate necessity to have sex with one another. Or don't you think that's the necessary outcome here?"

"Necessary, not by the laws of geometry," he said, "but by the laws of sexual attraction—probably more potent sources of persuasion, and compulsion, when it comes to the majority of the population."

"That's right, I said. "But the next point, Glaucon, is that unregulated coupling, or unregulated anything, is not [e] permissible in a city of happy people, and the rulers will forbid it."

"No," he said, "for it's not just."

"Then it's clear that the next step will be for us to make mating a sacred matter, to the very best of our ability; and it's the most beneficial kind that will be sacred."

"Absolutely." (Plato, *Republic* V, 458c–e)

6.25(b) . . . *and used, for example, to encourage valor*

"And among other prizes and rewards the young men who are good in war or other things must be given permission to have sex with the women [b] more often, since this will also be a good pretext for having them father as many of the children as possible." (Plato, *Republic* V, 460a–b)

6.26 *Plato's Athenian sees procreation as the natural purpose of sex*

ATHENIAN: The three impulses we distinguished by our three terms: the desire for "food" [d] (I think we said) and "drink," and thirdly "sexual stimulation."

CLINIAS: Yes, sir, we'll certainly remember, just as you tell us.

ATHENIAN: Splendid. Let's turn our attention to the bridal pair, and instruct them in the manner and method by which they should produce children. (And if we fail to persuade them, we'll threaten them with a law or two.)

CLINIAS: How do you mean?

ATHENIAN: The bride and groom should resolve to present the state with [e] the best and finest children they can produce. Now, when human beings cooperate in any project, and give due attention to its planning and execution, the results they achieve are always of the best and finest quality; but if they act carelessly, or are incapable of intelligent action in the first place, the results are deplorable. So the bridegroom had better deal with his wife and approach the task of begetting children with a sense of responsibility, and the bride should do the same, especially during the period when no [784a] children have yet been born to them. They should be supervised by women whom we have chosen (several or only a few—the officials should appoint the number they think right, at times within their discretion). These women must assemble daily at the temple of Eileithuia for not more than a third of the day, and when they have convened each must report to her colleagues any wife or husband of childbearing age she has seen who is concerned with anything but the duties imposed on him or her at the time of the [b] sacrifices and rites of their marriage. If children come in suitable numbers, the period of supervised procreation should be ten years and no longer. But if a couple remain childless throughout this period, they should part, and call in their relatives and the female officials to help them decide terms of divorce that will safeguard the interests of them both. If some dispute arises about the duties and interests of the parties, they must choose ten [c] of the Guardians of the Laws as arbitrators, and abide by their decisions on the points referred to them. The female officials must enter the homes of the young people and by a combination of admonition and threats try to make them give up their ignorant and sinful ways. If this has no effect, they must go and report the case to the Guardians of the Laws, who must resort to sterner methods. If even the Guardians prove ineffective, they should make the case public and post up the relevant name, swearing on their oath that they are unable to reform So-and-So. (Plato, *Laws* VI, 783c–784c)

6.27   But Plato, Xenophon, Aeschines, and Cebes at least
sometimes sanctioned relationships between older men and boys as well

The question is whether boys' lovers should be allowed to be with them [E] and pass their time with them, or whether, conversely, they should be kept from them and scared off from their company. For when I look at those fathers who speak their mind, and react to their children's lovers in a harsh and surly way, thinking it an unbearable outrage for them to be with their boys, I am cautious about proposing or advising it. But then again when I think of Socrates, Plato, Xenophon, Aeschines, Cebes, and that whole chorus of men who valued male-on-male love, and procured (*proagein*) adolescents with a view to an education in leadership and virtuous character, then I think [F] differently, and I am inclined toward emulating the example of those fine men. (Plutarch, *On the Education of Children* 11D–F = Aeschines 38)

Chapter 7: Alcibiades and Politics

None of the closest members of the Socratic circle was actively engaged in politics. Closest to the political scene, by birth and family connections, were Plato and Xenophon, but Plato evidently preferred philosophy, while Xenophon—after the civil war in Athens in 404–403 BCE—left home to become a mercenary general, and even to fight on the Spartan side against his fellow Athenians. Both writers nevertheless have much to say about political questions; indeed, more than a third of Plato's total output centers on politics: the ten books of the *Republic,* the twelve of the *Laws,* the *Statesman,* the *Gorgias* (both substantial works), and other minor works. Among the main topics in these are: (a) the best kind of political regime, and (b) the nature and acquisition of *politikê technê,* the "art of politics" or ruling. The latter is also the subject of Xenophon's long treatise on the education of Cyrus: the *Cyropaedia.*

Politics was a subject of interest to other Socratics too, as evidenced by a fair scattering, among the lists of their works, of dialogues or works named after political figures of one kind or another. And central to the treatment of the political art for many of them was Alcibiades—ward of the great Athenian general and statesman Pericles. We have already encountered him in Chapter 6 as a famous beauty and intimate of Socrates: he was also notorious for his chequered political career, having proved as ready to work for Athens' enemies as for Athens herself. His career, however, ultimately ended in failure; the Athenians' patience with him was finally exhausted, and he ended his life an exile, murdered partly at the instigation of the oligarchic faction at Athens that he had (sometimes) supported.

Socrates' close association with such a character was undoubtedly a major factor both in his own trial and in the repeated appearance of Alcibiades' name in and among the writings of the Socratics; just as Alcibiades would no doubt have been the star exhibit for the prosecution to support the charge against Socrates of corrupting the young, so Socrates' friends and followers would have felt bound to try to exonerate him from responsibility for Alcibiades' misconduct. Alcibiades, they argue, went astray *despite* the influence of Socrates, not because of it—a point which led them to use Alcibiades as an occasion for positive discussion on what it takes to be a political leader, and especially of what kind of expertise is required. Not surprisingly, virtue (*self*-control) is taken to be a prerequisite for the ability to control others, and a recurrent theme in works on Alcibiades seems to have been his humbling

191

(or even humiliation) by Socrates. Plato's *Alcibiades* revolves around this theme (**7.1**),[1] and so, apparently, did the *Alcibiades* of Aeschines (**7.4**). It also recurs in a section of the *Symposium* which could be thought of as a mini-*Alcibiades* itself (212c–223a, from which **7.2** and **6.11** are drawn: Alcibiades looks back on his time with Socrates, and regrets having turned his back on him; the dialogue ends with Socrates humiliating him as he had done before their breakup).

Other Socratics credited with an *Alcibiades* include Antisthenes, Euclides, and Phaedo (although, in their cases, we have no direct evidence about content). Xenophon is something of an exception here. He does write about Alcibiades, but he devotes his main treatment of the subject of ruling—the *Cyropaedia*—to someone he views as a positive exemplar of the perfect statesmanship, the Persian Cyrus I, founder in the sixth century BCE of the vast empire that continually threatened the Greeks in the fifth and fourth centuries. (Xenophon's *Hiero,* a dialogue between Hiero, "tyrant" of Syracuse from 478 to 466 BCE, and the poet Simonides, is a kind of miniature counterpart of the *Cyropaedia*.) The pattern of Alcibiades' career may, in any case, have been too close to that of Xenophon's own—that of an Athenian cavalryman who went on to enter service first with the Persians, then with the Spartans—to be an entirely safe subject for extended discussion. In Xenophon's *Memorabilia,* his examples of youthfully aspiring politicians are Glaucon, Plato's brother (**7.5**); Charmides, Plato's uncle (**7.6**) (associated with, but not a member of, the murderous oligarchic grouping known as the "Thirty Tyrants"); and—in the extended dialogue that constitutes *Memorabilia* 4.2—Euthydemus. (For an extract, see **2.16**.)

Attitudes toward politicians who were held in more general respect vary significantly. The requirements for political expertise proposed by Plato's Socrates (and his unnamed visitor from Elea in the *Statesman*) tend to be so high that they can hardly be matched by any politician, whether past or contemporary (**7.7**, **7.8**, **7.11**; cf. *Phaedrus* 278c for Solon); they are, as the Eleatic says, simply ignorant of what true statesmanship, or the art of politics, is about: that is, making people into better people. The same is implied by the provocative claim of Plato's Socrates in the *Gorgias,* that he himself is the only true statesman alive (**7.18**), even as he does his best to keep out of actual politics altogether. But other Socratics may have been less austere in their judgments, at

---

1. I.e., the *First Alcibiades,* also known as the *Alcibiades Major*—assuming it to be genuine; its authenticity has been, and continues to be, a matter of debate in modern scholarship. (Another dialogue, known as the *Second Alcibiades* or *Alcibiades Minor,* also attributed to Plato, is generally agreed to be spurious.)

least on statesmen of the past—particularly Xenophon, with his examples of Cyrus and Hiero. Both, of course, are non-Greek, which is significant; but compare also **7.3**, which may tell us something of his view of Pericles; and **7.5** (with which compare Xenophon, *Symposium* 8.39; *Memorabilia* 4.2.2) on Themistocles, Greek commander at the battle of Salamis in 480 BCE. Themistocles also turns up in Aeschines as an example for Alcibiades of political know-how (**7.4**).

The question of what makes for a good statesman is naturally bound up with what makes for a good state. Existing states are generally reckoned to be far from perfect. Athens comes in for particular criticism from the Athenian in Plato's *Laws* (he is for example thoroughly contemptuous of some of the victories on which the Athenians most prided themselves: **7.28**), and Athens and Thebes are compared unfavorably to Sparta by Antisthenes (**7.26–27**, **7.29**)—who is not uncritical of the Spartans, either (**7.30**).[2] (Antisthenes' general position perhaps has something in common with that implied by Plato's Athenian visitor in *Laws* I, on the way Spartan and Cretan laws encourage a part, but only a part, of virtue: the military sort.) Antisthenes lays against democracy, in particular, the charge of ignorance that Plato's Socrates makes against all politicians (**7.25**). Xenophon, to judge by his behavior both before and after his departure from Athens, was also a convinced antidemocrat. Not that the Socratics favored tyranny, at least in its usual manifestation (**7.35–39**). Where we have evidence, the Socratics appear to have favored an enlightened autocracy (as Xenophon, implicitly, at **7.24**; and, more explicitly, in the *Hiero*), or aristocracy (as in Plato's *Republic,* which is governed by a plurality of philosopher kings and queens: see **7.19**). In the *Laws,* this is expressed as a mixture of monarchy and democracy that avoids the excesses of both forms (*Laws* III, 693d–e), along with the problems of human frailty and corruptibility (**7.21**). (Other Platonic models for a better society appear in **7.20–22**.)

As well as reflection on constitutions, and rulership, we also find thought given to the subject of laws. (The urgency here is perhaps connected with their perceived role as preceptors of the young: cf. discussion in Ch. 5.) Aeschines is quoted for his deflationary view on the status of written law (see **1.28**), which perhaps has something in common with the view of the Eleatic visitor's musings in Plato's *Statesman* that they are an imperfect substitute for the use of wisdom (**7.31**); compare Aristippus at **7.32–33**. (Compare, also, the dialogue

---

2. For more criticism of Athens, cf. the—presumably ironical—speech of Aspasia in Plato's *Menexenus*.

between Xenophon's Socrates and Hippias at **3.35**.) For Plato on this subject, the reader should also consult *Crito* 50a–54d (of which **5.4** is a part), *Republic* I, 338c–347e—and, of course, the *Laws* itself, which gives a special twist to the conventional idea that we become virtuous by obeying the laws (Ch. 5, p. 147; cf. **7.3**) in suggesting that law in its pure form is the product of reason, the divine in us (**7.21**, esp. 714a).

If none of the Socratics was engaged directly *in* politics, then, at least some of them were certainly engaged *with* politics as a subject. They saw philosophy as a more wholesome activity than climbing the greasy pole (cf. **7.14–15**); but at the same time they generally recognized the need for rulers with the right qualities (e.g., **7.6**), and sometimes proposed ways in which philosophy itself could contribute. Thus, at the most basic level, Socrates' conversations with young, aspiring politicians in Plato and Xenophon tend to have the effect of showing that to be a good politician one needs to be with a Socrates and do dialectic. But it was not all so hands-off. Plato apparently went to Syracuse three times, to visit, then to stay, at the court of the tyrants of Syracuse, Dionysius I and his son Dionysius II. Reports place Aeschines and Aristippus there too—and this is credible enough, since we have independent evidence that Dionysius I, at least, had a habit of inviting intellectuals of various kinds to his court.[3] His son, it is true, had something of a reputation as a philistine, but nevertheless seems himself to have invited—or summoned—Plato. The seventh of the *Letters* attributed to Plato (see **7.44**), if it is genuinely by Plato, will be the most valuable evidence in this context, and would probably remain so even if it was written not by Plato but by someone close to him both in time and otherwise. It is, in any case, as useful as many of the anecdotes preserved for us of exchanges between Socratics and Dionysius (father or son), some of which are included below (**7.36–43**; see also **2.7**, **3.5**, **3.23**, **4.18**). At least one of them, **4.18**, must be fictional: the reports of Socratics in Syracuse generally tend not to mention Antisthenes, and it is hard to see what might have taken this austere figure there. But the other anecdotes appear sufficiently in-character, and in general sufficiently plausible, given our other evidence, to earn them a place in the present chapter.

---

3. Note, though, that the anecdotes we have usually fail to specify whether Dionysius I or II is meant.

Texts

i. On the Requirements for Ruling: The "Political Art"

7.1(a) Plato's *Socrates questions Alcibiades' qualifications for political leadership . . .*

SOCRATES: Right then; you plan, as I say, to come forward and advise the Athenians some time soon. Suppose I stopped you as you were about to take the podium and asked, "Alcibiades, what are the Athenians proposing to discuss? You're getting up to advise them because it's something you know better than they do, aren't you?" What would you reply?

ALCIBIADES: Yes, I suppose I would say it was something that I know better than they do. [d]

SOCRATES: So it's on matters you know about that you're a good adviser.

ALCIBIADES: Of course.

SOCRATES: Now the only things you know are what you've learned from others or found out for yourself; isn't that right?

ALCIBIADES: What else could I know?

SOCRATES: Could you ever have learned or found out anything without wanting to learn it or work it out for yourself?

ALCIBIADES: No, I couldn't have.

SOCRATES: Is that right? Would you have wanted to learn or work out something that you thought you understood?

ALCIBIADES: Of course not.

SOCRATES: So there was a time when you didn't think you knew what you now understand. [e]

ALCIBIADES: There must have been.

SOCRATES: But I've got a pretty good idea what you've learned. Tell me if I've missed anything: as far as I remember, you learned writing and lyre playing and wrestling, but you didn't want to learn aulos playing. These are the subjects that you understand—unless perhaps you've been learning something while I wasn't looking; but I don't think you have been, either by night or by day, on your excursions from home.

ALCIBIADES: No, those are the only lessons I took.

SOCRATES: Well then, is it when the Athenians are discussing how to spell a word correctly that you'll stand up to advise them? [107a]

ALCIBIADES: Zeus! I'd never do that!

SOCRATES: Then is it when they're discussing the notes on the lyre?

ALCIBIADES: No, never.

SOCRATES: But surely they're not in the habit of discussing wrestling in the Assembly.

ALCIBIADES: Certainly not. (?Plato, *Alcibiades* 106c–107a)[4]

7.1(b) . . . *and those of established leaders as well* . . .

SOCRATES: Well, who are the ones making the mistakes? Surely not the ones who know?

ALCIBIADES: Of course not.

SOCRATES: Well, since it's not those who know, and it's not those who [118a] don't know and know they don't know, is there anyone left except those who don't know but think they do know?

ALCIBIADES: No, they're the only ones left.

SOCRATES: So this is the ignorance that causes bad things; this is the most disgraceful sort of stupidity.

ALCIBIADES: Yes.

SOCRATES: And isn't it most harmful and most contemptible when it is ignorance of the most important things?

ALCIBIADES: Very much so.

SOCRATES: Well, can you name anything more important than what's just and admirable and good and advantageous?

ALCIBIADES: No, I really can't.

SOCRATES: But aren't those the things you say you're wavering about?

ALCIBIADES: Yes.

SOCRATES: So, if you're wavering, it's obvious from what we've said that [b] not only are you ignorant about the most important things, but you also think you know what you don't know.

ALCIBIADES: I guess that's right.

---

4. For the contested status of the *Alcibiades*, see n.1 above.

SOCRATES: Good god, Alcibiades, what a sorry state you're in! I hesitate to call it by its name, but still, since we're alone, it must be said. You are wedded to stupidity, my good fellow, stupidity in the highest degree—our discussion and your own words convict you of it. This is why you're rushing into politics before you've got an education. You're not alone in this [c] sad state—you've got most of our city's politicians for company. There are only a few exceptions, among them, perhaps, your guardian, Pericles.

ALCIBIADES: Yes, Socrates, and people do say that he didn't acquire his expertise all by himself; he kept company with many experts like Pythoclides and Anaxagoras. Even now, despite his advanced age, he consults with Damon for the same purpose.

SOCRATES: Really? Have you ever seen any expert who is unable to make others expert in what he knows? The person who taught you how to read and write—he had expertise in his field, and he made you and anybody else he liked expert as well, didn't he?

ALCIBIADES: Yes.

SOCRATES: And will you, having learned from him, be able to teach somebody else? [d]

ALCIBIADES: Yes.

SOCRATES: And isn't it the same with the music teacher and the gymnastics teacher?

ALCIBIADES: Certainly.

SOCRATES: I think we can be pretty sure that someone understands something when he can show that he has made someone else understand it.

ALCIBIADES: I agree.

SOCRATES: Well then, can you tell me who Pericles has made into an expert? Shall we start with his sons?

ALCIBIADES: But Socrates, both of his sons turned out to be idiots! [e] (?Plato, *Alcibiades* 117e–118e)

7.1(c) . . . *and Alcibiades in his arrogance draws the conclusion that character rather than training will see him through*

SOCRATES: Very well. What do you propose for yourself? Do you intend to remain in your present condition, or practice some self-cultivation?

ALCIBIADES: Let's discuss it together, Socrates. [b] You know, I do see what you're saying and actually I agree—it seems to me that none of our city's politicians has been properly educated, except for a few.

SOCRATES: And what does that mean?

ALCIBIADES: Well, if they were educated, then anyone who wanted to compete with them would have to get some knowledge and go into training, like an athlete. But as it is, since they entered politics as amateurs, there's no need for me to train and go to the trouble of learning. I'm sure [c] my natural abilities will be far superior to theirs. (?Plato, *Alcibiades* 119a–c)

7.2 Plato's *Alcibiades* elsewhere confesses to being shamed by Socrates

"Socrates is the only man in the world who has made me feel shame—ah, you didn't think I had it in me, did you? Yes, he makes me feel ashamed: I know perfectly well that I can't prove he's wrong when he tells me what I should do; yet, the moment I leave his side, I go back to my old ways: I cave in to my desire to please the crowd. My whole life has become one constant effort to escape from him and keep away, but when I see him, [c] I am deeply ashamed, because I'm doing nothing about my way of life, though I have already agreed with him that I should. Sometimes, believe me, I think I would be happier if he were dead. And yet I know that if he dies I'll be even more miserable. I can't live with him, and I can't live without him! What *can* I do about him?" (Plato, *Symposium* 216b–c)

7.3 Xenophon's Alcibiades left Socrates before the real lesson was learned

It's said that before he was twenty Alcibiades had the following discussion with Pericles, his own guardian and Athens' first citizen; the subject was the laws.

[41] "Tell me, Pericles: are you in a position to teach me what a law is?"

"That I surely am," replied Pericles.

"Teach me, then, by the gods!" said Alcibiades; "because when I hear certain people being praised for upholding the law, I reflect that no one can be deserving of such praise if he doesn't know what a law is."

[42] "What you're looking for, Alcibiades, is not at all difficult," replied Pericles, "if what you want to know is what a law is: laws are

all the enactments approved by the people in assembly, whereby they announce what we should and shouldn't do."

"Is that with the thought that we should do what's good for us, or what's bad?"

"Zeus, lad!" he exclaimed. "What's good, not bad."

[43] "And if it's not the people in majority, but—as happens where there's an oligarchy—it's just a few who come together and lay down rules about what the citizens should do, what do these count as?"

"Whatever rules the sovereign part of the city lays down after due deliberation," said Pericles, "is called law."

"And what if a tyrant is in power over the city and he lays down for the citizens what they should do? Are his rules law too?"

"If a tyrant is in power," Pericles said, "the rules he lays down are called laws too."

[44] "But force, Pericles," asked Alcibiades, "and absence of law—what is that? Isn't it when the stronger man makes the weaker do what he, the stronger, decides by violence instead of persuasion?"

"I believe so," replied Pericles; "I retract my claim that the rules a tyrant lays down without persuading people constitute law."

[45] "And when the few enact their rules not by persuading the majority but by exerting its power, is that or is it not a case of using force?"

"I think," said Pericles, "that anything one person makes another do without having persuaded him, whether by enactment or otherwise, is a case of force and not law."

"In that case, what the whole people enacts when it exerts power over those with money, and hasn't persuaded them, will similarly be a case of force and not law?"

[46] "I can tell you, Alcibiades," said Pericles, "when we were your age we were clever at this sort of thing too. We used to practice just the sort of tricky arguments that you seem to me to going in for presently."

To which Alcibiades replied, "Pericles, if only I'd been with you when you were even cleverer at these things than you are now!"

[47] Well, as soon as [Critias and Alcibiades] thought they had the advantage over the politicians of the day, they stopped coming to Socrates; they were generally disenchanted with him, and in particular they disliked being cross-examined about things they got wrong. They tried politics themselves, but actually it was politics that had first taken them to Socrates. (Xenophon, *Memorabilia* 1.2.40–47)

7.4 *Aeschines' Socrates (perhaps quoted from his* Alcibiades*) uses Themistocles in an attempt to put Alcibiades in his place*

Let us consider the sorts of things Aeschines tells us about Themistocles—the Aeschines who was a companion of Socrates and a fellow pupil with Plato:

"Now that you have had the cheek to criticize the life of Themistocles," [said Socrates to Alcibiades,] "think what sort of person it is that you have thought it right to attack. Think to yourself: where does the sun rise, and where does it set?"

"That's not hard to say, Socrates."

"Then has it ever troubled you to reflect that one man rules over the territory that stretches for the length of the sun's course—the one called Asia?"

"Certainly—it's the Great King."

"So you'll know that he mounted an expedition against us and the Spartans, thinking that if he took these two cities he would readily subdue the rest of the Greeks. He so terrified the Athenians that they abandoned their land and fled to Salamis, and having elected Themistocles as general, they allowed him to do what he wished in governing their affairs. The greatest hopes they had for survival lay in whatever he would decide to do on their behalf. Themistocles was not downcast by the situation and the fact that the Greeks' resources in terms of ships, infantry, and money were considerably inferior to the King's, because he knew that unless the King turned out a better strategist than he was, the huge quantity of his other resources would be of no great advantage to him; and he understood that the advantage usually lay with whichever side had people in charge that were superior in virtue. And then the King saw that his own position was weaker, on a day when he encountered a man better than he was. Themistocles so easily handled the king's forces, despite their vast numbers, that after he had defeated him at sea he tried to persuade the Athenians to break up the enemy's pontoon bridge. When he failed to persuade them, he reported to the King that the city's decision was the opposite of what it actually was: he said that the Athenians had told him to destroy the bridge, but he opposed it, as a way of trying to save the King and his entourage. So not only do we and other Greeks think Themistocles responsible for saving us; the King himself, whom Themistocles had defeated, actually thought he owed his survival to him and no one else. That's how much wiser Themistocles proved than the King. The result was that when Themistocles was an exile from home the King paid him back as if he had been his savior, and among other gifts he made him ruler over the whole of Magnesia, so that even though he was an exile his situation was better than that of many Athenians who stayed at home, fine and good though they were thought to be. So who else at that time could justly be said to have the greatest power than Themistocles, when he, as general of the Greeks, overthrew the man who lorded it over everything from the rising of the sun to its setting? And then consider, Alcibiades," I said, "that even for such a person as that his wisdom was not enough, great as it was, to prevent his being exiled and deprived of his rights by his city, but fell short. What, then, do you suppose will be in store for inferior people who take no care of themselves? Is it not amazing that they succeed even in small matters? And don't condemn me," I said, "Alcibiades, as if I have eccentric and atheistic views of chance and of divine matters, if I attribute all Themistocles' actions to knowledge, and if I hold that no mere chance was responsible for these deeds of his. I could much more easily prove to you that those who hold views opposite to mine are atheists than they could me, given that *they* suppose that good fortune attends equally on the bad and the good, and not that the fine and good, just because they are more pious, are better provided for in terms of what comes from the gods." (Aelius Aristides, *In Defense of the Four* 348 = Aeschines 50; part = **3.51**)

7.5 Xenophon's Socrates also counsels **Glaucon** against a hasty entry into politics

When Ariston's son Glaucon set his sights on becoming the city's leading statesman and tried to address the Assembly despite not yet being twenty years old, no one else of his family and friends could prevent him from being dragged away from the podium and becoming a laughing-stock. But Socrates, who was friendly toward him on account of both Charmides, Glaucon's son, and Plato,[5] prevented him all by himself. [2] When he met up with him, he first got his attention with words to this effect:

"Have you made up your mind to become our leading statesman, Glaucon?" he said.

"Indeed I have, Socrates," he replied.

"Well, that's certainly a fine ambition, if ever there was one," he said. "If you succeed, you'll clearly be able to get anything you desire; you'll have the means to help your friends, promote your family's fortune, enhance your country's influence, and make a name for yourself first in

---

5. It may be interesting to note that this is the only occurrence of Plato's name in Xenophon's works. (Plato for his part never names Xenophon at all.)

our city, then in Greece generally, and perhaps, like Themistocles, even among foreigners. Wherever you are, all eyes will be on you."

[3] Glaucon began to swell with pride at the sound of these words, and he was happy to linger. Whereupon Socrates said, "This much is clear, isn't it, Glaucon: if you want to be held in esteem, you need to help your city?"

"Certainly," he said.

"Then by all means, don't be coy," he said. "Tell us the first thing you'll do to benefit your city."

[4] Glaucon went silent, as if considering for the first time where he would start. Then Socrates said, "If you wanted to improve a friend's fortune, you'd try to make him wealthier. Wouldn't you likewise try to make your city wealthier?"

"Certainly," he said.

[5] "Would it be wealthier if its revenues increased?"

"That stands to reason," he said.

"Tell us, then," he said, "what are the city's current sources and amounts of revenue? You've clearly considered the issue, so as to get the most out of any sources that are underperforming and to add any that are being overlooked."

"Honestly," replied Glaucon, "I haven't given it any thought."

[6] "Well," he said, "if you've overlooked this detail, at least tell us about the city's expenditures, since you also clearly intend to eliminate any superfluous ones."

"Frankly," he said, "I haven't had time for that yet either."

"So shall we defer the business of making the city wealthier?" he asked. "After all, how can anyone oversee expenses and revenues if he isn't even familiar with them?"

[7] "Well, Socrates," said Glaucon, "it's also possible to enrich a city from its enemies' resources."

"That's certainly true, provided that the city is stronger than its enemies," replied Socrates. "But if it's weaker, it could even lose what it already had."

"That's true," he said.

[8] "So," he replied, "anyone who intends to offer advice regarding whom to attack should know the strength both of his own city and of its enemies, so that he may recommend going to war if his city is stronger but urge caution if it turns out to be weaker than its enemies."

"That's correct," he said.

[9] "Then first tell us the respective strength of our city's army and navy, and next that of our enemies," he replied.

"Frankly," he said, "I couldn't tell you that off the top of my head."
"Well, if you have it written down somewhere, fetch it," he said. "I really would like to hear it."
"To be honest, I don't even have it written down yet," he replied.
[10] "So shall we also hold off on military advice, at least for the time being?" he asked.
"You probably haven't gotten around to reviewing these things because of their magnitude and the fact that you're just starting out as our leading statesman. But I'm sure that you've already given careful consideration to the city's defenses, and that you know both how many of our garrisons are strategically placed and how many aren't, as well as how many border guards are competent and how many aren't. And I'm sure that you'll recommend enlarging the strategically placed garrisons and abolishing the superfluous ones."

. . .

[16] [Socrates] added, "Be careful that your desire for distinction doesn't have the opposite effect, Glaucon. Don't you see how risky it is for someone to say or do things he doesn't understand? Reflect on others you know who are the kind of people to say or do things they obviously don't understand. Do you think that their conduct wins them more praise and admiration or blame and contempt? [17] Then reflect on those who actually understand what they both say and do. You'll find, I suggest, that in every endeavor the people awarded distinction and admiration consist of those with the best understanding, whereas the ones who endure infamy and contempt consist of the most ignorant. [18] So, if your desire is to be distinguished and admired in the city, try to achieve the best understanding possible of the things you want to do. If you try your hand at politics after you've outdone everyone else in this regard, it wouldn't surprise me if you easily achieved your desired goal." (Xenophon, *Memorabilia* 3.6.1–10 and 16–18)

7.6 *On the other hand,* **Xenophon***'s Socrates encourages someone with the right talents to use them*

When he observed that Charmides, Glaucon's son, was reluctant to speak in the Assembly or to take part in politics despite being a remarkable man and more capable than contemporary politicians, he said, "Tell me, Charmides, if someone were good enough to win the garland at our most prestigious competitions, and so bring honor upon himself and enhance the reputation of his native land throughout Greece, but refused to compete, what kind of man would you consider him to be?"

"Clearly a sissy and a coward," he said.

[2] "And if someone were able to enhance his country's influence," he replied, "and so bring honor upon himself by taking part in politics, but shrank from doing so, wouldn't it be reasonable for him to be considered a coward?"

"I suppose," he said. "But why are you asking me this?"

"Because I think that you, despite your ability, shrink from taking part in things that are your shared responsibility as a citizen," he said.

[3] "What do you base your criticism on?" replied Charmides. "In what kind of endeavor have you observed this ability of mine?"

"In your interactions with politicians," he said. "I see that whenever they consult you about something, you give good advice; and whenever they make mistakes, you properly criticize them."

[4] "Private conversation isn't the same thing as public debate, Socrates," he said.

"But someone skilled at counting doesn't count any worse in a crowd than alone," he said, "and the string players who play best when by themselves also excel in public performance."

[5] "Don't you see that modesty and timidity are rooted in human nature, and that they manifest themselves much more in crowds than in private company?" he asked.

"In fact," he said, "I'm eager to instruct you on precisely this point: though you aren't modest in the wisest company or timid among the strongest, you're embarrassed to speak in the presence of simpletons and weaklings. [6] Who among them makes you embarrassed? Is it the clothes makers? Or the shoemakers, or the carpenters? Or the smiths, the farmers, the merchants—or the businessmen from the marketplace who worry about what they can buy cheaply and sell at a profit? Because they're the ones who make up the Assembly. [7] How is your behavior any better than that of someone who can beat trained athletes but is afraid of rank amateurs? You easily engage in conversation with our city's leading citizens, some of whom actively dislike you, and you're far superior to those actively engaged in political dialogue; and yet you still balk at speaking in front of people who've never given a thought to politics and have nothing against you, because you're afraid of being ridiculed."

[8] "Well, don't you think that members of the Assembly frequently ridicule people who present sound arguments?" he said.

"Yes, and so do the others," he replied. "That's why I'm surprised: you handle those people easily whenever they do it, but you think that you won't be able to deal at all with the ones in the Assembly. [9] Don't be ignorant of yourself, my dear friend, and don't make the mistake most people make. In their eagerness to pry into other people's business, they don't take the time to subject themselves to scrutiny. Don't dodge this responsibility; pay special attention to yourself. And don't neglect public affairs if you're at all able to improve them. If they go well, not just the other citizens but also your friends and you yourself will reap not inconsiderable benefits." (Xenophon, *Memorabilia* 3.7.1–9)[6]

ii. Politicians as Impostors

7.7 Plato's *Socrates (at his trial) reports his failure to find wisdom in a politician*

"I went to one of those reputed wise, thinking that there, if anywhere, I could refute the oracle and say to it: 'This man is wiser than I, but you said I was.' Then, when I examined this man—there is no need for me to tell you his name, he was one of our politicians—my experience was something like this: I thought that he appeared wise to many people and especially to himself, but he was not. I then tried [d] to show him that he thought himself wise, but that he was not. As a result he came to dislike me, and so did many of the bystanders. So I withdrew and thought to myself: 'I am wiser than this man; it is likely that neither of us knows anything worthwhile, but he thinks he knows something when he does not, whereas when I do not know, neither do I think I know; so I am likely to be wiser than he to this small extent, that I do not think I know what I do not know.'" (Plato, *Apology* 21b–d; preceding and following text is in **3.54(a)**)

7.8 *A visitor from Elea in* **Plato**, *to Socrates' younger namesake, on how surprisingly robust cities are, given the quality of those who rule them*

"Do we wonder, then, Socrates, at all the evils that turn out to occur in such constitutions [i.e., all existing types], and all those that will turn out for them, when a foundation of this sort underlies them, one of carrying out their functions [302a] according to written rules and customs without knowledge—which if used by another expertise would manifestly destroy everything that comes about through it? Or should we rather wonder at something else, namely at how strong a thing a

---

6. Cf. also the account given by Plato's Socrates in **3.16** of the natural qualities required by a future ruler in a philosophically ruled city.

city is by its nature? For in fact cities have suffered such things now for time without limit, but nevertheless some particular ones among them are enduring and are not overturned. Yet many from time to time sink like ships, and perish, and have perished, and will perish in the future through the depravity of their steersmen and sailors, who [b] have acquired the greatest ignorance about the greatest things—although they have no understanding at all about what belongs to the art of statesmanship, they think they have completely acquired this sort of expert knowledge, most clearly of them all. . . . [303c] So then we must also remove [sc. from the scope of our account of what statesmanship is] those who participate in all these constitutions, except for the one based on knowledge, as being, not statesmen, but experts in faction; we must say that, as presiding over insubstantial images, on the largest scale, they are themselves of the same sort, and that as the greatest imitators and magicians they turn out to be the greatest sophists among sophists." (Plato, *Statesman* 301e–302b and 303c)

7.9 Xenophon's Socrates on the false pretenses of the orators

On still another occasion, Antiphon was questioning him about how he thought he could equip others for political life when he did not participate in politics himself, or whether he was even capable of doing so. "Which would be a better way for me to participate in politics, Antiphon," he said, "doing so on my own, or seeing to it that as many people as possible are competent to do so?"

[7.1] Let us consider whether he turned his companions' attention toward virtue by also discouraging them from false pretense. He always used to say that there was no better path to a good reputation than for someone actually to become as good at something as he wanted to seem. This is what he taught to prove his point:

[2] "Let's ponder," he said, "what someone who isn't a good flutist should do if he wants to be thought one. Shouldn't he imitate good flutists in the trappings of their art? To begin with, since they own fancy equipment and lead a sizeable entourage, he should do the same. Next, since many people admire them, he should also recruit hordes of admirers. But by no means should he undertake an actual performance, or else he'll become a laughingstock and be exposed straightaway as not just a poor flutist but a fraud. Besides, if he spends a lot of money without deriving any benefit, and earns a bad reputation on top of that, how could he avoid a life fraught with hardship, frustration, and derision? [3] Likewise, let's reflect on what would befall someone who wanted to appear to be a good commander or boat pilot, supposing he

weren't. Wouldn't it be distressing if he set his heart on being thought competent at these functions but weren't persuasive? And yet wouldn't it be even more miserable if he did persuade people, considering that someone with no experience appointed to pilot a ship or lead an army would obviously end up destroying those he least wanted to and bringing shame and harm upon himself?"

[4] He similarly declared that there was no benefit in being thought rich, courageous, and powerful if one were not actually so, since, he said, such people are assigned tasks beyond their abilities; and if they proved unable to do what they were thought to be competent at, they would not be forgiven. [5] He called anyone who employed persuasion to rob somebody of money or goods a big fraud, but he called the biggest fraud by far someone who, despite his own worthlessness, deceived people by convincing them that he was competent to govern the state. Personally, I think that he also discouraged his companions from false pretense by engaging in these kinds of conversations. (Xenophon, *Memorabilia* 1.6.15–7.5)

7.10 *Antisthenes' disdain for the orators (and* **Plato***)*

Again, Antisthenes, in his second *Cyrus,* abuses Alcibiades by saying he was perverted in his relations with women as well as in his general way of life. He claims Alcibiades slept with his mother, his daughter, and his sister, "in the Persian manner." [D] His dialogue *Statesman* includes invective against all public speakers at Athens, his *Archelaus* against the orator Gorgias, while his *Aspasia* slanders Pericles' sons Xanthippus and Paralus—one of them, he says, shared a house with Archestratus, whose occupation resembled that of women in a cheap brothel, and the other was a companion and intimate of Euphemus, famous for poking vulgar and heartless fun at anybody he met; and he altered Plato's name to the lewd and vulgar "Satho" ["Dick"], publishing his dialogue against him under this title. [E] For in the eyes of these people there is no one who gives good advice; no general is wise, no sophist is worth anything, no poet is useful, no populace capable of reason—only Socrates is, who spends his time with Aspasia's flute girls where they work, and converses with Piston the breastplate maker, and instructs the courtesan Theodote on how to seduce her lovers, as Xenophon represents him in the second book of the *Memorabilia*.[7] (Athenaeus, *The Learned Banqueters* 5, 220C–E = Antisthenes 141 + 204 + 203 + 142 + 147)

---

7. See **6.3** (from what is actually the third book of the *Memorabilia*, at least as we have it).

7.11 Plato's Socrates suggests that Pericles could not make people virtuous

"Am I following what you are saying?" I [Socrates] asked. "You appear to be talking about the art of citizenship, and to be promising to make men good citizens."

"This is exactly what I claim, Socrates," he [Protagoras] said.

"Well, this is truly an admirable technique you have developed," I said, "if indeed [b] you have. There is no point in my saying to you anything other than exactly what I think. The truth is, Protagoras, I have never thought that this could be taught, but when you say it can be, I can't very well doubt it. It's only right that I explain where I got the idea that this is not teachable, not something that can be imparted from one human being to another. I maintain, along with the rest of the Greek world, that the Athenians are wise. And I observe that when we convene in the Assembly and the city has to take some action on a building project, we send for builders to advise us; if it has to do with the construction of ships, we send for [c] shipwrights; and so forth for everything that is considered learnable and teachable. But if anyone else, a person not regarded as a craftsman, tries to advise them, no matter how handsome and rich and well-born he might be, they just don't accept him. They laugh at him and shout him down until he either gives up trying to speak and steps down himself, or the archer police remove him forcibly by order of the board. This is how they [d] proceed in matters which they consider technical. But when it is a matter of deliberating on city management, anyone can stand up and advise them, carpenter, blacksmith, shoemaker, merchant, ship captain, rich man, poor man, well born, low born—it doesn't matter—and nobody blasts him for presuming to give counsel without any prior training under a teacher. The [e] reason for this is clear: They do not think that this can be taught. Public life aside, the same principle holds also in private life, where the wisest and best of our citizens are unable to transmit to others the virtues that they possess. Look at Pericles, the father of these young men here. He [320a] gave them a superb education in everything that teachers can teach, but as for what he himself is really wise in, he neither teaches them that himself nor has anyone else teach them either, and his sons have to browse like stray sacred cattle and pick up virtue on their own wherever they might find it. Take a good look at Clinias, the younger brother of Alcibiades here. When Pericles became his guardian he was afraid that he would be corrupted, no less, by Alcibiades. So he separated them and placed Clinias in Ariphron's house and tried to educate him there. Six months later he [b] gave him back to Alcibiades because he couldn't do anything with him. I could mention a great many more, men who are good themselves but have never succeeded in making anyone else better, whether family members or total strangers." (Plato, *Protagoras* 319a–320b)

7.12 *Antisthenes on the need for virtuous leaders*

"What ruined cities," [Antisthenes] said, "was when they were unable to distinguish bad men from good." (Diogenes Laertius 6.5 = Antisthenes 71)

7.13 *The same*

[Antisthenes] said it was strange to weed out thistles from corn, and the useless in war, but not to get rid of the bad elements in government. (Diogenes Laertius 6.6 = Antisthenes 73)

iii. The Philosopher and Politics

7.14 *Xenophon's Aristippus prefers freedom to enjoy pleasures over politics*

I think that he also encouraged his companions to exercise self-control in matters of food, drink, sex, sleep, cold, heat, and hard work by saying things of the following kind. Once, when he recognized that a certain companion of his was lacking self-control in these regards, he said, "Tell me, Aristippus, if you needed to take two young men and raise them so that one would be a competent ruler and the other wouldn't even aspire to power, how would you go about raising each of them? If you care to, let's examine the matter starting from the basics, as it were, with nutrition."

Aristippus replied, "Nutrition does strike me as the place to start, since no one could even survive without nourishment."

[2] "So it stands to reason that the desire for food arises in both when the time is right?"

"It does," he said.

"Then which of the two would you accustom to taking care of pressing business over gratifying his belly?"

"The one being raised to govern, of course," he replied, "so that state business isn't neglected during his tenure."

"So likewise, whenever they're thirsty," he said, "should we endow the same one with the ability to hold off from drinking?"

"Certainly," he replied.

[3] "And which one should we endow with mastery over sleep, such that he's able to go to bed late, to get up early, or to stay awake if need be?"

"The same one as well," he replied.

"What about mastery over sexual desires, such that these don't prevent him from taking action when necessary?" he asked.

"The same one as well," he replied.

"What about not shirking hard work, but submitting to it willingly? Which one should we endow with this disposition?"

"Also the one being raised to govern," he replied.

"What about the ability to learn whatever item's useful for overpowering one's enemies? Which one would it be more appropriate to endow with this?"

"Far and away the one being raised to govern," he said, "since without this kind of knowledge none of the rest would be of any use."

[4] "Don't you think that whoever's raised in this manner is less likely than any other creature to be captured by his enemies? Some of these other creatures, as you know, get lured in by their stomach—hunger drives even some especially timid ones to take the bait and get caught—while others are ensnared through drink."

. . .

[7] "Now, if we assign people with mastery over all these things to the class of those fit to govern, shall we assign the ones incapable of doing them to the class of people who won't even aspire to power?"

He agreed to this as well.

"Well, then, given your familiarity with each of these respective classes, have you ever considered to which of the two you ought to assign yourself?"

[8] "I certainly have," said Aristippus, "and by no means do I include myself in the class of those who want to govern. In fact, as much effort as it takes for a person to meet his own needs, I think that only a complete fool wouldn't let this suffice, but would take on the added burden of meeting the rest of the citizens' needs as well. What could be more foolish than for someone to sacrifice many of the things he personally wants while exposing himself to possible prosecution if, as head of state, he fails to deliver on all the things his country wants? [9] States claim the right to treat their rulers in the same way I treat my slaves: I expect my attendants to lavish me with everything I need without laying their own hands on anything; likewise, states think that their rulers should provide them with every possible good while personally

abstaining from all of them. I would therefore place in the class of men fit to govern, and raise accordingly, those who want to have the many troubles associated with trying to provide both for themselves and for others. Myself, however, I put in the class of those who want to live as easily and pleasantly as possible."

[10] Socrates replied, "So do you want us to examine also whether those ruling or those being ruled lead more pleasant lives?"

"Certainly," he said.

"Let's start with the nations with which we're familiar. In Asia, the Persians rule, while the Syrians, Phrygians, and Lydians are ruled. In Europe, the Scythians rule, while the Maiotians are ruled. And in Africa, the Carthaginians rule, while the Libyans are ruled. So which of these do you think lead more pleasant lives? Or among Greeks, of which you're one yourself, do you think the conquerors or the conquered lead more pleasant lives?"

[11] "Well, rest assured," said Aristippus, "that I don't put myself in the class of slaves either. But I think that there's a middle road between these, which I try to travel. It runs through neither ruling nor slavery, but through freedom, which is the road most conducive to happiness."

[12] "Well," said Socrates, "if this road bypassed humanity in the way it bypasses ruling and slavery, you might be on to something. But if you expect to live among human beings without either ruling or being ruled, and you won't willingly serve those who do rule, I think that you can see how expert the stronger are at causing grief for the weaker, whether states or individuals, and treating them like slaves. [13] Or haven't you noticed how the stronger slash crops and chop down trees that others have sown and planted, and use every means to harrass the weaker who withhold service, until finally they convince them to accept enslavement over fighting against their superiors? And as for the private sphere, aren't you aware how the courageous and powerful profit by reducing the cowardly and powerless to servitude?"

"Well," he said, "you should know that as a personal precaution I don't confine myself to any particular nationality; I am a stranger everywhere."

[14] "That's certainly a clever trick you describe," replied Socrates. "So does no one harm strangers ever since Sinis, Sciron, and Procrustes died? Yet even today the participants in the governments of these countries establish laws to protect themselves from harm, and they get the support of friends from outside their immediate family, erect fortifications around their cities, acquire arms to fend off aggressors, and secure foreign allies besides. And despite having all of these advantages, they

still suffer harm. [15] You, on the other hand, have none of these things. You spend much of your time on the open road, where the majority of people come to harm. You're also in a weaker position than any citizen of whatever state you visit, and a likely target for would-be aggressors. Do you imagine that you'll avoid harm anyway, just because you're a stranger? Are you confident because the states themselves publicly guarantee your safe passage coming and going? Or is it because you fancy yourself the kind of person who would be of no use to any master, even as a slave? After all, who would want to have as part of his household someone who enjoys living luxuriously but refuses to do any work?

[16] "Let's consider further how masters deal with servants like this. Don't they keep their lust in check by starving them, deter them from stealing by denying them access to wherever valuables are kept, prevent them from running away by chaining them up, and drive away their laziness by beatings? Or what do you do whenever you discover one of your servants behaving like this?"

[17] "I punish them in every way until I force them to submit," he said. "But, Socrates, what about those people raised in the art of governance, which you seem to identify with happiness? If they're going to be subjected to hunger, thirst, cold, sleep deprivation, and to undergo voluntarily every other kind of hardship, how are they any better off than people forced to suffer? Personally, I don't see what difference it makes whether the same skin is flogged voluntarily or involuntarily, or, in general, whether the same body is beset by all these hardships voluntarily or involuntarily, except that anyone who willingly submits to suffering is a fool to boot." (Xenophon, *Memorabilia* 2.1.1–4 and 7–17 = Aristippus 163)

7.15 *Antisthenes recommends cautious engagement with politics*

Asked how one should approach government, Antisthenes said, "As with fire: neither get too close, in case you burn, nor be too far away, in case you freeze." (Stobaeus, *Selections* 4.4.28 = Antisthenes 70)

7.16 *Plato's Socrates thinks the (true?) philosopher won't even know his way to the marketplace*

THEODORUS: No, no, Socrates. Let us review the philosophers . . .

SOCRATES: Very well, then; we must review them, it seems, since you have made up your mind. But let us confine ourselves to the leaders; why bother about the second-rate specimens? To begin with, then, [d] the philosopher grows up without knowing the way to the marketplace, or the whereabouts of the law courts or the council chambers or any other place of public assembly. Laws and decrees, published orally or in writing, are things he never sees or hears. The scrambling of political cliques for office; social functions, dinners, parties with flute girls—such doings never enter his head even in a dream. So with questions of birth—he has no more idea whether a fellow citizen is high-born or humble, or whether he has inherited some taint from his forebears, male or female, than he has [e] of the number of pints in the sea, as they say. And in all these matters, he knows not even that he knows not; for he does not hold himself aloof from them in order to get a reputation, but because it is in reality only his body that lives and sleeps in the city. His mind, having come to the conclusion that all these things are of little or no account, spurns them and pursues its wingéd way, as Pindar says, throughout the universe, "in the deeps beneath the earth" and geometrizing its surfaces, "in the heights above the heaven," astronomizing, [174a] and tracking down by every path the entire nature of each whole among the things that are, never condescending to what lies near at hand.

THEODORUS: What do you mean by that, Socrates?

SOCRATES: Well, here's an instance: they say Thales was studying the stars, Theodorus, and gazing aloft, when he fell into a well; and a witty and amusing Thracian servant girl made fun of him because, she said, he was wild to know about what was up in the sky but failed to see what was in front of him and under his feet. The same joke applies to all who [b] spend their lives in philosophy. It really is true that the philosopher fails to see his nextdoor neighbor; he not only doesn't notice what he is doing, he scarcely knows whether he is a man or some other kind of creature. The question he asks is, What is Man? What actions and passions properly belong to human nature and distinguish it from all other beings? This is what he wants to know and concerns himself to investigate. You see what I mean, Theodorus, don't you?

THEODORUS: Yes, and what you say is true.

SOCRATES: This accounts, my friend, for the behavior of such a man when [c] he comes into contact with his fellows, either privately with individuals or in public life, as I was saying at the beginning. Whenever he is obliged, in a law court or elsewhere, to discuss the things that lie at his feet and before his eyes, he causes entertainment not only to Thracian servant girls but to all the common herd, by tumbling into wells and every sort of difficulty through his lack of experience. His clumsiness is awful and gets him a reputation for fatuousness. On occasions when personal scandal is the topic of conversation, he never has anything at all of his own to contribute; he knows nothing to the detriment of anyone, never having [d] paid any attention to this subject—a lack of resource which makes him look very comic. And again, when compliments are in order, and self-laudation, his evident amusement—which is by no means a pose but perfectly genuine—is regarded as idiotic. When he hears the praises of a despot or a king being sung, it sounds to his ears as if some stockbreeder were being congratulated—some keeper of pigs or sheep, or cows that are giving him plenty of milk; only he thinks that the rulers have a more difficult and treacherous animal to rear and milk, and that such a man, [e] having no spare time, is bound to become quite as coarse and uncultivated as the stock farmer; for the castle of the one is as much a prison as the mountain fold of the other. When he hears talk of land—that So-and-So has a property of ten thousand acres or more, and what a vast property that is, it sounds to him like a tiny plot, used as he is to envisage the whole earth. When his companions become lyric on the subject of great families, and exclaim at the noble blood of one who can point to seven wealthy ancestors, he thinks that such praise comes of a dim and limited [175a] vision, an inability, through lack of education, to take a steady view of the whole, and to calculate that every single man has countless hosts of ancestors, near and remote, among whom are to be found, in every instance, rich men and beggars, kings and slaves, Greeks and foreigners, by the thousand. When men pride themselves upon a pedigree of twenty-five ancestors, and trace their descent back to Heracles, the son of Amphitryon, [b] they seem to him to be taking a curious interest in trifles. As for the twenty-fifth ancestor of Amphitryon, what *he* may have been is merely a matter of luck, and similarly with the fiftieth before him again. How ridiculous, he thinks, not to be able to work that out, and get rid of the gaping vanity of a silly mind. On all these occasions, you see, the philosopher is the object of general derision, partly for what men take to be his superior manner, and partly for his constant ignorance and lack of resource in dealing with the obvious.

THEODORUS: What you say exactly describes what does happen, Socrates. (Plato, *Theaetetus* 173c–175b)

7.17 Plato's Socrates describes his own inexperience of the ways of the wider world . . .

"I tell you, Polus, I'm not one of the politicians. Last year I was elected to the Council by lot, and when our tribe was presiding and I had to call [474a] for a vote, I came in for a laugh. I didn't know how to do it. So please don't tell me to call for a vote from the people present here. If you have no better 'refutations' than these to offer, do as I suggested just now: let me have my turn, and you try the kind of refutation I think is called for. For I do know how to produce one witness to whatever I'm saying, and that's the man I'm having a discussion with. The majority I disregard. And I do know how to call for a vote from one man, but I don't even discuss things with the majority." (Plato, *Gorgias* 473e–474a)

7.18 . . . yet he had earlier claimed that he himself may be the only true expert in politics of his generation . . .

SOCRATES: I hope you won't say what you've said many times, that anyone who wants to will put me to death. That way I, too, won't repeat my claim that it would be a wicked man doing this to a good man. And don't say that he'll confiscate any of my possessions, either, so I won't reply that when he's done so he won't know how to use them. Rather, just as he unjustly confiscated them from me, so, having gotten them, he'll [c] use them unjustly too, and if unjustly, shamefully, and if shamefully, badly.

CALLICLES: How sure you seem to me to be, Socrates, that not even one of these things will happen to you! You think that you live out of their way and that you wouldn't be brought to court perhaps by some very corrupt and mean man.

SOCRATES: In that case I really am a fool, Callicles, if I don't suppose that anything might happen to anybody in this city. But I know this well: that [d] if I do come into court involved in one of those perils which you mention, the man who brings me in will be a wicked man— for no good man would bring in a man who is not a wrongdoer—and it wouldn't be at all strange if I were to be put to death. Would you like me to tell you my reason for expecting this?

CALLICLES: Yes, I would.

SOCRATES: I believe that I'm one of a few Athenians—so as not to say I'm the only one, but the only one among our contemporaries—to take up the true political craft and practice the true politics. This is because the speeches I make on each occasion do not aim at gratification but at what's [e] best. They don't aim at what's most pleasant. And because I'm not willing to do those clever things you recommend, I won't know what to say in court. And the same account I applied to Polus comes back to me. For I'll be judged the way a doctor would be judged by a jury of children if a pastry chef were to bring accusations against him. Think about what a man like that, taken captive among these people, could say in his defense, if somebody were to accuse him and say, "Children, this man has worked many great evils on you, yes, on you. He destroys the youngest among [522a] you by cutting and burning them, and by slimming them down and choking them he confuses them. He gives them the most bitter potions to drink and forces hunger and thirst on them. He doesn't feast you on a great variety of sweets the way I do!" What do you think a doctor, caught in such an evil predicament, could say? Or if he should tell them the truth and say, "Yes, children, I was doing all those things in the interest of health," how big an uproar do you think such "judges" would make? Wouldn't it be a loud one?

CALLICLES: Perhaps so.

SOCRATES: I should think so! Don't you think he'd be at a total loss as [b] to what he should say?

CALLICLES: Yes, he would be.

SOCRATES: That's the sort of thing I know would happen to me, too, if I came into court. For I won't be able to point out any pleasures that I've provided for them, ones they believe to be services and benefits, while I envy neither those who provide them nor the ones for whom they're provided. Nor will I be able to say what's true if someone charges that I ruin younger people by confusing them or abuse older ones by speaking bitter words against them in public or private. I won't be able to say, that is, [c] "Yes, I say and do all these things in the interest of justice, my 'honored judges'"—to use that expression you people use—nor will I be able to say anything else. So presumably I'll get whatever comes my way. (Plato, *Gorgias* 521b–522c)

7.19(a) . . . *and elsewhere proposes that philosophers should rule* . . .

"Until philosophers rule as kings," I [Socrates] said, "or those who are now called kings and leading men genuinely and adequately philosophize, that is, until [d] political power and philosophy entirely coincide, while the many natures who at present pursue either one exclusively are forcibly prevented from doing so, cities will have no rest from evils,

Glaucon, nor, I think, will the human race. And, until this happens, the constitution we've been describing in [e] theory will never be born to the fullest extent possible or see the light of the sun. It's because I saw how very paradoxical this statement would be that I hesitated to make it for so long, for it's hard to face up to the fact that there can be no happiness, either public or private, in any other city." (Plato, *Republic* V, 473c–e)[8]

7.19(b) *... just as a ship should be captained by an expert*

"What the most decent people experience in relation to their city," [I (Socrates) said, to Adimantus,] "is so hard to bear that there's no other single experience like it. Hence to find an image of it and a defense for them, I must construct it from many sources, just as painters paint goat-stags by combining the features of different things. Imagine, then, that something like the following happens on a ship or on many ships. The shipowner is bigger and stronger than everyone else on board, but [b] he's hard of hearing, a bit short-sighted, and his knowledge of seafaring is equally deficient. The sailors are quarreling with one another about steering the ship, each of them thinking that he should be the captain, even though he's never learned the art of navigation, cannot point to anyone who taught it to him, or to a time when he learned it. Indeed, they claim that it isn't teachable and are ready to cut to pieces anyone who says that it is. They're always crowding around the shipowner, begging [c] him and doing everything possible to get him to turn the rudder over to them. And sometimes, if they don't succeed in persuading him, they execute the ones who do succeed or throw them overboard, and then, having stupefied their noble shipowner with drugs, wine, or in some other way, they rule the ship, using up what's in it and sailing while drinking and feasting, in the way that people like that are prone to do. Moreover, they call the person who is clever at persuading or forcing the shipowner to let them rule a 'navigator,' a [d] 'captain,' and 'one who knows ships,' and dismiss anyone else as useless. They don't understand that a true captain must pay attention to the seasons of the year, the sky, the stars, the winds, and all that pertains to his craft, if he's really to be the ruler of a ship. And they don't believe there is any craft that would enable him to determine how he should steer the ship [e] whether the others want him to or not, or any possibility of mastering this alleged craft or of practicing it at the same time as the craft of navigation. Don't you think that the true captain will be called a real

---

8. Cf. **7.44(a)** (at 326a–b).

stargazer, a babbler, and a good-for-nothing by those who sail in ships governed in that way, in which such things happen?" (Plato, *Republic* VI, 488a–e)

7.19(c) *Nor is it impossible that it should happen (or have happened in the past)*

"So," [I (Socrates) said,] "if something either has happened, in the endless reach of past time, or is now happening in some region far beyond the ken of us Greeks, or else will happen at some time in the future, to compel top philosophers to take charge of a city, on this point we're [d] ready and willing to fight our corner: that the regime we've described has come into existence, and exists, or will exist, only when the Muse of philosophy herself takes control of a city. It's not impossible for her to do so—we're not talking about something that's impossible; just difficult—that much we're agreed about."

"That's my opinion, anyway," said Adimantus.

"But the majority don't share your opinion—is that what you are going to say?" I asked.

"They probably don't," he replied. (Plato, *Republic* VI, 499c–d)

iv. Other Reflections on the Ideal Society

7.20 *Plato's Socrates (with **Glaucon**) on the "healthy" city*

"First, then," [I (Socrates) said,] "let's see what sort of life our citizens will lead when they've been provided for in the way we have been describing. They'll produce bread, wine, clothes, and shoes, won't they? They'll build houses, work naked [b] and barefoot in the summer, and wear adequate clothing and shoes in the winter. For food, they'll knead and cook the flour and meal they've made from wheat and barley. They'll put their honest cakes and loaves on reeds or clean leaves, and, reclining on beds strewn with yew and myrtle, they'll feast with their children, drink their wine, and, crowned with wreaths, hymn the gods. They'll enjoy sex with one another but bear no more [c] children than their resources allow, lest they fall into either poverty or war."

"It seems that you make your people feast without any delicacies," Glaucon interrupted.

"True enough," I said, "I was forgetting that they'll obviously need salt, olives, cheese, boiled roots, and vegetables of the sort they cook in the country. We'll give them desserts, too, of course, consisting of figs, chickpeas, and beans, and they'll roast myrtle and acorns before the fire, drinking [d] moderately. And so they'll live in peace and good health, and when they die at a ripe old age, they'll bequeath a similar life to their children."

"If you were founding a city for pigs, Socrates," he replied, "wouldn't you fatten *them* on the same diet?"

"Then how should I feed these people, Glaucon?" I asked.

"In the conventional way. If they aren't to suffer hardship, they should recline on proper couches, dine at a table, and have the delicacies and [e] desserts that people have nowadays."

"All right, I understand. It isn't merely the origin of a city that we're considering, it seems, but the origin of a *luxurious* city. And that may not be a bad idea, for by examining it, we might very well see how justice and injustice grow up in cities. Yet the true city, in my opinion, is the one we've described, the healthy one, as it were. But let's study a city with a [373a] fever, if that's what you want. There's nothing to stop us. The things I mentioned earlier and the way of life I described won't satisfy some people, it seems, but couches, tables, and other furniture will have to be added, and, of course, all sorts of delicacies, perfumed oils, incense, prostitutes, and pastries. We mustn't provide them only with the necessities we mentioned at first, such as houses, clothes, and shoes, but painting and embroidery must be begun, and gold, ivory, and the like acquired. Isn't that so?"

"Yes." [b]

"Then we must enlarge our city, for the healthy one is no longer adequate. We must increase it in size and fill it with a multitude of things that go beyond what is necessary for a city—hunters, for example, and artists or imitators, many of whom work with shapes and colors, many with music. And there'll be poets and their assistants, actors, choral dancers, contractors, and makers of all kinds of devices, including, among other things, those needed for the adornment of women. And so we'll need more servants, [c] too. Or don't you think that we'll need tutors, wet nurses, nannies, beauticians, barbers, chefs, cooks, and swineherds? We didn't need any of these in our earlier city, but we'll need them in this one. And we'll also need many more cattle, won't we, if the people are going to eat meat?"

"Of course." (Plato, *Republic* II, 372a–373c)

7.21 The Athenian in **Plato**'s Laws *describes a mythical idyll with a moral for us*

"The traditional account that has come down to us tells of the wonderfully happy life people lived then [i.e., in the age of Cronus], and how they were provided with everything in abundance and without any effort on their part. The reason is alleged to be this: Cronus was of course aware that human nature, as we've explained, is never able to take complete control of all human affairs without being filled with arrogance [d] and injustice. Bearing this in mind, he appointed kings and rulers for our states; they were not men, but beings of a superior and more divine order—*daimones*.[9] We act on the same principle nowadays in dealing with our flocks of sheep and herds of other domesticated animals: we don't put cattle in charge of cattle or goats in charge of goats, but control them ourselves, because we are a superior species. So Cronus too, who was well-disposed to man, did the same: he placed us in the care of the *daimones,* a superior order of beings, who were to look after our interests—an easy enough [e] task for them, and a tremendous boon to us, because the results of their attentions were peace, respect for others, good laws, justice in full measure, and a state of happiness and harmony among the races of the world. The story has a moral for us even today, and there is a lot of truth in it: where the ruler of a state is not a god but a mortal, people have no respite from toil and misfortune. The lesson is that we should make every effort to imitate the life men are said to have led under Cronus; we should run our public and our private life, our homes and our cities, in obedience to what [714a] little spark of immortality lies in us, and dignify these edicts of reason with the name of 'law.' But take an individual man, or an oligarchy, or even a democracy, that lusts in its heart for pleasure and demands to have its fill of everything it wants—the perpetually unsatisfied victim of an evil greed that attacks it like the plague—well, as we said just now, if a power like that controls a state or an individual and rides roughshod over the laws, it's impossible to escape disaster." (Plato, *Laws* IV, 713c–714a)

7.22 The Athenian in **Plato**'s Laws *again: we should aim to approximate to the best*

"The next move in this game of legislation is as unusual as going 'across the line' in checkers, and may well cause surprise at first hearing. But

---

9. See Ch. 10.

reflection and experience will soon show that the organization of a state is almost bound to fall short of the ideal. You may, perhaps—if you don't know what it means to be a legislator without dictatorial powers—refuse to countenance such a state; nevertheless the right procedure is to describe not only the ideal society but the second and third best too, and then leave [b] it to anyone in charge of founding a community to make a choice between them. So let's follow this procedure now: let's describe the absolutely ideal society, then the second best, then the third. On this occasion we ought to leave the choice to Clinias, but we should not forget anyone else who may at some time be faced with such a choice and wish to adopt for his own purposes customs of his native country which he finds valuable.

[c] "You'll find the ideal society and state, and the best code of laws, where the old saying 'friends' property is genuinely shared' is put into practice as widely as possible throughout the entire state. Now I don't know whether in fact this situation—a community of wives, children, and all property—exists anywhere today, or will ever exist, but at any rate in such a state the notion of 'private property' will have been by hook or by crook completely eliminated from life. Everything possible will have been done to throw into a sort of common pool even what is by nature 'my own,' [d] like eyes and ears and hands, in the sense that to judge by appearances they all see and hear and act in concert. Everybody feels pleasure and pain at the same things, so that they all praise and blame with complete unanimity. To sum up, the laws in force impose the greatest possible unity on the state—and you'll never produce a better or truer criterion of an absolutely perfect law than that. It may be that gods or a number of the children of gods inhabit this kind of state: if so, the life they live there, [e] observing these rules, is a happy one indeed. And so men need look no further for their ideal: they should keep this state in view and try to find the one that most nearly resembles it." (Plato, *Laws* V, 739a–e)[10]

---

10. For the ideal described here, cf. the city described at length in the part of the *Republic* that follows **7.20**, and the city of Atlantis described at the beginning of Plato's *Timaeus* and in the companion work *Critias*.

v. On Actual Societies

7.23 *Plato's Socrates (with* **Glaucon***) classifies
existing constitutions into four types*

"You said, if I [Glaucon] remember, that there were four types of constitution remaining[11] that are worth discussing, each with faults that we should observe, and we should do the same for the people who are like them. Our aim was to observe them all, agree which man is best and which worst, and then determine whether the best is happiest and the worst most wretched or whether it's otherwise. I was asking you which four constitutions you had in mind when Polemarchus and Adimantus interrupted. [b] And that's when you took up the discussion that led here."

"That's absolutely right," I [Socrates] said.

"Well, then, like a wrestler, give me the same hold again, and when I ask the same question, try to give the answer you were about to give before."

"If I can," I replied.

"So what I'd really like to hear," he said, "is what four constitutions you had in mind."

[c] "That's not a difficult task," I said. "They're the ones that have names. First, there's the constitution praised by most people, namely, the Cretan or Laconian. The second, which is also second in the praise it receives, is called 'oligarchy' and is filled with a host of evils. The next in order, and antagonistic to it, is democracy. And finally there is genuine tyranny, surpassing all of them, the fourth and last of the diseased cities. Or can you think of another type of constitution—I mean another whose form is distinct from these? Dynasties and purchased kingships and other constitutions [d] of that sort, which one finds no less among the barbarians than among the Greeks, are somewhere intermediate between these four."

"There are certainly many strange ones people talk about," he said. (Plato, *Republic* VIII, 544a–d)

7.24 **Xenophon** *on the inferiority of most societies
to (his idealization of) Cyrus' Persia*

It once occurred to me to reflect how many democracies have been overthrown by people who wanted to be governed in some other way

---

11. I.e., apart from the ideal, described in the body of the *Republic*.

than a democracy—and how many monarchies and oligarchies likewise have been destroyed by their own people. I reflected too on how some of those individuals who have aspired to absolute power have been quickly deposed, whereas others, if they have managed to stay in power for any length of time, are marveled at for their wisdom and good fortune. It also seemed to me that I had observed that even in private households people could not impose their authority as masters on their slaves, whether they had more than the usual numbers or just a few. [2] I also thought to myself that cowherds are rulers too—over their cattle; and horse breeders over their horses; and in general everybody we call a "herdsman" can reasonably be counted as ruling over the animals they have in their charge. And I saw myself observing that these animal herds went along with their herdsmen more willingly than human beings do with their rulers: they move in whichever direction the herdsman directs them, they graze in the places he guides them to, they keep out of the ones he makes off-limits; and then they allow their keepers to enjoy, just as they like, the profits that come from them. Again, I have never known herds to conspire against their keepers, by disobeying them or keeping them from their profits. In fact they are harsher toward animals from other herds than they are to their rulers, the very people who benefit from them. By contrast there is no one against whom human beings are readier to conspire than those they see endeavoring to rule over them.

[3] As I reflected on all this, my conclusion was that for anyone born human it was easier rule over any creature other than human beings. But then I observed that there was Cyrus, a Persian, who acquired huge numbers of human subjects, of cities and of nations, and they all obeyed him—and that compelled me to change my mind. Perhaps after all it was not impossible, or even difficult, to rule over human beings, provided one goes about it in a knowledgeable way. At any rate we know that Cyrus' subjects willingly submitted to his rule even if they lived many, many days' march away, or even months; some of them had never even seen him, and knew for sure that they never would, and yet still they remained his willing subjects. [4] The reason lies in his superiority to other kings, whether they have inherited their thrones or acquired them through their own efforts. There are large numbers of Scythians, for example, yet the Scythian king would never be able to rule over another nation in addition to his own; he is happy enough if he can continue in power over the Scythians. So too with the Thracian king and the Thracians, the Illyrian with the Illyrians, and so on with other nations, or so we hear. At any rate the European ones are

said still to be autonomous and independent of one another. Cyrus, on the other hand, faced with Asiatic nations that were similarly autonomous, started with a small expedition of Persians and ended as ruler, by consent, of Medes and then of Hyrcanians. He then conquered the Syrians, the Assyrians, the Arabians, the Cappadocians, the peoples of both Phrygias, Lydians, Carians, Phoenicians, Babylonians; he became ruler of the Bactrians, the Indians, the Cilicians, not to mention the Sacians, the Paphlagonians, and the Magadidae—and many, many other nations one doesn't even know the names of. He became ruler of the Greeks in Asia, too, and crossing the sea established his power over the Cypriots and the Egyptians. [5] And he established himself over all these nations when they did not speak the same language as him or as each other. Despite that he was able to reach out over all this vast area through the fear that he instilled, great enough to paralyze everyone and prevent any resistance; and simultaneously he was able to inspire so great a desire in everyone to please him that they never wished to be ruled again by anyone's judgment but his. The races that he brought under him in this way were so many in number that it would be hard to travel through them all, in whichever direction one started from the royal palace, whether to east or west, north or south.

[6] Thinking this man to be someone deserving of our admiration, I have accordingly examined his origins, his natural endowments, and what sort of education he enjoyed, in order to discover how he became so outstanding as a ruler of human beings. So I shall now try to set out what I have heard and what I think I understand of him. (Xenophon, *Cyropaedia* 1.1.1–6)

7.25 *Antisthenes against democratic appointment to positions requiring expertise*

[Antisthenes] used to advise the Athenians to pass a vote that donkeys were horses; when they thought that unreasonable, he said, "Well, generals are made here without their having learned anything, but just by a show of hands." (Diogenes Laertius 6.8 = Antisthenes 72)

7.26 *Antisthenes admires the manliness of Sparta . . .*

Antisthenes, himself an Athenian, said on visiting Sparta from Athens that he was coming from the women's quarters into the men's. (Aelius Theon, *Preliminary Exercises* 5, ii. 105.6 Spengel = Antisthenes 7)

7.27 . . . and thinks it morally superior to Thebes

Seeing the Thebans thinking much of themselves after the battle of Leuctra [sc. against the Spartans], Antisthenes the Socratic said that they were no different from little boys giving themselves airs for giving their tutor (*paidagogos*) a good beating. (Plutarch, *Life of Lycurgus* 30.6 = Antisthenes 10)

7.28 *The Athenian in **Plato**'s Laws describes the ignoble impulses behind the Athenians' response to Persian invasion under King Xerxes*

"They could think of only one hope, and a thin, desperate hope it was; but there was simply no other. Their minds went back to the previous occasion, and they reflected how the victory they won in battle had been gained in equally desperate [c] circumstances. Sustained by this hope, they began to recognize that no one but they themselves and their gods could provide a way out of their difficulties. All this inspired them with a spirit of solidarity. One cause was the actual fear (*phobos*) they felt at the time, but there was another kind too, encouraged by the traditional laws of the state. I mean the 'fear' they had learned to experience as a result of being subject to an ancient code of laws. In the course of our earlier discussion we have called this fear 'modesty' (*aidôs*) often enough,[12] and we said that people who aspire to be good must be its slave. A coward, on the other hand, is free of this particular kind of fear and never experiences it. But if fright (*deos*) had not taken over the coward on this occasion, he and his fellow cowards would never have combined to defend themselves or protected temples, tombs, fatherland, and friends and relatives as well, in the way they did." (Plato, *Laws* III, 699b–c)

7.29 Antisthenes *mocks Athenian pretensions*

Antisthenes, son of Antisthenes, an Athenian. He was said not to be a true-born Athenian; hence his retort to the person who criticized him for it: "And the mother of the gods was a Phrygian." In fact people thought he had a Thracian mother; which when he had distinguished himself at the battle of Tanagra allowed Socrates to claim that he'd never have acquired such nobility if both his parents had been Athenian. He himself, by way of pouring scorn on the Athenians for preening themselves on being earth-born, used to say they were no better born than snails or locusts. (Diogenes Laertius 6.1 = Antisthenes 8)

---

12. Cf. *Laws* I, 647a, II, 671d.

7.30 Antisthenes' *ambivalence over Athens, Thebes, and Sparta*

And Hermippus[13] says that [Antisthenes] had originally set out in the assembly at the Isthmian games both to attack and to praise Athenians and Thebans and Spartans; but that he cried off when he saw that rather a lot of people had come from those cities. (Diogenes Laertius 6.2 = Antisthenes 9)

vi. On Laws

7.31 Plato's *Eleatic points out that laws are a blunt instrument in need of wise oversight*

YOUNG SOCRATES: The rest of it, visitor, seems to have been said in due measure; but that ideal rule may exist even without laws was something harder for a hearer to accept.

VISITOR: You got in just a little before me with your question, Socrates. [294a] For I was about to ask you whether you accept all of this, or whether in fact you find any of the things we have said difficult to take. But as it is it's already apparent that we'll want a discussion of this matter of the correctness of those who rule without laws.

YOUNG SOCRATES: Quite.

VISITOR: Now in a certain sense it is clear that the art of the legislator belongs to that of the king; but the best thing is not that the laws should prevail, but rather the kingly man who possesses wisdom. Do you know why?

YOUNG SOCRATES: What then is the reason?

VISITOR: That law could never accurately embrace what is best and most just for all at the same time, [b] and so prescribe what is best. For the dissimilarities between human beings and their actions, and the fact that practically nothing in human affairs ever remains stable, prevent any sort of expertise whatsoever from making any simple decision in any sphere that covers all cases and will last for all time. I suppose this is something we agree about?

YOUNG SOCRATES: Certainly.

VISITOR: But we see law bending itself more or less toward this very thing; [c] it resembles some self-willed and ignorant person, who allows

---

13. Fifth-century BCE comic poet.

no one to do anything contrary to what he orders, nor to ask any questions about it, not even if, after all, something new turns out for someone which is better, contrary to the prescription which he himself has laid down.

YOUNG SOCRATES: True; the law does absolutely as you have just said with regard to each and every one of us.

VISITOR: Then it is impossible for what is perpetually simple to be useful in relation to what is never simple?

YOUNG SOCRATES: Very likely.

VISITOR: Why then is it ever necessary to make laws, [d] given that law is not something completely correct? We must find out the cause of this.

YOUNG SOCRATES: Certainly.

VISITOR: Now with you, too, people train in groups in the way they do in other cities, whether for running or for anything else, for competitive purposes?

YOUNG SOCRATES: Yes, very frequently.

VISITOR: Well, now let's recall to mind the instructions that expert trainers give when they're in charge of people in such circumstances.

YOUNG SOCRATES: What are you thinking of?

VISITOR: That they don't suppose there is room for them to make their prescriptions piece by piece to suit each individual, giving the instruction [e] appropriate to the physical condition of each; they regard it as necessary to make rougher prescriptions about what will bring physical benefit, as suits the majority of cases and a large number of people.

YOUNG SOCRATES: Right.

VISITOR: And it's just for this reason that, as it is, they give equally heavy exercises to the group as a whole, starting them off together and stopping them together in their running, wrestling, and the rest of their physical exercises.

YOUNG SOCRATES: That's so.

VISITOR: Then let's suppose the same about the legislator too, the person [295a] who will direct his herds in relation to justice and their contracts with one another: he will never be capable, in prescribing for everyone together, of assigning accurately to each individual what is appropriate for him.

YOUNG SOCRATES: What you say certainly sounds reasonable.

VISITOR: Instead he will, I think, set down the law for each and every one according to the principle of "for the majority of people, for the majority of cases, and roughly, somehow, like this," whether expressing it in writing or in unwritten form, legislating by means of ancestral customs. (Plato, *Statesman* 293e–295a)

7.32–33 *Aristippus thinks that laws do for others what philosophy does for the wise*

[7.32] Asked once what advantage philosophers have, he [Aristippus] said, "If all the laws are taken away, we shall go on living in a similar way." (Diogenes Laertius 2.68 = Aristippus 105)

[7.33] This makes it clear that legislation itself is necessarily only about those who are equal, both in birth and in capacity. There is no law for men of outstanding quality; they are themselves the law. Anyone who tried to legislate for them would be ridiculous; they would probably say what Antisthenes had the lions say when the hares harangued them and tried to claim equal rights for all. (Aristotle, *Politics* 2.13, 1284a11–17 = Antisthenes 68)

vii. The Socratics, Tyrants, and Tyranny

7.34 *Antisthenes on the problem with tyrants*

Antisthenes the philosopher said ordinary people had a greater regard to piety than tyrants; when asked why, he said that with ordinary people it was criminals that were done away with, while with tyrants it was those who had done nothing wrong. (Stobaeus, *Selections* 4.8.31 = Antisthenes 75)

7.35–39 *Aristippus against tyranny*

[7.35] Aristippus, the philosopher from Cyrene, said that kingship was as different from tyranny as law from lawlessness and freedom from slavery. (Stobaeus, *Selections* 4.8.18 = Aristippus 41)

[7.36] From Aristippus: when Dionysius [the tyrant of Syracuse] said to him, "I've not benefited from you one bit," Aristippus replied, "True;

if you had, you'd have put a stop to your tyranny as if it were the sacred disease." (Stobaeus, *Selections* 4.8.23 = Aristippus 41)

[7.37] When he [Aristippus] was asking for money, and [Dionysius] said, "But you told me the wise man wouldn't want for anything," he replied, "Give me some, and let's discuss the matter." So Dionysius did, and Aristippus said, "So do you see? There's nothing I want for." When Dionysius said to him: "Let a man take his wares to a tyrant's court, | And he's his slave, no matter if he freely comes,"[14] Aristippus retorted, "He has no master, if he freely comes." (Diogenes Laertius 2.82 = Aristippus 40 + 30)

[7.38] Once when he was being forced by Dionysius to say something philosophical, he said, "How funny! You're learning from me what to say, and yet you're telling me when to say it!" When Dionysius took offense at this, and made him sit at the bottom of the table, Aristippus said, "You just wanted to give bottom place more prestige." (Diogenes Laertius 2.73 = Aristippus 36)

[7.39] Once when he [Aristippus] was asking something of Dionysius in relation to a friend, and did not get what he wanted, he fell at his feet; and when some one criticized him for it, he said: "Don't blame me, blame Dionysius for only listening through his feet." (Diogenes Laertius 2.79 = Aristippus 37)

7.40–41 *Aeschines paid court to Dionysius*

[7.40] And they say that poverty made him [Aeschines] go to Sicily, to Dionysius, and that he was disregarded by Plato, but supported by Aristippus; and that he received gifts from Dionysius after giving him some of his dialogues. (Diogenes Laertius 2.61 = Aristippus 22; part of **11.2**)

[7.41] And Polycritus of Mende[15] in the first book of his *On Dionysius* says that he [Aeschines] lived with the tyrant until he was deposed and Dion returned to Syracuse, reporting that Carcinus the tragic poet was also with him. A letter of Aeschines to Dionysius is said to exist. (Diogenes Laertius 2.63 = Aeschines 13; **1.24** follows)

---

14. Dionysius is quoting from a lost play of Sophocles (fr. 873 *TrGF*).
15. A historian of the mid–fourth century BCE (*FGrH* 559).

7.42 **Plato** and **Aristippus** *invited to the court of Dionysius*

When the one [Dionysius] went on trying to give and the other [Plato] refusing gifts of money, lots of it and many times over, Aristippus of Cyrene, who was there, said it was safe for Dionysius to be so bighearted; he offered little to people like him who wanted more, and a lot to Plato who would never take anything. (Plutarch, *Life of Dion* 19.3 = Aristippus 27)

7.43 **Plato** and **Aristippus** *at the court of Dionysius*

Helicon of Cyzicus, one of Plato's associates, predicted an eclipse of the sun. When his prediction proved correct, the tyrant was impressed and gave him a talent of silver. But Aristippus made fun of the other philosophers present, and claimed that he too could predict something no one expected. When they asked him to tell, he said, "Well then, I predict that it won't be long before Plato and Dionysius become enemies." (Plutarch, *Life of Dion* 19.7 = Aristippus 28)

7.44(a)–(b) *From a letter purporting to be* **Plato's** *description of his own visits to Syracuse, motivated by a desire to educate and advise the tyrant*

[7.44(a)] At last I came to the conclusion that all existing states are badly governed and the condition of their laws practically incurable, without some miraculous remedy and the assistance of fortune; and I was forced to say, in praise of true philosophy, that from her height alone was it possible to discern what the nature of justice is, either in the state or in [b] the individual, and that the ills of the human race would never end until either those who are sincerely and truly lovers of wisdom come into political power, or the rulers of our cities, by the grace of God, learn true philosophy. It was with this conviction [i.e., that politics should be united with philosophy] that I arrived in Italy and Sicily for the first time. When I arrived and saw what they call there the "happy life"—a life filled with Italian and Syracusan banquets, with men gorging themselves twice a day and never sleeping alone at night, and following all the [c] other customs that go with this way of living—I was profoundly displeased. For no man under heaven who has cultivated such practices from his youth could possibly grow up to be wise—so miraculous a temper is against nature—or become temperate, or indeed acquire any other part of virtue. Nor could any city enjoy tranquility, no matter how good its laws, [d] when its men think they must spend their all on excesses, and be easygoing about everything except the feasts and the drinking bouts and the pleasures of love that they pursue with professional zeal. . . . The rulers in [these cities] will not even hear mention of a just and equitable constitution. (?Plato, *Letters* VII, 326a–d)

[7.44(b)] When I arrived [i.e., in Syracuse, for the third time], I thought my first task was to prove whether Dionysius was really on fire with philosophy, or whether the many reports that came to Athens were without foundation. Now there is a certain way of putting this to the test, a dignified way and quite appropriate to tyrants, especially to those whose heads are full of half-understood doctrines, which I saw at once upon my arrival was particularly the case with Dionysius. You must picture to such men the extent of the undertaking, describing what [c] sort of inquiry it is, with how many difficulties it is beset, and how much labor it involves. For anyone who hears this, who is a true lover of wisdom, with the divine quality that makes him akin to it and worthy of pursuing it, thinks that he has heard of a marvelous quest that he must at once enter upon with all earnestness, or life is not worth living; and from that time forth he pushes himself and urges on his leader without ceasing, until he has reached the end of the journey or has become capable of doing without [d] a guide and finding the way himself. This is the state of mind in which such a man lives; whatever his occupation may be, above everything and always he holds fast to philosophy and to the daily discipline that best makes him apt at learning and remembering, and capable of reasoning soberly with himself; while for the opposite way of living he has a persistent hatred. Those who are really not philosophers but have only a coating of opinions, like men whose bodies are tanned by the sun, when they see how much learning is required, and how great the labor, and how orderly [e] their daily lives must be to suit the subject they are pursuing, conclude that the task is too difficult for their powers; and rightly so, for they are [341a] not equipped for this pursuit. But some of them persuade themselves that they have already sufficiently heard the whole of it and need make no further effort. Now this is a clear and infallible test to apply to those who love ease and are incapable of strenuous labor, for none of them can ever blame his teacher, but only himself, if he is unable to put forth the efforts that the task demands.

It was in this fashion that I then spoke to Dionysius. I did not explain everything to him, nor did he ask me to, for he claimed to have already [b] a sufficient knowledge of many, and the most important, points because of what he had heard others say about them. Later, I hear, he wrote a book on the matters we talked about, putting it forward as his own teaching, not what he had learned from me. Whether this is true I do not know. I know that certain others also have written on these same matters; but who they are they themselves do not know. So much at least I can affirm with [c] confidence about any who have written or propose to write on these questions, pretending to a knowledge of the problems with which I am concerned, whether they claim to have learned from me or from others or to have made their discoveries for themselves: it is impossible, in my opinion, that they can have learned anything at all about the subject. There is no writing of mine about these matters, nor will there ever be one. (?Plato, *Letters* VII, 340b–341c)

7.45 *Hostile sources supposed that the Socratics who went to Syracuse were motivated by greed*

These were the devices [Damis] used to try to cajole Apollonius[16] into not rejecting what he might be offered. But Apollonius, as if by way of joining his side of the argument, said, "But Damis, surely you were going to give me some examples? These include Aeschines son of Lysanias, who went off to Dionysius in Sicily for the sake of money; and Plato is said to have traversed Charybdis three times in pursuit of Sicilian riches; and then there are Aristippus of Cyrene and Helicon of Cyzicus and Phyto when he was exiled from Rhegium, who buried themselves so deep in Dionysius' treasure-houses that they barely surfaced again." (Philostratus, *Life of Apollonius of Tyana* 1.35.1 = Aristippus 25)

---

16. Apollonius of Tyana, the subject of Philostratus' hagiography, was a first-century CE Pythagorean who became the object of a cult later on.

Chapter 8: Aspasia and the Role of Women

It is presumably not coincidental that Alcibiades was a focus for the Socratics' thinking about erotics as well as politics: any successful society has to negotiate interpersonal relationships, and the Socratics in particular are committed to personal encounter as the model for dialectic, the basis for virtue, and the starting point for true political education. So it is perhaps no surprise that Alcibiades had a female counterpart in the Socratics' discussions as well: Aspasia.

Aspasia was what has been described as Pericles' "de facto wife" for the twenty years or so up to his death; he could not legally marry her, as a foreigner (from Miletus, in Greek Ionia), according to legislation he himself proposed. She was apparently on close terms with members of Socrates' circle, starting with Socrates himself (**8.3**, **8.7**), and she plainly left her mark on them: Aeschines and Antisthenes both wrote dialogues entitled *Aspasia* (see **8.1–9** and **8.13–14**, respectively), and Plato's *Menexenus* (see **8.10**) might as well have been named after her, since most of it is in her voice, albeit mediated by Socrates. Their views about her seem to have been somewhat ambivalent, ranging between apparent, if perhaps sometimes qualified, approval (Aeschines, Plato, Xenophon) to apparent hostility (Antisthenes). Aspasia is either genuinely wise, whether about supposedly "female" subjects (**8.11–12**) or in general (**8.2–3**, **8.6**, **8.9–10**); or she is a foreign woman exercising her female charms over the greatest statesman of the age (**8.13–14**); or else she is something of a mixture of both things (as in **8.4–5**—if, as seems likely, these passages in their original contexts were comparing her to the powerful women being described). In her role as a wise woman, Aspasia becomes a kind of seer without the religious trappings, comparable to—and perhaps a model for—the female Mantinean seer Diotima who taught Socrates about love (*Symposium* 201d–212a, of which **6.1(b)** is an excerpt). If we take Aspasia's Funeral Speech in the *Menexenus* as a knowing parody, it might not be entirely fanciful to see her as a sort of prototype for the philosopher-queens of Plato's *Republic*.

The ambivalence over Aspasia reflects a certain ambivalence over the status of women in general. The standard contemporary view of women as not just different from but inferior to men is reflected in Plato's works (**8.19–24**) as it is in Xenophon's (cf. his account of what he evidently sees as an ideal marital relationship: **8.18**).[1] Women who are available for extramarital sex are blithely commodified by Antisthenes

---

1. And see all of *On Household Management* 7–8.

(see **6.20–22**) and Aristippus (**8.15–16** in addition to **6.24**). Yet, as we have already seen, Antisthenes thought that excellence in a woman is the same as that in a man (**3.3**.[12]); and in both of his major political works, Plato has the leading character put the case that the current unequal treatment of women is contrary to reason (**8.27**; and see the whole discussion about the nature and roles of women from which this comes: *Republic* V, 451c–466c), and that it is an extraordinary and potentially damaging waste for a city to neglect the education of its female citizens, cordoning them off into different roles (**8.28**).

Texts

i. Aeschines' Aspasia

8.1–9 *Most, perhaps all, of these passages derive from* **Aeschines'** *dialogue, the* Aspasia. *His Aspasia is inspired by strong women of the past, and an inspiring teacher of eloquence and wisdom*

[8.1] Most of the philosophers tend naturally to be more abusive than the comic poets, to go by Aeschines the Socratic, for example. . . . [B] In his *Aspasia*, too, he calls Hipponicus son of Callias[2] a "nimcompoop," and Ionian women in general "adulteresses" and "gold diggers." (Athenaeus, *The Learned Banqueters* 5, 220A–B = Aeschines 61)

[8.2] Next we must put down an image of her wisdom and understanding.[3] Here we shall need many models, most of them ancient, and one itself Ionic in origin: those who painted and crafted it were Aeschines, Socrates' companion, and Socrates himself, most accurate of all craftsmen in that they worked with love. They proffered that famous Aspasia, from Miletus, with whom the most marvelous Olympian [Pericles] himself lived, as no mean image of understanding, to go by the degree of her experience, her political acumen, her quick and sharp wit—all of which we need to transfer to our own image with true precision. (Lucian, *Images* 17 = Aeschines 60)

---

2. Hipponicus was an Athenian general who married the ex-wife of Pericles, which could explain his presence in the *Aspasia*. (Cf. **8.14**.)
3. Lucian is describing Panthea, a feminine paragon.

[**8.3**] As for your honoring knowledge more than anything, Socrates, I hear that you frequently go out of your way to introduce young people to one teacher or another; [c] I gather you're someone that even urges Callias to send his son to Aspasia's, the Milesian—a man, to a woman's—and [d] that you visit her yourself, at your age, and that even she isn't a sufficient teacher for you. . . . (Maximus of Tyre, *Philosophical Orations* 38, 4b–d = Aeschines 60)

[**8.4**] Rhodogyne, queen of the Persians, so Aeschines the philosopher tells us, brought the Persian kingship to the greatest of heights. So great was her courage in action, he says, and so fearsome was she, that once when she was in the middle of doing her hair, and heard that some of the nations had rebeled, she left her hair half done, and didn't finish braiding it until she had put a stop to the peoples just referred to and brought them under control. This is why a golden statue of her was put up that had half its hair braided up on the head, the other half flowing loose. (Anonymous, *Treatise on Women* 8 = Aeschines 63)

[**8.5**] They say that she [Aspasia] emulated Thargelia, an Ionian woman from a previous age, by targeting the most powerful men. [4] This Thargelia, with an attractive appearance and charm combined with cleverness, bedded a large number of Greek men, and brought all those who associated with her over to the King, sowing the seeds of Medism in their cities through them because of their power and importance. [5] Some say that Pericles' enthusiasm for Aspasia was because of her wisdom and political expertise; witness the fact that sometimes Socrates used to visit her, with his associates, and his companions brought their wives in to her to listen, even though the business she presided over wasn't decent, or respectable—grooming young girls as prostitutes. [6] Aeschines the Socratic says that Lysicles the sheep dealer, too, from being a person of low birth and humble talents became first among the Athenians through his association with Aspasia after the death of Pericles. (Plutarch, *Life of Pericles* 24.3–6 = Aeschines 64 + 66)

[**8.6**] Aspasia the Milesian is also said to have sharpened up Pericles' speaking style in the manner of Gorgias. (Philostratus, *Letters* 73.28 = Aeschines 65; **1.25** follows)[4]

---

4. **1.25** purports to be a quotation from a work by Aeschines called *On Thargelia*, but (as no such title is attested in the catalogue of his works) may in fact come from the *Aspasia*: cf. **8.5**.

[8.7] Aspasia: daughter of Axiochus, from Miletus, wife of Pericles, had experience of philosophizing with Socrates, as Diodorus says in his treatise *On Monuments*.[5] After Pericles' death she married again, to Lysicles the sheep dealer, and had a son from him called Poristes; she made Lysicles a very clever speaker, as she had also trained Pericles in public oratory, as Aeschines the Socratic says in his dialogue,[6] and Plato, and similarly Callias in his *Men in Fetters*. Cratinus calls her a "tyrant" in his *Chirones*.[7] (Scholium to Plato, *Menexenus* 235e = Aeschines 66)

[8.8] At about this time Aspasia was put on a charge of impiety, her prosecutor being Hermippus the comic poet, who made the additional charge that she received free women in the house for Pericles. . . . [3] He interceded for her, shedding many tears before the court on her behalf, as Aeschines tells us, and pleading with the jurors. (Plutarch, *Life of Pericles* 32.1 and 3 = Aeschines 67)

[8.9] Induction is the form of speech that uses undisputed facts to win the assent of the person one is addressing; by means of this assent it brings him to accept things that are more doubtful because they resemble what he has already assented to. Thus in a work by Aeschines the Socratic Socrates tells us that Aspasia had the following conversation with Xenophon's wife and Xenophon himself: "Please tell me, wife of Xenophon: if your neighbor had a better piece of gold jewelry than you have, would you prefer hers or yours?" "Hers," replied Xenophon's wife. "What if she had better clothes and other woman's finery than you have, would you prefer yours or hers?" "Hers, obviously!" "So here's the next question," said Aspasia: "what if she had a better husband than you have—would you prefer your husband or hers?" When the woman blushed at this, [52] Aspasia then started talking to Xenophon himself: "Please tell me, Xenophon: if your neighbor had a better horse than yours is, would you prefer your horse or his?" "His," replied Xenophon. "What if he had a better farm than you have? Which farm would you then prefer to have?" "The better one, clearly," he said. "And if he had a better wife than you have, would you prefer yours or his?" At which point Xenophon himself fell silent too. Aspasia went on,

---

5. Diodorus Periegetes (*FGrH* 372), a historian of the fourth century BCE.

6. I.e., the *Aspasia*?

7. Cratinus (519–422 BCE) was a comic poet. The title of this play might be a reference to Chiron, the Centaur who was Achilles' teacher; it could also mean "worse/inferior [people]."

"Since both of you have failed to give me the one answer I wanted to hear, I'll say for myself what each of you is thinking. Both you, woman, want to have the best husband, and you, Xenophon, want more than anything to have the finest wife. So unless you two can bring it about that there is no better man or finer woman on earth, then plainly what you'll always lack much more than anything is what you think best, namely that you, Xenophon, should be husband of the best woman possible, and that she be married to the best man possible." (Cicero, *On Rhetorical Invention* 1.51–52 = Aeschines 70)

ii. Aspasia in Plato and Xenophon

8.10 *Plato's Socrates prefaces his recitation of a funeral speech composed by Aspasia*

MENEXENUS: You're forever making fun of the orators, Socrates. This time, though, I don't think that the one who's chosen is going to have an easy time of it; the selection is being made at the last minute, so perhaps the speaker will be forced practically to make his speech up as he goes.

SOCRATES: Nonsense, my good man. [d] Every one of those fellows has speeches ready-made, and, besides, even making up this kind of speech as you go isn't hard. Now if he were obliged to speak well of the Athenians among the Peloponnesians or the Peloponnesians among the Athenians, only a good orator could be persuasive and do himself credit; but when you're performing before the very people you're praising, being thought to speak well is no great feat.

MENEXENUS: You think not, Socrates?

SOCRATES: No, by Zeus, it isn't.

MENEXENUS: Do you think that *you* could deliver the speech, [e] if that were called for, and the Council were to choose you?

SOCRATES: In fact, Menexenus, there would be nothing surprising in my being able to deliver it. I happen to have no mean teacher of oratory. She is the very woman who has produced—along with a multitude of other good ones—the one outstanding orator among the Greeks, Pericles, son of Xanthippus.

MENEXENUS: What woman is that? But obviously you mean Aspasia?

SOCRATES: Yes, I do—her and Connus, son of Metrobius. [236a] These are my two teachers, he of music, she of oratory. Surely it's no surprise that a man with an upbringing like that should be skilled in speaking! But even someone less well educated than I—a man who had learned music from Lamprus and oratory from Antiphon the Rhamnusian—even he, despite these disadvantages, could do himself credit praising Athenians among Athenians.

MENEXENUS: And what would you have to say if the speech were yours to make?

SOCRATES: On my own, very likely nothing; but just yesterday in my lesson [b] I heard Aspasia declaim a whole funeral oration on these same dead. For she heard that the Athenians, just as you say, were about to choose someone to speak. Thereupon she went through for me what the speaker ought to say, in part out of her head, in part by pasting together some bits and pieces thought up before, at the time when she was composing the funeral oration which Pericles delivered, as, in my opinion, she did.

MENEXENUS: And can you remember what Aspasia said?

SOCRATES: I *think* I can. Certainly she taught it to me herself— [c] and I narrowly escaped a beating every time my memory failed me.

MENEXENUS: So why don't you go ahead and repeat it?

SOCRATES: I'm afraid my teacher will be angry with me if I divulge her speech.

MENEXENUS: Have no fear, Socrates. Speak. I shall be very grateful, whether you're pleased to recite Aspasia's speech or whoever it is. Only speak.

SOCRATES: But perhaps you will laugh at me if I seem to you, old as I am, to go on playing like a child.

MENEXENUS: Not at all, Socrates. In any case, just speak the speech. (Plato, *Menexenus* 235b–236c)

8.11 *Xenophon's* Socrates learns from Aspasia that matchmakers should tell the truth . . .[8]

"All right, then," replied Socrates, "this much I'm allowed to say about you to anyone you want to make friends with. Now, if you'll give me permission to say further that you're devoted to your friends; that

---

8. For Socrates as matchmaker and procurer: see **6.3–5**.

nothing pleases you more than good friends; that you take as much pride in your friends' achievements as in your own, and as much pleasure in their success, which you never stop devising ways to promote; and that you recognize that a man's virtue consists in outdoing his friends in kindness and his enemies in malice, then I think that I'd prove a very useful companion in your quest for good friends."

[36] "Why are you acting as if it's not up to you to say whatever you want about me?" asked Critobulus.

"It most certainly isn't, as I once heard Aspasia say. She said that good matchmakers have success at bringing people together only when the messages they convey back and forth are true and they refuse to pay false compliments, since the victims of any deception end up hating both one another and the matchmaker alike. I'm convinced that this is sound advice, and so I don't consider myself at liberty to pay you any compliments unless they're true."

[37] "So, Socrates," said Critobulus, "you're the kind of friend who will help me out if I'm somehow qualified myself to make friends, but who will otherwise refuse to make up something to say on my behalf."

"Do you think I'd benefit you more, Critobulus, by paying you false compliments or by convincing you to try to become a good man?" replied Socrates. (Xenophon, *Memorabilia* 2.6.35–37)

8.12 . . . *and about a woman's role in household management*

"It seems to me [Socrates] that there is a certain age at which both horses and people at once become useful and then go on improving. And I can show you that married women too can be treated by their husbands either in such a way as to become their partners in helping make the household prosper, or so as to inflict the greatest damage on it."

[11] "And should we blame the husband for that, Socrates, or the wife?" [asked Critobulus].

"For the most part," said Socrates, "if a sheep is in a bad way, we blame the shepherd, and if a horse is vicious we generally criticize the rider; with a wife, if she does badly when she is being taught the right things by her husband, it's probably right that the wife should bear the blame, but if he failed to teach her what is right and proper and dealt with her on the basis that she didn't know, then wouldn't it be right for the blame to attach to the husband? [12] In any case, Critobulus," said Socrates, "since we're all friends here, come clean with us: is there anyone you trust with more of the important things than your wife?"

"No, there isn't," he said.

"And is there anyone you talk to less than you do to your wife?"

"There certainly aren't many," he replied.

[13] "And you married her when she was the youngest she could have been, and had seen and heard as little of things as she could have done?"

"Certainly I did."

"Then it would be much more surprising if she knew what to say and do than if she made mistakes."

[14] "But what about the people you claim have good wives, Socrates—have they educated them themselves?"

"There's nothing like investigating a question like this. I'll introduce you to Aspasia, who will explain all this to you more knowledgeably than I could. [15] I think the wife who is a good partner in the household is the one whose contribution to it is the matching opposite of her husband's. Generally speaking what comes in does so because of what the husband does, whereas most of the expenditure that goes out is by dispensation of the wife; and if all this happens as it should, then households become more prosperous, whereas if it goes wrong they go downhill." (Xenophon, *On Household Management* 3.10–15)

iii. Antisthenes' Aspasia

8.13–14 *Like Aeschines,* **Antisthenes** *wrote an* Aspasia, *from which these passages may derive. There is a further fragment at* **7.10**.

[8.13] Antisthenes the Socratic says that [Pericles] was in love with Aspasia, and kissed the woman twice daily, when he left the house and when he came back in. (Athenaeus, *The Learned Banqueters* 13, 589E = Antisthenes 143)

[8.14] Pericles' affection for Aspasia appears to have been of a somewhat erotic sort. He had a wife who was related to his family, who had previously been married to Hipponicus,[9] to whom she bore the rich Callias; with Pericles she bore Xanthippus and Paralus. Then, when they tired of living with one another, he gave her away, with her consent, to someone else. He himself took Aspasia, [8] for whom he conceived an extraordinary passion: they say he embraced her with kisses

---

9. Cf. **8.1**.

every day both when he left for the agora and when he came back. (Plutarch, *Life of Pericles* 24.7–8 = Antisthenes 143)

iv. Aristippus on Prostitutes[10]

8.15 When a prostitute said to him, "I'm pregnant, and you're the father," he said, "You no more know that than if you were going through a patch of prickly rushes and claimed that you'd been pricked by *this* one." (Diogenes Laertius 2.81 = Aristippus 88)

8.16 When someone criticized him for living with a prostitute, he asked, "Would it make any difference to take a house that had had many previous residents or none?" "No." "What about sailing in a ship in which thousands had sailed before, as against one that no one had sailed in?" "Not at all." "Then there's no difference between living with a woman many men have used before and living with one no one has." (Diogenes Laertius 2.74 = Aristippus 90)

v. Plato and Xenophon on Women

8.17 *Plato's Meno sets out the conventional difference between male and female virtue, while Socrates seeks for what they have in common*

SOCRATES: Let us leave Gorgias out of it, since he is not here. But Meno, by the gods, what do you yourself say that virtue is? Speak and do not begrudge us, so that I may have spoken a most unfortunate untruth when I said that I had never met anyone who knew, if you and Gorgias are shown to know.

MENO: It is not hard to tell you, Socrates. [e] First, if you want the virtue of a man, it is easy to say that a man's virtue consists of being able to manage public affairs and in so doing to benefit his friends and harm his enemies and to be careful that no harm comes to himself; if you want the virtue of a woman, it is not difficult to describe: she must manage the home well, preserve its possessions, and be submissive to her husband; the virtue of a child, whether male or female, is different again, and so is that of an elderly man, if you want that, or if you

---

10. Cf. also **3.43–44**.

want that of a free man [72a] or a slave. And there are very many other virtues, so that one is not at a loss to say what virtue is. There is virtue for every action and every age, for every task of ours and every one of us—and, Socrates, the same is true for wickedness.

SOCRATES: I seem to be in great luck, Meno; while I am looking for one virtue, I have found you to have a whole swarm of them. But, Meno, to [b] follow up the image of swarms, if I were asking you what is the nature of bees, and you said that they are many and of all kinds, what would you answer if I asked you: "Do you mean that they are many and varied and different from one another insofar as they are bees? Or are they no different in that regard, but in some other respect, in their beauty, for example, or their size or in some other such way?" Tell me, what would you answer if thus questioned?

MENO: I would say that they do not differ from one another in being bees.

SOCRATES: If I went on to say: "Tell me, what is this very thing, Meno, [c] in which they are all the same and do not differ from one another?" Would you be able to tell me?

MENO: I would.

SOCRATES: The same is true in the case of the virtues. Even if they are many and various, all of them have one and the same form which makes them virtues, and it is right to look to this when one is asked to make [d] clear what virtue is. Or do you not understand what I'm saying?

MENO: I think I understand, but I certainly do not grasp what it being asked, at any rate as fully as I want to.

SOCRATES: I am asking whether you think it is only in the case of virtue that there is one for man, another for woman, and so on, or is the same true in the case of health and size and strength? Do you think that there is one health for man and another for woman? Or, is there the same [e] form everywhere, if there's health, whether in a man or in anything else whatever?

MENO: The health of a man seems to me the same as that of a woman.

SOCRATES: And so with size and strength? If a woman is strong, she will be strong by virtue of the same form, and the same strength? By "the same" here, what I have in mind is that the strength in question is no different insofar as one is talking about being strong, whether it's a man or a woman. Or do you think there is a difference?

MENO: I do not think so.

SOCRATES: And will there be any difference in the case of virtue, [73a] insofar as being virtue is concerned, whether it be in a child or an old man, in a woman or in a man?

MENO: I think, Socrates, that somehow this is no longer like those other cases.

SOCRATES: How so? Did you not say that the virtue of a man consists of managing the city well, and that of a woman of managing the household?

MENO: I did.

SOCRATES: Is it possible to manage a city well, or a household, or anything else, while not managing it moderately and justly?

MENO: Certainly not.

SOCRATES: Then if they manage justly and moderately, [b] they must do so with justice and moderation?

MENO: Necessarily.

SOCRATES: So both the man and the woman, if they are to be good, need the same things, justice and moderation.

MENO: So it seems.

SOCRATES: What about a child and an old man? Can they possibly be good if they are unrestrained and unjust?

MENO: Certainly not.

SOCRATES: But if they are moderate and just? [c]

MENO: Yes.

SOCRATES: So all human beings are good in the same way, for they become good by acquiring the same qualities.

MENO: It seems so. (Plato, *Meno* 71d–73c)

8.18 *Xenophon's Socrates on the ideal wife*

"Well now," said [Ischomachus], "in answer to your question, Socrates, I certainly don't spend my time in the house. The fact is that my wife is herself quite capable of running things there herself."

[4] "That's just what I'd really like you to tell me about, Ischomachus," I said: "Did you educate your wife yourself, to give her the qualities she needs, or did you receive her from her father and mother already knowing the things that belong to her sphere?"

[5] "What could she have known when I received her, Socrates? She came to me when she was not yet fifteen, and up till then she'd been kept under careful control, so that she should see and hear and say as little as possible. [6] Surely you'll think it quite sufficient if she came knowing no more than how to take some wool and turn out a cloak, and having seen no more than that the spinning is given to serving-women? Though I tell you, Socrates, she certainly arrived very well educated in matters of the stomach, which in my view is the greatest lesson both a man and a woman has to learn."

[7] "But in other respects, Ischomachus," I asked, "did you take on her education yourself, to make her competent to oversee her side of things?"

"Zeus! No," said Ischomachus, "or at least not until I'd sacrificed and prayed that I'd really succeed in teaching and she in learning what was best for both of us."

[8] "And did your wife join in sacrifice and prayer with you?" I asked.

"Certainly she did," replied Ischomachus, "with many a promise that by the gods, she'd become what she should; and it was clear that she wasn't going to neglect her lessons."

[9] "By the gods, Ischomachus!" I exclaimed. "Describe for me what you first tried to begin teaching her. I'd sooner hear you tell me that than have you describe the finest athletic contest or horse race."

[10] Ischomachus replied, "Well Socrates, since I'd already found her docile, and sufficiently domesticated to carry on a conversation, I put this sort of question to her: 'Tell me, wife, have you understood why I took you and your parents gave you to me? [11] You're obviously as aware as I am that there was no shortage of others for either of us to share a bed with. But I reckoned for myself and your parents for you who would be the best person for me and you to share a house and children with, and I chose you, your parents chose me out of the possibles. [12] Now if god grants that we have children at some point, then will be the time to think about them, and how best to educate them; for this is another blessing for us to share, the two of us—the best possible allies in life, the best possible support in old age. That is what children are. But for now it is this house that we share between us. [13] I declare everything I have, to go into the common stock, and you have deposited everything you brought with you. Nor should we calculate which has contributed the numerically greater amount; what we must keep well in mind is that it is whichever of us is the better partner that will make the more valuable contribution.'

[14] "My wife's reply to me, Socrates, was 'What could *I* do to contribute? What power do I have to do anything? It all depends on you. My task, my mother said, is to be virtuous (*sôphronein*).'
[15] "'Zeus!' I said. 'That, wife, was just what my father said *I* had to do. But virtue for both for man and for wife is surely a matter of acting so that what they have is kept in the best condition, and as much as possible is added to it by means of what is fine and just.'
[16] "'And what do you see,' asked my wife, 'that I could possibly do to help augment what we have?'
"'Zeus!' I said, 'it's the things the gods made in your power and sanctioned by the law—that's what you must try to do as best you can.'
[17] "'And what are these?' she asked.
"'Things that I think are of great importance,' I said, '—as great as the tasks that fall to the bee who leads in the swarm. [18] It seems to me, wife,'" Ischomachus said he said to her, "'that the gods too used great forethought in creating this yoking together, as people call it, of female and male, to ensure the best outcomes for the partnership. [19] First of all this yoking is established for the making of children together, so that the species of living creatures may continue in existence. Secondly, for human beings at least, it allows them to acquire carers for themselves in their old age. Thirdly, human beings do not live out in the open air, like flocks and herds, but need shelter, obviously. [20] But if they're going to have something to put in their covered store, they need someone to do the outside work. Ploughing, sowing, planting, grazing—these are all outside tasks, and these supply what is necessary. [21] Again, when the produce is brought in to the shelter, someone is needed to keep it safe and work at the things that have to be done inside. Shelter is needed for the rearing of newborn offspring, the making of food from the crops, or again the production of clothes from the wool. [22] And since both outside and inside tasks require both hard work and attention, well,'" Ischomachus said (so he told Socrates), "'it seems to me that god for that very reason adapted the nature of the woman to work and care for things inside, the nature of the man for the things outside. [23] He made the man's body and his soul more able to endure cold and heat, journeys and campaigns—and that's why he imposed the outside tasks on him; whereas,'" he said he said, "'with the woman, by having made her body naturally less tolerant of these things god seems to me to have assigned the inside tasks to her. [24] And knowing that he'd assigned the feeding of newborn offspring to the woman, making it part of her nature, he also gave her a greater love for the newborn babies than he did to the man. [25] And

since he'd assigned her the task of guarding over the produce brought into the shelter, and knew that when it comes to guarding things a fearful soul is no bad thing, god also gave her a larger share of fear than he did the man; equally, knowing that the one with the outside tasks would have to provide any defense against injustice, he gave the man a larger share of boldness. [26] But because there must be give and take between both, he has pooled memory and caring attention to detail between them, so that you could never tell whether it's the female sex or the male that has more of them. [27] Also pooled by him between them is control (*enkrateia*) over the things [i.e., in them] that need to be controlled, and the license to whichever of them may be the better, whether the man or the woman, to derive the greater benefit from this good. [28] And because the natures of the two are not well adapted to all the same things, they have a greater need of one another, and the yoking between them is all the more beneficial, each of them making up for the deficiencies of the other.'" (Xenophon, *On Household Management* 7.3–28)

8.19(a) Plato's Socrates makes women the weaker sex . . .

"We'd be right, then," [I (Socrates) said,] "to delete the lamentations of famous men [sc. from the list of approved poetry], leaving them to women (and not even to good women, either) and to cowardly men, so that those we say we are training to guard our city will disdain [388a] to act like that." (Plato, *Republic* III, 387e–388a)

8.19(b) . . . and more prey to non-rational desire

"One finds all kinds of diverse desires, pleasures, and pains, mostly in children, women, household slaves, and in those of the inferior majority who are called free." (Plato, *Republic* IV, 431b–c)

8.20 Plato's Timaeus on the inferiority of women, and the biological basis for differences in desire between the sexes

"Let us proceed, then," [said Timaeus,] "to a discussion of this subject in the following way. According to our likely account, all male-born humans who lived lives of cowardice or injustice were reborn in the second generation as women. [91a] And this explains why at that time the gods fashioned the desire for sexual union, by constructing one ensouled living thing in us, one in women. This is how they made them in each case: There is [in a man] a passage by which fluids exit from the body, where it receives the liquid that has passed through the lungs down into the kidneys and on into the bladder and expels it under pressure of air. From this passage they bored a connecting one into the compacted marrow that runs from [b] the head along the neck through the spine. This is in fact the marrow that we have previously called 'seed.' Now because it has soul in it and had now found a vent [to the outside], this marrow instilled a life-giving desire for emission right at the place of venting, and so produced the love of procreation. This is why, of course, the male genitals are unruly and self-willed, like an animal that will not be subject to reason and, driven crazy by its desires, seeks to overpower everything else. The very same causes [c] operate in women. A woman's womb or uterus, as it is called, is a living thing within her with a desire for childbearing. Now when this remains unfruitful for an unseasonably long period of time, it is extremely frustrated and travels everywhere up and down her body. It blocks up her respiratory passages, and by not allowing her to breathe it throws her into extreme emergencies, and visits all sorts of other illnesses upon her until finally [d] the woman's desire (*epithumia*) and the man's passion (*erôs*) bring them together, and, like plucking the fruit from a tree, they sow the seed into the ploughed field of her womb, living things too small to be visible and still without form. And when they have again given them distinct form, they nourish these living things so that they can mature inside the womb. Afterward, they bring them to birth, introducing them into the light of day. That is how women and females in general came to be." (Plato, *Timaeus* 90e–91d)

8.21–24 *Plato's Athenian assumes the inferiority of women . . .*

[8.21] "In addition, we shall have to distinguish, in a rough and [e] ready way, the songs suitable for men and those suitable for women, and give each its proper mode and rhythm. It would be terrible if the words failed to fit the mode, or if their meter were at odds with the beat of the music, which is what will happen if we don't match properly the songs to each of the other elements in the performance—elements which must therefore be dealt with, at any rate in outline, in our legal code. One possibility is simply to ensure that the songs men and women sing are accompanied by the rhythms and modes imposed by the words in either case; but our regulations about female performances must be more precise than this and be based on the natural difference between the sexes. So an elevated manner and a tendency toward manliness must be regarded as characteristic of the male, while a tendency to orderliness and moderation must be presented—in theory and law alike—as a peculiarly feminine trait." (Plato, *Laws* VII, 802d–e)

[8.22] "No one is to possess a shrine in his own private home. When a man takes it into his head to offer sacrifice, he is to go to the public shrines in order to do so, and he should hand over his offerings to the priests and [e] priestesses responsible for consecrating them; then he, and anyone else he may wish to participate, should join in the prayers. The grounds for these stipulations are as follows. To establish gods and temples is not easy; it's a job that needs to be very carefully pondered if it is to be done properly. Yet look at what people usually do—all women in particular, invalids of every sort, men in danger or any kind of distress, or conversely when they have just won a measure of prosperity: they dedicate the first thing that [910a] comes to hand, they swear to offer sacrifice, and promise to found shrines for gods and spirits and children of gods. And the terror they feel when they see apparitions, either in dreams or awake—a terror which recurs later when they recollect a whole series of visions—drives them to seek a remedy for each individually, with the result that on open spaces or any other spot where such an incident has occurred they found the altars and shrines that fill every home and village." (Plato, *Laws* X, 909d–910a)

[8.23] "So let's define some limits now: a man must tell no lie, commit no deceit, and do no [917a] fraud in word or deed when he calls upon the gods, unless he wants to be thoroughly loathed by them—as anyone is who snaps his fingers at them and swears false oaths, or (though they find this less offensive) tells lies in the presence of his superior. Now the 'superiors' of bad men are the good, and of the young their elders (usually)—which means that parents are the superiors of their offspring, men are (of course) the superiors of women and children, and rulers of their subjects." (Plato, *Laws* XI, 916e–917a)

[8.24] "When men take to damning and cursing each other [935a] and to calling one another rude names in the shrill tones of women, these mere words, empty though they are, soon lead to real hatreds and quarrels of the most serious kind." (Plato, *Laws* XI, 934e–935a)

8.25 . . . *but he also gives them a role in judicial proceedings*

"Whenever a man and his wife find it impossible to get on with each other because of an unfortunate incompatibility of temperament, the case must [930a] come under the control of ten men—middle-aged Guardians of the Laws—and ten of the women in charge of marriage, of the same age." (Plato, *Laws* XI, 929e–930a)

8.26 Plato's Socrates compliments their linguistic conservatism

"Women, who are the best preservers of the ancient language . . ." (Plato, *Cratylus* 418b)

8.27 Plato's Socrates proposes that while women may be weaker than men, they have the same range of capacities

"Therefore," I [Socrates] said, "if the male sex is seen to be different from the female with regard to a particular craft or way of life, we'll say that the relevant one must be assigned to it. But if it's apparent that they differ only in this respect, that the females bear children while the males beget them, we'll say that there has been no kind of proof that women are different from [e] men with respect to what we're talking about, and we'll continue to believe that our guardians and their women must have the same way of life."

"And rightly so," [Glaucon] said.

"Next, we'll tell anyone who holds the opposite view to instruct us in this: With regard to what craft or way of life involved in the constitution [455a] of the city are the natures of men and women not the same but different?"

"That's a fair question, at any rate."

"And perhaps he'd say, just as you did a moment ago, that it isn't easy to give an immediate answer, but with enough consideration it should not be difficult."

"Yes, he might say that."

"Shall we ask the one who raises this objection to follow us and see whether we can show him that no way of life concerned with the management [b] of the city is peculiar to women?"

"Of course."

"'Come, now,' we'll say to him, 'give us an answer: Is this what you meant by one person being naturally well suited for something and another being naturally unsuited? That the one learned it easily, the other with difficulty; that the one, after only a brief period of instruction, was able to find out things for himself, while the other, after much instruction, couldn't even remember what he'd learned; that the body of the one adequately served his thought, while the body of the other opposed his. [c] Are there any other things besides these by which you distinguished those who are naturally well suited for anything from those who are not?'"

"No one will claim that there are any others."

"Do you know of anything practiced by human beings in which the male sex isn't superior to the female in all these ways? Or must we make a long story of it by mentioning weaving, baking cakes, and cooking vegetables, in which the female sex is believed to excel and in which it is most ridiculous [d] of all for it to be inferior?"

"It's true," he said, "that one sex is much superior to the other in pretty well everything, although many women are better than many men in many things. But on the whole it is as you say."

"Then, my friend, there is no way of life concerned with the management of the city that belongs to a woman because she's a woman or to a man because he's a man, but the various natures are distributed in the same way in both creatures. Women share by nature in every way of life just as men do, though [e] in all of them women are weaker than men."

"Certainly." (Plato, *Republic* V, 454d–455e)

8.28(a)–(b) *Plato's unnamed Athenian argues for equality of education*

[8.28(a)] ATHENIAN: Let me stress that this law of mine will apply just as much to girls as [e] to boys. The girls must be trained in precisely the same way, and I'd like to make this proposal without any reservations whatever about horse riding or athletics being suitable activities for males but not for females. You see, although I was already convinced by some ancient stories I have heard, I now know for sure that there are pretty well countless numbers of [805a] women, generally called Sarmatians, round the Black Sea, who not only ride horses but use the bow and other weapons. There, men and women have an equal duty to cultivate these skills, so cultivate them equally they do. And while we're on the subject, here's another thought for you. I maintain that if these results can be achieved, the state of affairs in our corner of Greece, where men and women do *not* have a common purpose and do *not* throw all their energies into the same activities, is absolutely stupid. Almost every state, under present conditions, is only half a state, and develops only half its potentialities, whereas with the same cost and [b] effort, it could double its achievement. Yet what a staggering blunder for a legislator to make!

CLINIAS: I dare say. But a lot of these proposals, sir, are incompatible with the average state's social structure. However, you were quite right when you said we should give the argument its head, and only make up our minds when it had run its course. You've made me reproach myself [c] for having spoken. So carry on, and say what you like.

ATHENIAN: The point I'd like to make, Clinias, is the same one as I made a moment ago, that there might have been something to be said against our proposal, if it had not been proved by the facts to be workable. But as things are, an opponent of this law must try other tactics. We are not going to withdraw our recommendation that so far as possible, in education [d] and everything else, the female sex should be on the same footing as the male. Consequently, we should approach the problem rather like this. Look: if women are *not* to follow absolutely the same way of life as men, then surely we shall have to work out some other program for them?

CLINIAS: Inevitably.

ATHENIAN: Well then, if we deny women this partnership we're now prescribing for them, which of the systems actually in force today shall we adopt instead? What about the practice of the Thracians and many other peoples, who make their women work on the land and mind sheep [e] and cattle, so that they turn into skivvies indistinguishable from slaves? Or what about the Athenians and all the other states in that part of the world? Well, here's how we Athenians deal with the problem: we "concentrate our resources," as the expression is, under one roof, and let our women take charge of our stores and the spinning and wool working in general. Or we could adopt the Spartan system, Megillus, which is a compromise. [806a] You make your girls take part in athletics and you give them a compulsory education in the arts; when they grow up, though dispensed from working wool, they have to "weave" themselves a pretty hardworking sort of life which is by no means despicable or useless: they have to be tolerably efficient at running the home and managing the house and bringing up children—but they *don't* undertake military service. This means that even if some extreme emergency ever led to a battle for their state and the lives [b] of their children, they wouldn't have the expertise to use bows and arrows, like so many Amazons, nor could they join the men in deploying any other missile. They wouldn't be able to take up shield and spear and copy Athena, so as to terrify the enemy (if nothing more) by being seen in some kind of battle array gallantly resisting the destruction threatening their native land. Living as they do, they'd never be anything like tough enough to imitate the Sarmatian women, who by comparison with such [c] femininity would look like men. Anyone who wants to commend your Spartan legislators for this state of affairs had better get on with it: I'm not going to change *my* mind. A legislator should go the whole way and not stick at half measures; he mustn't just regulate the men and allow the women to live as they like and wallow in expensive luxury. That would be to give the state only half the loaf of prosperity instead of the whole of it. (Plato, *Laws* VII, 804d–806c)

[8.28(b)] ATHENIAN: We are establishing gymnasia for all physical exercises of a military [e] kind—archery and deployment of missiles in general, skirmishing, heavy-armed fighting of every variety, tactical maneuvers, marches of every sort, pitching camp, and also the various disciplines of the cavalryman. In all these subjects there must be public instructors paid out of public funds; their lessons must be attended by the boys and men of the state, and the girls and women as well, because they too have to master all these techniques. While still girls, they must practice every kind of dancing and fighting in armor; when grown women, they must play their part in maneuvering, [814a] getting into battle formation and taking off and putting on weapons, if only to ensure that if it ever proves necessary for the whole army to leave the state and take the field abroad, so that the children and the rest of the population are left unprotected, the women will at least be able to defend them. On the other hand—and this is one of those things we can't swear is impossible—suppose a large and powerful army, whether Greek or not, were to force a way into the country and make them fight a desperate battle for the very existence of the state. It would be a disaster for their [b] society if its women proved to have been so shockingly ill-educated that they couldn't even rival female birds, who are prepared to run every risk and die for their chicks fighting against the most powerful of wild animals. What if, instead of that, the women promptly made off to temples and thronged every altar and sanctuary, and covered the human race with the disgrace of being by nature the most lily-livered creatures under the sun?

CLINIAS: By heaven, sir, no state in which that happened could avoid [c] disgrace—quite apart from the damage that would be caused.

ATHENIAN: So let's lay down a law to the effect that women must not neglect to cultivate the techniques of fighting, at any rate to the extent indicated. These are skills which all citizens, male and female, must take care to acquire. (Plato, *Laws* VII, 813d–814c)

Chapter 9: God and the World

The predominant thematic focus of most members of the Socratic circle on ethics (cf. Ch. 2) was a deliberate and self-conscious break with earlier traditions of natural philosophy which, on the whole, they thought pointless (see **9.1–8**; also **3.1**; and Xenophon in **5.16**, for the more moderate view that they are useful only to a certain extent). This is not, however, to say that they did not have views about other things, including, importantly, the nature of the divine; on this score, they held views which were every bit as radical in their own ways as those of the Presocratic "scientists." They would certainly have disagreed with the idea of the divine "intellect" proposed by Anaxagoras, controlling and ordering the elements, and were even further removed from the conceptions of an Empedocles, a Heraclitus, or an Anaximenes, who found divinity in the elements themselves. But their rational, provident gods, concerned for the well-being of the universe as a whole and of mankind in particular (**9.14–26**; see also Euclides in **2.33**), were quite unlike the capricious and colorful gods of Greek polytheistic tradition.

Were they, then, themselves guilty of the charge brought against Socrates, of "not believing in the gods the city believes in" (**10.14**)? Probably not. For one thing, there is nothing in our evidence that suggests that the Socratics' views were actually incompatible with their expression in conventional religious forms (cf. Antisthenes in **9.11–12**; Xenophon, especially in **10.16**). For another, the ways in which the Socratics talk about the gods might be close to the way in which at least some ordinary Athenians would have talked in private conversation. (Thanks to their practice of writing dialogues, we know quite a lot about how the Socratics talked to each other; we know rather less about how other educated people talked among themselves.) And ordinary language contained phrases like "god willing" (*an theos thelêi*), too, and used "god" (*theos*) in the singular in a way that allowed reference to the divine in general, without commitment to particular gods recognized by the poets or in religious practice.

What is certain is that a degree of radicalism in theology among the Socratics does not by any means imply a simple rationalism. We have seen Plato and Xenophon treating piety as a requirement of a good human life (**3.51–59**), and Plato representing Socrates as a servant of god (**3.53–55**). Xenophon's Socrates believes in divination (see **9.23**.[12], **5.16**.[10]), and is a strict observer of the conventional pieties (**3.56–58**). Likewise, in the foundation of his ideal city in the *Republic*, Plato's Socrates makes the conventional proposal that it will be for the

Apollo of Delphi to "establish temples, sacrifices, and other forms of service to gods, *daimones*,[1] and heroes; then, for the dead, the proper forms of burial, and all the other things that must be done for those in Hades to keep them favorable to us" (*Republic* V, 427b). The visitor from Athens in Plato's *Laws* is also clear that the punishment of the bad and the reward of the good is a matter of divine ordinance—or, more specifically, is ordained by the traditional, Olympian gods (e.g., Plato, *Laws* X, 904e–905a).

Plato stands out in one respect, however. Most members of the circle avoided "scientific" speculation about the nature of the cosmos that goes beyond this; Plato did not (indeed, Themistius in **9.3** pointedly omits him from the "true chorus of Socrates" on this ground). His *Timaeus* is a large-scale exposition on the nature of the universe, its origins, its structure, and its constituent elements and their interactions. Perhaps conscious of associations in the popular mind between natural philosophy or astronomy with out-and-out atheism (cf. **9.2(b)**), Plato has Timaeus describe the process of the formation of the universe as the work of a divine craftsman (his exposition of the work even begins with a hymn to the gods, at 27c). Readers since antiquity have wondered whether this "creator god" is to be taken literally: like other members of Socrates' circle, Plato usually restricted himself to talking of the gods' ordering or creating of things in the universe, not creating the universe itself (although Xenophon comes close in **9.16** to an "argument from design"). But what is abundantly clear is that he, like them, is quite sure that the universe is not to be explained by merely mechanical factors.

Texts

i. What Should We Study?

9.1 *Xenophon's Socrates questioned by a Syracusan circus master: isn't he "the thinker," who thinks about useless things?*

With that sort of talk going on, the Syracusan saw that the company were enjoying one another's company instead of paying attention to his

---

1. See Ch. 10.

show, so he maliciously asked Socrates, "Socrates, are you the one they call 'the thinker'?"

"Well, isn't that better," replied Socrates, "than if they said I had no thought in my head?"

"Yes, if it weren't for the fact that you're supposed to be a thinker about things up there in the heavens."

[7] "Well," asked Socrates, "do you know of anything more heavenly than the gods?"

"No, but it's not the gods people say you're concerned with; they say you concern yourself with the least beneficial things."

"Even in that case I'd be concerned with the gods," said Socrates, "for they *at least benefit* us from up there by raining on us and giving us light. Sorry about the pun, but it's your fault for giving me trouble."

[8] "Well, let that pass. But tell me the distance between us in flea feet; people say that's the sort of geometry you do."[2] (Xenophon, *Symposium* 6.6–8)

9.2(a) *Plato's Socrates insists that Aristophanes misrepresented his interests . . .*

"Let us then take up the case from its beginning. What is the accusation [b] from which arose the slander in which Meletus trusted when he wrote out the charge against me? What did they say when they slandered me? I must, as if they were my actual prosecutors, read the affidavit they would have sworn. It goes something like this: Socrates is guilty of wrongdoing in that he busies himself studying things in the sky and below the earth; he makes the worse into the stronger argument, and he teaches these same [c] things to others. You have seen this yourself in the comedy of Aristophanes, a Socrates swinging about there, saying he was walking on air and talking a lot of other nonsense about things of which I know nothing at all. I do not speak in contempt of such knowledge, if someone is wise in these things—lest Meletus bring more cases against me—but, gentlemen, I have no part in it, and on this point I call upon the majority of you as witnesses. I think it right that all those of you who have heard me conversing, and [d] many of you have, should tell each other if anyone of you has ever heard me discussing such subjects to any extent at all. From this you will learn that the other things said about me by the majority are of the same kind." (Plato, *Apology* 19a–d; followed by **5.3**)

---

2. This is how Socrates is engaged in Aristophanes, *Clouds* 144 ff.

9.2(b) *. . . and that he is not to be confused with Anaxagoras*

SOCRATES: You are a strange fellow, Meletus. Why do you say this? Do I not believe, as other men do, that the sun and the moon are gods?

MELETUS: No, by Zeus, gentlemen of the jury, for he says that the sun is stone and the moon, earth.

SOCRATES: My dear Meletus, do you think you are prosecuting Anaxagoras? Are you so contemptuous of these men and think them so ignorant of letters as not to know that the books of Anaxagoras of Clazomenae are full of those [e] theories, and further, that the young men learn from me what they can buy from time to time for a drachma, at most, in the bookshops, and ridicule Socrates if he pretends that these theories are his own, especially as they are so absurd? Is that, by Zeus, what you think of me, Meletus, that I do not believe that there are any gods?

MELETUS: That is what I say, that you do not believe in the gods at all. (Plato, *Apology* 26d–e)

9.3 *Cebes, Phaedo, Aristippus, Aeschines restricted themselves to human affairs*

For this reason the ancient figure of Socrates, whom one might call the father and founder of wisdom of the more valuable sort, did not think even so that he should look into other things—some of it he said made no difference to us, while knowledge of the rest was beyond us—and devoted all his research to good things and bad things and how a human being, and a household and a city, become happy; and he praised Homer for claiming that one should investigate above all "what in your halls is bad and what good."[3] The true chorus of Socrates stuck within these limits: Cebes, Phaedo, Aristippus, Aeschines. (Themistius, *Orations* 35.5 = Aristippus 166)

9.4 *Aristippus saw no value in purely theoretical studies as mathematics*

This is why nothing is demonstrated through this cause in mathematics, nor is there any proof which appeals to better or worse: absolutely no mention at all is made of any of this sort of thing. That is why some sophists, including Aristippus, criticized them: in all the other

---

3. Homer, *Odyssey* 4.392 (but in its original context the sense is "what in your halls has been badly done and what well").

arts, even practical crafts like carpentry and shoemaking, everything is explained by what is better or worse; but mathematical arts make no claims about what is good and bad. (Aristotle, *Metaphysics* B, 996a29–b1 = Aristippus 170)

9.5 *The **Socratics** think physics and astronomy "useless" . . .*

Some philosophers, and especially followers of Socrates, say that to do physics and meddle with astronomy is pointless and useless, and think one should not bother with such things. (Diogenes of Oenoanda fr. 4 col. ii = Aristippus 167)

9.6 *. . . ethics and politics are all that matter to them*

For these things, and many others, are absolutely useless for ethics and the so-called political virtues and actions, and likewise for the cure of psychological affections. [14] Xenophon wrote well about them, not only condemning them himself for their uselessness, but saying that Socrates took the same view. [15] The other companions of Socrates agree with him, as well as Plato himself, who added the study of nature to philosophy, but gave its discussion to Timaeus, not Socrates. (Galen, *On the Doctrines of Hippocrates and Plato* 9.7.13–15 = Aristippus 169)

9.7 *The same*

In Socrates' time the method in question [i.e., the approach to nature through an understanding of causation] had gained more ground, but in this period the study of nature itself ceased, and those active in philosophy turned their attention to practical and political excellence. (Aristotle, *On the Parts of Animals* I.1, 642a29–31)

9.8 ***Euclides*** *is even against a certain kind of theology*

When Euclides the philosopher was asked by someone what sort of beings the gods were, and what pleased them, he said, "I don't know about the rest of it, but what I do know for sure is that they hate busybodies." (*Vatican Sayings* 277 = Euclides 17)[4]

---

4. But this did not stop him offering thoughts of his own on the nature of the divine: see **2.33** ("god" is a name for the good).

9.9 *But* **Plato**'*s Socrates insists that mathematics and astronomy do have ethical value, if their potential is properly understood*

"And what about astronomy?" [I (Socrates) asked.] "Shall we [include it too, in the education of the future rulers of Callipolis]? Or do you disagree?"

"That's fine with me," [d] said [Glaucon], "for a better awareness of the seasons, months, and years is no less appropriate for a general than for a farmer or navigator."

"You amuse me!" I said. "You're like someone who's afraid that the majority will think he is prescribing useless subjects. It's no easy task—indeed it's very difficult—to realize that in every soul there is an instrument that is purified and rekindled by such subjects when it has been blinded and destroyed [e] by other ways of life, an instrument that it is more important to preserve than ten thousand eyes, since only with it can the truth be seen. Those who share your belief that this is so will think you're speaking incredibly well, while those who've never been aware of it will probably think you're talking nonsense, since they see no benefit worth mentioning in these subjects. So decide right now which group you're addressing. Or are your [528a] arguments for neither of them but mostly for your own sake—though you won't begrudge anyone else whatever benefit he's able to get from them?"

"The latter," he said: "I want to speak, question, and answer mostly for my own sake."

"Then let's fall back to our earlier position," I went on, "for we were wrong just now about the subject that comes after geometry."

"What was our error?" he asked.

I replied, "After plane surfaces, we went on to revolving solids before dealing with solids by themselves. But the right thing to do is to take up the third [b] dimension right after the second. And this, I suppose, consists of cubes and of whatever shares in depth."

"You're right, Socrates," he said, "but this subject hasn't been developed yet."

"There are two reasons for that," I said. "First, because no city values it, this difficult subject is little researched. Second, the researchers need a director, for, without one, they won't discover anything. To begin with, such a director is hard to find, and, then, even if he could be found, those who [c] currently do research in this field would be too arrogant to follow him. If an entire city helped him to supervise it, however, and took the lead in valuing it, then he would be followed. And, if the subject was consistently and vigorously pursued, it would soon be developed. Even now, when it isn't valued and is held in contempt by the majority and is pursued by researchers who are unable to give an account of its usefulness, nevertheless, in spite of all these handicaps, the force of its charm has caused it to develop somewhat, so that it wouldn't be surprising if it were further developed even as things stand."

[d] "Indeed," he said, "the subject does have outstanding charm. But explain more clearly what you were saying just now. The subject that deals with plane surfaces I think you took to be geometry."

"Yes."

"And at first you put astronomy after it, but later you went back on that."

"Yes," I said; "in my haste to go through them all, I've only progressed more slowly. The subject dealing with the dimension of depth was next. But because it [e] is in a ridiculous state, I passed it by and spoke of astronomy (which deals with the motion of things having depth) after geometry."

"That's right."

"Let's then put astronomy as the fourth subject," I said, "on the assumption that solid geometry will be available if a city takes it up."

"That seems reasonable," he replied. "And since you reproached me before for praising astronomy in a vulgar manner, I'll now praise it your way, for I think it's [529a] clear to everyone that astronomy compels the soul to look upward and leads it from things here to things there."

"It may be obvious to everyone except me," I said; "that's not my view about it."

"Then what *is* your view?" he asked.

"As it's practiced today by those who teach philosophy, it makes the soul look very much downward."

"How so?"

"In my opinion," I said, "your conception of 'higher studies' is a good deal too generous, for if someone were to study something by leaning his head back and studying ornaments on a ceiling, it looks as though you'd say [b] he's studying not with his eyes but with his understanding. Perhaps you're right, and I'm foolish, but I can't conceive of any subject making the soul look upward except one concerned with that which is, and that which is is invisible. If anyone attempts to learn something about sensible things, whether by gaping upward or squinting downward, I'd claim—since there's no knowledge of such things— that he never learns anything and [c] that, even if he studies lying on his back on the ground or floating on it in the sea, his soul is looking not up but down."

"You're right to reproach me," he said, "and I've been justly punished, but what did you have in mind when you said that astronomy must be learned in a different way from the way in which it is learned at present if it is to be a useful subject for our purposes?"

"It's like this," I said. "We should consider the decorations in the sky to be the most beautiful and most exact of visible things, seeing that they're embroidered on a visible surface. But we should consider their motions to fall [d] far short of the true ones—motions that are really fast or slow as measured in true numbers, that trace out true geometrical figures, that are all in relation to one another, and that are the true motions of the things carried along in them. And these, of course, must be grasped by reason and thought, not by sight. Or do you think otherwise?"

"Not at all."

"So," I said, "we should use the embroidery in the sky as a model in the study of these other things. If someone experienced in geometry were to come upon plans very carefully drawn and worked out by Daedalus or [e] some other craftsman or artist, he'd consider them to be very finely executed, but he'd think it ridiculous to examine them seriously in order to [530a] find the truth in them about the equal, the double, or any other ratio."

"How could it be anything other than ridiculous?"

"In that case," I asked him, "don't you think that a real astronomer will feel the same when he looks at the motions of the stars? He'll believe that the craftsman of the heavens arranged them and all that's in them in the finest way possible for such things. But as for the ratio of night to day, of days to a month, of a month to a year, or of the motions of the stars to any of them or to each other, don't you think he'll consider it strange to believe that they're [b] always the same and never deviate anywhere at all or to try in any sort of way to grasp the truth about them, since they're connected to body and visible?"

"That's my opinion anyway," he responded, "now that I hear it from you."

"So it's by means of problems," I said, "that we'll pursue the study of astronomy, as we do that of geometry, and we'll leave the things in the sky to one side, if we're truly going to use astronomy to make the naturally intelligent part of the soul useful instead of useless."

"The task you're prescribing is a lot harder," he remarked, "than anything now attempted in astronomy."

"And I suppose," I added, "that if we are to be of any benefit as lawgivers, our prescriptions for the other subjects will be of the same kind." (Plato, *Republic* VII, 527c–530c)

ii. The Nature of God

9.10 *Plato's Socrates in conversation with Euthyphro (a self-proclaimed religious expert): are the gods really as they are conventionally agreed to be?*

EUTHYPHRO: These people themselves [6a] believe that Zeus is the best and most just of the gods, yet they agree that he bound his father because he unjustly swallowed his sons, and that he in turn castrated his father for similar reasons. But they are angry with me because I am prosecuting my father for his wrongdoing. They contradict themselves in what they say about the gods and about me.

SOCRATES: Indeed, Euthyphro, this is the reason why I am a defendant in the case, because I find it hard to accept things like that being said about the gods, and it is likely to be the reason why I shall be told I do wrong. [b] Now, however, if you, who have full knowledge of such things, share their opinions, then we must agree with them, too, it would seem. For what are we to say, we who agree that we ourselves have no knowledge of them? Tell me, by the god of friendship, do you really believe these things are true?

EUTHYPHRO: Yes, Socrates, and so are even more surprising things, of which the majority has no knowledge.

SOCRATES: And do you believe that there really is war among the gods, [c] and terrible enmities and battles, and other such things as are told by the poets, and other sacred stories such as are embroidered by good writers and by representations of which the robe of the goddess is adorned when it is carried up to the Acropolis? Are we to say these things are true, Euthyphro? (Plato, *Euthyphro* 5e–6c)

9.11 *Antisthenes: there are many religions, but one god . . .*

According to Antisthenes in his book *On Nature*, by convention there are many gods but in nature there is one. (*PHerc* 1428, fr. 21, from Philodemus, *On Piety* = Antisthenes 179)

9.12 ... and god is like nothing else

This was not a Cynic concept, but as an associate of Socrates Antisthenes declares, "God is unlike anyone [or: anything]; which is why no one can learn about him from a likeness." (Clement of Alexandria, *Exhortation* 6.71.2 = Antisthenes 181)

9.13 *Plato's* Socrates (here with Adimantus) thinks the gods unchanging

"A god, then," [I (Socrates) said,] "is simple and true in word and deed. He doesn't change himself or deceive others by images, words, or signs, whether in visions or in dreams."

[383a] "That's how it appears to me, too," he said, "as I listen to your argument."

"You agree, then," I asked, "that this is our second pattern for speaking or composing poems about the gods: they are not sorcerers who change themselves, nor do they mislead us by falsehoods in words or deeds?"

"I agree."

"So, even though we praise many things in Homer, we won't approve of the dream Zeus sent to Agamemnon, nor of Aeschylus when he makes [b] Thetis say that Apollo sang in prophecy at her wedding:

> About the good fortune my children would have,
> Free of disease throughout their long lives,
> And of all the blessings that the friendship of the gods would
>   bring me,
> I hoped that Phoebus' divine mouth would be free of falsehood,
> Endowed as it is with the craft of prophecy.
> But the very god who sang, the one at the feast,
> The one who said all this, he himself it is
> Who killed my son.

"Whenever anyone says such things about a god, we'll be angry with him, [c] refuse him a chorus, and not allow his poetry to be used in the education of the young, so that our guardians will be as god-fearing and godlike as human beings can be." (Plato, *Republic* II, 382e–383c)

9.14 *Plato's* Socrates contrasts the divine with the material: the former controls the latter

"And now I should try to tell you [i.e., Phaedrus] why living things are said to include both mortal and immortal beings. All soul looks after all that lacks a soul, [c] and patrols all of heaven, taking different shapes at different times. So long as its wings are in perfect condition it flies high, and the entire universe is its dominion; but a soul that sheds its wings wanders until it lights on something solid, where it settles and takes on an earthly body, which then, owing to the power of this soul, seems to move itself. The whole combination of soul and body is called a 'living thing,' or 'animal,' and has the designation 'mortal' as well. Such a combination cannot be immortal, not on any reasonable account. In fact it is pure fiction, based neither on [d] observation nor on adequate reasoning, that a god is an immortal living thing which has a body and a soul, and that these are bound together by nature for all time—but of course we must let this be as it may please the gods, and speak accordingly." (Plato, *Phaedrus* 246b–d)

9.15 Plato's Socrates (with **Hermogenes**) on god as an organizing force immanent in the universe

"It's easy to figure out that 'justice' (*dikaiosunê*) is the name given to the comprehension of the just (*dikaiou sunesis*), but the just itself is hard to understand. It seems that many people agree with one another about it [d] up to a point, but beyond that they disagree. Those who think that the universe is in motion believe that most of it is of such a kind as to do nothing but give way, but that something penetrates all of it and generates everything that comes into being. This, they say, is the fastest and smallest thing of all; for if it were not the smallest, so that nothing could keep it out, or not the fastest, so that it could treat all other things as though they were standing still, it wouldn't be able to travel through everything. However, since it is governor and penetrator (*diaïon*) of everything else, [e] it is rightly called 'just' (*dikaion*)— the *k* sound is added for the sake of euphony. As I was saying before, many people agree about the just up to [413a] this point. As for myself, Hermogenes, because I persisted at it, I learned all about the matter in secret—that this is the just and the cause, since that through which (*di' ho*) a thing comes to be is the cause. Indeed, someone told me that it is correct to call this *'Dia'* (Zeus) for that reason. Even when I'd heard this, however, I persisted in gently asking, 'If all this is true, my friend, what actually *is* the just?' Thereupon, they think I am [b] asking too many questions and demanding the impossible, and they tell me that I have already learned enough. Then they try to satisfy me by having each tell me his own view. But they disagree with each other. One says that the just is the sun, since only the sun governs all of the things that are, penetrating (*diaiôn*) and burning (*kaôn*) them. Well satisfied, I tell this fine answer to one of the others, but he ridicules me by asking if I think nothing just ever happens in human affairs once the sun has set. So [c] I persist, and ask him to tell me what *he* thinks the just is, and he says that it is fire (*to pur*)—but that isn't easy to understand. Another says that it isn't fire, but the heat itself that is in fire. Another says that all these explanations are ridiculous, and that the just is what Anaxagoras talks about, namely, mind; for he says that mind is self-ruling, mixes with nothing else, orders the things that are, and travels through everything. Thereupon, my friend, I am even more perplexed than when I set out to learn what the just is. However, the goal of our investigation was the *name* 'just,' and it seems to have been given for the reasons we mentioned." (Plato, *Cratylus* 412c–413d)

9.16 Xenophon's Socrates (with Aristodemus) on signs of intelligence in the structure of things within the universe

I shall first relate what I once heard him say on the subject of religion during a conversation with the man they call "Little Aristodemus." When Socrates discovered that he neither sacrificed to the gods nor made use of divination, and even mocked those who did, he said, "Tell me, Aristodemus, are there any people you've come to admire for their wisdom?"

"Of course," he said.

[3] "Tell us their names," he said.

"Well, for epic poetry, I especially admire Homer; for dithyrambs, Melanippides; for tragedy, Sophocles; for sculpture, Polyclitus; and for painting, Zeuxis."

[4] "Who seems to you more deserving of admiration: the makers of senseless, static images or the makers of intelligent, dynamic, living creatures?"

"By far the makers of living creatures, provided that they're really products of design rather than mere chance."

"Between things with no clear purpose and those that clearly provide some benefit, which would you judge to be products of chance and which of design?"

"It stands to reason that the ones serving some benefit would be products of design."

[5] "Don't you think it was for the benefit of human beings that their original creator endowed them with each of their various sense organs, such as eyes to see what's visible and ears to hear what's audible? What

good would smells do us, if we hadn't been endowed with noses? And how could we perceive sweet or bitter tastes, or any pleasures of the palate, unless we'd been outfitted with a tongue to discern them? [6] And don't other things besides these also resemble products of forethought to you? Take, for instance, the fact that the eye, because of its fragility, has eyelids for gates, which are open whenever we need to use it but closed during sleep. Or that eyelashes form a natural filter so that winds don't do any damage. Or that eyebrows stick out above our eyes so that the sweat from our brow doesn't hurt them. Or that our hearing takes in every sound without ever filling up. Or that the front teeth of every animal are suited to cutting, while the molars are suited to grinding up what they get from the front teeth. Or that the mouth, which animals use to ingest the things they desire, is positioned near the eyes and nose, but the channels for excrement, given its offensive nature, divert and carry it as far away as possible from the sense organs. Do you have any doubt as to whether these effects of so much forethought are products of chance or design?"

[7] "Good heavens, no!" he said. "If you look at it this way, they really do seem like the handiwork of some wise and benevolent craftsman."

"What about the fact that the desire to procreate is instinctive? Or that mothers have an instinctive desire to nurture? Or that their offspring crave life and fear death most of all?"

"By all means, these also look like the contrivances of someone who planned for living creatures' existence."

[8] "And do you seem to have any intelligence of your own?"

"Well, ask away, and you'll get your answer."

"Do you think that nothing intelligent exists anywhere else, despite knowing that your body contains only a small fraction of the large amount of earth in existence, and a tiny fraction of the large volume of water, and that your share of the presumably vast quantities of each of the other elements comprising your body is small?[5] Do you imagine that you got hold of intelligence all for yourself by some stroke of luck, and that the order exhibited by these immense, infinitely large masses is the result, as you suppose, of some blind force?"

[9] "In fact, I do, since, unlike the craftsmen of things made here and now, I don't see the responsible parties."

---

5. The hint here that our intelligence is not only made by, but derives from, a cosmic source is made an explicit argument by Plato's Socrates: see **4.2**.

"You also don't see your own mind, which controls your body. By this line of reasoning, you could say that you do nothing by design but everything by chance."

[10] Aristodemus said, "Rest assured, Socrates, I don't hold the divine in contempt, but I do consider it too magnificent to need my service."

"Well, the more magnificent the object that deigns to serve you," Socrates said, "the more you should honor it."

[11] "You can be sure that I wouldn't neglect the gods if I thought that they had any concern for humanity," said Aristodemus.

"So you think that they don't have any concern? In the first place, they made human beings the only animal to stand erect, and his erect posture enables him to see farther in front, to better observe things overhead, and to be less prone to injury. Then, while they gave all the other land animals feet, which provide only for locomotion, on human beings they added hands, which we use to accomplish most of the things that account for our greater happiness. [12] In addition, while all animals have a tongue, they made only the human one capable of touching different parts of the mouth at different times to produce articulate sounds so as to communicate all our wants to each other. And then there's the fact that they grant all other animals the pleasures of sex during only a fixed time of year, while they allow us to enjoy them continuously right up to old age.

[13] "Nor was god satisfied with merely attending to the body. On the contrary, and most importantly, the mind he implanted in humans is also the very best. In the first place, what other animal's mind is even aware of the existence of the gods, who are responsible for the finest examples of order on the grandest scale? What class of animal other than human beings worships gods? And what sort of mind is more adept than the human one at taking precautions against hunger, thirst, cold, or heat; or at helping fight disease; or at building up strength through exercise; or at seeking out knowledge; or more adept at remembering whatever it hears, sees, or learns? [14] Isn't it perfectly obvious to you that human beings live like gods in comparison with other animals in virtue of our natural superiority in both mind and body? If someone were to have a human being's mental capacity but a cow's body, he wouldn't be able to do what he wanted. Nor would there be any advantage to having hands without intelligence. But you, who are lucky enough to have both of these most precious possessions, don't think that the gods take care of you? What will they have to do for you to believe that they're concerned for you?"

[15] "I'll believe it when they send advisors to tell me what I should and shouldn't do, just as you claim that they send them to you."

"Don't you think that they're advising you as well whenever they advise the Athenians through divination in response to some inquiry? Or whenever they warn the Greeks, or the whole human race, by sending signs and wonders? Or do you think that they single you out for neglect? [16] Do you think that the gods would have implanted in the human race the idea that they can cause benefit or harm unless they really could, or that people would never have realized that they'd been duped this whole time? Can't you see that the most venerable and wisest of human institutions—states and nations—are the most devout, and that the most sensible times of life are the ones most concerned with religion?

[17] "Bear in mind also, my friend," he continued, "that the intellect inside you directs your body however it wants. You should therefore imagine that the intelligence present in the universe arranges everything in whatever way it pleases. You shouldn't suppose that your eye is capable of seeing for miles but god's eye is incapable of seeing everything at once; or that your mind is capable of considering events both here and in Egypt and Sicily but god's intelligence isn't competent to attend to everything simultaneously. [18] It's by helping other people and doing favors for them that you discover who's willing to reciprocate, and by asking advice that you learn who's reasonable. In the same way, if by your service you put to the test the gods' willingness to counsel you on matters that aren't apparent to human understanding, you'll come to recognize that the divine is great and grand enough to see everything at once, to hear everything, to be present everywhere, and to attend to everything simultaneously." (Xenophon, *Memorabilia* 1.4.2–18; part = **10.7**)

9.17 *Plato has* **Glaucon** *agree with Socrates that god is a kind of plantsman*

"God knew this, I [Socrates] think, and wishing to be the real maker of the [d] truly real bed and not just *a* maker of *a* bed, he made it to be one in nature."

"Probably so."

"Do you want us to call him its 'plantsman' (*phutourgos*) or something like that?"

"That seems to fit," [Glaucon] said, "given that it's through nature that he has made both this and everything else he has made." (Plato, *Republic* X, 597d)

9.18 *Plato's visitor from Elea proposes something similar*

VISITOR: But now, since he's included among experts in imitation, first we obviously have to divide productive expertise in two. We say imitation [b] is a sort of production, but of copies and not of the things themselves. Is that right?

THEAETETUS: Absolutely.

VISITOR: First of all, production has two parts.

THEAETETUS: What are they?

VISITOR: Divine and human.

THEAETETUS: I don't understand yet.

VISITOR: If you remember how we started, we said production was any capacity that causes things to come to be that previously were not.

THEAETETUS: I remember.

VISITOR: Take animals and everything mortal, [c] including plants and everything on the earth that grows from seeds and roots, and also all lifeless bodies made up inside the earth, whether fusible or not. Are we going to say that anything besides the craftsmanship of a god makes them come to be after previously not being? Or shall we rely on the saying and the widespread belief that . . . ?

THEAETETUS: That what?

VISITOR: Are we going to say that nature produces them by some spontaneous cause that generates them without any thought, or by a cause that works by reason and divine knowledge derived from a god?

THEAETETUS: I often shift back and forth on that from one view to the other, [d] maybe because of my age. When I'm focusing on you now, and supposing that you think they come to be by the agency of a god, that's what I think too.

VISITOR: Fine, Theaetetus. If we thought you were the kind of person who might believe something different in the future we'd try to use some cogent, persuasive argument to make you agree. But since I know what [e] your nature is and I know, too, that even without arguments from us it will tend in the direction that it's pulled toward now, I'll let the issue go. It would take too much time. I'll assume divine expertise produces the things that come about by so-called nature, and that human expertise produces the things that humans compound those things into. According to this account there are two kinds of production, human and divine. (Plato, *Sophist* 265a–e)

9.19 Plato's unnamed Athenian, on god as craftsman

ATHENIAN: So let's not treat god as less skilled than a mortal craftsman, who applies the same expertise to all the jobs in his own line whether they're big or small, and gets more finished and perfect results the better he is at his work. We must not suppose that god, who is supremely wise, [903a] and willing and able to superintend the world, looks to major matters but—like a faint-hearted lazybones who throws up his hands at hard work—neglects the minor, which we established were in fact *easier* to look after.

CLINIAS: No sir, we should never entertain such notions about gods. It's a point of view that would be absolutely impious and untrue.

ATHENIAN: Well, it looks to me as if we've given a pretty complete answer to this fellow who's always going on about the negligence of heaven.

CLINIAS: Yes, we have.

ATHENIAN: At any rate, our thesis has forced him to admit he was wrong. [b] But I still think we need to find a form of words to *charm* him into agreement.

CLINIAS: Well, my friend, what do you suggest?

ATHENIAN: What we say to the young man should serve to convince him of this thesis: "The supervisor of the universe has arranged everything with an eye to its preservation and excellence, and its individual parts play appropriate active or passive roles according to their various capacities. These parts, down to the smallest details of their active and passive functions, have each been put under the control of ruling powers that have [c] perfected the minutest constituents of the universe. Now then, you perverse fellow, one such part—a mere speck that nevertheless constantly contributes to the good of the whole—is you, you who have forgotten that nothing is created except to provide the entire universe with a life of prosperity. You forget that creation is not for your benefit: *you* exist for the sake of the universe. Every doctor, you see, and every skilled craftsman always works for the sake of some end product as a whole; he handles his materials so that they will give the best results in general, and makes [d] the parts contribute to the good of the whole, not vice versa. But you're grumbling because you don't appreciate that your position is best not only for the universe but for you too, thanks to your common origin. And since a soul is allied with different bodies at different times, and perpetually undergoes all sorts of changes, either self-imposed or produced by some other soul, the divine checkers-player has nothing else to do except promote a soul with a promising character to a better situation, and relegate one that is deteriorating to an inferior, as is appropriate in each case, so that [e] they all meet the fate they deserve."

CLINIAS: How so?

ATHENIAN: I fancy I could explain how easy it could be for gods to control the universe. Suppose that in one's constant efforts to serve its interests one were to mold all that is in it by *transforming* everything (by turning fire into water permeated by soul, for instance), instead of producing variety from a basic unity or unity from variety, then after the first or [904a] second or third stage of creation everything would be arranged in an infinite number of perpetually changing patterns. But in fact the supervisor of the universe finds his task remarkably easy.

CLINIAS: Again, how so?

ATHENIAN: This. Our King saw (i) that all actions are a function of soul and involve a great deal of virtue and a great deal of vice, (ii) that the combination of body and soul, while not an eternal creation like the gods sanctioned by law, is nevertheless indestructible (because living beings could never have been created if one of these two constituent factors [b] had been destroyed), (iii) that one of them—the good element in soul—is naturally beneficial, while the bad element naturally does harm. Seeing all this he contrived a place for each constituent where it would most easily and effectively ensure the triumph of virtue and the defeat of vice throughout the universe. With this grand purpose in view he has worked out what sort of position, in what regions, should be assigned to a soul to match its changes of character; but he left it to the individual's acts of [c] will to determine the *direction* of these changes. You see, the way we react to particular circumstances is almost invariably determined by our desires and our psychological state. (Plato, *Laws* X, 902e–904c)

9.20 Plato's *Timaeus* on goodness as the motivation of the demiurge, a creator god who creates the universe as a whole

TIMAEUS: . . . So we should accept the likely tale on these matters. It behooves us not to look for anything beyond this.

SOCRATES: Bravo, Timaeus! By all means! We must accept it as you say we should. This overture of yours was marvelous. Go on now and let us have the work itself.

TIMAEUS: Very well then. Now why did he who framed this whole [e] universe of becoming frame it? Let us state the reason why: He was good, and one who is good can never become jealous of anything. And so, being free of jealousy, he wanted everything to become as much like himself as was possible. In fact, men of wisdom will tell you (and you couldn't do [30a] better than to accept their claim) that this, more than anything else, was the most preeminent reason for the origin of the world's coming to be. The god wanted everything to be good and nothing to be bad so far as that was possible, and so he took over all that was visible—not at rest but in discordant and disorderly motion—and brought it from a state of disorder to one of order, because he believed that order was in every way better than disorder. Now it wasn't permitted (nor is it now) that one who is [b] supremely good should do anything but what is best. Accordingly, the god reasoned and concluded that in the realm of things naturally visible no unintelligent thing could as a whole be better than anything which does possess intelligence as a whole, and he further concluded that it is impossible for anything to come to possess intelligence apart from soul. Guided by this reasoning, he put intelligence in soul, and soul in body, and so he constructed the universe. He wanted to produce a piece of work that would be as excellent and supreme as its nature would allow. This, then, in keeping with our likely account, is how we must say divine [c] providence brought our world into being as a truly living thing, endowed with soul and intelligence. (Plato, *Timaeus* 29d–30c)

9.21 Plato's *Timaeus* on further gods created by the divine craftsman

"This, then, was the reason why all those everlasting and unwandering stars—divine living things which stay fixed by revolving without variation in the same place—came to be. Those that have turnings and thus wander in that sort of way came to be as previously described.

"The Earth he devised to be our nurturer, and, because it winds around [c] the axis that stretches throughout the universe, also to be the maker and guardian of day and night. Of the gods that have come to be within the universe, Earth ranks as the foremost, the one with greatest seniority.

"To describe the dancing movements of these gods, their juxtapositions and the back-circlings and advances of their circular courses on themselves; to tell which of the gods come into line with one another at their conjunctions and how many of them are in opposition, and in what order and at which times they pass in front of or behind one another, so that some are occluded from our view to reappear once again, thereby bringing terrors [d] and portents of things to come to those who cannot reason—to tell all this without the use of visible models would be labor spent in vain. We will make do with this account, and so let this be the conclusion of our discussion of the nature of the visible and generated gods.

"As for the other spiritual beings [*daimones*], it is beyond our task to know and speak of how they came to be. We should accept on faith the assertions of those figures of the past who claimed to be the offspring of gods. They must surely have been well informed about their own ancestors. So we [e] cannot avoid believing the children of gods, even though their accounts lack plausible or compelling proofs. Rather, we should follow custom and believe them, on the ground that what they claim to be reporting are matters of their own concern. Accordingly, let us accept their account of how these gods came to be and state what it is. Earth and heaven gave birth to Ocean and Tethys, who in turn gave birth to Phorcys, Cronus, and Rhea and all the gods in that generation. [41a] Cronus and Rhea gave birth to Zeus and Hera, as well as all those siblings who are called by names we know. These in turn gave birth to yet another generation. In any case, when all the gods had come to be, both the ones who make their rounds conspicuously and the ones who present themselves only to the extent that they are willing, the begetter of this universe spoke to them. This is what he said:

"'O gods, works divine whose maker and father I am, whatever has come to be by my hands cannot be undone but by my consent. Now [b] while it is true that anything that is bound is liable to being undone, still, only one who is evil would consent to the undoing of what has been well fitted together and is in fine condition. This is the reason why you, as creatures that have come to be, are neither completely immortal nor exempt from being undone. Still, you will not be undone nor will death be your portion, since you have received the guarantee of my will—a greater, more sovereign bond than those with which you were bound when you came to be. Learn now, therefore, what I declare to you. There remain still three kinds of mortal beings that have not yet been begotten; and as long as they have not come to be, the universe will be incomplete, for it will still [c] lack within it all the kinds of living things it must have if it is to be sufficiently complete. But if these creatures came to be and came to share in life by my hand, they would rival the gods. It is you, then, who must turn yourselves to the task of fashioning these living things, as your nature allows. This will assure their mortality, and this whole universe will really be a completed whole. Imitate the power I used in causing you to be. And to the extent that it is fitting for them to possess something that shares our name of "immortal," something described as divine and ruling within those of them who always consent to follow after justice and after you, I [d] shall begin by sowing that seed, and then hand it over to you. The rest of the task is yours. Weave what is mortal to what is immortal, fashion and beget living things. Give them food, cause them to grow, and when they perish, receive them back again.'" (Plato, *Timaeus* 40b–41d)

9.22 *Aristippus* on divine providence

He [Aristippus] said that, altogether, praying for good things and asking anything from god was ridiculous. For doctors do not give food or drink when the sick man asks for it, but when they think it will be useful. (*Vatican Sayings* 32 = Aristippus 132)

9.23 *Xenophon's* Socrates on the gods' benevolence

In the first place, he tried to make his companions think soundly about the gods. Different people who were present at different conversations of his on the subject have given their accounts of them. I myself was present for the following conversation he had with Euthydemus.

[3] "Tell me, Euthydemus," he said, "has it ever occurred to you to consider how much care the gods have taken to provide for humanity's needs?"

"No, in fact, it hasn't," replied Euthydemus.

"Well," he said, "do you realize that our first need is for light, which the gods provide us?"

"Of course," he replied. "If we didn't have light, we'd be as good as blind, despite our eyes."

"Besides that, we need rest, and they provide us a perfect resting time in night."

[4] "This certainly deserves our gratitude too," he said.

"And since the sun is bright and illuminates for us the times of day, along with everything else, while nighttime is more dim because of its darkness, didn't they make the stars shine at night to mark its passing for us, and doesn't this allow us to satisfy many of our needs?"

"That's right," he said.

"Plus, doesn't the moon reveal to us not only the successive stages of the night but also those of the month?"

"Certainly," he said.

[5] "And what about the fact that they've made the earth yield food for us in response to our need and arranged for this purpose the seasons, which supply us not only all kinds of things we need but also things for our enjoyment?"

"This really shows their benevolence," he said.

[6] "What about supplying us with water, a gift so precious that, together with the earth and the seasons, it causes everything that's useful for us to sprout and grow; helps in our own nourishment; and combines with all the things that nourish us to make them more easily digestible, beneficial, and pleasant? Or the fact that, because we need so much of it, they supply it to us in such abundance?"

"This shows forethought," he said.

[7] "What about their gift of fire, a defense against cold and darkness and an aid in every craft and all the various things people devise for their own benefit? In short, there isn't anything of practical benefit worth mentioning that human beings devise without fire."

"This shows their benevolence even more," he said.

[8] "And what about the fact that the sun's approach after the winter solstice ripens some things and withers others whose time has passed; and that, once it's done this, it doesn't keep coming closer but turns back, careful not to cause us any harm from overheating? Or that once it's receded to the point beyond which we'd clearly freeze from the cold, it turns back and approaches again and makes its revolutions in that part of the heavens where it can do us the most good?"

"This certainly gives every appearance of being done for the benefit of humanity," he said.

[9] "And what about the fact that, since we clearly couldn't endure either the heat or the cold if they came on suddenly, the sun approaches and recedes so gradually that we arrive at either extreme without even noticing?"

"I'm already beginning to wonder whether the gods do anything but care for human beings," said Euthydemus. "The only sticking point for me is the fact that all the other animals also share in these benefits."

[10] "But isn't it also clear," said Socrates, "that these animals themselves are born and reared for the sake of humanity? What other living thing derives as many advantages from goats, sheep, cattle, horses, and donkeys as human beings do? In my opinion, people get more out of these than they do from plants. They certainly get no less in terms of nourishment and commercial benefit. Many nations don't use plant life for sustenance but live off the nourishment from the milk, cheese, and meat they get from their livestock. And everyone tames and domesticates the animals that are useful and employs them as help in war and for many other tasks."

"I agree with you on this point," he said, "especially considering how animals far stronger than us are brought under human control to such an extent that we can use them however we want."

[11] "And what about the fact that they've endowed human beings with senses suited for perceiving the great variety of beautiful and beneficial objects, and that allow us to enjoy everything that's good? Or that they've implanted in us the power of reason, whereby we can reflect on the objects of our perception and commit them to memory, and so come to understand their respective benefits and to devise various means for enjoying what's good and avoiding what's bad? [12] Or that they've given us the power of expression, which allows us through instruction to impart and share with one another everything that's good, to establish laws, and to participate in government?"

"The gods certainly do seem to devote a great deal of care to human beings, Socrates."

"And what about the help they give us, because of our inability to discern our future interests, by revealing through divination to those who consult them what a given outcome will be and by teaching them how to achieve the best result?"

"They seem to treat you more friendly than everyone else, Socrates," he said, "at least if it's true that they warn you what to do and not to do without even being asked."[6]

[13] "You'll know for yourself that I'm telling the truth if, instead of waiting for the gods to appear to you in physical form, you're content to worship and honor them for their works, which you do see. Bear in mind that even the gods themselves suggest as much: the other gods who grant us blessings don't reveal themselves along with their gifts, and the same is true especially of the one who orders and maintains the entire universe, which encompasses every genuinely good thing that

---

6. An allusion to Socrates' *daimonion*: see Ch. 10.

he constantly supplies—fresh, sound, untouched by age, and reliably at his service quicker than thought—for our use. While he is manifest in the greatness of his works, he himself nevertheless remains unseen in his administration of them. [14] Bear in mind that even the sun, which seems visible to everyone, doesn't allow people to get a clear look at it; if anyone tries to gaze at it without the proper respect, it takes away their sight. You'll find that even the gods' agents are invisible. The thunderbolt is clearly hurled from overhead and overpowers everything it meets, but no one sees it coming, striking, or going. No one sees the winds themselves, but their effects are obvious to us, and we can sense their approach. Even our mind, which has a share of divinity if anything human does, is itself unseen, though it obviously reigns within us. In recognition of these facts, we shouldn't despise things unseen but rather come to appreciate their power from their effects and honor the divine." (Xenophon, *Memorabilia* 4.3.2–14; followed by **3.58**)

9.24 *Plato's Socrates believes that the gods will not neglect a good man*

"You too must be of good hope as regards death, gentlemen of the jury, [d] and keep this one truth in mind, that a good man cannot be harmed either in life or in death, and that his affairs are not neglected by the gods." (Plato, *Apology* 41c–d; preceded by **4.16**, followed by **10.8**)

9.25 *Plato's Socrates, in conversation with Adimantus, argues that god is responsible only for good, never for what is bad*

"Then not only is god, being god, in fact good," [I (Socrates) said,] "but he must be said to be so?"
  "What else?"
  "And surely nothing good is harmful, is it?"
  "I suppose not."
  "And can what isn't harmful do harm?"
  "Never."
  "Or can what does no harm do anything bad?"
  "No."
  "And can what does nothing bad be the cause of anything bad?"
  "How could it?"
  "Moreover, the good is beneficial?"
  "Yes."
  "It is the cause of doing well?"
  "Yes."

"The good isn't the cause of all things, then, but only of good ones; it isn't the cause of bad ones."

"I agree entirely," he [Adimantus] said. [c]

"In that case," I said, "since god is good, he will not be—as most people claim—the cause of everything that happens to human beings but of only a few things, and of many things he is not the cause; for good things are far fewer than bad ones in our lives. We must treat him alone as responsible for the good things, and find some other cause for the bad ones, not god." (Plato, *Republic* II, 379b–c)

9.26 *Xenophon's Socrates exhorts* **Chaerecrates** *to recognize the duty on us to use our divine gifts well*

"At the moment, you two are like a pair of hands that god designed to cooperate with one another, but that have given this up and turned to hindering each other; or like a pair of feet designed by providence to work in tandem, but that have lost sight of this fact and get in each other's way. [19] Wouldn't it be gross stupidity and a great misfortune to use for harm things designed to benefit? And yet, as I see it, god designed two brothers to be more beneficial to one another than two hands or feet or eyes or anything else people have that form a natural pair. If the hands need to perform two tasks at the same time that are more than about six feet apart, they can't; the feet can't reach two spots even six feet apart at the same time; and the eyes, which seem to have the longest range, can't simultaneously see objects both in front of and behind them, even at a closer distance. But two brothers who are friends can simultaneously act for each other's benefit even when they're far apart." (Xenophon, *Memorabilia* 2.3.18–19)

Chapter 10: Lesser Divinities and Socrates' "Sign"

While there is tendency among the Socratics to think about the divine as a *unified* providential force, it is unlikely that any of them thought there was only one god. (Euclides in **2.33** comes closest to saying that; but even he is quoted as talking about "gods" in **9.8**.) What is more, we saw in passing that there may be a hierarchy of gods: Plato in the *Timaeus* distinguishes an eternal creator god from gods who are in their turn created by him (**9.21**); **9.14** and **10.6** show that he thought that even souls are, or come close to being, divine (cf. **4.2**; and Xenophon at **9.16**). One way of distinguishing the highest god(s) from lower divine beings in Greek is by calling the latter *daimones* (singular: *daimôn*) as opposed to *theoi* (singular: *theos*). In fact, either word *can* be used of any god; but when the distinction is intended, it is often to draw attention to the role of *daimones* in mediating between the celestial gods and humans—helped by the fact that the word *daimôn* can also refer to our individual fortunes, or fortune in general. (Cf. p. 28 on the word *eudaimonia,* which we are translating as "happiness.")

The Socratics seem in general to have been interested in observing the distinction between *theoi* and *daimones* (examples in **10.1–6**), and they have a particular reason to be interested in the "demonic" realm. This is the striking claim that Socrates' friend and enemies alike consistently report him as having made, namely that he had some kind of special relationship with the divine through his own *daimonion*—something unspecified, but *daimôn*-related: see **10.7–15**; also **3.59**, **5.7**, **6.7**, **9.23**.[12]. There was much speculation in antiquity over what exactly it was—that is, how Socrates experienced it: as some sort of voice perhaps (**10.12, 10.13(b)**), or in a sneeze (**10.13(a)**)? There was disagreement too about the scope of its message. The advice Xenophon's Socrates derives from it is about both what to do and what not to do, and even (as in **10.14**.[4]) about what others should do; for Plato's Socrates, on the other hand, the *daimonion* only intervenes to *prevent* him from doing things he would otherwise have done.

Plato and Xenophon seem to be more interested in the *daimonion* than other members of the circle, perhaps for the same reason that they are most interested in issues of piety in general (cf. Ch. 3): the charge against Socrates of "not believing in the gods (*theoi*) the city believes in, but other new *daimonia*" (**10.14**; cf. Plato, *Apology* 24b–c). It is true that the direct access to the divine that Socrates seemed to claim was unheard of, certainly outside the world of poetry. But according to

Xenophon and Plato, to have used that claim as a basis for a charge of impiety was to misunderstand both Socrates and the nature of piety (see Ch. 3 and Ch. 5). In addition to the *daimonion*, we have seen that Xenophon's Socrates looks to conventional forms of divination (**5.16**.[10], **9.23**.[12]) as sources of divine guidance—as did Xenophon himself, by his own account in **10.16**. He also believes in the power of dreams to foretell the future, and his army looks for omens from sacrifices. The Platonic Socrates, likewise, talks as if he believes in the predictive power of dreams (**10.17–18**), and the art of the seer, which he describes as "more perfect and more admirable" than the art of prediction from birds (**6.18**.[244c]); the "likely story" told about the world by Plato's Timaeus includes interesting remarks about diviners and divination in the context of a discussion of the role of the liver in the human body (see *Timaeus* 71e–72b). In fact, for both Xenophon and Plato the phenomenon of the *daimonion* probably counts as a kind of divination, or *mantikê* (see **10.19**, where Plato's Socrates makes the link more or less explicit), but it is divination of a unique kind (cf. **10.9** [496c]).

Texts

10.1 *Euclides thinks humans have a "double* daimôn*" . . .*

And Euclides the Socratic said that all of us without any exception had a double *daimôn* assigned to us. One can establish that from Lucilius' book of satires.[1] (Censorinus, *Birthday Book* 3.3 = Euclides 11)

10.2 *. . . perhaps this very pairing of sleep and old age?*

From Euclides: sleep is a younger, boyish *daimôn* who is easily persuadable and can readily be escaped; whereas this other one is grey-haired and old, especially located in older people, not easily persuaded and immune to entreaty. It's a hard task to be rid of this second *daimôn*, when once he's made his appearance, because he doesn't pay attention to what's said, because he's deaf, and you can't get anything through to him by pointing things out, because he's blind. (Stobaeus, *Selections* 3.6.63 = Euclides 11)

---

1. Lucilius was a second-century BCE Roman poet.

10.3 Plato's Socrates *(claiming to recount a first-hand report from someone who died and came back to life) on one's* daimôn *as one's fate*

"When the souls arrived at the light, they had to go to Lachesis right away. There a speaker arranged them in order, took from the lap of Lachesis a number of lots and a number of models of lives, mounted a high pulpit, and spoke to them: 'Here is the message of Lachesis, the maiden daughter of Necessity: "Ephemeral souls, this is the beginning of another cycle that will end in death. No *daimôn* will be allotted to you; the choice of *daimôn* will be your own. The one who has the [e] first lot will be the first to choose a life to which he will then be bound by necessity. Virtue knows no master; each will possess it to a greater or less degree, depending on whether he values or disdains it. The responsibility lies with the one who makes the choice; the god has none."'" (Plato, *Republic* X, 617d–e)

10.4 *The* daimôn *as personal guide according to* **Plato's Phaedo's** *Socrates—reporting "what we are told" (by persons unspecified)*

"But [d] now that the soul appears to be immortal, there is no escape from evil or salvation for it except by becoming as good and wise as possible, for the soul goes to the underworld possessing nothing but its education and upbringing, which are said to bring the greatest benefit or harm to the dead right at the beginning of the journey yonder.

"We are told that when each person dies, the *daimôn* who was allotted to him in life proceeds to lead him to a certain place, whence those [e] who have been gathered together there must, after being judged, proceed to the underworld with the guide (*hêgemôn*) who has been appointed to lead them thither from here. Having there undergone what they must and stayed there the appointed time, they are led back here by another guide after [108a] long periods of time. The journey is not as Aeschylus' Telephus describes it. He says that only one single path leads to Hades, but I think it is neither one nor simple, for then there would be no need of guides; one could not make any mistake if there were but one path. As it is, it is likely to have many forks and crossroads; and I base this judgment on the sacred rites and customs here.

"The well-ordered and wise soul follows the guide and is not without familiarity with its surroundings, but the soul that is passionately attached [b] to the body, as I said before, hovers around it and the visible world for a long time, struggling and suffering much until it is led away by force and with difficulty by its appointed *daimôn*. When the impure soul which has performed some impure deed joins the others after being involved in unjust killings, or committed other crimes which are akin to these and are actions of souls of this kind, everybody shuns it and turns away, [c] unwilling to be its fellow traveler or its guide (*hêgemôn*); such a soul wanders alone completely at a loss until a certain time arrives and it is forcibly led to its proper dwelling place. On the other hand, the soul that has led a pure and moderate life finds fellow travelers and gods to guide it, and each of them dwells in a place suited to it.

"There are many strange places upon the earth, and the earth itself is not such as those who are used to discourse upon it believe it to be in nature or size, as someone has convinced me." (Plato, *Phaedo* 107d–108c)

10.5 Plato *has the wise Diotima explain to his Socrates why Erôs is a* daimôn *and not a god (*theos*)*

"Yet everyone agrees he [Love] is a great god," I said.

"Only those who don't know?" she said. "Is that how you mean 'everyone'? Or do you include those who do know?"

"Oh, everyone together."

And she laughed. [c] "Socrates, how could those who say that he's not a god at all agree that he's a great god?"

"Who says that?" I asked.

"You, for one," she said, "and I for another."

"How can you say this!" I exclaimed.

"That's easy," said she. "Tell me, wouldn't you say that all gods are beautiful and happy? Surely you'd never say a god is not beautiful or happy?"

"Zeus! Not I," I said.

"Well, by calling anyone 'happy,' don't you mean they possess good and beautiful things?"

"Certainly." [d]

"What about Love? You agreed he needs good and beautiful things, and that's why he desires them—because he needs them."

"I certainly did."

"Then how could he be a god if he has no share in good and beautiful things?"

"There's no way he could, apparently."

"Now do you see? You don't believe Love is a god either!"

"Then, what could Love be?" I asked. "A mortal?"

"Certainly not."

"Then, what is he?"

"He's like what we mentioned before," she said. "He is in between mortal and immortal."

"What's that you're saying, Diotima?"

"He's a great *daimôn*, [e] Socrates. Everything that is *daimonion*, you see, is in between god and mortal."

"What is their function?" I asked.

"They are messengers who shuttle back and forth between the two, conveying prayer and sacrifice from men to gods, while to men they bring commands from the gods and gifts in return for sacrifices. Being in the middle of the two, they round out the whole and bind fast the all to all. [203a] Through them all divination passes, through them the art of priests in sacrifice and ritual, in enchantment, prophecy, and sorcery. Gods do not mix with men; they mingle and converse with us through the *daimonion* instead, whether we are awake or asleep. He who is wise in any of these ways is a *daimonios* man, but he who is wise in any other way, in a profession or any manual work, is merely a mechanic. These *daimones* are many and various, then, and one of them is Love." (Plato, *Symposium* 202b–203a)

10.6 Plato's Socrates (with **Hermogenes**) suggests that human souls might become daimones

SOCRATES: Do you know what Hesiod says *daimones* are?

HERMOGENES: No, I don't remember.

SOCRATES: Do you remember that he speaks of a golden race, which was the first race of human beings to be born?

HERMOGENES: Yes, I remember that.

SOCRATES: He says this about it:
Since this race has been eclipsed by fate,
They are called sacred *daimones;* they live on earth, [398a]
And are good, warding off evil and guarding mortal men.[2]

HERMOGENES: So what?

---

[2] A version of Hesiod, *Works and Days* 121–23, perhaps deliberately modified by Plato. Our text reads: "Since this race has been hidden by the earth, | They are *daimones* through the will of Zeus, | Good, living above ground, and guarding mortal men."

SOCRATES: Well, I don't think he's saying that the golden race is by nature made of gold, but that it is good and fine. I consider it a proof of this that he calls us a "race of iron."
HERMOGENES: That's true.
SOCRATES: So don't you think that if someone who presently exists were [b] good, Hesiod would say that he too belonged to the golden race?
HERMOGENES: He probably would.
SOCRATES: Are good people any different from wise ones?
HERMOGENES: No, they aren't.
SOCRATES: It is principally because daemons are wise and knowing (*daêmones*), I think, that Hesiod says they are named *daimones*. In our older Attic dialect, we actually find the word *daêmones*. So, Hesiod and many other poets speak well when they say that when a good man dies, he has a great destiny and a great honor and becomes a *daimôn*, [c] which is a name given to him because it accords with wisdom. And I myself assert, indeed, that every good man, whether alive or dead, is daemonic, and is correctly called a "daemon." (Plato, *Cratylus* 397e–398c)

10.7 *Xenophon's Aristodemus: the gods send Socrates "advisors"*

"What will [the gods] have to do for you to believe that they're concerned for you?"

[15] "I'll believe it when they send advisors to tell me what I should and shouldn't do, just as you claim they do you." (Xenophon, *Memorabilia* 1.4.14–15; part of **9.16**)

10.8 *The* daimonion *of* **Plato's** *Socrates only prevents him from doing wrong*

"A surprising thing has happened to me, jurymen—you I would rightly call jurymen [i.e., those who have now voted to acquit him]. At all previous times that familiar prophetic power from my *daimonion* frequently opposed me, even in small matters, when I was about to do something wrong, but now that, as you can see for yourselves, I was faced with what one might think, and what is generally thought to be, the [b] worst of evils, the god's sign has not opposed me, either when I left home at dawn, or when I came into court, or at any time that I was about to say something during my speech. In other talks it often held me back in the middle of my speaking, but now it has opposed no word or deed of mine. What do I think is the reason for this? I will tell you. What has happened to me may well be a good thing, and those of us who believe death [c] to be an evil are certainly mistaken. I have convincing proof of this, for it is impossible that my familiar sign would not have opposed me if I was not about to do something good. . . . What has happened to me now has not happened of itself, but it is clear to me that it was better for me to die now and to escape from trouble. That is why the sign did not oppose me at any point. So I am certainly not angry with those who convicted me, or with my accusers." (Plato, *Apology* 40a–c and 41d; the passage omitted = **4.16** + **9.24**)

10.9 *The* daimonion *keeps* **Plato's** *Socrates out of politics* . . .

"Then there remains, Adimantus, only a very small group who consort with philosophy in a way that's worthy of her: a noble and well-brought up character, for example, kept down by exile, who remains with philosophy [b] according to his nature because there is no one to corrupt him, or a great soul living in a small city, who disdains the city's affairs and looks beyond them. A very few might be drawn to philosophy from other crafts that they rightly despise because they have good natures. And some might be held back by the bridle that restrains our friend Theages—for he's in every way qualified to be tempted away from philosophy, but his physical illness [c] restrains him by keeping him out of politics. Finally, my own case is hardly worth mentioning—my *daimonion* sign—because it has happened to no one before me, or to only a very few. Now, the members of this small group have tasted how sweet and blessed a possession philosophy is." (Plato, *Republic* VI, 496a–c)

10.10 . . . *kept him away from Alcibiades until the time was right* . . .

"I was the first man to fall in love with you, son of Clinias [Alcibiades], and now that the others have stopped pursuing you I suppose you're wondering why I'm the only one who hasn't given up—and also why, when the others pestered you with conversation, I never even spoke to you all these years. Human causes didn't enter into it; I was prevented by opposition of some *daimonion* sort, the effect of which you'll hear about later on. But now it no longer prevents me, so here I am. I'm confident it won't prevent me in the future either." (?Plato, *Alcibiades* 103a–b)[3]

---

3. For the contested status of the *Alcibiades*, see Ch. 7 n.1.

10.11 ... *prevents him from missing a philosophical encounter* ...

CRITO: I have no objection, Socrates, if you really think well of the plan. But first explain to me what the wisdom of the two men is, to give me some idea of what we are going to learn.

SOCRATES: You shall hear at once, since I can't pretend that I paid no attention to the pair. As a matter of fact, I did just that and remember [e] what was said and will try to recount the whole thing from the beginning. As good luck would have it, I was sitting by myself in the undressing room just where you saw me and was already thinking of leaving. But when I got up, my customary *daimonion* sign put in an appearance. So I [273a] sat down again, and in a moment the two of them, Euthydemus and Dionysodorus, came in. (Plato, *Euthydemus* 272d–273a)

10.12 ... *and stops him from leaving blasphemy unrepented*

SOCRATES: My friend, just as I was about to cross the river, the familiar [c] divine (*daimonion*) sign came to me which, whenever it occurs, holds me back from something I am about to do. I thought I heard a voice coming from this very spot, forbidding me to leave until I made atonement for some offense against the gods. In effect, you see, I am a seer, and though I am not particularly good at it, still—like people who are just barely able to read and write—I am good enough for my own purposes. I recognize my offense clearly now. In fact, the soul too, my friend, is itself a sort of seer; that's [d] why, almost from the beginning of my speech, I was disturbed by a very uneasy feeling, as Ibycus puts it, that "for offending the gods I am honored by men." But now I understand exactly what my offense has been.

PHAEDRUS: Tell me, what is it?

SOCRATES: Phaedrus, that speech you carried with you here it—was horrible, as horrible as the speech you made me give. (Plato, *Phaedrus* 242b–d)

10.13(a) *An explanation of Socrates'* daimonion *attributed to* **Terpsion** ...

"So you imagine, then, Theocritus," replied Galaxidorus, "that Socrates' *daimonion* had some special and extraordinary power to tip the balance of reason, bypassing the ordinary requirement that in matters unclear and unproven the man should put it to the test and confirm it? For just as a single weight does not tip the scales by itself, [581A] but only inclines the whole to itself when added on one side of an equilibrium, so too a sneeze or a remark or any indication of that sort is too light to incline a mind of substance to action; but when it has been combined with one or other of two opposing reasonings, it solves the impasse by destroying the balance, and thus allows movement and impulse."

"Just so, Galaxidorus," my father [Caphisias' father, Polymnis] broke in. "I heard it myself from one of the Megarians, who heard it from Terpsion, that Socrates' *daimonion* was a sneeze, whether his own or someone else's. So if someone sneezed to the right of him, whether behind [B] or in front, he proceeded with his action, but if it was to his left, he turned aside; while if it was his own sneezing, if it occurred when he was about to act it endorsed the action, whereas if it occurred when he was already acting it checked him and stopped his impulse to go ahead." (Plutarch, *On Socrates' Daimonion* 580F–581B)[4]

10.13(b) . . . *and another (more subtle) put in the mouth of* **Simmias**

They were already some way on with an inquiry of no mean sort; it was the one Galaxidorus and Pheidolaus had embarked on shortly before, when they started puzzling over what the [C] substance and force was of Socrates' so-called *daimonion*. We didn't hear how Simmias responded to Galaxidorus' contribution, but speaking for himself, he said that he'd once asked Socrates about it, and not received a reply. For that reason he had never asked again. But he had often witnessed Socrates describing as "impostors" anyone who claimed to have seen some divine phenomenon with their own eyes, while paying close attention to those who said that they had heard a voice of some sort, and questioning them in detail. "The suspicion thus occurred to us," Simmias said, "as we considered the matter in private among ourselves, that Socrates' *daimonion* was perhaps not a vision but rather a perception [D] of a voice of some kind, or else an apprehension of some form of words that in some odd way attached itself to him—just as in sleep there is no sound and yet we have the impression of certain things being said, and think that we are

---

4. Plutarch's dialogue *On Socrates' Daimonion* (probably written around the turn of the second century CE) is a fictionalized discussion somewhat on the model of Plato's dialogues, and similar caution should be exercised about the historicity of the views he puts in the mouths of his characters. More so, perhaps: we have no way of knowing how well Plutarch or his audience knew the views of Terpsion (who left no writings) or Simmias (although he did).

actually hearing people speaking. To some people this kind of impression takes the form of a genuine dream, which occurs because the body is calm and at rest, when they're asleep; when they're awake their souls hardly give a hearing to their superiors—crowded in by the tumult of the passions and surrounded by wants, they are unable to listen or apply their minds to what is shown to them. Socrates' intellect, by contrast, was pure and free from the passions, and he barely involved himself in the necessities [E] of the body, so that he was sensitive and delicate, and sharply responsive to what touched him. And what touched him, one may guess, was no voice, but rather words of a *daimôn* attaching themselves to his understanding, soundlessly, by the very force of what they were showing him. Sound is like a blow, the soul forcibly receiving what is being said through the ears when we encounter each other. By contrast the intellect of our superior draws the well-endowed soul by the touch of the thought, with no need for blows, and the soul responds unforced to the slackening and tightening of its impulses, no passions [F] intervening, its movements as easy and smooth as its reins are slack. That should be no surprise, when we see the hulks of great merchantmen being turned by tiny steering oars, or potters' wheels whirling round evenly at the touch of a fingertip: though soulless, the smoothness of their construction makes them respond readily to the mover. The soul of a human being, strung with a thousand impulses like so many woven cords, is by far the most responsive of all instruments, if it is handled appropriately, needing the lightest touch to move it toward the object of its thought. [589A] For in this case it is toward the intellect that the sources of the passions and impulses tend, and when the intellect is shaken they are dragged with it and convulse and taughten the human being for action. It is here that one grasps the true power of thought. Insensate bones, sinews, flesh stuffed full with fluids, a great bulk made up of all this lying there inactive—and the very fact of the soul's putting something in its mind and setting in train an impulse toward it makes the whole rise up and with all its parts straining together fly like a bird toward the action. Nor is it hard, let alone an impossible task, to envisage the mode of movement, of coordination and of suggestion [B] by which the soul, having thought, uses its impulses to draw the bulk of the whole along with it. But if the mind's thought moves things so effortlessly, with not a word spoken, I hardly think it should be hard to believe that intellect and soul should be guided by a superior intellect and a diviner soul, which touches it from outside in the way that only thought can touch thought, like the reflection of light. For in truth we recognize each other's thinking like people groping in the dark, using only speech, whereas the thoughts of the gods (*daimones*), who have light, shine out for those able to see, without the need for the verbs and nouns [C] that humans use as tokens in their intercourse with each other, who only see the shadows and images of each other's thoughts, not grasping them as they are—unless, that is, they enjoy the presence of that special and divine (*daimonion*) light I spoke of. Yet in a way the phenomenon of speech itself may serve to allay the doubts of the skeptical. Air, when impressed with articulate sounds, turns at once into spoken language and brings a thought to the soul of the hearer. So it should be no matter for surprise if the air turned out to be susceptible enough to conform itself to the thought of the gods (*daimones*) too, and imprint the thinker's thoughts on certain divine, exceptional individuals. Just as sappers' blows [D] from deep beneath the earth pass through everything else unnoticed, but are caught and re-echoed by bronze shields, so what the gods (*daimones*) say passes over everyone and finds resonance only in those of untroubled character and unruffled soul—the very people we call "sacred," even "divine" (*daimonioi*). Ordinary people think that divinity (*to daimonion*) only visits those who are asleep, and they think it an astonishing and incredible idea that its words should affect the thinking of people who are awake and in possession of their faculties in a similar way; it's as if one should suppose a musician is using his lyre when it is unstrung, and doesn't touch it, or use it, when it has been properly set up and tuned. They don't see the reason for their misunderstanding, which is [E] their own disharmony and inner confusion, from all of which our companion Socrates was quite free, as the oracle given to his father, when Socrates was still a boy, predicted: it instructed that he should leave his son to do whatever came to his mind, not force him or guide him, but give his impulses free play, praying for him to Zeus Agoraeus and the Muses but otherwise not interfering with him, evidently on the grounds that he [F] had a guide (*hêgemôn*) in him for life that was superior to a thousand teachers and tutors. That, Pheidolaus, is the way it occurred to us to think about Socrates' *daimonion* when he was alive, and we've gone on to think about it like that now he's dead; we treat with contempt those who bring in overheard remarks or sneezes to explain it." (Plutarch, *On Socrates' Daimonion* 588B–589F)

10.14 Xenophon *links the* daimonion *to the charges against Socrates* . . .

I have often wondered by what possible arguments Socrates' prosecutors persuaded the Athenians that he deserved death at the hands of the state. The indictment against him went something like this: "Socrates is guilty of not recognizing the gods (*theoi*) recognized by the state and of introducing new divinities (*daimonia*). He is also guilty of corrupting young men." [2] As to the first charge, that he did not recognize the gods recognized by the state, what sort of proof could they possibly produce? He offered sacrifices openly and often, both at home and upon the city's public altars, and he made no secret of his use of divination. It was common knowledge that Socrates claimed that his *daimonion* gave him signs which actually seems to me the main reason that they charged him with "introducing new divinities." [3] He was not introducing anything newer than people who believe in divination and use birds, oracles, signs, and sacrifices for the purpose. They don't suppose that the birds or those they meet by chance know for themselves what will benefit the inquirer; rather they suppose them to be the means by which the gods indicate what this is. And that was [Socrates'] position too. [4] But whereas most people claim that they are deterred or encouraged by portents or chance encounters, Socrates said just what he thought: he claimed that his *daimonion* conveyed messages. He even advised many of his companions what to do and not to do based on what he claimed was the divine sign's warning. Those who obeyed him benefited, and those who did not regretted it. (Xenophon, *Memorabilia* 1.1.1–4)

10.15 . . . *as does* **Plato's** *Euthyphro*

SOCRATES: He [Meletus] says that I am a [b] maker of gods, and on the ground that I create new gods (*theoi*) while not believing in the old gods (*theoi*), he has indicted me for their sake, as he puts it.

EUTHYPHRO: I understand, Socrates. This is because you say that the *daimonion* keeps coming to you. So he has written this indictment against you as one who makes innovations in religious matters, and he comes to court to slander you, knowing that such things are easily misrepresented to the crowd. (Plato, *Euthyphro* 3a–b)

10.16 Xenophon *(writing in the third person about himself) says that he consulted the Delphic oracle about his expedition to the east as a mercenary*

So Xenophon read the letter, and consulted with Socrates the Athenian about his journey. Socrates suspected that friendship with Cyrus would be held against him by the city because of the obvious enthusiasm with which Cyrus had fought alongside Sparta against Athens, and he advised Xenophon to go [6] to Delphi and consult the god about his journey. Xenophon went, and asked Apollo to which of the gods he should sacrifice and pray if he was to follow his intended route with the greatest possible honor, flourish, and return safe. In response, Apollo ordained [7] to which gods he should sacrifice. When he returned, he told Socrates what the response had been; and when Socrates heard it, he criticized him for not first asking whether it would be better for him to take his journey or to stay—rather than asking, as he did, to know how he could complete the journey with as much honor as possible. (Xenophon, *Anabasis* 3.1.5–7)

10.17 Plato's *Socrates has a dream that portends his death* . . .

SOCRATES: Why have you come so early?

CRITO: I bring bad news, Socrates, not for you, apparently, but for me and all your friends the news is bad and hard to bear. Indeed, I would count it among the hardest.

SOCRATES: What is it? [d] Or has the ship arrived from Delos, at the arrival of which I must die?

CRITO: It has not arrived yet, but it will, I believe, arrive today, according to a message some men brought from Sunium, where they left it. This makes it obvious that it will come today, and that your life must end tomorrow.

SOCRATES: May it be for the best. If it so please the gods, so be it. However, I do not think it will arrive today.

CRITO: What indication have you of this? [44a]

SOCRATES: I will tell you. I must die the day after the ship arrives.

CRITO: That is what those in authority say.

SOCRATES: Then I do not think it will arrive on this coming day, but on the next. I take to witness of this a dream I had a little earlier during this night. It looks as if it was the right time for you not to wake me.

CRITO: What was your dream?

SOCRATES: I thought that a beautiful and comely woman dressed in white [b] approached me. She called me and said: "Socrates, may you arrive at fertile Phthia on the third day."

CRITO: A strange dream, Socrates.

SOCRATES: But it seems clear enough to me, Crito. (Plato, *Crito* 43c–44b)

10.18 . . . *and another that gives him his commission*

"Cebes intervened and said: 'By Zeus, yes, Socrates, you did well to remind me. Evenus asked me the day before yesterday, as others had [d] done before, what induced you to write poetry after you came to prison, you who had never composed any poetry before, putting the fables of Aesop into verse and composing the hymn to Apollo. If it is of any concern to you that I should have an answer to give to Evenus when he repeats his question, as I know he will, tell me what to say to him.'

"'Tell him the truth, Cebes,' he said, 'that I did not do this with the idea of rivaling him or his poems, for I knew that would not be easy, but I [e] tried to find out the meaning of certain dreams and to satisfy my conscience in case it was this kind of art they were frequently bidding me to practice. The dreams were something like this: the same dream often came to me in the past, now in one shape now in another, but saying the same thing: "Socrates," it said, "practice and cultivate the arts." In the past I imagined that it was instructing and advising me to do what I was doing, such as [61a] those who encourage runners in a race, that the dream was thus bidding me to do the very thing I was doing, namely, to practice the art of philosophy, this being the highest kind of art, and I was doing that. But now, after my trial took place, and the festival of the god was preventing my execution, I thought that, in case my dream was bidding me to practice this popular art, I should not disobey it but compose poetry. [b] I thought it safer not to leave here until I had satisfied my conscience by writing poems in obedience to the dream. So I first wrote in honor of the god of the present festival.'" (Plato, *Phaedo* 60c–61b)

10.19 *The gods, in fact, communicate with* **Plato**'s
Socrates in a range of different ways

"But what I do, as I [Socrates] say, I do because the god has assigned it to me, whether he communicates through oracular responses, or dreams, or any other means gods use to assign whatever task it may be to human beings." (Plato, *Apology* 33c)

Chapter 11: Debates and Rivalries

The passages in this last, brief section should be treated with some caution as history: they are contradictory and patently based on questionable extrapolation from the dialogues in some cases (**11.1, 11.2, 11.7**). But they serve other useful purposes for us. They provide an ancient perspective on the Socratics as a community, and their published works as artifacts of that community, properly read in the context of its conversations. The very fact that the attribution of some dialogues—whole corpora in some cases—is hotly contested (**11.2**; see also details in the Index of Socratics) shows both the importance and the difficulty of establishing whose voice is in play when the very medium of much philosophical debate is *itself* fictionalized conversation between historical characters.

> Readers interested in pursuing later ancient constructions of Socrates' circle and the interactions of it members should also read the *Socratic Epistles* (cf. Introduction p. ix with n.3.).

Texts

11.1 Plato versus *Xenophon, Antisthenes, Aeschines*

Xenophon does not seem to have been well disposed toward him [Plato]: as if in competition with each other, they have written similar works: a *Symposium,* an *Apology of Socrates,* and records of conversations on ethics. Again, one of them wrote a *Republic,* the other the *Education of Cyrus.* And in the *Laws,* Plato says that his *Education* is a fiction: Cyrus is not like that. Both mention Socrates, but never each other—except that Xenophon mentioned Plato in *Memorabilia* 3.[1]

[35] It is said that Antisthenes was going to read one of his writings and invited Plato to be present. When he asked what he was going to read, he said that it was a denial of contradiction. "So how can you write about that?" asked Plato, and proceeded to show him that the

---

1. See **7.5**.[1].

argument was self-refuting; at which he wrote a dialogue against Plato called *Satho*.² From then on they were always at odds with each other.

They say that Socrates heard Plato reading his *Lysis:* "Heracles!" he said: "What a lot of lies this young man is telling about me." For the man had written a lot of things that Socrates never said.

[36] Plato was also on bad terms with Aristippus. In *On the Soul,* anyway, he slanders him as not having been there when Socrates died, although he was close by in Aegina.³

They also say there was a certain rivalry between him and Aeschines, who was himself held in high regard by Dionysius. The report is that when poverty drove him to Sicily, Plato ignored him, but Aristippus stuck by him. And the words he ascribed to Crito, advising [Socrates] in the prison about escaping, Idomeneus⁴ says were actually said by Aeschines; Plato transferred them to Crito out of malice. (Diogenes Laertius 3.34–36 = Antisthenes 148 + Aristippus 15 + Aeschines 3)

11.2 *Plato slights **Aeschines** and favors **Aristippus**; the authenticity of **Aeschines**' dialogues is put in question*

Aeschines, an Athenian, son of Charinus the sausage maker (or Lysanias, as some say), was industrious from childhood; which is why he never left Socrates. Hence Socrates' remark, "Only the sausage maker's son knows how to honor me." Idomeneus said that it was he who advised Socrates to escape when he was in prison, not Crito. Plato ascribed his words to Crito, because Aeschines was too fond of Aristippus.

Aeschines was slandered, especially by Menedemus of Eretria,⁵ for stealing most of his dialogues from Socrates, having got them from Xanthippe. The so-called "headless ones"⁶ are very casual, and do not get across the vigor of Socrates; these Peristratus of Ephesus⁷ agrees are not by Aeschines. [61] Of the seven dialogues in question Persaeus⁸

---

2. Cf. Ch. 1 for the issue of contradiction; **7.10** for the *Satho*.

3. *Phaedo* 59c.

4. An Epicurean philosopher writing around the turn of the third century BCE.

5. A later member of the Elian school (which traced its roots to Phaedo); flourished around the turn of the third century BCE.

6. For the mysterious term "headless" (*akephaloi*) see the Index of Socratics under "Aeschines."

7. Otherwise unknown.

8. Of Citium: third-century BCE Stoic.

thinks most are by Pasiphon the Eretrian,⁹ who ascribed them to Aeschines. He also fabricated Antisthenes' *Cyrus Minor, Heracles,* and *Alcibiades,* and works by other authors besides. Anyway, the works of Aeschines which bear the hallmark of a Socratic character are seven: the first was *Militiades,* which explains its relative weakness; then *Callias, Axiochus, Aspasia, Alcibiades, Telauges,* and *Rhino.*¹⁰

They say that poverty made him go to Sicily, to Dionysius, and that Plato ignored him, but Aristippus stuck by him;¹¹ and that he received gifts from Dionysius after giving him some of his dialogues. [62] When he returned to Athens, he lacked the nerve to set up as a teacher [lit.: play the sophist], since Plato and Aristippus and their respective followers were then enjoying a high reputation; but he gave paid lectures. Subsequently he wrote judicial speeches for victims of injustice. That is why Timon¹² spoke of "Aeschines' persuasive force | In writing."

When he was oppressed by poverty, they say that Socrates told him to borrow from himself by cutting down what he ate.

Aristippus too suspected [the authenticity of] his dialogues— anyway, they say that when he was reading one of them in Megara, Aristippus mocked him by saying, "Where did you get all that, you thief?" (Diogenes Laertius 2.60–62, including Aeschines 13, 22, 28 + Antisthenes 43, 141 + Aristippus 15, 22, 23; part = **7.40**)

11.3 *Plato lords it over* **Phaedo** *and* **Aeschines**

Aeschines was a poor man and had one single follower, Xenocrates, of whom Plato stripped him, and in Phaedo's case he took charge by stopping the slavery case;¹³ in general his natural stance toward all of Socrates' pupils was that of a stepmother. (Athenaeus, *The Learned Banqueters* 11, 507C = Aeschines 21)

11.4 *But elsewhere,* **Plato** *sticks up for* **Aeschines**

It is well said that one should do something for one's friends especially when they are angry or in trouble, and look out for their interests and needs; and it is no less friendly to speak out for them if they feel they have been ignored or slighted by others, and put in a word for them.

---

9. Early-third-century BCE member of the Elian school.
10. For the text and sense of this, we follow Beall (2010).
11. Cf. **11.1**.[36] above.
12. Of Phlius (320–230 BCE): philosopher and author of satirical verses.
13. Cf. Ch. 6, p. 167.

As when Plato was in trouble and under suspicion with Dionysius: he asked for a meeting, and Dionysius granted the request, thinking that Plato was coming over because of some criticism he had to make of him. But Plato spoke to him as follows: "Dionysius, if you saw that someone [D] ill disposed to you had sailed into Sicily with the intention of doing you some harm, but did not find his opportunity, would you allow him to sail home again and see him go unpunished?" "Far from it, Plato!" said Dionysius. "It is not only what one's enemies do that should be hated and punished, but what they intend." "So," said Plato, "if someone comes here with good intentions and wants to bring about some good for you, but you don't give him the opportunity, is it appropriate to let him go unthanked and neglected?" Dionysius asked whom he meant. "Aeschines," he said: "he is a man as decent in character as any of Socrates' companions, and his conversation can improve anyone he spends time with. [E] He sailed a long way to get here so that he could do philosophy with you—and he is ignored." That moved Dionysius so much that he at once embraced Plato and kissed him, admiring his good will and magnanimity. And he treated Aeschines with noble generosity. (Plutarch, *On Telling Flatterers from Friends* 67C–E = Aeschines 11)

11.5 *Antisthenes* thinks **Plato** *conceited*

[Antisthenes] used to mock Plato for being conceited. So there was a procession, and seeing a spirited horse, he said to Plato: "I always thought you'd make a good horse—a show horse"; he said it also because Plato would keep on praising the horse. And once when he went to see him when he was ill, and saw the dish into which Plato had vomited, said, "I see the bile in there, but I don't see the conceit!" (Diogenes Laertius 6.7 = Antisthenes 27)

11.6 *Plato* thinks *Antisthenes* obtuse

Some of the ancients did away with qualities altogether, while agreeing that there were things possessing qualities: like Antisthenes, who when in dispute with Plato said, "Plato, I see a horse; I don't see horseness"—to which he replied, "That's because you have the eye that sees horses, but you haven't acquired the one that's needed to think about horseness." (Simplicius, *On Aristotle's Categories* 208.28–32 Kalbfleisch = Antisthenes 149)

11.7 Both **Xenophon** and **Plato** disliked **Aristippus** . . .

Xenophon was not well disposed to him [Aristippus]; that is why he presents his attack on pleasure as a dialogue in which Socrates attacks Aristippus.[14] Theodorus too, in his *Sects,* abuses him;[15] and so does Plato in his *On the Soul,* as I have noted elsewhere.[16] (Diogenes Laertius 2.65 = Aristippus 15)

11.8 . . . and **Aristippus** was critical of **Plato**

Or like Aristippus, who said when Plato was saying something a bit too dogmatically (as Aristippus thought): "But surely our friend never said anything like that"—meaning Socrates. (Aristotle, *Rhetoric* 2.23, 1398b29–31 = Aristippus 16)

11.9 How **Aristippus** saved his friendship with **Aeschines**

He [Aristippus] got angry with Aeschines, and after a bit said: "Shall we give it up and stop this nonsense? Or are you going to wait until someone else does it for us over the wine?" He replied, [83] "Gladly!" Aristippus said, "Well, then, remember that I came to you first, as the elder." And Aeschines said: "Right, by Hera! You're right. And you're much better than me. I caused the enmity, you the friendship." (Diogenes Laertius 2.82–83 = Aristippus 24)

11.10 **Aeschines** for his part criticized **Critobulus**

The majority of the philosophers have been ruder than the comic poets—even Aeschines the Socratic, who makes fun of Crito's son Critobulus in the *Telauges* for being unwashed and uneducated. (Athenaeus, *The Learned Banqueters* 5, 220A = Aeschines 61)

---

14. Cf. **7.14**.
15. We have no secure means of identifying this Theodorus.
16. See **11.1.**[36].

Bibliography

i. Primary Material

Cooper, J. M. (1997). *Plato: Complete Works* (Indianapolis: Hackett Publishing Co.).

Gagarin, M., and Woodruff, P. (1995). *Early Greek Political Thought from Homer to the Sophists* (Cambridge: Cambridge University Press). [Includes another translation of the *Ajax* and *Odysseus* of Antisthenes.]

Giannantoni, G. (1990) (ed.). *Socratis et Socraticorum Reliquiae*. 4 vols. (Naples: Bibliopolis). [*SSR*][1]

Malherbe, A. J. (1977). *The Cynic Epistles: A Study Edition*. Society of Biblical Literature Sources for Biblical Study 12. (Missoula, Mont.: Scholars Press). [Includes translations of letters ascribed to members of the Socratic circle. See Introduction p. ix with n.3.]

McKirahan, R. D. (2011). *Philosophy before Socrates: An Introduction with Texts and Commentary*. 2nd ed. (Indianapolis: Hackett Publishing Co.).

Rossetti, L. (1980). "Ricerche sui 'Dialoghi Socratici' di Fedone e di Euclide," *Hermes* 108: 182–200. [Covers evidence for Phaedo's *Zopyrus* not in *SSR*.]

Sanders, K. R. [forthcoming]. *Xenophon: Memorabilia, Apology, Symposium, Oeconomicus*. Translated, with introduction. (Indianapolis: Hackett Publishing Co.).

Seddon, K. (2005). *Epictetus' Handbook and the Tablet of Cebes: Guides to Stoic Living* (London / New York: Routledge).

Sprague, R. K. (ed.) (1972). *The Older Sophists:* A Complete Translation by Several Hands of the Fragments in *Die Fragmente der Vorsokratiker* edited by Diels-Kranz. With a new edition of Antiphon and of Euthydemus. (Columbia: University of South Carolina Press).

ii. References and Selected Further Reading

Beall, E. F. (2010). "Diogenes Laertius on Aeschines the Socratic's Works," *Hermes* 129: 142–44.

---

1. Not to be confused with his *Socraticorum Reliquiae*, 3 vols. (Naples: Bibliopolis, 1981), which it supersedes.

Boys-Stones, G. R. (2004). "Phaedo of Elis and Plato *On the Soul*," *Phronesis* 49: 1–23.

Brancacci, A. (2003). "Zwei verlorene Schriften des Antisthenes," *Rheinisches Museum* 146: 259–78.

Claus, D. B. (1981). *Toward the Soul: An Inquiry into the Meaning of Psyche before Plato*. Yale Classical Monographs 2. (New Haven: Yale University Press).

Danzig, G. (2010). *Apologizing for Socrates: How Plato and Xenophon Created Our Socrates* (Lanham, Md.: Lexington Books).

Decleva Caizzi, F. (2006). "Minor Socratics," in M. L. Gill and P. Pellegrin (eds.), *A Companion to Ancient Philosophy* (Malden, Mass./Oxford: Blackwell), 119–35.

Dorion, L.-A., and Menn, S. (2007). "Xenophon's Socrates," in S. Ahbel-Rappe and R. Kamtekar (eds.), *A Companion to Socrates* (Malden, Mass./Oxford: Blackwell), 93–109.

Ford, A. (2010). "Σωκρατικοὶ λόγοι in Aristotle and Fourth-Century Theories of Genre," *Classical Philology* 105: 221–35.

Gera, D. L. (2007). "Xenophon's Socrateses," in M. Trapp (ed.), *Socrates from Antiquity to the Enlightenment* (Aldershot, Eng.: Ashgate), 33–50.

Lampe, K. (2010). "'Socratic Therapy' from Aeschines of Sphettus to Lacan," *Classical Antiquity* 29: 181–221.

Lévystone, D. (2005). "La figure d'Ulysse chez les Socratiques: Socrate polutropos," *Phronesis* 50: 181–214.

McQueen, E. I., and Rowe, C. J. (1989). "Phaedo, Socrates, and the Chronology of the Spartan War with Elis," *Méthexis* 2: 1–18.

Morrison, D. R. (1987). "On Professor Vlastos' Xenophon," *Ancient Philosophy* 7: 9–22.

———. (1994). "Xenophon's Socrates as Teacher," in P. A. Vander Waerdt (ed.), *The Socratic Movement* (Ithaca: Cornell University Press), 181–208.

Nails, D. (2002). *The People of Plato: A Prosopography of Plato and Other Socratics* (Indianapolis: Hackett Publishing Co.).

Prince, S. (2005). "Socrates, Antisthenes, and the Cynics," in S. Ahbel-Rappe and R. Kamtekar (eds.), *A Companion to Socrates* (Malden, Mass./Oxford: Blackwell), 75–92.

Rossetti, L. (2003). "Le dialogue socratique in statu nascendi," *Philosophie Antique* 1: 11–35. Reprinted as Rossetti (2011): 23–51.

——— (2011). *Le dialogue socratique* (Paris: Belles Lettres). [A collection of previously published articles by Rossetti, in French translation.]

Wolfsdorf, D. (2008). "Hesiod, Prodicus, and the Socratics on Work and Pleasure," *Oxford Studies in Ancient Philosophy* 35: 1–18.

Worman, N. (2002). *The Cast of Character: Style in Greek Literature* (Austin: University of Texas Press).

Wörner, E. (1897–1902). "Palladion," in W. H. Röscher (ed.), *Ausführliches Lexikon der griechischen und römischen Mythologie* (Leipzig: Teubner), vol. 3.1: 1301–24.

iii. Web Resource

www.socratica.eu/socratica/ by Livio Rossetti and Alessandro Stavru, complementing a series of conferences and publications on the Socratics for which they have been responsible.

Index of Socratics

This index covers *SSR* passage numbers and other named references to members of the circle (as defined in the Introduction, at p. ix–xi). Since it also lists the works we are told they wrote (and indexes them to references and quotations in the volume),[1] a prefatory word about the *Sôkratikos logos* (Socratic discussion) is in order.

Aristotle attributes the invention of this distinctively Socratic form of writing to one Alexamenos of Teos (listed for this reason below), although the credit for it is also given to Simon of Athens (also listed below). The dialogues of Plato and Xenophon are presumably a reasonable guide to the general form—although, along with Aeschines, they were already considered in antiquity to be head and shoulders above the rest stylistically. But two things in particular should be borne in mind. First of all, most of these works were very much shorter than most surviving dialogues: this is obvious when twenty or thirty are said to have made up a single volume. Some of the pseudo-Platonic dialogues we have give a sense of this: the *Halcyon,* for example, is barely three pages long in Brad Inwood's translation in Cooper (1997); see also the *Ajax* and *Odysseus* of Antisthenes (Ch. 1, Appendix).

Secondly, although many of these Socratic writings were clearly "dialogues," it is equally clear that many (including, indeed, the *Ajax* and *Odysseus*) were not. There is some recognition of this in later catalogues, and "dialogues" and "writings" (*sungrammata*) are sometimes distinguished (Aristippus' works, for example, are collectively called "dialogues" in the version of the catalogue which excludes the *Diatribes,* but "writings" in the version that includes them). On the other hand, the tendency to think of the dialogue as the Socratic form par excellence leads to its being used as an umbrella term for all sorts of works—including, as will be seen, treatises and letters.

In general, it is well to remember that the lists of Socratic works that we have come to us courtesy of the work of later ancient scholars. We should be aware that they are responsible not only for the classification and arrangement of these works, but also, in some cases no doubt, for their titles, and in all cases for their attribution. There was a fair amount of disagreement over this last issue in the case of works ascribed to Plato

---

1. But for extracts from surviving works by Plato and Xenophon, see the Index of Sources.

already; but this is nothing compared to the arguments there seem to have been in the case of other Socratics. Two different, though overlapping, catalogues exist for Aristippus, for example, although some maintained he wrote nothing at all (Diogenes Laertius 2.84). Suspicions of false attribution and deliberate plagiarism are rife; and Aeschines was even accused of having bought the works he passed off as his own from Socrates' wife Xanthippe (**11.2**).

After each Socratic's name (and before the catalogue of their works, where relevant), we note the evidence used to justify their inclusion in this list, and any blood tie with another member of the circle. We have kept other comments to a bare minimum; fuller biographical information is readily available elsewhere, especially in the excellent Nails (2002). The following abbreviations are used: DL = Diogenes Laertius; *Ap.* = Plato, *Apology; Mem.* = Xenophon, *Memorabilia; Phd.* = Plato, *Phaedo.*

AESCHINES of Sphettos (Athens) (*Ap.* 33e, *Phd.* 59b; cf. DL 2.47). Son of Lysanias (see below). **Dialogues** (DL 2.61 [see **11.2**]): *Miltiades; Callias; Axiochus; Aspasia* [cf. **1.25**,[2] **8.1–9**]; *Alcibiades* [cf. **3.51, 6.19, 7.4**]; *Telauges* [cf. **11.10**]; *Rhino. "Akephalos"* **dialogues** (*Suda* αι.346):[3] *Phaedo; Polyaenus; Draco; Eryxias; On Virtue; Erasistrati; Scythians.* **Other works** (DL 2.62): law court speeches [cf. the *Defense of Phaeax* mentioned at **1.24**]; *Letter to Dionysius* [**7.41**]. **Contested** (DL 2.105):[4] *Nicias; Medius; Cobbler Discussions.*

SSR VI A
3: **11.1**
7: **1.26**
11: **11.4**
13: **1.24, 7.41, 11.2**
21: **11.3**
22: **11.2**
28: **11.2**
38: **6.27**
50: **3.51, 7.4**

---

2. The speech *On Thargelia* mentioned here was probably part of the *Aspasia*.
3. Cf. Diogenes Laertius 2.60. The meaning of the term *"akephalos"* (literally: "headless") is obscure. Plato uses it of a speech at *Phaedrus* 264c, and of a story at *Laws* VI, 752a; in these cases, it could mean "without a preface" or, more likely, "without a main point." We are not helped by the use of *Akephaloi* as the alternative title for a surviving work spuriously attributed to Plato (see below, under "Plato").
4. See below, under "Phaedo."

53: **6.19**
60: **8.2, 8.3**
61: **8.1, 11.10**
63: **8.4**
64: **8.5**
65: **1.25, 8.6**
66: **8.5, 8.7**
67: **8.8**
70: **8.9**
93: **1.28**
95: **2.21**
Also named in: **6.27, 7.41, 7.45, 9.3, 11.9.**

ALEXAMENOS of Teos. Writer of the first *Sôkratikoi logoi* according to Aristotle (fr. 72 Rose³ = Athenaeus, *The Learned Banqueters* 11, 505c) (but see under "Simon," below). Otherwise unknown.

ANTIPHON of Kephisia (Athens) (*Ap.* 33e). Father of Epigenes (see below). (Not to be confused with the sophist of the same name who appears in the works of Xenophon.)

ANTISTHENES of Athens (*Phd.* 59b; cf. DL 2.47). Progenitor of the Cynical movement by way of his student Diogenes of Sinope. **Writings** (according to the ten-volume arrangement in DL 6.15–18): **I.** *On Diction* or *On Figures of Speech*; *Ajax* or *Speech of Ajax* [see Ch. 1, Appendix]; *Odysseus* or *On Odysseus* [see Ch. 1, Appendix]; *Defense of Orestes* or *On Forensic Speechwriters*; *Carbon Copy*⁵ or *Lysias and Isocrates*; *To Isocrates: The Absence of Witnesses*; **II.** *On the Nature of Animals*; *On Making Children* or *On Marriage* (erotic); *On the Sophists* (physiognomical); *On Justice and Courage* (protreptic) in three books [cf. **1.23**]; *On Theognis* in five books; **III.** *On the Good*; *On Courage*; *On Law* or *On the Republic*; *On Law* or *On the Honorable and Just*; *On Freedom and Slavery*; *On Belief*; *On a Guardian* or *On Persuading*; *On Victory* (to do with household management); **IV.** *Cyrus*;† *Heracles Major* or *On Strength*;* **V.** *Cyrus* or *On Kingship*;† *Aspasia* [cf. **7.10, 8.13–14**]; **VI.** *Truth* [cf. **1.23**]; *On Arguing* (contradictory); *Satho* or *On Contradiction* in three books [cf. **7.10, 11.1**]; *On Language*; **VII.** *On Education* or *Names* in five books; *On the Use of Names* (eristic); *On Question and Answer*; *On Opinion and Knowledge* in four books; *On Dying*; *On Life and Death*; *On Those in Hades*; *On Nature* in two books [cf. **9.11**]; *Questions on Nature* in two books; *Opinions* or *Eristic*; *Problems*

---

5. This is a rather speculative translation of *Isographê*—literally "equal writing"; but a word *isographon* is attested meaning "copy."

Concerning Learning; **VIII.** *On Music*; *On Interpreters*; *On Homer*; *On Injustice and Impiety*; *On Calchas*; *On a Spy*; *On Pleasure*; *On the Odyssey*; **IX.** *On the Staff*; *Athena* or *On Telemachus*; *On Helen and Penelope*; *On Proteus*; *Cyclops* or *On Odysseus*; *On the Use of Wine* or *On Drunkenness* or *On the Cyclops*; *On Circe*; *On Amphiaraus*; *On Odysseus and Penelope and On the Dog*;[6] **X.** *Heracles* or *Midas*;* *Heracles* or *On Prudence or Strength*;* *Cyrus* or *The Beloved*;† *Cyrus* or *The Spies*;† *Menexenus* or *On Ruling*; *Alcibiades* [**11.2**]; *Archelaus* or *On Kingship* [cf. **7.10**; **11.2**]. **Other titles attested:** *Statesman* [cf. **7.10**]; *Cyrsas* (Cicero, *Letters to Atticus* 12.38.5).[7]

  * candidates for the *Heracles* mentioned in **2.23**, **3.4**, and **11.2**.
  † candidates for "the second [of his books on?] *Cyrus*" mentioned in **7.10**, and the *Cyrus Minor* of **11.2**.

SSR V A
7: **7.26**
8: **7.29**
9: **7.30**
10: **7.27**
11: **1.23**
14: **6.7**
27: **11.5**
32: **4.18**
37: **4.19**
43: **11.2**
53: Ch. 1, Appendix
54: Ch. 1, Appendix
56: **6.23**
57: **6.21**
58: **6.20**
60: **6.22**
68: **7.33**
70: **7.15**
71: **7.12**
72: **7.25**
73: **7.13**
75: **7.34**
78: **3.33**
82: **3.2**

---

6. Or possibly two titles: *On Odysseus and Penelope* and *On the Dog*.
7. This title is usually "corrected" in editions of Cicero to *Cyrus*, but Brancacci (2003) connects it with **4.17** and argues that it was part of one of Antisthenes' works on death.

83: **3.34**
98: **2.23**
99: **3.4, 3.62**
100: **1.2**
103: **3.6**
104: **3.20**
105: **3.21**
106: **3.19**
114: **2.11**
118: Ch. 2 n. 4
122: **2.12**
123: **3.45**
127: **2.13**
134: **2.4, 3.3**
141: **7.10, 11.2**
142: **7.10**
143: **8.13, 8.14**
145: **1.23**
147: **7.10**
148: **11.1**
149: **11.6**
151: **1.4**
152: **1.9**
159: **1.13**
160: **1.5**
161: **5.19**
163: **5.14**
173: **1.27**
176: **4.20**
177: **4.21**
178: **4.22**
179: **9.11**
181: **9.12**
185: **5.22**
186: **5.25**
187: **1.21**
188: **5.29**
189: **5.30**
190: **5.31**
191: **5.28**
192: **3.15**
193: **4.9**
194: **5.23**

195: **5.24**
198: Ch. 6, n. 1.
199: Ch. 6, n. 1.
203: **7.10**
204: **7.10**
Not in *SSR*: **4.17**. Appears in Xenophon's *Symposium* and *Memorabilia* (cf. **6.3**.[17]).

APOLLODORUS of Phaleron (*Ap.* 33e, *Phd.* 59b). Relays the account of the party in Plato's *Symposium* told to him by Aristodemus (below). Also appears in Xenophon's *Apology* and *Memorabilia*. Named in **6.3**.[17], **6.8**.

ARISTIPPUS of Cyrene (*Phd.* 59b; cf. DL 2.47). Founded a school at Cyrene whose later members were known as "Cyrenaics." **Dialogues** (DL 2.84): twenty-five in one volume, including: *Artabazus*; *To the Shipwrecked*; *To Exiles*; *To a Beggar*; *To Lais*; *To Porus*; *To Lais, on the Mirror*; *Hermeias*; *A Dream*; *To Someone Over a Drink*; *Philomelus*; *To His Household*; *To Those Reproaching Him for Keeping Old Wine and Concubines*; *To Those Reproaching Him for Dining Expensively*; *Letter to His Daughter Arete*; *To Someone Training for the Olympics*; *Interrogation*; *Interrogation II*; *An Anecdote for Dionysius*; *Another Anecdote, about the Image*; *Another Anecdote, about the Daughter of Dionysius*; *To One Who Thought Himself Slighted*; *To One Attempting to Advise*. **Other titles attested:** *History of Libya* in three books (DL 2.83); *Six Diatribes* (DL 2.84). **Alternative list of "writings"** (DL 2.85): *On Education*; *On Virtue*;[8] *Protreptic*; *Artabazus*; *The Shipwrecked*; *The Exiles*; *Six Diatribes*; *Three Anecdotes*; *To Lais*; *To Porus*; *To Socrates*; *On Luck*. **Doubtful attestations** (Ibn al-Qifti, *History of Learned Men* 70.15 Lippert): *On the Operation of Algebra*; *On the Division of Numbers*.[9]

SSR IV A
1: **5.7**
15: **11.1, 11.2, 11.7**
16: **11.8**
22: **7.40, 11.2**
23: **11.2**
24: **11.9**
25: **7.45**
27: **7.42**
28: **7.43**
30: **7.37**

---

8. Or perhaps: *On Arete* (his daughter)? (Cf. the *Letter to His Daughter Arete* above.)
9. This is doubtful not least because Aristippus apparently disdained mathematics: see **9.4**.

31: **3.5**
36: **7.38**
37: **7.39**
40: **7.37**
41: **7.35, 7.36**
49: **4.12**
51: **2.7**
87: **3.44**
88: **8.15**
90: **8.16**
93: **6.24**
95: **6.13**
96: **3.43**
104: **1.1**
105: **7.32**
106: **3.23, 3.24**
116: **1.12**
120: **3.25**
121: **5.17**
122: **5.18**
124: **3.10, 5.13**
125: **5.9**
126: **5.11**
127: **5.12**
128: **5.10**
129: **5.8**
132: **9.22**
139: **4.10**
163: **7.14**
166: **9.3**
167: **9.5**
169: **9.6**
170: **9.4**
173: **2.6**
174: **2.8, 2.9**

Appears in Xenophon's *Memorabilia*. Also named in **2.10, 2.22**. (And is perhaps in Antisthenes' mind in **2.11**?)

ARISTODEMUS of Kydathenaion (Athens) (*Symp.* 173ab). Source for the narrative of Apollodorus (above), which constitutes the bulk of Plato's *Symposium*. Interlocutor in Xenophon, *Memorabilia* 1.4: cf, **9.16, 10.7**. Also named in **6.11**.[218b].

CEBES of Thebes (*Phd.* 59c, *Mem.* 1.2.48). **Dialogues** (DL 2.125): *Tablet*;[10] *Seventh Day*; *Phrynicus*. Mentioned at Plato, *Crito* 45b. Interlocutor in Plato's *Phaedo*; also named in **6.3**.[17], **6.27**, **9.3**.

CHAERECRATES of Sphettos (Athens) (*Mem.* 1.2.48). Brother of Chaerephon (see below). Addressee of **9.26**.

CHAEREPHON of Sphettos (Athens) (*Ap.* 21a; *Mem.* 1.2.48). Brother of Chaerecrates (see above). Appears in Plato's *Gorgias* and *Charmides*, mentioned at Xenophon, *Apology* 14.

CLEOMBROTUS of Ambrakeia (*Phd.* 59c).

CRITO of Alopeke (Athens) (*Ap.* 33d, *Mem.* 1.2.48; cf. *Phd.* 59b). Father of Critobulus (see below). **Dialogues** (DL 2.121): seventeen in one volume: *That Learning Does Not Make Men Good*; *On Having Too Much*; *What Is Suitable* or *The Statesman*; *On the Beautiful*; *On Wrongdoing*; *On Tidiness*; *On Law*; *On the Divine*; *On Expertises*; *On Intercourse*; *On Wisdom*; *Protagoras* or *The Statesman*; *On Written Characters*; *On the Expertise of Poetry*; *On Learning*; *On Cognizing* or *On Knowledge*; *What Knowledge Is*. **Other titles attested** (Suda κ. 2451): *Socrates' Apology*. Interlocutor in Xenophon, *Memorabilia* 2.9. Appears in Plato's *Crito* (named for him), *Euthydemus*, and *Phaedo*. Also named in **6.16, 11.1, 11.2, 11.10**.

CRITOBULUS of Alopeke (Athens) (*Ap.* 33e, *Phd.* 59b). Son of Crito (see above). Appears in Plato's *Euthydemus*, and in Xenophon's *Memorabilia*, *Household Management* and *Symposium*. Named in **2.18, 6.16, 8.11, 8.12, 11.10**.

CTESIPPUS of Paeania (Athens) (*Phd.* 59b). Cousin of Menexenus (see below). Appears in Plato's *Lysis* and *Euthydemus* (cf. **1.10**).

EPIGENES of Kephisia (Athens) (*Ap.* 33e, *Phd.* 59b). Son of Antiphon (see above). An interlocutor in Xenophon, *Memorabilia* 3.12.

EUCLIDES of Megara (*Phd.* 59c; DL 2.47). Founded a school at Megara (known variously as the Megarian, Eristic, or Dialectic school), whose

---

10. A work called *Tablet*, attributed to Cebes, survives (see, e.g., Seddon 2005), but is generally held to be a much later work.

subsequent members did important work in logic. **Dialogues** (DL 2.108): *Lamprias*; *Aeschines*; *Phoenix*;[11] *Crito*; *Alcibiades*; *Erotics*.
SSR II A
3: **1.11**
11: **10.1, 10.2**
17: **9.8**
18: **5.5**
30: **2.33**
31: **2.31, 2.32**
32: **3.17**
34: **1.14**
Narrator of Plato's *Theaetetus*.

GLAUCON of Kollytos (Athens). Brother of Plato (see below). **Dialogues** (nine in one volume) (DL 2.124): *Phidylus*; *Euripides*; *Amytichus*; *Euthias*; *Lysithides*; *Aristophanes*; *Cephalus*; *Anaxiphemus*; *Menexenus*. (DL also knows of, but does not list, thirty-two further dialogues of doubtful authenticity.) Interlocutor in Plato's *Republic* and, with Apollodorus (above), in the frame of the *Symposium*. Mentioned at Plato, *Parmenides* 126a. Appears in Xenophon's *Memorabilia*: see **7.5**; also named in **7.6**.

HERMOGENES of Alopeke (Athens) (*Phd.* 59b, *Mem.* 1.2.48). Appears in Plato's *Cratylus* and in Xenophon's *Memorabilia, Symposium, Apology*, and *Hellenica*. Speaker in **3.59**; addressee in **4.5**.

LYSANIAS of Sphettos (Athens) (*Ap.* 33e). Father of Aeschines (see above). (But cf. **11.2**.) Also named in **7.45**.

MENEXENUS of Athens (*Phd.* 59b). Cousin of Ctesippus (see above). Interlocutor in Plato's *Menexenus* and *Lysis*.

PHAEDO of Elis (*Phd.* 57a; DL 2.47). Founded a school at Elis originally known as the Elian school. (It became known as the Eretrian school from the time of Menedemus, around the turn of the third century BCE.) **Genuine Dialogues** (DL 2.105): *Zopyrus* [cf. **4.11**]; *Simon*.[12] **Doubtful dialogues** (DL 2.105): *Nicias*; *Medius*, also ascribed to Aeschines or

---

11. Since most of the other titles in this list give the names of people (and "Erotics" simply describes the subject matter of the work), it seems most probable that "Phoenix" is also the name of a man (perhaps the very man mentioned in **6.8**). But it might, among other things, refer to a Phoenician—or to the mythical bird.

12. Phaedo's Simon was apparently a cobbler (Phaedo 16–18 *SSR*), and may be connected with the *Cobbler Discussions*. Cf. also Simon, below.

Polyaenus; *Antimachus* or *The Ambassadors*; *Cobbler Discussions*, also ascribed to Aeschines. **Alternative list** (Suda φ.154): *Zopyrus*; *Medius*; *Simon*; *Antimachus* or *The Ambassador*; *Nicias*; *Simmias*; *Alcibiades*; *Critolaus*.
SSR III A
1: p. 167
12: **5.6**
Not in SSR: **4.11**.
Narrator of Plato's *Phaedo*. Also named in: **1.14, 9.3, 11.3**.

PHAEDONDAS (or PHAEDONDES) of Thebes (*Phd.* 59c, *Mem.* 1.2.48).

PLATO of Kollytos (Athens) (*Ap.* 34a, *Phd.* 59b). Brother of Glaucon (see above). Founded a school in Athens known as "the Academy" (cf. Introduction, p. viii). **Dialogues (extant)** (as listed at DL 3.57–61 in the arrangement of their first-century BCE editor, Thrasyllus):[13] **I.** *Euthyphro* or *On the Holy* (peirastic); *Socrates' Apology* (ethical) [cf. **11.1**]; *Crito* or *What Is to Be Done* (ethical); *Phaedo* or *On the Soul* (ethical) [cf. **11.1, 11.7**]; **II.** *Cratylus* or *On the Correctness of Names* (logical); *Theaetetus* or *On Knowledge* (peirastic); *Sophist* or *On Being* (logical); *Statesman* or *On Kingship* (logical); **III.** *Parmenides* or *On Ideas* (logical); *Philebus* or *On Pleasure* (ethical); *Symposium* or *On the Good* (ethical) [cf. **11.1**]; *Phaedrus* or *On Love* (ethical); **IV.** *Alcibiades* or *On the Nature of Man* (maieutic); *Alcibiades II* or *On Prayer* (maieutic); *Hipparchus* or *The Love of Profit* (ethical); *Rival Lovers* or *On Philosophy* (maieutic); **V.** *Theages* or *On Philosophy*; *Charmides* or *On Temperance* (peirastic); *Laches* or *On Courage* (maieutic); *Lysis* or *On Friendship* (maieutic) [cf. **11.1**]; **VI.** *Euthydemus* or *Eristic* (anatreptic); *Protagoras* or *Sophists* (endeictic); *Gorgias* or *On Rhetoric* (anatreptic); *Meno* or *On Excellence* (peirastic); **VII.** *Hippias I* or *On the Beautiful* (anatreptic); *Hippias II* or *On Falsehood* (anatreptic); *Ion* or *On the Iliad* (peirastic); *Menexenus* or *Funeral Oration* (ethical); **VIII.** *Clitophon* or *Protreptic* (ethical); *Republic* or *On the Just* (political) [cf. **11.1**]; *Timaeus* or *On Nature* (physical); *Critias* or *Atlanticus* (ethical); **IX.** *Minos* or *On Law* (political); *Laws* or *On Law Giving* (political) [cf. **11.1**]; *Epinomis* or *Nocturnal Conversation* or *Philosopher* (political); thirteen *Letters* (ethical). **Spurious works (extant)** (DL 3.62): *Midon* or *Horse Breeder*; *Eryxias* or *Erasistratus*;

---

13. Thrasyllus classes some dialogues as "gymnastic" ("for training purposes"): these include peirastic dialogues, which are supposed to test a reader's preconceived ideas, and maieutic dialogues (alluding to Plato's characterization of Socrates as a "midwife": see **6.5**), which help readers develop their own new and better thoughts. Others are agonistic (argumentative): these include anatreptic dialogues, which overthrow beliefs; and endeictic dialogues, which set out to prove something.

Halcyon; *Akephaloi* or *Sisyphus*;[14] *Axiochus*; *Phaeacians*; *Demodocus*; *Swallow*; *Seventh Day*; *Epimenides*. **Also extant under Plato's name:** *On Justice*; *On Excellence*; *Definitions*. Named in **2.31, 2.34, 2.35, 2.36, 2.37, 2.38, 3.5, 6.27, 7.5** [Xenophon], **7.10, 7.40, 7.42, 7.43, 7.45, 8.7, 9.6, 11.1, 11.2, 11.3, 11.4, 11.5, 11.6, 11.7, 11.8.**

SIMMIAS of Thebes (*Phd.* 59c, *Mem.* 1.2.48). **Dialogues** (DL 2.124): twenty-three in one volume: *On Wisdom; On Reasoning; On Music; On Words*;[15] *On Courage; On Philosophy; On Truth; On Written Characters; On Teaching; On Expertise; On Presiding; On the Decent; On What Is to Be Chosen and Avoided; On a Friend; On Knowing; On the Soul; On Living Well; On the Possible; On Money; On Life; What Is Beautiful; On Taking Care; On Love*. Interlocutor in Plato's *Phaedo*; also mentioned at *Crito* 45b and *Phaedrus* 242b. Named in **6.3.**[17], **10.13(b)**.

SIMON of Athens. His historicity has been doubted; it is possible that his name was derived from Phaedo's *Simon* (see above) and attached to the following works. According to DL 2.123, he invented the *Sôkratikos logos* (but see Alexamenos, above). **Dialogues** (DL 2.122–23): thirty-three in one volume, known as the **Cobbler Dialogues**: *On the Gods; On the Good; On the Beautiful; What Is the Beautiful; On the Just* in two books; *On Virtue, That It Is Not Teachable; On Courage* in three books; *On Law; On Popular Leadership; On Honor; On Composition; On Enjoyment; On Love; On Philosophy; On Knowledge; On Music; What Is the Beautiful?; On Teaching; On Dialogue; On Judgment; On Being; On Number; On Taking Care; On Working; On the Love of Profit; On False Pretension; On the Beautiful*. **Other works** (DL 2.123): *On Deliberating; On Reason* or *On Suitability; On Wrongdoing*.

TERPSION of Megara (*Phd.* 59c). Appears in Plato's *Theaetetus*. Named in **10.13(a)**.

THEAGES of Anagyrous (Athens) (*Ap.* 33e). Interlocutor in the pseudo-Platonic *Theages*. Named in Plato's *Republic*: see **10.9**.

THEODOTUS of Athmonon (Athens) (*Ap.* 33e).

---

14. *Akephaloi* literally means "the headless." In the plural like this and otherwise unqualified, it could make one think of the "headless" creatures of Herodotus, *Histories* 4.191.15–16; but that has no obvious relevance to the surviving *Sisyphus* (a short dialogue about deliberation). Cf. also n. 3 above.

15. *Epê*: perhaps "epics"; or again "sayings."

XENOPHON of Erchia (Athens). Usually (under) described as a "historian," he was also a soldier and a philosopher. (It was an encounter with his *Memorabilia* that is supposed to have interested Zeno of Citium, founder of Stoicism, in Socrates: DL 7.2.) **Works (extant)** (as listed at DL 2.47): *Anabasis*; *Cyropaedia* [cf. **11.1**]; *Hellenica*; *Memorabilia* [cf. **7.10**]; *Symposium* [cf. **11.1**]; *Oeconomicus*; *On Horsemanship*; *Hunting*; *Cavalry Commander*; *Apology of Socrates* [cf. **11.1**]; *On Revenues*; *Hiero* or *The Tyrannical Man*; *Agesilaus*; *Constitution of the Athenians and Spartans*. Also named in **1.5**, **1.26**, **6.27**, **9.6**, **11.1**, **11.7**.

Index of Sources

Acron, pseudo-. Anonymous scholia falsely attributed to the 3rd-century CE Roman grammarian
   Scholia on Horace (ed. O. Keller, in *Pseudacronis scholia in Horatium vetustiora*, 2 vols., Leipzig: Teubner, 1902–1904): ii. 264.14–22: **6.13**

Aelian, Claudius. 2nd-/3rd-century CE Roman teacher of rhetoric
   Historical Miscellany: 14.6: **2.8**

Aelius Aristides, *see* Aristides, Aelius

Aelius Theon, *see* Theon, Aelius.

Alexander of Aphrodisias. 2nd-century CE follower of Aristotle
   On Aristotle's Metaphysics (ed. Hayduck, in *CAG*, vol. 1): 434.25–435.20: **1.9**

Alexis. 4th-century BCE Greek comic poet
   fragments (PCG): 98: **2.36**

Amphis. 4th-century BCE Greek comic poet
   fragments (PCG): 6: **2.37**

anonymous
   Treatise on Women (ed. and tr. D. Gera, in *Warrior Women*, Leiden: Brill, 1996). A brief collection of anecdotes, mainly drawn from 5th- and 4th-century BCE writers: 8 [p. 8]: **8.4**

Antonius Melissa. Probably an 11th-century CE monk (*SSR* refers to him as "Antonius Monachus"); his work is a compilation of anecdotes drawing on earlier compilations.
   Commonplaces (ed. J.-P. Migne, in *Patrologia Graeca*, vol. 136, Paris: Garnier Frères, 1863): II, 34.43 [col. 1092]: **4.10;** II, 34.42 [col. 1092]: Ch. 6 n.7

Aristides, Aelius. 2nd-century CE Greek orator
   In Defense of Oratory, Against Plato: 61: **6.19(a)**; 62: **6.19(b)**; 74: **6.19(c)**; 217–18: **1.28**

   In Defense of the Four, Against Plato: 348: **3.51, 7.4**

Index of Sources 315

Aristotle. 4th-century BCE philosopher and pupil of Plato
Metaphysics: B, 996a29–b1: **9.4**
Nicomachean Ethics: VII.13, 1153b19–20: Ch. 2, n. 4
On the Parts of Animals: 1.1, 642a29–31: **9.7**
Politics: 3.13, 1284a11–17: **7.33**
Rhetoric: 2.23, 1398b29–31: **11.8**

Aristoxenus of Tarentum. 4th-century BCE pupil of Aristotle
Harmonics (ed. R. da Rios, in *Aristoxenus: Elementa Harmonica*, Rome: Accademia dei Lincei, 1954): 39.4–40.4: **2.34**

Athenaeus. 2nd-/3rd-century CE rhetorician and grammarian
The Learned Banqueters (a.k.a., *Deipnosophistae*): 5, 220A–B: **8.1**; 5, 220A: **11.10**; 5, 220C–E: **7.10**; 11, 507C: **11.3**; 12, 513A: **2.13**; 12, 534C: Ch. 6 n.1; 12, 544A–B: **2.9**; 13, 589E: **8.13**

Censorinus. 3rd-century CE Roman grammarian
Birthday Book: 3.3: **10.1**

Cicero. 1st-century BCE Roman statesman and Academic philosopher
On Academic Scepticism (a.k.a., *Academica*): 2.129: **2.31**
On Rhetorical Invention: 1.51–52: **8.9**
Tusculan Disputations: 4.80: **4.11**

Clement of Alexandria. 2nd-century CE Christian thinker
Exhortation: 6.71.2: **9.12**

Dio of Prusa ("Chrysostom"). 1st-/2nd-century CE member of the "second sophistic" (a movement combining interests in literature, rhetoric, and philosophy)
Orations: 53 (36).4–5: **5.23**

Diogenes Laertius. 3rd-century CE historian of philosophy
Lives and Views of Famous Philosophers: 2.20: **1.26**; 2.30: **1.11**; 2.60–62: **11.2**; 2.61: **7.40**; 2.63: **1.24, 7.41**; 2.65: **5.7, 11.7**; 2.66: **2.7**; 2.68: **1.1, 7.32**; 2.69: **3.23, 3.44, 5.8**; 2.70: **1.12, 3.24, 5.9**; 2.71: **4.12, 5.18**; 2.72: **5.10**; 2.73: **3.25, 7.38**; 2.74–75: **3.43**; 2.74: **8.16**; 2.78: **3.5**; 2.79: **7.39**; 2.80: **5.17**; 2.81: **8.15**; 2.82–83: **11.9**; 2.82: **7.37**; 2.106: **2.33**; 2.107: **1.14**; 3.34–36: **11.1**; 6.1: **1.23, 7.29**; 6.2: **7.30**; 6.3: **1.4, 6.21**,

6.23; 6.4: **4.22, 6.22**; 6.5: **4.20, 4.21, 7.12**; 6.6: **1.2, 7.13**; 6.7: **11.5**; 6.8: **2.11, 7.25**; 6.10–13: **3.3**; 6.11: **2.4, 6.20**; 6.18: **4.19**; 6.103: **5.19**; 6.104: **2.23**; 6.105: **3.4, 3.62**; 7.161: **3.17**

Diogenes of Oenoanda. 2nd-century CE Epicurean
fragments (ed. and tr. M. F. Smith, in *Diogenes of Oenoanda: The Epicurean Inscription*, Naples: Bibliopolis, 1993): fr. 4, col. ii: **9.5**

Elias. 6th-century CE Platonist philosopher
On Aristotle's Categories (ed. Busse, in *CAG*, vol. 18.1): 109.18–22: **1.13**

Epictetus. 1st-/2nd-century CE Stoic philosopher
Discourses: 1.17.10–12: **1.5**

Eusebius. 3rd-/4th-century CE Christian thinker
Preparation for the Gospel: 14.18.31: **2.6**

Galen. 2nd-century CE physician and philosopher
On the Doctrines of Hippocrates and Plato: 9.7.13–15: **9.6**

Lactantius. 3rd-/4th-century CE Christian thinker
Divine Institutes: 3.12.9: **2.32**

Lucian. 2nd-century CE Roman satirical writer
Images: 17: **8.2**

Maximus of Tyre. 2nd-century CE Platonist member of the "second sophistic" (cf. Dio of Prusa, above)
Philosophical Orations: 38, 4b–d: **8.3**

Olympiodorus. 6th-century CE Platonist philosopher
On Plato's Alcibiades (ed. L. G. Westerink, in *Olympiodorus: Commentary on the First Alcibiades of Plato*, 2nd ed., Amsterdam: Hakkert, 1982): 28.21–22: Ch. 6, n. 1

Philippides. 4th-century BCE Greek comic poet
fragments (PCG): 6: **2.38**

Philo of Alexandria. 1st-centuries BCE/CE Jewish philosopher
How Every Good Man Is Free: 28: **3.19**

Index of Sources 317

Philodemus. 1st-century BCE Epicurean philosopher and poet
 On Piety (ed. T. Gomperz, in *Philodem Über Frömmigkeit*, Leipzig: Teubner, 1866): *PHerc* 1428 fr. 21 [7ª, p. 72]: **9.11**

Philostratus. 2nd-/3rd-century member of the "second sophistic" (cf. Dio of Prusa, above)
 Letters: 73.28–34: **1.25**; 73.28: **8.6**
 Life of Apollonius of Tyana: 1.35.1: **7.45**

Plato
 Alcibiades (authenticity debated): 103a–b: **10.10**; 106c–107a: **7.1(a)**; 117e–118e: **7.1(b)**; 119a–c: **7.1(c)**; 129c–130c: **4.3**

 Apology: 17a–c: **1.31**; 19a–d: **9.2(a)**; 19d–20c: **5.3**; 20d + 21a-c + 22e–23b: **3.54(a)**; 21b–d: **7.7**; 26d–e: **9.2(b)**; 28d–30b: **3.54(b)**; 30a–b: **2.17**; 33c: **10.19**; 40a–c + 41d: **10.8**; 40c–41c: **4.16**; 41c–d: **9.24**

 Charmides: 154b–d: **6.6(a)**; 155b–d: **6.6(b)**; 156b–157c: **4.14**; 164a–165c: **1.8**; 173d–174d: **2.5**; 174b–175a: **3.47**

 Cratylus: 397e–398c: **10.6**; 399d–400b: **4.1**; 412c–413d: **9.15**; 418b: **8.26**

 Crito: 43c–44b: **10.17**; 49a–d: **2.27**; 51c–52a: **5.4**

 Euthydemus: 272d–273a: **10.11**; 278e–279c: **2.19(a)**; 279c–280b: **3.61**; 280b–282a: **2.19(b)**; 283e–284c: **1.10(a)**; 285d–286b: **1.10(b)**

 Euthyphro: 3a–b: **10.15**; 5e–6c: **9.10**; 11b–d: **1.19**; 12c–d: **3.52**; 13d–15c: **3.53**

 Gorgias: 462b–466a: **1.30**; 470d–471a: **2.3**; 473e: **1.17**; 473e–474a: **7.17**; 474b: **2.28**; 481c–d: **6.10**; 482a–b: **1.18**; 491c–e: **3.41**; 492e–494e: **4.8**; 505a–c: **3.46**; 521b–522c: **7.18**

 Laches: 198a–199e: **3.50**

 Laws: III, 699b–c: **7.28**; IV, 709e–710a: **3.11**; IV, 713c–714a: **7.21**; V, 739a–e: **7.22**; VI, 783c–784c: **6.26**; VII, 802d–e: **8.21**; VII, 804d–806c: **8.28(a)**; VII, 810e–812a: **5.21**; VII, 813d–814c: **8.28(b)**; X, 902e–904c: **9.19**; X, 909d–910a: **8.22**; XI, 916e–917a: **8.23**; XI, 929e–930a: **8.25**; XI, 934e–935a: **8.24**; XII, 967d–968a: **3.29**

 Lesser Hippias: 375d–376c: **3.38**

 Letter VII (authenticity debated): 326a–d: **7.44(a)**; 340b–341c: **7.44(b)**

Lysis: 204a–c: **6.2(a)**; 206c: **6.2(b)**; 216b–218c: **2.25(a)**; 220c–221e: **2.25(b)**

Menexenus: 235b–236c: **8.10**

Meno: 71d–73c: **8.17**; 77b–78b: **2.2**; 87–89e: **3.13**

Phaedo: 60c–61b: **10.18**; 64c–66a: **4.15**; 68a–69b: **3.27**; 82a–c: **3.28**; 84e–85b: **3.55**; 92d: **1.15**; 98d–99c: **2.30**; 107d–108c: **10.4**

Phaedrus: 237b–c: **1.6**; 237c–238c: **6.14**; 242b–d: **10.12**; 244a–245c: **6.18**; 246b–d: **9.14**; 247b–c: **5.20**; 270c–272c: **1.22**

Philebus: 11a–c: **2.20(a)**; 29d–31a: **4.2**; 33c–35d: **4.7**; 63d–65b: **2.20(b)**

Protagoras: 309a–b: **6.9**; 319a–320b: **7.11**; 329b–330b: **3.18(a)**; 342a–347b: **5.26**; 349a–351a: **3.18(b)**; 351c–e: **2.14**; 358a–c: **3.48**; 361a–c: **3.18(c)**

Republic: I, 329b–d: **6.12**; I, 349a–350c: **3.39**; I, 352d–353e: **3.7**; II, 357b–358a: **2.26**; II, 372a–373c: **7.20**; II, 379b–c: **9.25**; II, 382e–383c: **9.13**; III, 387e–388a: **8.19(a)**; III, 403a–c: **6.17**; IV, 430e–431b: **3.42**; IV, 431b–c: **8.19(b)**; IV, 433b–d: **3.12**; IV, 442a–d: **3.30**; IV, 443b–444a: **3.36**; V, 454d–455d: **8.27**; V, 458c–e: **6.25(a)**; V, 460a–b: **6.25(b)**; V, 473c–e: **7.19(a)**; VI, 485a–486b: **3.16**; VI, 488a–e: **7.19(b)**; VI, 496a–c: **10.9**; VI, 499c–d: **7.19(c)**; VI, 500c–d: **3.31**; VI, 504d–506e: **2.29(a)**; VI, 507b–509c: **2.29(b)**; VII, 518e–519b: **3.26**; VII, 527c–530c: **9.9**; VIII, 544a–d: **7.23**; IX, 573a–c + 573d–574a: **6.15**; IX, 588b–589b: **3.37**; X, 597d: **9.17**; X, 617d–e: **10.3**

Sophist: 223a–b: **5.2**; 263e: **1.3**; 265a–e: **9.18**

Statesman: 266d: **1.16**; 293e–295a: **7.31**; 301e–302b + 303c: **7.8**; 304c–d: **1.29**

Symposium: 173a–b: **6.8**; 177e: **6.1(a)**; 201d: **6.1(b)**; 202b–203a: **10.5**; 204e–205a: **2.1**; 210a–e: **4.6**; 216b–c: **7.2**; 216d–219e: **6.11**

Theaetetus: 150a–151b: **6.5**; 153b–c: **5.15**; 173c–175b: **7.16**

Timaeus: 29d–30c: **9.20**; 40b–41d: **9.21**; 90e–91d: **8.20**

Plutarch. 1st-/2nd-century CE Platonist philosopher
    Life of Dion: 19.3: **7.42**; 19.7: **7.43**

    Life of Lycurgus: 30.6: **7.27**

    Life of Pericles: 24.3–6: **8.5**; 24.7–8: **8.14**; 32.1 + 3: **8.8**

On the Education of Children: 11D–F: **6.27**

How the Young Should Listen to Poetry: 33C: **5.24**

On Telling Flatterers from Friends: 67C–E: **11.4**

On Socrates' Daimonion: 580F–581B: **10.13(a)**; 588B–589F: **10.13(b)**

Dialogue on Love: 750D–E: **6.24**

On Stoic Self-contradictions: 1039E–1040A: **3.21**

fragments (ed. and tr. F. H. Sandbach, in *Plutarch's Moralia*, vol. 15, Cambridge, Mass./London: Harvard University Press, 1987): 42: **5.11**

Porphyry. 3rd-century CE Platonist philosopher
Questions on Homer's Iliad (ed. H. Schrader, in *Porphyrii Quaestionum homericarum ad Iliadem pertinentium reliquias*, Leipzig: Teubner, 1880–1882): on 11.636 [p. 168.15–16]: **5.28**

Questions on Homer's Odyssey (ed. H. Schrader, in *Porphyrii Quaestionum homericarum ad Odysseam pertinentium reliquias*, Leipzig: Teubner, 1890): on 1.1 [p. 1.1–3.2]: **1.21**; on 7.257 [p. 69, n. 2]: **5.29**; on 9.106 [p. 86.14–87.6]: **5.30**; on 9.525 [pp. 94.26–95.3]: **5.31**

pseudo-Acron: *see* Acron, pseudo-

scholia on the *Iliad*
(ed. H. Erbse, in *Scholia Graeca in Homeri Iliadem (scholia vetera)*, 5 vols., Berlin: de Gruyter, 1969–1988): on 15.123 [iv. 35.24–26 (test.)]: **3.15**; on 23.66 [v. 377.40–42]: **4.9**

scholia on Plato
(ed. W. C. Greene, in *Scholia Platonica*, Haverford, Penn.: Haverford College, 1938): on *Menexenus* 235e [pp. 182–83]: **8.7**

Seneca. 1st-century CE Stoic philosopher
Letters: 94.41: **5.6**

Sextus Empiricus. 2nd-century CE Pyrrhonist philosopher
Outlines of Pyrrhonism: 3.181: **2.12**

Simplicius. 6th-century CE Platonist philosopher
On Aristotle's Physics (ed. Diels, in *CAG*, vol. 9): 151.6–11: **2.35**

On Aristotle's Categories (ed. Kalbfleisch, in *CAG*, vol. 8): 208.28–32: **11.6**

Stobaeus, Joannes. 6th-century CE complier of a didactic anthology
Selections (a.k.a., *Eclogues*): 2.31.52: **5.5**; 2.31.68: **5.14**; 2.31.76: **1.27**; 2.8.26: **2.21**; 3.6.63: **10.2**; 4.4.28: **7.15**; 4.8.18: **7.35**; 4.8.23: **7.36**; 4.8.31: **7.34**

Suda (a.k.a., Suidas). 10th-century CE encyclopedia: σ.829.60–63 ("Socrates"): **4.17**; φ.154 ("Phaedo"): p. 167

Themistius. 4th-century CE statesman and orator
Orations: 35.5: **9.3**

Theodoret. 5th-century Christian thinker
Cure for Greek Maladies: 3.53: **3.45**

Theon, Aelius. Teacher of rhetoric; probably 1st century CE
Preliminary Exercises (ed. L. von Spengel, in *Rhetories Graeci*, 3 vols., Leipzig: 1853–1856): 5 [ii. 105.6]: **7.26**

Vatican Sayings. An anonymous collection of anecdotes known formally as the *Gnomologium Vaticanum*, found in a 14th-century CE manuscript in the Vatican library (Vat. gr. 743) (ed. L. Sternbach, in "De Gnomologio Vaticano inedito," *Wiener Studien* 9 [1887], 175–206 + 10 [1888], 1–49 + 211–60 + 11 [1889], 43–64 + 192–242): 5: **4.18**; 12: **3.20**; 32: **9.22**; 33: **5.12**; 34: **3.10, 5.13**; 277: **9.8**

Xenophon.
Anabasis: 3.1.5–7: **10.16**

Apology: 11–12: **3.59**

Cyropaedia ("*Education of Cyrus*"): 1.1.1–6: **7.24**; 4.1.38–40: Ch. 3, n. 1.

On Household Management (a.k.a., *Oeconomicus*): 1.10–15: **2.18**; 3.10–15: **8.12**; 7.3–28: **8.18**

On Hunting: 13.1–9: **5.1**

Memorabilia: 1.1.1–4: **10.14**; 1.1.16: **3.1**; 1.1.6–9: **3.32**; 1.2.1–5: **3.40**; 1.2.18–20: **3.6**; 1.2.40–47: **7.3**; 1.2.53–54: **4.4**; 1.2.56–59: **5.27**; 1.3.1: **3.56**; 1.3.2: **2.24**; 1.3.3: **3.57**; 1.3.6–8: **4.13**; 1.3.8–15: **6.16**; 1.4.2–18: **9.16**; 1.4.14–15: **10.7**; 1.5.4–5: **3.8**; 1.6.15–7.5: **7.9**; 2.1.1–4 + 7–17: **7.14**; 2.1.23–30: **2.10**; 2.3.18–19: **9.26**; 2.6.35–37: **8.11**; 3.11:

6.3; 3.6.1–10 + 16–18: **7.5**; 3.7.1–9: **7.6**; 3.8.2–3: **2.22**; 3.9.1–3: **3.49**; 3.9.14–15: **3.60**; 3.9.4: **3.22**; 3.9.5–7: **3.14**; 4.2.31–35: **2.16**; 4.3.15–17: **3.58**; 4.3.2–14: **9.23**; 4.4.1–5 + 7-25: **3.35**; 4.4.5–7: **1.20**; 4.5.1–12: **3.9**; 4.6.1: **1.7(a)**; 4.6.14–15: **1.7(b)**; 4.7.1–10: **5.16**; 4.8.6–7: **2.15**

Symposium: 3.10: **6.4**; 3.3–4: **3.33**; 3.5–6: **5.22**; 4.1–5: **3.34**; 4.34–44: **3.2**; 4.6: **5.25**; 6.6–8: **9.1**; 8.12–16: **4.5**; 8.3–6: **6.7**